# Recovering the Voice in
# Our Techno-Social World

# Recovering the Voice in Our Techno-Social World

*On the Phone*

Deborah Eicher-Catt

LEXINGTON BOOKS
Lanham • Boulder • New York • London

Published by Lexington Books
An imprint of The Rowman & Littlefield Publishing Group, Inc.
4501 Forbes Boulevard, Suite 200, Lanham, Maryland 20706
www.rowman.com

6 Tinworth Street, London SE11 5AL

Copyright © 2020 by The Rowman & Littlefield Publishing Group, Inc.

Quotations from Mladen Dolar, *A Voice and Nothing More*, published by The MIT Press, are provided courtesy of The MIT Press.

*All rights reserved.* No part of this book may be reproduced in any form or by any electronic or mechanical means, including information storage and retrieval systems, without written permission from the publisher, except by a reviewer who may quote passages in a review.

British Library Cataloguing in Publication Information Available

**Library of Congress Cataloging-in-Publication Data**

ISBN: 978-1-7936-0527-6 (cloth : alk. paper)
ISBN: 978-1-7936-0528-3 (electronic)
ISBN: 978-1-7936-0529-0 (pbk. : alk. paper)

# Contents

| | |
|---|---|
| Acknowledgments | vii |
| Introduction: Speaking and Listening from the Heart | 1 |
| 1  On the *Phone* | 23 |
| 2  Our Digital Age of Distraction and Our Increasing Techno-Social Dilemma | 45 |
| 3  Enchantments and Their Inauthenticity: The Play of Amusements | 67 |
| 4  Echoes of the Acousmatic Voice in Cyberspace: The Impersonal Self | 97 |
| 5  The Murder of the *Phone* in Plain Sight: The Voice of Articulation | 119 |
| 6  The Enchanting *Phone* as Phenomenological Event: The Voice of Enunciation | 155 |
| 7  The Pivotal Nature of Voice: *Interper-sónal* Relationality and Its Authenticity | 187 |
| 8  Resonance, Resilience, and Re-Enchantment: Voicing the Heart of the Matter | 221 |
| Bibliography | 251 |
| Index | 265 |
| About the Author | 279 |

# Acknowledgments

A book such as this does not materialize without the support of many people. Initial research for this project was provided by a sabbatical grant, funded by The Pennsylvania State University during fall semester 2016. I especially wish to thank the local Penn State York administration, in particular Robert Farrell, for always supporting my scholarly efforts. I received numerous travel grants from Penn State York to share these ideas with my colleagues at various academic conferences and was awarded a research development grant that helped defray editing costs in the final stages of manuscript preparation. My Presidential Address at the 2018 Semiotic Society of America conference in Berea, Kentucky, formed the foundation for this book where I argued for a re-enchantment of human communication as a voiced act of interpersonal resilience.

My fellow communicologists Frank J. Macke, Marian Zielinski, Igor Klyukanov, Galina Sinekopova, Ron and Millie Arnett, Janie Harden Fritz, Garnet Butchart, Andrew Smith, and Pat Arneson have always encouraged my academic pursuits through their interest in my work. I am thankful for the comaraderie and friendship that our fellowship has spawned and always look forward to participating in the chorus of voices we create when we gather together. I am indebted, of course, to my academic mentors, Richard L. Lanigan and Thomas J. Pace, for teaching me the value of academic inquiry in the first place but also the importance of grounding that inquiry in lived experience.

The chapters of this book are new work products. I have received permissions to publish from journals where a chapter draws upon previous work. An earlier version of portions of chapter 3 on my interpretation of Merleau-Ponty's notion of ambiguity was published as "The Authenticity in Ambiguity: Appreciating Maurice Merleau-Ponty's Abductive Logic as Communicative Praxis" in *The Atlantic Journal of Communication* 13, no. 2 (2005): 113–134. An earlier version of portions of chapter 3 on cyberspace and its inauthentic enchantments and portions of chapter 7 on authentic enchantments were published as "A Prelude to a Semioethics of Dialogue: The Aesthetics of Enchantment in a New Key," in *Language and Dialogue* 7, no. 1 (2017): 100–119. I am grateful to these journals for granting permission to publish. I also wish to thank MIT Press for allowing me to reprint excerpts from Mladen Dolar's book, *A Voice and Nothing More.*

On a more personal note, I am blessed to have my sons Ty Joshua Yurkovic and Zachary Thomas Yurkovic in my life. They continually inspire me to remain open to the questions life presents and allow me to experience, firsthand, what it means to speak and listen "heart-to-heart." I thank them for their loving encouragement to remain steadfast to my heart's pursuits and for modeling, each in their own way, an aesthetics of communication that is truly inspiring. In addition to my daughter-in-law Terra Yurkovic, I also want to thank my brother, Robert Eicher and his wife, Lynne, step-son Marcus Sanford and his wife Michelle, brother-in-law Ben Catt and his wife Carol, and good friends Sharon Maughan, Sue and Jim Weinrich, Deb and Tony Adair, and Thom Green and David Blanchard. The sentiments expressed in this book echo my experiences of "being with" each of you in deeply satisfying and immediate ear-to-ear relations.

My undergraduate research assistant, Sidra Veriatch, was extremely helpful and I appreciated the many valuable discussions we had on the impact of electronic connectivity on relationality, especially for the younger generations. I also want to acknowledge all of my students in my advanced interpersonal class during spring 2019 where we explored together the impact of the digital age on human relationships. I benefited greatly from our interactions. I am grateful to my copy editor, Emmalee Torisk (from Duquesne University), who was as wonderful to work with as she was efficient and I wish to thank my editor at Lexington Press, Nicolette Amstutz, for believing in this project from the beginning and seeing it through to production. I also appreciate the insightful feedback from my reviewer who helped to strengthen my arguments. The wonderful cover is the original artwork of my sister-in-law, Lynne Wheaton Eicher, who creatively captured the meaning of heart-to-heart as an enchanting sound phenomenon. Thank you, Lynne, for the sentiment you captured with your beautiful brush strokes.

Last, but certainly not least, I wish to acknowledge my husband, friend, and colleague, Isaac E. Catt. While our mutual philosophical interests have fueled many a stimulating discussion between us, it is merely just being with you—heart-to-heart—that continues to make life truly enchanting. Thank you for being the voice of reason, of love, of mutuality in its natural and wild unfolding. This book is dedicated to you.

# Introduction

## *Speaking and Listening from the Heart*

It was serendipitous on Valentine's Day 2019 that I ran across an online article about Amazon's personal digital voice assistant, Alexa. I had been contemplating for some time the impact our digital world seems to have on how we view our most intimate of relationships. The article was written by a technologist who was espousing the "awesome" ways we could use Alexa on Valentine's Day.[1] Setting aside momentarily the awkwardness of appealing to an electronic auditory device on matters pertaining to the heart, the writer encouraged us to see how easily Alexa could set the mood of the day by playing appropriate music or, if lightheartedness was our goal, by telling us jokes or stories with love themes. These functions seem frivolous enough and merely echo (pun intended) some of the playful functions offered by various applications on our smartphones, electronic tablets, or other electronic devices.

A bit more disturbing to me were three other ways promoted by the author that Alexa could interject (dare I say intervene) in our most intimate of love relationships. It was suggested that by enabling the *Love Notes* function on Alexa, our loved one could retrieve a Valentine's Day message randomly chosen from over 100 programmed into the device. The operating assumption here seems to grossly miss the mark of what a love note is supposed to represent—the unique feelings we have toward a unique other expressed uniquely in our own words. The logic behind *Love Notes* is that, apparently, nothing says a relationship is deeply held in our hearts more than sending a randomized love note. Really? Wondering if that logic now nourishes our relationships, I read on.

If we do not have a bona fide lover in our lives, Alexa could apparently help with that, too. Saying, "Play me a love podcast" results in learning relationship skills from a so-called expert in hopes of capturing that special someone. This logic is also flawed, given that it dismisses the crucial point that relationships are not one-way endeavors that merely require honing a certain set of skills. Relationships, instead, are organically co-constructed communicatively between two people, requiring constant adaptation and negotiation. Relationality is not a one size fits all affair. Unfortunately, this important point is typically obscured in our contemporary culture. Our digital age (or information age, if you prefer) amplifies the value we place on information retrieval within cyberspace as opposed to genuine communication, that is, the accomplishment of a shared understanding that emerges spontaneously between two human beings. So, receiving information, instruction, or advice about love from a distant, unknown other does not really challenge our current zeitgeist too much, given the highly mediated environment in which we live. The constant barrage of mass-mediated instructional messages about relationships from online/print magazines, entertainment news, dating websites, TED Talks, podcasts, social media sites, and the like is quickly becoming the new norm.[2] We now more than ever exist within digitalized webs of symbolic meaning where the importance of our analogical experiences is too often relegated to the back seat of our mobile lives. Analogue experiences are not premised upon an either/or digital logic but rather on perceptions based upon relationality itself, using immediate contextual cues of relation to register differences of perception within those very relations.

Perhaps the most disturbing programmable feature Alexa presents is the "Be My Valentine" oral command. Here, Alexa functions as your Valentine's Day date, showering you with words to lift your spirits and make you feel special and loved. This is the ultimate example of anthropomorphism, which is especially troubling given that we are dealing with the context of love, intimacy, and human relationality. This disconcerting feature easily blurs the boundaries between what constitutes human relationships based upon a reciprocity of genuine affectual sensibilities involving two human beings and human/machine social interaction.[3] Where are we headed as a culture, I wondered, when our co-constructed senses of love and intimacy are electronically wired and programmed into *another* that is nothing but a smart or intelligent device? Moreover, the "Be My Valentine" feature only magnifies a one-way view of love and intimacy—a narcissistic view, where others are expected to nourish our own well-being without the obligatory human response that genuine love requires. If our sense of self can now be hardwired by a shallow programmable talking machine that asks nothing of us in return, how authentic and viable is our sense of self in the end? How meaningful can those types of interactions actually be? I am disheartened by Alexa's ostensible "awesomeness" when it comes to love's enactment and hope that the article did not receive that many hits; or, if it did, it struck the same chord with others as it did with me. In any case, Alexa leaves me silently chanting the popular 1960s Supremes song "Where Did Our Love Go" for the rest of the afternoon. I am psychologically unsettled, to say the least.

The above description of Alexa (a thoroughly disembodied auditory voice machine) as a supposed *personal* tool of the heart begins to address a key communication problematic within contemporary life. That is, how should we approach a growing techno-social dilemma we face when it comes to developing and maintaining healthy and satisfying self and other relations, especially given the constant intervening of our electronic technologies within such a delicate human dynamic? No one disagrees that we now live in a thoroughly entangled techno-social world where the boundaries of human and electronic connectivity are increasingly blurring. We have ready access to a plethora of intelligent devices and awesome applications in contemporary life that are advertised, of course, as merely being in service to our expanding needs and desires. At the same time, we are presented with a new set of challenges when it comes to sustaining healthy habits of discourse in our most immediate relations with others especially, I will argue, when it comes to our *vocality*. With the advent of electronic forms of connectivity that are increasingly text-based and visual, we are beginning to run the risk of actually de-voicing our interactions. Or, at the very least, we are beginning to devalue the importance of the sounding voice (Greek word, *phone*) in establishing our mutuality of relations.[4] As psychologist, medical researcher, and author James Lynch articulates, "for the first time in history we electronically removed the voice from the body (through technology). We're speaking from no place to nobody, and there are no feelings left."[5]

We are reminded of phenomenologist and media theorist Walter Ong's observations concerning the contrast between visual and oral-aural modes of thought and action. As he suggests, visual and auditory media within a given culture activate different aspects of our senses, producing different cultural habits of thought, action, and knowledge.[6] It is to an examination of these new habits of discourse that this book is devoted. For true to their very nature as philosopher John Dewey attests, habits are "always silent and present" in lived experience and yet "express the fundamental nature of being-in-the-world."[7] Our new habits of discourse thus call for careful scrutiny given our increasing preferences for visual and textual digitalized forms of interaction. These new habits problematize our relationality and call for what I will describe as a re-enchantment of human communication.

So, even though electronic information technologies have significantly increased our overall connectivity and made that connectivity much more efficient, herein I echo the growing concern about the impact such a social landscape is having on our overall well-being and the well-being of our relationships.[8] Technology companies and new media marketers are even acknowledging the growing concern by promoting digital wellness seminars and software applications.[9] One of the key communicative challenges I see in our current techno-social world is this: How do we find a healthy balance between our new mediated forms of electronic connectivity that are now dominating our cultural scene and the traditional modes of interaction and conversation provided by face-to-face (or what I will call immediate *ear-to-ear*) transactions? Given that the very social fabric of our lives is rapidly being rewoven on digitalized looms of our own making, I think such a question is timely. I do not think that even Walter Ong in his thorough and insightful historical writings on the topic of media anticipated the extent to which our new electronic forms would come to dominate our social landscape. As I aim to show, these new forms of electronic media should not be taken lightly as innocent or neutral aspects of our everyday existence, presuming they are just examples of technological advances among many in our cultural history. While our new *information technologies* definitely have their advantages (especially in terms of speed and efficiency of connection and information transfer), they also modify both the content of our discourse with others and the very nature or characteristics of the relations that necessarily emerge. This book is about exploring both of these social and personal consequences.[10]

Herein, I shall refer to our new media of connectivity as *information technologies* instead of *communication technologies*. These two designations are often used interchangeably and quite unreflectively in our cultural lexicon, especially by media companies and those who market technological goods and services. This confusion is unfortunate, given that they are not the same and their theoretical muddle diminishes the importance that real communication has in our lives. Information exchange or information transfer does not constitute communication, in and of itself, as a guarantee. For example, the act of sending a text to someone does not guarantee that we have achieved communication. This is because communication requires a mutual acknowledgment on the part of the addresser and the addressee that a shared understanding (code condition in semiotic terms) has emerged between self and other in the process of constructing meaning. That shared meaning may occur when we send a text, but there is no guarantee at the outset that it will happen. Moreover, the operating logics of each theoretical perspective are quite different. Information exchange or transmission (as it is sometimes called) is premised upon a logic of uncertainty reduction between a sender and receiver (to use the mechanical metaphor), derived principally from Shannon and Weaver's initial mathematical model of information transfer based upon either/or digital choices within a mechanical system.[11] So as not to be misunderstood here, information exchange or transmission is a worthy goal in many instances of interaction. We could not successfully maneuver in the social world without it. However, as we shall see when it comes to constituting relationality in its most rewarding instances of interpersonal depth and understanding, the mere sending and receiving of messages often leaves us wanting—or at least leaves us at the superficial level of message exchange where meaning may be only presumed. The underlying premise of communication entails information exchange, but it also incorporates the either/or logic of message production within a both/and mutuality of emergent meaning. Said differently, while each interlocutor's digital choices of linguistic expressions and perceptions (the semiotic components of discourse) are a part of the process, an analogue of relationality is necessarily constituted phenomenologically within the spontaneous and organic embodied unfolding of meaning that transpires between speaker and listener. Thus, all of our new media technologies are increasing the value of connectivity through efficient information sharing, but we cannot necessarily call them communication technologies. That designation, I believe, is too presumptuous.[12] Technology critic and psychologist Sherry Turkle of the Massachusetts Institute of Technology acknowledges this very distinction. We now have an explosion of electronic *connectivity* at the expense of real conversation and *communication* with one another.[13] Therefore, being electronically connected does not guarantee that communication occurs. In some instances, I would argue, it produces just the opposite: misunderstandings through bypassing, where interlocutors talk (text?) past one another and never really establish a firm ground from which a mutuality of meaning might arise organically between them.[14]

While the contents of this book could be read as a dystopian response to our techno-culture that appears to be deeply pathological (for example, many say we are now living in a culture of distraction that is eroding our ability to even think logically), my aim is not quite as negative but more modest in tone. I wish merely to preclude a forgetfulness of some of the important qualities of human communication that speaking with another ear-to-ear necessarily foreground. The title of this book is thus accentuating the importance of the Greek word for voice (*phone*) in a digital world where we increasingly appeal to our electronic devices (phones) to connect or try to communicate with others.

Sound and vocal theorist Michel Chion helps us understand the phenomenological duality of speaking and listening that Lynch highlights in the quotation above. Chion suggests that human beings in their habituated behaviors are both voco-centric (sound producers) and verbo-centric (what he specifies as language users). And while Walter Ong is right to claim that orality itself is not an ideal (we cannot, for example, return to a primarily orally based culture as found in ancient times), I will contend that neither should one aspect of our expressive/perceptive existence (our voco-centric natures, for example) be dismissed in favor of the other (in this case, our verbo-centric capacities).[15] As we understand from the symbolic interactionists (George Herbert Mead, for example) and the pragmatists (such as William James, John Dewey, and Charles Sanders Peirce), the kinds of interactions we have in the social world and the habits of discourse we develop, constituted as I will explain both semiotically and phenomenologically, bear significantly on our overall sense of self and our social well-being. Developing Peirce's ideas about habits as fixations of belief[16] and their impact on our sense of self, Dewey describes in *Human Nature*, "all habits are demands for certain kinds of activity; and they constitute the self. In any intelligible sense of the word will, they *are* will. They form our effective desires and they furnish us with our working capacities. They rule our thoughts, determining which shall appear and be strong and which shall pass from light into obscurity."[17]

Given our current techno-social culture, we increasingly spend our waking days and sometimes waking nights *on the phone*. This is rapidly becoming our new habit of discourse. Here, I am using the phrase *on the phone* as a general, inclusive term that speaks to our daily use of many electronic forms of connectivity, such as cell phones, computers, electronic tablets, and the like.[18] We are plugged in or wired, as we say, and maneuvering (often in fragmented and distracted ways) within the virtual world of cyberspace. We are surfing the web, catching up on emails, texting, ordering goods and services, playing games, checking Instagram, and so on. Regardless of the activity, in the process we often *phubb* others who are physically present to our immediate awareness, that is, we ignore the felt-presence of others while we scroll and manipulate the various screens and tabs on our devices. As it is described, "phubbing can severely disrupt your present-moment, in-person relationships" while we look at our cell phones instead.[19] These new habits of interaction are important given that they radically shape interaction quality. Research indicates, for example, that the mere presence of a phone either on the dinner table or at informal social gatherings influences face-to-face conversational quality.[20] The presence of the phone on the social scene is a distraction that inhibits the development of interpersonal closeness and trust, and reduces a felt-sense of empathy between relational partners. Obviously, these kinds of distracting communicative behaviors, over a period of time, will erode the relational ties that bind, for we know that such ties require a more in-depth attending to the other in speaking and listening. Distraction, after all, means literally to draw apart.

Herein, I describe our fascinations with new electronic media as forms of *enchantment*, although I suggest that these forms seldom nourish a deeper appreciation of our relationality. I will argue that they also can undermine our ethical relations with others. I label these forms of enchantment *inauthentic*. Unlike Max Weber's contention back in the early twentieth century, I do not conceptualize our current modern (or postmodern, if you will) life as completely disenchanted, at least not in the way he theorized.[21] To briefly review, Weber theorized that the rise of industrialization in the modern world fueled the rise of rational, scientific thinking. Consequently, such a worldview relegated the mythical, mysterious, or ineffable aspects of life (the aesthetically enchanting aspects) to the margins of human existence.[22] Weber contends that a disenchanted world is devoid of an appreciation for the aesthetic—the beautiful, mystical elements of our embodied connections, especially given their historical link to the sacred. Unlike the qualities of mastery and control we associate with rationality, enchantment, on the other hand, signifies the metaphysical or ineffable qualities of human existence that semiotically leave us spellbound in a momentary experience of phenomenological wonder and awe. Such affectual and aesthetic experiences of enchantment are thought, therefore, to be in direct opposition to the logical rationality that has been characteristic of Western philosophy since Plato and expanded by the rise of secular thinking at the dawn of modernity. Weber theorized "the natural world and all areas of human experience become . . . understood as less mysterious; defined, at least in principle, as knowable, predictable and manipulable by humans."[23] With his proclamation of the disenchantment of the world, Weber was in effect acknowledging the birth of the secular world. Often correlating the rise of secularization with the rise of disenchantment, social theorists have long sought to reconcile the world of spirit, or *geist*, with nature or, said differently, religion with science.[24] Not all social theorists agree with Weber's assessment. Richard Jenkins, for example, directly challenges Weber's grand narrative about the disenchantment of the world. He contests the very theoretical ground from which Weber builds his argument. Jenkins asserts that the premodern world known for its enchanting qualities also exhibited the disconnection and fragmentation typically associated with modernity. Thus, the pre-modern could also be characterized as exhibiting disenchanted qualities.[25]

In what follows, I align with Jenkins's theoretical position and claim that our contemporary world shows signs of a unified or wholistic enchanted imaginary that is anything but completely rational. We still live in a world of enchantments, in other words, although our mystical or mythical thinking as an aesthetic has merely morphed into other cultural, symbolic forms that are no longer tied directly to the orthodoxy of religion. McPherson and Taylor agree.[26] These new forms of enchantment now nourish a new social imaginary, one that I argue is increasingly based upon our burgeoning electronic fascinations and their attendant symbolic interfaces. These new electronic information technologies are enchanting, as their auditory etymology suggests, because they *call* or *summon* us to experience them in intensely profound sensory ways. And indicative of most experiences of enchantment as historically conceived, our electronic devices appear uncanny. That is, they simultaneously reflect intelligent and ineffable or mysterious qualities. After all, with a couple of touches on our cell phones, we are instantaneously connected to family and friends. Also important is the fact that our current electronic enchantments seem to echo the historical connotations of enchantment that describe them as "deluding or spellbinding," signifying the negative connotations ascribed to them.[27] This negative aspect marks the power of enchantments to supposedly captivate our conscious experience and beguile us. It also accentuates our supposed disempowerment in the long run. I have more to say on this point in the chapters that follow.

And yet, I will theoretically develop the contours of enchantment as an aesthetic experience so as to recuperate what I see as its positive experiential aspects, especially as they relate to human interactions. Echoing my sentiments here, Michael Saler believes what he calls the "ironic imagination" holds promise as a way to experience enchantments without beguilement; in other words, experience enchantments in their positive or more productive form.[28] Fleshing out these ideas further, I frame my discussions of enchantment within the discipline of communicology, using its paradigm methodology of semiotic phenomenology. While my approach is distinct in this regard, it also echoes other theorists' reassessments of enchantment, especially when it comes to its potential for sparking imaginative thinking and facilitating an ethical generosity toward others.[29] With its etymological association to the German word *stimmung*, meaning mood, which also refers metaphorically to sound, I insist that certain enchantments can possibilize an important attunement or *resonance* among self, other, and world.[30] Such a theoretical move of recuperation for the concept of enchantment is already underway across several disciplines, as researchers explicate the heuristic value of enchantment as a sensory trope of discourse.[31] I suggest, therefore, that other forms of enchantments we experience and in particular the immediate sounding of another's voice within ear-to-ear relations can manifest positive relational outcomes. This is because the enchanting voices of self and other empower a relational *tonality* from which positive transformative experiences might arise.[32] I label these types of enchantments *authentic*, especially since their auditory aesthetic qualities are prominently featured within self and other relations. Of course, it is the very fading of these forms of enchantment in our de-vocalized soundscape[33] that prompts our pursuit of a re-enchantment of human communication in the first place. After all, I contend that we increasingly see a general escalation of disenchanting enchantments, a term coined by social theorist George Ritzer to describe the effects of the McDonaldization of society.[34] I will speak to a kind of overall cultural disenchantment we currently see that fosters a particularly insidious and growing apathy toward life in general. The positive delight of enchantment, in other words, can turn rapidly into despair.[35]

Taking the lead from psychoanalyst and social critic Sherry Turkle, I have thus become increasingly concerned about the changing habits of our communication practices with one another in dyadic encounters within our current media-saturated environment.[36] Based upon her decades of research with people of all ages, she declares that we would now rather "text than talk"[37] to one another. She is correct. Apparently 2008 was the watershed year when the number of text messages sent on our phones surpassed the number of voice calls made in the United States.[38] Millennials and Generation Z give us the most direct example of this textual trend, although many of us from other generations are increasingly making such discursive choices as well. Indicative of this trend, voice mail within the business world is also waning. Major companies like Coca-Cola and JPMorgan Chase are eliminating office voice mail altogether. A recent *Harvard Business Review*[39] essay actually urges companies to dump voice mail; this is shocking given that voice mail has served as the premier electronic message storage and retrieval system for many years. It is argued that, as a communication medium, voice mail is no longer essential and has become as clunky and irrelevant as our use of carbon paper.[40] Within my own professional life of academia, I find academic departments at major universities across the country eliminating office phones altogether. The logic is, of course, that office phones are no longer needed. Nowadays everyone emails or texts instead of making phone calls. These examples are not mere exceptions. They are becoming the cultural zeitgeist of our times. If we are texting, emailing, or Instagramming rather than talking on the phone, then we are drastically changing our habits of thought, discourse, and action. Following Peirce's pragmatism, these habits significantly shape our subsequent behaviors. So, we are currently witnessing how the form of our communication with one another (the media used) significantly shapes the content of what is expressed—theoretical issues familiar to the field of media ecology.[41]

In terms of the form of this electronic media trend, it appears we are engaging in more hyper-textual/visual forms of information sharing than ever before. We write texts, tweets, and emails, and we send along pictures for supplementary illustration. This supports philosopher Jacques Ellul's contention that with the rise of modernity we witness the "unconditional victory of the visual and images."[42] Brain researcher and author Richard Restak agrees and is concerned in particular that this new barrage of images now dominates our social landscape. And while images—unlike writing or speaking—require less thought or analysis to be grasped, textual forms of the visual plunge us into the world of abstraction. Both forms—images and text, Restak asserts, significantly alter brain neuropathways and thereby alter their functioning.[43] In any case, this means that our increased preference for textual/visual forms of connectivity transpires at the expense of our immediate vocality with one another. When I recently asked my students if they talk on the phone, they laughed and said, "Of course, if we are video-chatting. We wouldn't just call someone. . . That would be weird." The proclivity to appeal to these hyper-textual/visual forms of connection indicates a devocalizing discursive trend within our electronic culture that should give us pause.

As we know from phenomenological studies on voice and sound, the sounding voice impresses us differently than the visual representation of another (whether face-to-face or through electronic mediation), and these impressions are significant in terms of our depth of shared experience when it comes to our relationality.[44] The position I take is different from the one advanced by Walter Ong in an essay titled "Wired for Sound" in his book *The Barbarian Within*, written in 1962. As Ong claims, our modern developments in communications, "while they have not slighted the visual, have given more play to the oral-aural."[45] He prophesizes that with the advent of electronic media sound would find a renewed currency in cultural life after its diminishment by typography, especially given the rising popularity of the telephone, radio, and television at the time of his writing. Hence, he claims that within electronic culture we enter a time of secondary orality, when sound and voice become once again prominent features of everyday life. I suggest his theoretical assessments on this point miss the mark. I will have more to say about this in subsequent chapters.

I believe the voice's distinction as immediate sound, which transgresses the visual or symbolic in its immersive qualities, should not go underappreciated as an aesthetic aspect of relational experience. The human voice in its embodied materiality ironically evokes the invisible, immaterial aesthetic qualities of human interactions and experience more than any other sensibility. As Ong admits, sound reveals interiors and "For man the paradigm of sound is voice, in which communication between man and man (man is the deepest of interiors) flowers as in no other sensory manifestation. Voice is alive."[46] I argue in the chapters to follow (and accentuating the sonic aspects of the speaking voice) that the real *per-sónal* aspects of the other come readily to the fore within the dynamic inter-immediacy of voiced relations.[47] Concerning changes in content or what we actually say to another within our hyper-textual/visual forms of connectivity, I explicate how such written forms also abbreviate discourse. Regrettably, abbreviated discourses necessarily abbreviate our relationality, or the depth and quality of the messages sent and received.

Given the above, it is also not surprising that the *lost art of conversation* is a growing social concern. At the time of this writing, a cursory review on Google indicates that this lost art has almost 400,000,000 web entries. It seems that culturally we are beginning to recognize a problem here.[48] Beneficial conversation with another, which equates to a more intense ear-to-ear mutual sharing and personal vulnerability, requires both a specific form of discourse and a more well-developed or elaborate explication of a given subject matter (content). In his history of conversation as a declining art, essayist Stephen Miller admits that conversation's appeal as a form of social interaction has waxed and waned over the centuries. Its assessed value has fluctuated greatly depending upon social, political, and economic circumstances as well as competing philosophical movements. However, he does contend that our current conversational avoidance devices (such as our smartphones) are radically changing the relevance we now place upon it.[49] Sherry Turkle's latest book, *Reclaiming Conversation*, echoes his concern. She suggests that conversation, in its immediate actual form (not virtual or robotic), lays the very groundwork for our development of a healthy sense of self and an ethical orientation toward the other. Her main concern is the steady decline in empathy we see in our younger generations, which, of course, requires deeper levels of listening, speaking, and shared understanding to evolve.[50] She shares a disturbing statistic: There has been a forty percent decline over the last twenty years or so in the markers for empathy among college students.

While I am not attempting to contribute to a discourse that pathologizes our current techno-culture or view it, in other words, as a general social disease that must be treated,[51] I do intend to draw parallels between our increased text- and image-based forms of connectivity (and our abbreviated content of interaction, which maintains a level of relational superficiality) and the general rise of anxiety and depression we see in America. I believe a strong argument can be made for their correlation, especially if we acknowledge the important role actual communication has in our lives.[52] According to the latest national survey completed by the American Psychological Association in May 2018, Americans' anxiety levels experienced a sharp increase in 2017.[53] Similarly, reports suggest that depression is "skyrocketing" in America.[54] Our increased levels of anxiety and depression, particularly among the younger generations, indicate what I call an overall feeling of *existential dissonance*, drawing from my sensory trope of enchantment as sound. This dissonance is partially exacerbated by the discordant and fragmented relationships that such a techno-culture seems to privilege. Thus, our *culture of distraction* can be viewed as an essential thread within this growing, disturbing social ecology. Relationality and particularly one that nourishes a healthy sense of self and empathy toward the other depends upon a particular economy of attention that demands a focused listening to or attending to the voice of the other in its immediacy. Ironically, our experience of existential dissonance within our techno-culture thus heralds a new sense of overall disenchantment with the world—however, it is one unlike what Weber initially described. We are becoming enchanted (mystified) by our electronic forms of connectivity at the same time that we also are left disheartened and disenchanted with life more generally. I submit that an essential aesthetics within lived experience is fading as we move toward the virtual aesthetics of high-definition visuals and digitalized sound reproduction. A re-enchantment of human communication is thus warranted, one that calls us toward one another in a mutuality of aesthetic presence in order to listen to the immediate sounding of our voices together.

My main argument is that with the rise of techno-culture, where we appear to always be *on the phone*, we are actually, quite ironically, propelling ourselves toward an unexamined acceptance of the actual murder of the *phone* (Greek word for voice/sound). The title of this book announces the double meaning of the word *phone* by signifying the importance of the immediate sounding voice to our successful re-enchantment of human communication. The voice is an existential calling that should not be dismissed. I explore how our increased enchantments with electronic media signal a corresponding devaluation of the sounding human voice within discursive practices. While video chats and podcasts are, of course, common auditory modes of connectivity with our electronic culture, I remind my readers that these ways of connecting are highly mediated.[55] In other words, these forms transpire within the abstracted world of representation, and because of this, they produce a distancing effect when it comes to interpersonal relations even as they celebrate connectivity. In such instances, the other in discourse is removed from the immediate auditory effects of a felt embodied materiality of voices coming together in their full aesthetic presence. Although we continue to hear the other in such electronic instances of interaction, the nuances of his/her voice (the *grain* of it, as semiotician Roland Barthes would say)[56] are sacrificed in their electronic modulation and distortion.[57] The voices of self and other are obviously important media of cyberspace, yet their mediated forms eclipse the value our voices have as unique aesthetic particularities. Even more importantly, such mediation subordinates our voices to acts of representation within a given signifying system.

Additionally, whether we are engaged in immediate ear-to-ear or highly mediated contexts of speaking, the essential aspects of the particular voice of another often go underappreciated, given our predominant acceptance of voice as merely a tool in service to the signifying/symbolic order of things—to our expressiveness as intelligibility. I aim to evoke its equally important aesthetic characteristics without turning the sounding voice into a mere fetish object to consciousness, as psychoanalyst Jacques Lacan contends.[58] In pursuit of a delicate balance between the two, I draw from phenomenological and semiotic writings on voice and sound to make the case that there are significant ineffable qualities of the voice in its immediate pure sounding that need to be revived. As we consider the ramifications of our changing sensorium at this moment in time, this theoretical move is especially important. Otherwise, these significant qualities of the voice may become lost to us, particularly given our habitual proclivity to subordinate voice to a semantic/symbolic system of meaning and relegate it to the parameters of our new social, mediated forms of discursive practices. After all, as we learn from poststructuralist theory, the timbre or grain of the voice points at the very locus of subjectivity and signals a paramount aspect of our embodiment.[59] Both the voice in service to intelligibility and the aesthetic dimensions of voice need to be heard and appreciated. I dispel any counterarguments that might pose such a theoretical move as essentialist or romantic, appealing in particular to the insights of Peirce and his philosophy of pragmatism. The pure voice, I insist, is a semiotic and phenomenological entailment, and with its enunciation, we may actualize more satisfying self and other relations.

The dual nature and function of voice as both intelligibility and ineffability thus warrants a philosophical framework that unpacks this duality and allows for an insightful hermeneutic of its contours and impact for a healthy and ethical relationality. I find the human science disciplinary approach of communicology particularly fruitful in this regard, especially given its methodological focus in phenomenology and semiotics.[60] As will be detailed later, I take the consciousness and experience of voice to be a co-constructed phenomenon through semiotic processes and phenomenological events of speaking and listening. This human science approach allows me to unpack how the human voice is both a part of the referential system of signification that it serves within the symbolic world (what I call the *voice of articulation*) and a primary semiotic, aesthetic medium of the body subject of a unique person (the *voice of enunciation*). We will find that our immediate vocality is not an aspect of *per-sónhood* that should be easily or readily dismissed as an outmoded habit of discourse, especially if we seek a balance between our electronic forms of connectivity and our traditional modes of immediate ear-to-ear interactions. Given that our existential habits, according to Dewey and Peirce, "operate on a level of experience which precedes any sort of deliberate, critical positing of distinct *objects* of reflection or consciousness,"[61] it behooves us to carefully examine them through a process of radical reflection. We must remember that our vocality originates from within an ineffable interior where the literal and figurative heart of a person dwells as a spiritual/soulful essence, an aspect of our being that should not go underappreciated in our fast-paced media-frenzied environment. If that vocality is not sufficiently heard, therefore, the soulful qualities of self and other are not actualized. As I unfold this idea in the pages that follow, I take this spiritual/soulful essence not as a divine manifestation of a transcendent deity. Instead, I develop a more secular conception of enchantment and our vocality, understanding them as vital, semiotic aesthetic forces that nonetheless permeate all human existence in powerful ways. I now turn to a brief description of each chapter.

Chapter 1, "On the *Phone*," describes the current media-saturated environment in which we live and sets up the problematic of the diminished value placed on the sounding voice within immediate self and other relations. I reference the smartphone's capabilities for multifarious connections in the world of cyberspace and note how, ironically, the *phone* (voice) is being eclipsed by the dominant video-centric and logo-centric forms of discourse we are increasingly using. I cite recent statistics on the degree to which we are *on the phone* and our other smart devices. I offer a hermeneutic of the space of cyber and the Internet and explore how sound and voice on these predominately logo- and video-centric media platforms are represented. In particular, I address the increasing popularity of social media platforms and question whether they are, indeed, prosocial. I make the case that electronic connectivity is dwindling our embodied sense of relationality.

Chapter 2, "Our Digital Age of Distraction and our Increasing Techno-Social Dilemma," reviews writings by recent social critics that describe our current culture as one of distraction[62] and discusses the contours of our new attention economy. I explore the cultural losses our age of distraction inculcates and examine how our new attention economy is impacting our ability to create sustained meaningful relationships. I reference several current trends concerning the re-engineering of humanity and the degree to which our new electronic media environment is changing not only our sensorium but also our brain functioning. What does it mean to enter the post-human world, especially in terms of our relationality?

Chapter 3, "Enchantments and Their Inauthenticity: The Play of Amusements," is where I introduce the sensory trope of enchantment as a way to understand the techno-social dilemma we face. I argue that it provides a means by which to re-enchant our understanding of human communication. I interpret the trope of enchantment as a phenomenological sign process. I then discuss our current fascination with our smart technologies and social robots as forms of enchantment, interpreting them as fleeting and disingenuous. I argue such enchantments exemplify the mere play of amusements and are thus predominantly inauthentic markers of communicative engagement.

In chapter 4, "Echoes of the Acousmatic Voice in Cyberspace: The Impersonal Self," I look closely at the structural elements of the voices we hear within cyberspace and on the Internet. I introduce sound theorist Michael Chion's idea of the *acousmatic voice*,[63] one in which the recognition of the bodily source or person from which it comes is occluded. I argue that the mediated acousmatic voice within the electronic networks of cyberspace has, unfortunately, replaced our appeal to the immediate sonic voice of the other. I suggest that such modes of interaction in cyberspace propel us toward what I call the *impersonal self*, that is, one whose depth of meaning and, hence, sense of self is as shallow as the forms of information exchange it engages in. I claim that these electronic interaction trends or new habits are based upon inauthentic enchantments because they do not herald enchantment's roots in the actual auditory particularity of being. Instead they contain our fascinations in the sedimented world of signification and the symbolic. I end this chapter by juxtaposing our increased levels of anxiety and depression in America with these inauthentic enchantments and argue that this social condition exhibits an effect known as disenchanting enchantments, as George Ritzer describes it.[64] I interpret this social condition sonically as a generalized case of *existential dissonance*, the social and personal consequences of such disturbing habits of discourse.

It is in chapter 5, "The Murder of the *Phone* in Plain Sight: The Voice of Articulation," that I explicate how the silenced or diminished value accorded the speaking voice resides in a long Western philosophical history of neglect. In lieu of voice, this tradition has been premised upon a visualist orientation. In an attempt to resurrect the immediacy of the sonic pure voice to its rightful theoretical position within human affairs and especially within the field of communication, I rely heavily upon Mladen Dolar's work[65] and Adriana Cavarero's writings.[66] Each of these authors provides a theoretical lens by which to make important distinctions between voice as articulation (in service to the realm of symbolic meaning) and the pure voice as semiotic and phenomenological (embodied) aesthetic enunciation. Through a discussion of Jacques Derrida's critique of a phonocentrism within Western scholarship, I uncover many of the philosophical weapons used to murder the *phone*. I end the chapter by explicating the voice of articulation, the talking corpse of the voice that now dominates the world of cyberspace.

"The Enchanting *Phone* as Phenomenological Event: The Voice of Enunciation" is chapter 6. Here I revive the sensory trope of enchantment as the signifier of sound as a way to emphasize the important role that *phone* as enunciation plays in our human relationality. My objective is to reintroduce *phone* as the salient embodied or phenomenological action within events of speaking and listening. Given the long-standing affiliation of sound with time and its inherent dynamic flow, the sounding voice of enunciation offers an appropriate counterbalance to the mediated voice within cyberspace in its predominant visual and fixed configurations. The voice of enunciation thus heralds our radical alterity through its aesthetic irruption into the dominant symbolic systems of meaning as a phenomenological felt event. I discuss Emmanuel Levinas's treatment of the Saying and the Said in light of its inadequate treatment of the voice. I contend that the voice of enunciation as I explicate it, however, reinvigorates our communicative relations with what I call a sense of the *wild*, that is, the untamed yet semiotic aspect of our pure potentiality as human beings. It is through the voice of enunciation as a natural summons to cultural experience that we come to a sensory appreciation for genuine auditory experiences in their natural semiotic reverberations.

In chapter 7, "The Pivotal Nature of Voice: *Interper-sónal* Relationality and its Authenticity," I elaborate on the key role the voice of enunciation plays as an existential pivot point within human experience. By understanding its pivotal nature, we begin to appreciate how the natural sounding of voices activates several dialectics and their subsequent semiotic and phenomenological negotiations. In addition to nature and culture, the voice activates the boundary conditions between the body and language, the ancient Greek's sense of *zoe* and *bios*, Aristotle's *phone semantike* and *logos*, self and other, and listening and speaking. I use the balcony scene in Shakespeare's play, *Romeo and Juliet* as an example of attending to the voice of enunciation. By keeping the voice of enunciation foremost in mind, our theory of human relationality shifts from an impersonal focus (enhanced by our appeals to merely the voice of articulation) to an actual *interper-sónal* one. I end the chapter by encouraging us to attend to these interper-sónal qualities of discursive practices given that within them we re-enchant our overall understanding of human communication and the value it has in our lives. Most important, we also constitute more authentic encounters with others.

In the last chapter (chapter 8), "Resonance, Resilience, and Re-Enchantment: Voicing the Heart of the Matter," I argue that by accentuating the interper-sónal aspects of discourse we possibilize interper-sónal *resonance* between self and other. I distinguish between the experience of resonance and echo, re-interpreting Jean-Luc Nancy's conceptualization.[67] I reference the myth of *Echo and Narcissus* as a symbol of both resonance and love lost. We find that unlike the representations of Echo and Narcissus, genuine interper-sónal encounters bring us to the very heart of the matter when it comes to understanding healthy and productive discursive habits. I equate the natural flow of authentic relatedness as a form of existential musicality which inheres within auditory events of speaking and listening bringing us heart-to-heart. These moments of aesthetic enchantment between self and other recapture a sense of our musicality as vibrant communicative creatures. It is within such moments of resonance that we find our true resilience as human beings.

What I offer in the chapters that follow is an informed theoretical assessment of our current socio-cultural condition when it comes to the *phone*. This is not a how-to book for creating better human relationships. That is anathema to my perspective on relationality as an organic unfolding or voicing between self and other. Nor am I advocating that we abandon our zest for cultural progress in terms of our electronic technological advancements. I, too, am a new media user of various kinds and appreciate its functionality in my life every day. My aim is quite simple: By redirecting our attention to the immediacy of the sounding voice of aesthetic enunciation, I hope to re-enchant our sense of human communication as an immediate aesthetic value in human experience by appealing to the sensory trope of enchantment. For me, above all, communication is not a tool nor is it a skill,[68] a claim unfortunately often propagated by the social science perspective in our discipline and technologists alike. So, my objective is to offer a repositioning of our philosophical understanding of relationality within its temporal flow as voiced, in order to remind us that human communication in its auditory mode is foremost the very means by which a good life, an authentic and ethical life, is built in immediate discursive practices, one moment of speaking and listening at a time. Georges Gusdorf reminds us of what we too often repress about the primary sensibility of the ear and sound: "The ear is the teacher of the voice."[69] To this I would reversibly add that the voice is also the teacher of the ear.

Perhaps we would be better off in our current socio-cultural circumstances of existential dissonance if we echoed the French in their traditional habit of what I will call interper-sónal greetings, greetings that accentuate the auditory nature of engagement and get at the heart of speaking and listening that I aim to explore. Upon being introduced to someone for the first time, they traditionally say, "Enchanté," which means "I am enchanted to meet you." I think the French are on to something. It seems to me that on such occasions the French are not interpreting the moment of meeting as delusionary or as if the other is casting a spell upon them, which is the typical negative connotation of the meaning of enchantment. Instead, it appears that this custom or auditory cultural code, if you will, acknowledges, from the outset, that being in the immediate auditory presence of others is a salient moment unlike others, an intense aesthetic experience. It is a moment in which our humanity is *called into being* by the other's voice in potentially unique and significant ways. Thus, by articulating "enchanté," they implicitly show a deference to the existential call or sounding of the other, interpreting it as a possible enchanting moment of auditory aesthetic importance, even if it might fail in the end to meet its full potentiality. For, as I will suggest, enchantment (in its authentic entailment at least) *is* a salient moment of relationality that interrupts our typical ways of being-in-the-world and enables a resiliency that we seem to so desperately need. Authentic enchantments mark an existential sign condition of potential openness to the other and the world that did not exist prior to its aesthetic enunciation. By focusing on the auditory presence of the other at such moments of introduction, the French perhaps unwittingly, but no less importantly, recognize that in such moments we are called to honor our companions—which nourishes a possible ethical generosity toward them. The French, in their cultural appreciation of semiotics and phenomenology, seem to understand well that relationality possibilizes enchantments and, reversibly, that authentic enchantments possibilize deeper moments of relationality. As a culture known historically for their appreciation of love and romance, with this traditional greeting they capture the very heart of the matter when it comes to the importance of our immediate speaking and listening. It is as if they well understand that the voice articulates the heart.[70]

## NOTES

1. Alina Bradford, "5 Awesome Ways to Use Alexa on Valentine's Day," *CNET,* February 13, 2019, https://www.cnet.com/how-to/alexa-on-valentines-day/.

2. Such contemporary trends indicate just how much relationships, in the digital age, have become a commodity form. See John W. Lannamann, "The Politics of Voice in Interpersonal Communication," in *Social Approaches to Communication*, ed. Wendy Leeds-Hurwitz (New York: Guilford Press, 1995), 114–34. As Lannamann (1995) says, the digital age is also a highly commercialized age of consumption where "desire cannot give way to satiation" (120). This age of consumption is propagated by what Max Horkheimer and Theodor Adorno identify as the "culture industry." See Max Horkheimer and Theodor Adorno, *Dialectic of Enlightenment*, trans. John Cumming (Frieberg: Herder and Herder, 1972).

3. It seems to me that such devices like the Amazon Echo smart speaker, which enables customers to interact with Alexa, are auditory precursors to welcoming full-fledged social robots into our homes in the not-too-distant future. Sherry Turkle's work at MIT, of course, addresses these virtual trends and raises serious concerns about the diminished status of real human relationality and empathy.

4. See John L. Locke, *The De-Voicing of Society: Why We Don't Talk to Each Other Anymore* (New York: Simon & Schuster, 1998).

5. See "The Consequences of Loneliness: Interview with James Lynch," Earl E. Bakken Center for Spirituality & Healing, University of Minnesota, accessed April 4, 2019, https://www.takingcharge.csh.umn.edu/consequences-loneliness-interview-james-lynch.

6. Walter Ong, *Orality and Literacy: The Technologizing of the Word* (New York: Routledge, [1982], 2002.

7. Victor Kestenbaum, *The Phenomenological Sense of John Dewey: Habit and Meaning* (Atlantic Highlands, NJ: Humanities Press, 1977): 24, 19.

8. The sources on this topic are enormous. One of the most compelling is from a former Google technologist now philosopher, James Williams, who I rely upon heavily in the chapters that follow. His book, *Stand Out of Our Light: Freedom and Resistance in the Attention Economy* (Cambridge: Cambridge University Press, 2018), speaks to the growing concern and possible remedies for our various technological addictions that are robbing us, he says, of our freedom to be fully human.

9. At the time of this writing, both Apple and Android systems have elaborate tracking mechanisms either installed on their upgraded phones or offered as easy-to-install applications so users can easily see statistics on how much they use various phone features and applications, even how many times they pick up their phones.

10. Of course, Plato, some 2,500 years ago, also expressed this same basic concern about how the forms of conversation we use (whether oral or written) necessarily influence what ideas or content can be shared. As he seemed to understand so long ago, the very content of our ideas provides the very *content* of our culture, of who we are collectively. To be clear, I am not a technological determinist, that is, one who believes that technological progress (which exists as an autonomous force outside our control) is the primary factor that influences the course of human history. Nor am I a technological instrumentalist, that is, one who believes that our technological advances are merely neutral tools we use for our own purposes. Instead, I like to call myself a *technological realist*, who believes that adoption of new media and reflection on its value and worth in society should go hand in hand; with new media comes cultural change. What are some of the consequences of cultural change?

11. Claude Shannon and Warren Weaver, *The Mathematical Theory of Communication* (Urbana: University of Illinois Press, 1949).

12. For example, I never use the word *communicator* in my own discourse to designate someone who is speaking in their expressivity because, for me, such a designation presupposes the accomplishment of communication that I am seeking in my expressions and forecloses the active perception of my words in the listener's conscious experience. Communication is thus *accomplished between* speaker and listener as an either/or and both/and logic of expression and perception as a reciprocal, reversible, and reflexive endeavor. It is never a one-sided affair like information exchange.

13. Sherry Turkle, *Reclaiming Conversation: The Power of Talk in a Digital Age* (New York: Penguin Books, 2015).

14. The distinction I am making here about the concepts of information exchange and communication was also made by communication and media theorist James Carey in his

insightful 1997 book, *Communication as Culture: Essays on Media and Society* (Boston: Unwin Hyman). Here, Carey advocates for a ritual view of communication, as opposed to the information model of transmission developed by Claude Shannon and Warren Weaver. See Claude Shannon and Warren Weaver, *The Mathematical Theory of Communication.*

15. Michel Chion, *Audio-Vision: Sound on Screen* (New York: Columbia University Press, 1994).

16. For a discussion on Peirce's notion of habit see: Charles Sanders Peirce, *The Collected Papers of Charles Sanders Peirce*, Vols. 1–6, eds. Charles Hartshorne and Paul Weiss (Cambridge: Belknap Press of Harvard University Press, 1931–1935), 5.538. References to Peirce's writings in *The Collected Papers* use the conventional format of citing volume followed by paragraph number.

17. John Dewey, *Human Nature and Conduct* (New York: The Modern Library, Random House, 1922): 25.

18. Being always *on the phone* is equated most often with cell phone addiction. See for example, "Cell Phone Addiction," *Psychguides,* accessed August 30, 2019, https://www.psychguides.com/behavioral-disorders/cell-phone-addiction/signs-and-symptoms/.

19. Jamie Ducharme, "'Phubbing' is Hurting Your Relationships. Here's What It Is," *Time,* March 29, 2018, http://time.com/5216853/what-is-phubbing/.

20. Andrew K. Przybylski and Netta Weinstein, "Can You Connect with Me Now? How the Presence of Mobile Communication Technology Influences Face-to-Face Conversation Quality," *Journal of Social and Personal Relationships* 30, no. 3 (May 2013).

21. Social theorist Jane Bennett agrees, as does sociologist Richard Jenkins. See Jane Bennett, *The Enchantment of Modern Life: Attachments, Crossings, and Ethics* (Princeton: Princeton University Press, 2001); Richard Jenkins, "Disenchantment, Enchantment and Re-Enchantment: Max Weber at the Millennium," *Max Weber Studies* 1, no. 1 (November 2000).

22. Max Weber, *The Protestant Ethic and the Spirit of Capitalism,* trans. Talcott Parsons (London: Unwin Hyman, 1989).

23. Jenkins, "Disenchantment, Enchantment and Re-Enchantment," 12.

24. See Gordon Graham, *The Re-Enchantment of the World: Art Versus Religion* (Oxford: Oxford University Press: 2007). Also, I believe communication theorist Gregory Bateson's work for much of his life takes up this key problematic. See Gregory Bateson and Mary Catherine Bateson, *Angels Fear: Towards an Epistemology of the Sacred* (New York: Bantam Books, 1987).

25. Jenkins, "Disenchantment, Enchantment and Re-Enchantment."

26. David McPherson and Charles Taylor, "Re-Enchanting the World: An Interview with Charles Taylor," *Philosophy & Theology* 24, no. 2 (2012).

27. As Michael T. Saler contends, at least since the middle ages enchantment had ambivalent meanings. "It signified both 'delight' in wonderful things and the potential to be placed under their spell, to be beguiled." See Saler, 2004, "Modernity, Disenchantment, and the Ironic Imagination," *Philosophy and Literature,* 28, no. 1, 138.

28. Ibid, 140.

29. Bennett, *The Enchantment of Modern Life*; Jane Bennett, *Vibrant Matter: A Political Ecology of Things* (Durham: Duke University Press, 2009); Akeel Bilgrami, "Occidentalism, the Very Idea: An Essay on Enlightenment and Enchantment," *Critical Theory* 32, no. 3 (2006); Akeel Bilgrami, *Secularism, Identity, and Enchantment* (Cambridge: Harvard University Press, 2014). See also Laura Zebuhr, "Sound Enchantment: The Case of Henry David Thoreau," *New Literary History* 48, no. 3 (Summer 2017).

30. Martin Heidegger refers to mood as one of the fundamental aspects of his existential structure of care. See Martin Heidegger, *Being and Time,* trans. John Macquarrie and Edward S. Robinson (Oxford: Blackwell, 1962), 176.

31. For a sampling of the cross-disciplinary appeal of using enchantment as a sensory trope in current scholarship, see the following: Arne Carlsen and Lloyd Sandelands, "First Passion: Wonder in Organizational Inquiry," *Management Learning* 46, no. 4 (2015); Patrick Curry, "Enchantment and Modernity," *PAN: Philosophy Activism Nature* 9 (2012); Louis E. Howe, "Enchantment, Weak Ontologies, and Administrative Ethics," *Administration & Society* 38, no. 4 (2006); Camilla Asplund Ingemark, "The Chronotope of Enchantment," *Journal of Folklore*

*Research* 43, no. 1 (2006); Sara Lyons, "The Disenchantment/Re-Enchantment of the World: Aesthetics, Secularization, and the Gods of Greece from Friedrich Schiller to Walter Pater," *Modern Language Review* 109, no. 4 (2014); George Ritzer and Todd Stillman, "The Postmodern Ballpark as a Leisure Setting: Enchantment and Simulated De-McDonaldization," *Leisure Sciences* 23, no. 2 (2001); Michael T. Saler, "Modernity, Disenchantment, and the Ironic Imagination;" Patrick Sherry, "Disenchantment, Re-Enchantment, and Enchantment," *Modern Theology* 25, no. 3 (2009); Paul Standish, "The Disenchantment of Education and the Re-Enchantment of the World," *Journal of Philosophy of Education* 50, no. 1 (2016); Jo A. Tyler, "Reclaiming Rare Listening as a Means of Organizational Re-Enchantment," *Journal of Organizational Change Management* 24, no. 1 (2011); Zebuhr, "Sound Enchantment."

32. Henry David Thoreau understood this positive capacity of enchantments well. Often referenced by literary scholars for his many references to nature's sounds and enchantments in his writings, Thoreau underscores the transformative potential of what I will call *authentic* enchantments. For discussions on this point, see Rochelle L. Johnson, "'This Enchantment Is No Delusion': Henry David Thoreau, the New Materialisms, and Ineffable Materiality," *Interdisciplinary Studies in Literature and Environment* 21, no. 3 (Summer 2014); Zebuhr, "Sound Enchantment."

33. Sound theorist and composer, R. Murray Schafer coined the term *soundscape* in his 1977 book, *The Tuning of the World* (New York: Knopf).

34. George Ritzer, *Enchanting a Disenchanted World: Revolutionizing the Means of Consumption* (Thousand Oaks: Pine Forge Press, 1999).

35. Marshall McLuhan speaks to this idea in his 1964 book, *Understanding Media: The Extensions of Man* (New York: McGraw Hill). In it he describes how technological advances can easily slip from being delightful to producing anxiety and a state of numbness and dread.

36. Sherry Turkle, *Alone Together: Why We Expect More from Technology and Less From Each Other* (New York: Basic Books, 2011).

37. Turkle, *Reclaiming Conversation*, 22.

38. Trista Kelley, "Study: You are More Likely to Die Walking with Headphones," *Times Union*, January 17, 2012, https://www.timesunion.com/news/article/Study-You-are-more-likely-to-die-walking-with-2578662.php.

39. Michael Schrage, "Time to Hang Up on Voice Mail," *Harvard Business Review*, September 30, 2013, https://hbr.org/2013/09/time-to-hang-up-on-voice-mail.

40. Neil Howe, "Why Millennials are Texting More and Talking Less," *Forbes*, July 15, 2015, https://www.forbes.com/sites/neilhowe/2015/07/15/why-millennials-are-texting-more-and-talking-less/#c5a207259752.

41. Media ecology is a growing body of scholarship that theorizes media as environments that radically shift our sense of self, other, and world. Some of the well-known media ecologists include Walter Ong and Neil Postman, although many others have also contributed greatly to the goals of exposing the media/technology/social interface. These others include Marshall McLuhan, Lewis Mumford, Christine Nystrom, Harold Innis, and Lance Strate. For an insightful introduction to the field see, Lance Strate, *Echoes and Reflections: On Media Ecology as a Field of Study* (Cresskill, NJ: Hampton Press, 2006).

42. Jacques Ellul, *The Humiliation of the Word*, trans. Joyce Main Hanks (Grand Rapids, MI: Eerdmans, 1985), 2.

43. Richard Restak, *The New Brain: How the Modern Age Is Rewiring Your Mind* (Emmaus: Rodale Publishers, 2003).

44. Don Ihde, *Listening and Voice: Phenomenologies of Sound* (Albany: State University of New York Press, 2007); Walter Ong, *The Presence of the Word: Some Prolegomena for Cultural and Religious History* (Binghamton: Global Publications State University of New York, [1967] 2000).

45. Walter J. Ong, *The Barbarian Within: And Other Fugitive Essays and Studies* (New York: Macmillan, 1962), 225.

46. Ong, *The Presence of the Word*, 309.

47. My intent is to accentuate the sonic characteristics of human relations and thus I will be designating self and other relations that are primarily based within vocality as *interper-sónal*.

48. For example, in Central Park in New York City, we find a new social engagement project called FreeConvo. Using inflatable plastic sofas that are positioned next to a sign that reads, "Free Conversation," passersby are encouraged to just sit for a while and talk with whomever willingly appears. The two men who launched the project in June 2018 work in finance and information technology and were convinced that no one talks to one another anymore. Communication scholar Sarah J. Tracy also notes this decline in conversation in a recent article entitled, "Let's Talk: Conversation as a Defining Moment for the Communication Discipline." See Tracy, 2019, *Health Communication,* DOI: 10.1080/10410236.2019.1593081.

49. Stephen Miller, *Conversation: A History of a Declining Art* (New Haven: Yale University Press, 2006).

50. Turkle, *Reclaiming Conversation.*

51. D. Travers Scott chronicles the historical pathologizing of technological advances as typical irrational responses to the advent of new technologies and calls this practice the operation of the "newness hypothesis." As Scott (2018) explains, "the newness hypothesis suggests that people fear social change and they project these fears onto new media as symbols of such change" (3). For more on this point, see D. Travers Scott, *Pathology and Technology: Killer Apps and Sick Users* (New York: Peter Lang, 2018).

52. My argument on this point (taken up in chapter 4) will be reconciled with Ong's contention that "a good many oral-aural cultures tend to manifest characteristic anxiety syndromes. . . ." See Ong, *The Presence of the Word,* 131. The nuance of acousmatic voices within cyberspace helps to support my position.

53. Peter Dockrill, "America Really Is in the Midst of a Rising Anxiety Epidemic," *Science Alert,* May 9, 2018, https://www.sciencealert.com/americans-are-in-the-midst-of-an-anxiety-epidemic-stress-increase.

54. Bill Hoffmann, "Report: Depression Is Skyrocketing in America," *Newsmax,* May 10, 2018, https://www.newsmax.com/newsfront/survey-depression-surge-america/2018/05/10/id/859531/.

55. Even talking on the telephone is a mediated experience, although less so.

56. Roland Barthes, *The Grain of the Voice: Interviews 1962–1980,* trans. Linda Coverdale (Los Angeles: University of California Press, 1991).

57. As vocal theorists Neumark, Gibson, and Van Leeuwen suggest, while the disembodied voice of networked culture is digitally "made transportable through time and space, or even artificially produced . . . [its] material qualities, [are] quite different. . . from those praised by Roland Barthes." See Norie Neumark, Ross Gibson, and Theo Van Leeuwen, eds., *Voice: Vocal Aesthetics in Digital Arts and Media* (Cambridge, MA: Massachusetts Institute of Technology, 2010), x.

58. See Mladen Dolar, *A Voice and Nothing More* (Cambridge: MIT Press, 2006), 4.

59. Ibid., 15.

60. For a preview of communicology, I refer you to Deborah Eicher-Catt and Isaac E. Catt, *Communicology: The New Science of Embodied Discourse* (Madison: Fairleigh Dickinson University Press, 2010). Also see Andrew R. Smith, Isaac E. Catt, and Igor E. Klyukanov, eds., *Communicology for the Human Sciences: Lanigan and the Philosophy of Communication* (New York: Peter Lang, 2018); Isaac E. Catt, *Embodiment in the Semiotic Matrix: Communicology in Peirce, Dewey, Bateson, and Bourdieu* (Madison: Fairleigh Dickinson University Press, 2017).

61. Kestenbaum, *The Phenomenological Sense of John Dewey,* 4.

62. Maggie Jackson, *Distracted: The Erosion of Attention and the Coming Dark Age* (Amherst: Prometheus Books, 2008).

63. Michel Chion, *The Voice in Cinema,* trans. Claudia Gorbman (New York: Columbia University Press, 1999).

64. Ritzer, *Enchanting a Disenchanted World.*

65. Dolar, *A Voice and Nothing More.*

66. Adriana Cavarero, *For More Than One Voice: Toward a Philosophy of Vocal Expression,* trans. Paul A. Kottman (Stanford: Stanford University Press, 2005).

67. Jean-Luc Nancy, *Listening,* trans. Charlotte Mandell (New York: Fordham University Press, 2007).

68. For an insightful discussion of this very distinction, see Isaac E. Catt, "Communication Is Not a Skill: Critique of Communication Pedagogy as Narcissistic Expression," in *Communicology: The New Science of Embodied Discourse,* eds. Deborah Eicher-Catt and Isaac E. Catt (Madison: Fairleigh Dickinson University Press, 2010): 131–50.

69. Georges Gusdorf, *Speaking (La Parole)*, trans. Paul T. Brockelman (Chicago: Northwestern University Press, 1965), 94.

70. John L. Locke, *The De-Voicing of Society: Why We Don't Talk to Each Other Anymore* (New York: Simon & Schuster, 1998).

*Chapter One*

# On the *Phone*

In this chapter, I describe the current media-saturated environment in which we live and set up the problematic of the diminished value placed on the immediate sounding voice within self and other relations. I begin by discussing our new online habits of discourse and the implications these taken-for-granted ways of electronically connecting have on our existential well-being. I offer a hermeneutic of cyberspace and the Internet, arguing that they are primarily hyper-textual/visual in composition rather than acoustic or sound based. Overall, I am beginning my pursuit of the important question: How do our new mediated environments impact our bodily comportment in the world and, most importantly, our relationality? I end by suggesting that our current electronic habits of connectivity are actually undermining our relationality using social media as an ironic example.

## EVERYDAY LIFE AND OUR ONLINE HABITS OF DISCOURSE

For most of us, everyday life is almost completely mediated by electronic technology in one way or another. Whether we are conscious of it or not, living within such a mediated environment has significantly changed our existential positioning in the world. As Joshua Meyrowitz argues, within such mediated environments there is an existential collapse of any traditional felt sense of place. This is because within the world of cyberspace existential boundaries tend to blur easily between fundamental aspects of daily life, such as the self and the other, what is considered public and private, the personal dimensions of lived experiences and the social, and what constitutes childhood and adulthood, to name but a few. As a result, we are increasingly nowhere and everywhere at the same time.[1] Hence, our new lived reality is not only significantly changing our cognitive habits but our existential positionality in the world and with it our perceptions of one another.

Within the short time span of about 20 years since the Internet was first introduced, we have quite unreflectively normalized our new habits of discourse by becoming full-fledged digital users. Unfortunately, our own habits of electronic connectivity remain, for the most part, personally unchallenged, reflecting the very pre-objective intentionality all habits entail, as the early pragmatist John Dewey theorized. Dewey reminds us that habits are illustrations of our pre-objective intentionality, existing below our conscious awareness most of the time. This idea originates, of course, in the philosophy of phenomenologist Edmund Husserl and is elaborated by phenomenologist Maurice Merleau-Ponty.[2] As is often the case, therefore, we are unaware of our electronic habits until an ignored loved one brings them to our attention or until we realize that too much time has been spent playing video games or engaging in other digitalized forms of entertainment instead of socializing with friends in immediate ear-to-ear contexts. Because habits exist at a pre-conscious level, it is important for us to bring them to conscious awareness through a phenomenological process of radical reflection that problematizes their taken-for-grantedness.

So, what is our new electronic normal? For most of us, we begin our day by surfing our favorite news sites and checking Twitter, LinkedIn, Facebook, Instagram, or our various email accounts. If we do so, we are considered quite normal, according to current studies on Americans' electronic habits. Throughout the day, we do more of the same. With business, industry, the medical world, government, and education (to name just a few) now fully operationalized online, the chances of not interacting on a given day with various constituencies in cyberspace or on the Internet is relatively low. Digital screens are appearing everywhere. We now have electronic screens placed in public places where they never were before—on individual tables at restaurants, on the backs of taxicab and airline seats, and over urinals, and, for only $12.99, an iPhone holster can be purchased for one's baby stroller.[3] So, we have come to anticipate being electronically connected in our daily lives, wired to a social world that mediates our existence in new and profound ways.

We are reminded of our new normal or taken-for-granted ways of being electronically mediated when we are without our phone or think that we have temporarily lost it. When this happens, panic often sets in immediately. This is not surprising given that nine out of ten people never leave home without it.[4] Increasingly, we find that the last item we touch before turning in for the evening is some kind of electronic device, be it our phones, e-readers, computers, or smart tablets. We are so thoroughly steeped in electronic connectivity that we can easily "spend the day transfixed by our screens, thumb twitching in the subways and elevators, glancing at traffic lights," so declares

James Williams, former technologist at Google now turned philosopher.[5] At issue is our increased preference for digitalized interaction at the expense of immediate ear-to-ear encounters. As Turkle describes it, we are beginning "to feel more at home in the world of screens. Among family and friends, among colleagues and lovers, we turn to our phones instead of each other. We readily admit we would rather send an electronic message or mail than commit to face-to-face meeting or a telephone call."[6] It appears we have arrived at a very different space of relationality through these very different habits of discourse. This is quickly becoming our new normal. We are almost always *on the phone*. Herein, I use the phrase *on the phone* in an inclusive way to signify various electronic devices such as smartphones, computers, notebooks, and e-readers.

The statistics documenting our new normal are staggering. To begin, as of 2018, there are an average of thirteen Internet-connected devices in the typical household in North America.[7] Although my husband and I do not consider ourselves technologically dependent, we have at least six devices between us! And, as reported by Williams, further studies have found that we use our devices hundreds of times per day, spending a third of our waking lives engaged with them.[8] Apple confirmed that users unlock their iPhones an average of 150 times a day, and a research firm conducting a study in 2016 found that we touch our phones about 2,617 times per day.[9] If that were not enough, our phones also prod us to keep engaged with them by constantly displaying electronic notifications and acoustic bings of various sorts: "Each day, the Android mobile operating system alone sends over 11 billion notifications to its more than 1 billion users."[10] It is not surprising, then, to learn from a 2015 Pew Research Center study on U.S. smartphone use that half of users say they could not live without their phone.[11]

But what does this new way of living entail exactly, especially in terms of our quality of being and habits of relating? What does it mean to be *on* the Internet and *in* cyberspace? How do these new mediated dimensions of spatiality and temporality impact our bodily comportment in the world and, most importantly, our relationality? Various forms of media significantly impact our ways of being in the world. This should not come as a surprise, especially for those theorists for whom media technologies are perceived and understood as salient environments that must be considered when reflecting upon the characteristics and qualities of cultural life. These theorists are known as media ecologists because they understand that new forms of media (including past inventions such as the printing press, television, or radio) upset a given socio-cultural ecology, often producing unbalanced social conditions when it comes to cultural life, at least until a new homeostasis can organically emerge. Media ecologists such as Marshall McLuhan, Walter Ong, Neil Postman, and Lance Strate have long argued that changing modes of media—such as the advent of radio, television, computers, and now smartphones and other devices—while often providing convenience and heightened connectivity also come with negative personal and social consequences, that is, they dramatically change our socio-cultural environments and ways of being. Neil Postman, for example, referencing Aldous Huxley's *Brave New World*, lamented in the 1980s that, with our increased reliance on television viewing (as opposed to book reading), we were running the risk of "amusing ourselves to death."[12] While he claimed that the personal consequences of our couch potato syndrome are psychologically significant, above all he was concerned about the impact that such a readily accessible digitalized visual medium would have on how we view the world, especially in the arena of political discourse. He thought television would reduce politics to mere show business. The fact that we elected a reality TV star as our forty-fifth president only lends support for his now prophetic argument. Central concerns of media ecologists are exemplified in the important questions they ask: What are we gaining with our media use in terms of our ways of perceiving and being in the world? What modes of perceiving, knowing, and understanding about our world are we potentially limiting and/or sacrificing with their use? Media theorist and cultural historian Walter Ong claims that changes in media over the course of history reorient the entire human psyche, and "man's relationship to the physical world around him, to his fellow men, to his own thought, and to himself radically changes."[13]

Our cultural forms of media—smartphones, electronic tablets, and the like—are aptly named; they *mediate* our conscious awareness of the world. Quite simply, media serve as connecting mechanisms that join sometimes quite disparate parts of a given interactive system—in this case, the socio-cultural system—the consequences of which often go unnoticed or unanticipated, as in Postman's critique of television. Ong reminds us that in our historical shifts and progressions from a primarily oral-aural (speaking-listening) culture to a print-typography culture (accelerated by the advent of the printing press) to our current electronic forms of communication (what he terms a *secondary orality*), there are also concomitant changes in our entire sensory interfaces with the world.[14] As a phenomenologist as well, that is, one who studies lived experiences as embodied occurrences of meaningful activity, Ong identifies these combinatory sensory interfaces our existential "sensorium."[15] He understands these sensory interfaces as the building blocks from which we construct life's meaning and significance. As Ong explains, "by the sensorium we mean here the entire sensory apparatus as an operational complex."[16] In other words, within each cultural milieu (orality, literacy, or electronic), we find different senses being activated over others, often creating an imbalance to our sensory experiences, where one will dominate over another. So, Ong associates orality with the auditory and literacy with the visual, emphasizing all the while that sensory experiences are culturally informed based upon our sensory preferences. For Ong and his mentor,

Marshall McLuhan, and others like anthropologist Constance Classen, sensory perception is not merely a physical act but also must be understood as historical and cultural.[17] In this regard, Ong shares close affinities with semiotic phenomenologists who claim that consciousness, or our awareness of the world in general, is a cultural act; it is informed by the very codes of language and discourse operable to a given group of people at a given moment in time. In his research on the differences between the media of orality, literacy, and electronic technologies, Ong asks quite directly this theoretical question: How do different forms of media impact how a given culture consciously senses the world—how we see, touch, taste, smell, and hear—as a combinatory ratio of sense experience? And, reciprocally, in what ways does the reorganization of our sensorium impact our relations with the world?

As a phenomenologist who follows the semiotic writings of Charles Sanders Peirce, I understand that such shifts in our sensorium are based upon variances in our modes of awareness of the world as communicative events. In other words, communicologists believe that awareness of the world and the meanings we derive from it are communicatively based; that is, they are largely shaped by the embodied signifying systems or code systems of which we are necessarily a part as cultural beings. Our interactions with signs (or objects to consciousness that appear to represent something else—an idea, a person, a place, or a thing) subsequently impact our phenomenological, embodied orientations toward self, other, and world. Our sensorium is thus best understood as a phenomenology of conscious experience that is heavily shaped by the cultural signs or code conditions we use to interpret (express and perceive) the world. Therefore, it is safe to assume that various media forms, including those that are highly digitized, symbolic, or auditory in their form impact our very sensory or phenomenological interfaces with the world in different ways. And although perception is varied according to the sensory stimuli presented in a given moment, it is best understood as a synthetic accomplishment of embodied experience.

A note of clarification is needed here in regard to my use of phenomenology in this endeavor, particularly given my desire to resuscitate an appreciation of the voice as sound. Phenomenology's traditional meaning is derived from *phainomenon*, which means "appearance" and stems from the word *phainein*, meaning "to show" or "expose to sight."[18] This historical association is unfortunate because it appears to uphold only a visualist orientation about the primacy of perception that, in its simplest or commonsense treatment, merely objectifies things of the world in space in an *a priori* realist fashion. Said differently, the word *phainein* seems to privilege sight over other sensory ways we perceive or take in the world. Although Edmund Husserl, the founder of phenomenology, theorized perception as a synthetic act, the very naming of phenomenology as an initial philosophical enterprise carries this unfortunate visualist connotation in its name. For those unfamiliar with the tenets of phenomenology, when it comes to the primacy of perception as our existential connection to the world, this visualist connotation might be misleading. We might assume that the phenomenology of perception refers primarily to the study of appearances or sight. Existential phenomenologist Maurice Merleau-Ponty and other continental philosophers writing during the mid-twentieth century offer important theoretical correctives that this unfortunate commonsense association presents. Specifically, Merleau-Ponty asserts that perception should be conceived as an original modality of consciousness that weds the subject-object duality as a *synthesis* of sensory experience. Perception is thus an embodied synthesis of sign characteristics in the world where meaning is arrived at phenomenologically through all the senses as a "style" of perceiving. Merleau-Ponty explains:

> The perceptual synthesis thus must be accomplished by the subject, which can both delimit certain perspectival aspects in the object, the only ones actually given, and at the same time go beyond them. This subject . . . is my body as the field of perception and action [*pratique*]—in so far as my gestures have a certain reach and circumscribe as my domain the whole group of objects familiar to me. Perception is here understood as a reference to a whole which can be grasped, in principle, only through certain of its parts or aspects. The perceived thing is not an ideal unity in the possession of the intellect, like a geometrical notion, for example; it is rather a totality open to a horizon of an indefinite number of perspectival views which blend with one another according to a given style, which defines the object in question.[19]

Thus, perception of objects to consciousness become stylized, according to Merleau-Ponty. Similarly, for followers of the pragmatist tradition, such as Dewey and Peirce, we could also say that perception becomes habitualized at the pre-objective level, developing psychic patterns of awareness that are then applied to subsequent thought and action. So, while phenomenology as a mode of inquiry appears to accentuate the visual elements of sensory experience as a study of appearances, this is not a restricted proposition about perception that most phenomenologists would corroborate. In his theoretical development of the sensorium, Ong understood as well that the senses work together, and yet, at the same time, we find different cultures developing different habits or styles of perception that exhibit particular sensory ratios. As Ong scholar Paul Soukup contends, "people can pattern and coordinate the world of sense experience differently. Because humans attend selectively to sense experience, they must make choices . . . [and] those choices are culturally informed."[20] Ong unwittingly acknowledges the signifying entailments involved in all sense perception.

It is beneficial to understand, therefore, that the spaces of cyber and the Internet present unique sensory characteristics that other objects to consciousness in our environment do not. Because of their unique aspects, we stylize our perceptions of them and develop habits of perception that go unquestioned. Thus, the spaces of cyber and the Internet are two powerful media forms of electronic connectivity, objects of consciousness that significantly shape our sensory experience and reciprocally implicate us in their ongoing maintenance. As Merleau-Ponty attests (and Dewey agrees), any interaction with our environment is highly dynamic and constitutes not a cause-and-effect relation as much as it displays a circularity of mutual, reciprocal implication. Merleau-Ponty declares that "situation and reaction are linked internally by their common participation in a structure in which the mode of activity proper to the organism is expressed. Hence they cannot be placed one after the other as cause and effect: they are two moments of a circular process."[21]

In our discussion of the reciprocal impact of these particular electronic forms, it is important to note that both cyberspace and the Internet appeared on the cultural scene only shortly before Ong's death. Much of Ong's argumentation about the promise of electronic communication that we find in many of his works, therefore, was written before technology's thorough elaboration and worldwide popularity as appealing virtual environments. Given my main concern with the immediacy of speaking and listening as oral-aural acts of communication and, in particular, the sounding voice as sensory experience, a brief summary of their attributes is in order.

## THE SPACE OF CYBER AND THE INTERNET

Originally coined by William Gibson in 1984 in his novel *Neuromancer*, the term *cyberspace* refers most generally to "any iteration of computer mediated virtuality, communicative device, or pseudo-spatial simulation."[22] As the name implies, cyberspace is understood to be a "mutually imagined environment" that while strictly speaking is not an actual space nonetheless operates as an "unbounded and multidimensional space" in which interactions take place.[23] In distinguishing cyberspace from the Internet, Phil Graham adds clarity: The Internet is a technological artifact that one goes *on*, whereas cyberspace is a virtually accessible cultural space that one goes *in*. The Internet constitutes the physically spatial medium that the virtually spatial medium of cyberspace inhabits.[24] As a consequence of their predominant spatial characteristics, both the Internet and cyberspace are often described in the literature as collapsing a linear sense of time, that is, accentuating a simultaneity to experience unlike other forms of media, like writing. Cyberspace thus transforms our experience in space to an abstraction of space and we begin to understand the reality of human relationships in cyberspace terms.[25]

As we move further into the twenty-first century, we find that the worlds of cyberspace and the Internet are increasingly video-centric and logo-centric in terms of their forms of sensory interface, thus accentuating the visual over the auditory. This progressive development was not anticipated by Ong. Instead, he theorized that modern developments in electronic communication would "give more play to the oral-aural" dimensions of experience.[26] To the contrary, our culture is described now as an image-based one, fueled in large part by our consumerist, capitalistic system where advertising and marketing provide its essential structure.[27] So, while the oral-aural continues to be an aspect of our culture more generally, we see an increasing visual dominance, especially if we take into account the widespread use of electronic logo-centric or textually based forms of connectivity. The modern field of graphic and digital design, for example, exploded with the advent of cyberspace and the Internet, as visual representation became the hallmark of website interfaces and online marketing. Given that print or textual representations (as logo-centric) are visual in nature as well (the primary characteristic of literate cultures, according to Ong), our new electronic media overwhelmingly seem to privilege visual media over the auditory. In his writings on technological change, philosopher Jacques Ellul agrees and specifically disputes Ong's prior summation by declaring that we now are witnessing the "unconditional victory of the visual and images"[28] over the auditory.

As a result, our digital landscape in terms of its sensory characteristics is primarily what I call hyper-textual/visual in composition rather than acoustic or sound based. Increasingly, we write tweets; we do not sing them. We write emails, blogs, and posts on Facebook; less frequently, we call people on the phone. We find business and industry using electronically produced voice message answering systems; speaking directly with another human being is now often the last resort when conducting business. At work, we enter textual data on computer screens, reducing the amount of time we actually orally interact with another. Here, we only have to think of the many contexts of customer service encounters we engage in every day, be it in a business setting or even at the doctor's office, to evidence this trend. For example, doctors and nurses now sit behind a computer screen in the examining room and talk to patients by periodically peering around it. The interaction and sensory perceptions of one another are dramatically changed by the fact that their chief concern appears to be accurately entering data into an electronic health network. While these preferences for the logo-centric aspects of information exchange are increasing, we also appeal to visual signs of iconicity as supplemental material, including, for example, photos we share on Instagram or Facebook or emojis within our texts. Consequently, I disagree with Ong's 1962 assessment that "modern developments in communications . . . specialize not in sight but in sound."[29] We must remember that at that time Ong was referencing the rise of radio as a medium and the predominance of sound over the visual in early television, acknowledging perhaps the unsophisticated quality of the pictures we initially saw in comparison to the more perfected sound quality that was then available.

Nowadays, video as primarily a visual medium is typically augmented by audio components. So, admittedly the auditory is still a component of our sensory experience. Both Ong and phenomenologist Don Ihde declare that with the advent of the electronic revolution, we have seen an increasing interest in sound in general. As Ihde claims,

> the electronic communications revolution has made us aware that once silent realms are in fact realms of sound and noise. The ocean now resounds with whale songs and shrimp percussions made possible by the extension of listening through electronic amplification. . . . It is not merely that the world has suddenly become noisier, or that we can hear further, or even that sound is somehow demandingly pervasive in a technological culture. It is rather that by living with electronic instruments our experience of listening itself is being transformed, and included in this transformation are the ideas we have about the world and ourselves.[30]

While the digitalization of sound is a burgeoning industry, it is this very transformation in "listening" (referred to above) and speaking that is my primary concern, especially given its impact on how we now view our ways of relating to one another. For while sound and the sounding voice are certainly aspects of cyberspace and the Internet (and our mainstream media), they both have become highly *mediated* through electronic editing and reproduction techniques. We have come to take this mediation of sound for granted. In their digitalization process, both sound and voice are abstracted from the immediacy of their original sounding so as to be efficiently reproduced for maximum circulation on the web. They are spatialized, as Ong would say.[31] This process illustrates what Ong describes as the depersonalization or degradation of sound by which we try to reduce sound, a temporal phenomenon, to the fixity of space. Moreover, we have become increasingly accustomed to attending to artificial voices that are completely electronically produced—for example, the iPhone's Siri, the Amazon Echo's Alexa, and the GPS devices in our cars. We must not forget that even the voices we hear when talking on our digitized telephones are mechanically modulated and distorted, transferred wirelessly and detached from their original bodily sources. Yet, these are the voices that are quickly becoming habitualized in our everyday sensory experience.

Digitized sound and voice on the Internet and within cyberspace are essentially abstractions or representations within virtuality, separate from the immediate or actual ear-to-ear sound emanations indicative of what Ong describes as primary orality, or what we experience whenever we are in the immediate auditory presence of the other. Hence, these latter immediate experiences of the sounding voice in their analogue form are now being replaced by the virtual, digitized, and symbolic forms—mass produced for mass consumption, which necessarily degrades sound when it comes to the speaking voice, according to Ong. It is not surprising, therefore, that we find a burgeoning new field of sound studies focused on effective and sophisticated sound and voice reproduction and editing.[32] While sound has been ignored by aesthetic theorists until just recently,[33] this trend was unfortunate, given that we know that it is the aesthetic dimensions of sound and voice in their original materiality that provide their most evanescent qualities.[34] Unmediated sound is the word's most native medium, so argues Ong,[35] although even the spoken word to which Ong refers is mediated existentially by the breath.[36] So, while voices in our new mediated environment are certainly present to our experience and comprise a component of our shifting sensorium, the voices within cyberspace, the Internet, and mainstream media are exceedingly filtered, regardless of whether they appear in written or oral forms. Paradoxically, while we are always *on the phone* using text- and image-based media, our immediate voices to one another are being replaced, muted, or significantly changed. I will have more to say about the implications of these sensory changes to our sensorium in the chapters that follow, particularly as they relate to the sounding voice.

Given Ong's predominant focus on the value of sound as word in his writings, he is led to refer to our developing electronic culture as *secondary orality*. However, I do not believe that Ong foresaw the degree to which the visual, through print and images rather than the auditory dimensions, would besiege our current media landscape, especially when it comes to our sociality. He even speaks to the difficulty at that time of theorizing the dimensions of the electronic in regard to communication, given the newness of its arrival upon the cultural scene. For example, he qualifies his assertions about the shift to secondary orality by admitting that "the full relationship of the electronically processed word to the orality-literacy polarity . . . is too vast a subject to be considered in its totality."[37] Furthermore, while Ong identifies our new electronic culture as a secondary orality, we find that he does so by using traditional oratory, that is, one speaker to an audience as an analogy, thereby emphasizing how our new electronic modes of connection enable us to reach larger and larger audiences (McLuhan's sense of the global village). As Ong suggests, "radio and television have brought major political figures as public speakers to a larger public than was ever possible before modern electronic developments."[38] Ironically, however, Ong does not conceive secondary orality as primarily auditory in nature and scope, even if he is emphasizing the notion of audiences. If he were alive today, I think he would acknowledge that the presence of the auditory elements within electronic media are merely reduced to their *second nature*, as I have mentioned previously, within the world of digitalized representation and signification.

Apparently, Ong chose the designation secondary orality to emphasize the group sense of mass audiences achieved through the efficiency of electronic connections. This notion of mass audiences undergirds Ong's discussions on secondary orality. Undoubtedly, electronic culture does produce mass audiences through its webs of mediated hyper-connectivity. However, as electronic culture has subsequently developed, sound plays an exceedingly minor role, especially in the communicative realm. Consequently, secondary orality does not signify an increase of the auditory as a primary aspect of its contours but its derivative. In other words, the designation of audience is no longer merely auditory in nature but constituted through highly sophisticated textual/visual means. The aural, from which Ong's secondary orality is based, is thus a misnomer. Admitting the likelihood of the logo-centric trend, Ong even states that "electronic devices are not eliminating printed books but are actually producing more"[39] textual materials. On the escalation of the visual dimensions within our electronic culture and their concordant spatial manifestations, Ong goes on to say that "the sequential processing and spatializing of the word, initiated by writing and raised to a new order of intensity by print, is further intensified by the computer, which maximizes commitment of the word to space and to (electronic) local motion and optimizes analytic sequentially by making it virtually instantaneous."[40] Ong theorizes that secondary orality is similar to primary orality, given that it fosters a communal sense of being in the world as an audience focused on the present moment. Perhaps if he were alive today, he would modify his designation from secondary orality to *secondary literacy*, in an effort to more adequately capture its textual/visual contours even as it retains its communal orientation. However, as I will discuss in a subsequent chapter, some social critics argue that nowadays our general literacy competency as a culture is increasingly in question.

In any case, for Ong, secondary orality is also quite different than primary orality because secondary orality is "based permanently on the use of writing and print, which are essential for the manufacture and operation of the equipment and for its use as well."[41] Furthermore, secondary orality (or secondary literacy, as I am suggesting) is also quite different. This is because, with its fundamental visual orientation as its predominant sensory mode, the importance of the once-valued primary oral-aural dimensions of communicative experience are more readily silenced or degraded, as Ong would say. Ong suggests that we can never return to a primary oral-aural state of being. I agree. However, this should not mean that preservation of some of the fundamental and humane qualities of the sounding voice in its immediacy should be abandoned or progressively forgotten as a qualitatively distinct habit of discourse. As current social theorist John L. Locke indicates in his assessment of the cultural direction in which we are headed with our electronic connectivity, we are witnessing an "undiagnosed social condition, a kind of functional 'de-voicing,' brought on by an insufficient diet of intimate talking."[42] Instead, we find a gluttony of video- and logo-centric electronic forms of connectivity, which are quickly muting the sounding voice in its originary expressivity as full aesthetic presence. We prefer to "text rather than talk"[43] to one another, as Turkle's research suggests. We seem to be becoming less appreciative of and able to distinguish between the boundary of "rich relations and meaningless hyper-connectedness, between abundance and chaos."[44] This trend is occurring, in part, because of the blurring of the boundary between the human and machine-enhanced or produced voice.

There is no doubt that our smart information technologies have proven advantageous. We have benefited greatly as a society from their development. We can connect more efficiently than ever before with people from across the globe, and the possibility of democratization has dramatically risen the world over by the advent of electronic information technologies. However, a theoretical assessment of our now dominant mediated social landscape is needed. Our main concern is the ongoing quality of human relationality, especially as it is configured by the human voice in its immediacy as sound. There is no longer any doubt that "the way we interact with each other has completely changed."[45] Being mediated by our electronic technologies is the new normal. As Thomas de Zengotita suggests, in our new mediated environment the real world dissolves into an optionality where our freedom to choose various ways of being (including being predominantly digitally represented in cyberspace) becomes its own condemnation of sorts.[46] It is time to survey the extent to which we are appealing to such electronic forms of connectivity and their impact on our overall relationality.

## ELECTRONIC CONNECTIVITY, SOCIAL MEDIA, AND OUR DWINDLING RELATIONALITY

I am not alone in harboring a concern about the quality of our relationships in the digital age. Many cultural critics today bemoan the toll that such a media-frenzied environment is having on human relationships.[47] Even international conferences aimed at extending the capabilities of digital media platforms are now including panel discussions on digital wellness in their conference programming.[48] Digital wellness refers to daily practices that encourage healthy electronic device use. Tech companies and independent application developers are also joining in by designing applications that serve to track our time spent online or on our phones. One such free application called Moment has been downloaded over eight million times at the time of this writing.[49] After all, the term *addiction* in our cultural lexicon has been paired with almost everything electronic, including computers, Internet surfing, video gaming, cell phone use, and texting (even while driving).[50] Concern over the addictive potential of computers and other electronic information technologies was expressed as early as the 1970s when pioneering computer scientist and technology critic Joseph Weizenbaum warned that people had become addicted, citing the need for withdrawal therapies.[51] It is no wonder then that human self-control and personal behavioral regulation are now identified as key burdens or concerns in our current media-saturated environment; our digital use can easily slip into self-indulgence and loss of personal control of not only our time but also our most fundamental goals in life. This theme of self-control as a driving force within our mediated culture will surface in the analyses that follow.

The typical counterargument we hear about our time spent online suggests that our new media platforms are actually enhancing our social connectivity and thereby increasing our relationality. If we quantify the time spent online, then this is probably true, especially if we consider social media platforms such as Facebook, Twitter, Reddit, YouTube, and Instagram. With the advent in 2005 of Web 2.0, we have witnessed an explosion of World Wide Web applications, such as blogs; microblogs like Twitter; social networking sites; video-, image-, and file-sharing platforms; and wikis. As described by Tim O'Reilly, who coined the term Web 2.0, Web 2.0 "is the network as platform, spanning all connected devices . . . [that because of its data-sharing capabilities creates] . . . an 'architecture of participation' . . . to deliver rich user experiences."[52] According to Christian Fuchs, the rise of the web's sociality functions has dramatically increased in the past several years—surpassing websites that were previously accessed strictly for informational purposes only. Given that, in 2011, Google broadened its functionality to include a social networking platform (Google+), it is not surprising that the websites receiving the most average daily visitors and page views in October 2015 were Google, Facebook, YouTube, Baidu, and Yahoo.[53]

The average monthly statistics regarding the most popular social media platforms as of October 2018 are also indicative of this rising trend in electronic sociality. At the time of this writing, Facebook has 166 million users, Instagram 114.43 million, Facebook Messenger 104.9 million, Twitter 67.18 million, Pinterest 57.21 million, and Snapchat 48.08 million. Of course, since the Cambridge Analytica scandal broke in March 2018, Facebook has experienced sharp declines in overall usership, especially among the youth cohort known as Generation Z. Part of Facebook's financial crisis was mitigated, however, by their previous acquisition of the now popular photo-sharing network Instagram in 2012 and WhatsApp in 2014. Worldwide, 3.028 billion people actively use social media, which is about forty percent of the world's population.[54] These numbers speak volumes about our growing appeals to social media as ways to connect with friends, family, and business associates. As of March 2019, Instagram had one billion monthly active users, with an average of 500 million people accessing the platform daily. How this volume of usage translates for the individual person is telling; during the last quarter of 2018, the average user spent about fifty-three minutes a day scrolling Instagram. That is almost an hour a day not spent conversing ear-to-ear with immediate others, reading a good book, or taking a walk. As of 2014, texting became the most common means by which to connect with others, especially those under the age of fifty.[55]

So, what do we mean when we refer to electronic social media? Some researchers define social media quite broadly, arguing that anything, like all media and all software, is social if it is a product of social processes. This notion is much too broad for our purposes here. Other theorists take a narrower definition following Karl Marx and stipulate that the social has to entail cooperative behaviors between or among social participants. This definition comes closer to the aspects of social media that I aim to address. While the research literature includes a plethora of definitions for social media, there are several essential characteristics we find across all of them. They are typically user centered and participatory, and they provide media-sharing capabilities through interconnected networks.

In many ways, the phrase *social media* is actually a misnomer, given that it encompasses qualities that I argue are anything but social. This is because, increasingly, social media have become less about supporting and inspiring us to open new avenues of dialogue with others that are, like most human relationships in the immediacy of experience, often complex, messy, and spontaneous. They do not encourage us to risk a bit of ourselves to create deeper levels of psychological vulnerability and intimacy. These are integral facets of human dialogue, at least if we follow the dialogic philosophers like Martin Buber who advocated for the "I-Thou" relation.[56] Instead, we find that social media are basically dominated by a capitalistic model of consumerist production bent on keeping users connected for financial gain. Such an orientation, by design, tends to transform the human other into an interchangeable part within the highly mediated networked interface. The other is automatically transformed into a commodity of exchange, be it monetary or informational. Buber identified such interactions as "I-It" encounters and argued vehemently against their enactment, given that he thought them detrimental in establishing deeper, more satisfying relational connections. Ong agrees on this point and states that with the evolution of our media environment into its technological phase, we have "in Buber's terminology . . . maximized the 'it' and minimized the 'I' and the 'thou' . . . maximizing the it, the objective, visual–tactile aspect of existence [that] necessarily accompanies the restructuring of the sensorium and of the psyche."[57] With the electronic instrumentality of the voice now circulating in cyberspace and on the Internet, according to vocal theorist, Theo Van Leeuwen, the human voice and humanity itself have become unfortunately "a surface phenomenon . . . a dressing up of a mechanical and relatively character-less foundation. What was once the core, the very vibration of the vocal cords, the very articulation of the vowel sound, now becomes a surface phenomenon, a bit of spicing added to an essentially characterless substance. A heart no longer beats inside."[58]

Demonstrating its surface characteristics, we find that the biggest technology companies are multibillion-dollar corporations whose main goal is marketing products and services to their users by keeping us engaged within fascinating digital interfaces. As former technologist James Williams indicates, we now erroneously assume that digital technologies fundamentally manage, manipulate, and move around information. This is an outdated notion that no longer accurately describes the reality of cyberspace functionality and design. Instead, Williams says electronic technologies are designing users who will keep their attention focused on consumer goods and services within the marketplace that social media platforms provide. He declares that what we now have in cyberspace is an "unprecedented system of intelligent, industrialized persuasion [that] poses [the greatest threat] to our freedom of attention."[59] Accordingly, Google and Facebook now comprise eighty-five percent (and rising) of Internet advertising's year-over-year growth.[60] The idea of the social as a means of enhancing dialogue as Buber's "I-Thou" relation, therefore, has now morphed into a primary means by which we are transformed into superficial commodities. To my way of thinking, the phrase *social media* has now become merely a floating signifier within our cultural milieu and capitalizes on the unfortunate fact that signs can be used to lie.[61]

The increase of so-called social media influencers speaks directly to this trend and to my argument. Such a person "has the power to affect purchase decisions of others because of his/her authority, knowledge, position or relationship with his/her audience."[62] Social media influencers are one of the fastest growing trends on social media platforms.[63] These are people who regularly post content and videos through popular streaming services and channels like YouTube, informing their audiences about the products they have contracted to promote. Expanding on prior research that showed that purchases by consumers are primarily based upon online reviews or peer testimony, these cyberspace celebrities are really marketing entrepreneurs—who, by disingenuously building relationships with their followers over social platforms, influence them to buy goods and services they have agreed to market.[64] The trend is remarkable for its popularity and accentuates the power of para-social interactions to shape not only behavior but also our sense of self-esteem. It is no wonder, then, that social media platforms typically promote not genuine interactions with others but status-seeking behaviors as branding of both goods and people rises to a whole new level of digitalized consumerism. "Digital advertising is by far the dominant business model for monetizing information on the Internet today. Many of the most widely used platforms, such as Google, Facebook, and Twitter, are at core advertising companies,"[65] so declares Williams, former executive of Google. As a former technology insider, his claim has credibility.

Social media are most often, therefore, "predicated on the cultural logic of celebrity, according to which the highest value is given to mediation, visibility, and attention,"[66] even for those of us who are not real celebrities. After all, we count how many likes or emojis we receive on posts, and that statistic becomes all important more often than not, at least in the moment. Social media platforms thus afford users what sociologist Pierre Bourdieu calls *social capital*, which is built from social visibility, and *cultural capital*, which is derived from increased reputation and value within the larger cultural context.[67] It is important not to forget that, in this case, social and cultural capital are virtually derived, that is, they are not actual, at least not in the sense that we typically use the word. Being virtual, they are fleeting and forever deferred as only a potentiality within the signifying order of things. It appears that for those who are regular social media users, the logic goes something like this: If we cannot garner social or cultural capital in the actual world, the virtual is the next best thing—or, perhaps in some cases, it is even better. The economic and political ramifications of this logic are enormous, given that the majority of social media followers are high-status wannabes who are lower to middle class. We might go so far as to say that social media platforms have become social pacifiers, especially for those who are otherwise socially, politically, and economically disenfranchised. When younger generations admit, as they have to media researcher Sherry Turkle, that they would rather interact in the virtual world than in the real world, it should concern us. As they indicate, the virtual world validates them in ways that immediate ear-to-ear relations with another does not. Many of the young teenage participants in Turkle's research admit that when at school they barely say anything to their friends. They rush home, however, so they can *talk* online through textual means.

In any case, we can legitimately begin to question our assumption that social media are, in fact, prosocial. They do not serve to enhance quality social relations that are deeper than mere cryptic exchanges of bits of information, whether textual or visual. As we see, the underlying logic is quite individualistic in nature and scope with very little quality sociality to it.[68] Too often, social media become a shallow source of self-validation, especially for those who feel psychologically isolated or lonely. This is in direct contrast to the "tribal or communal" qualities that Ong thought are indicative of primarily oral-aural cultures.[69] And while we have repeatedly heard the arguments that online identities can be beneficial for folks who are otherwise interpersonally shy or reserved, the fact of the matter is that such identities are digitally formed to serve someone's self-esteem—and not in the interest of mutual caring or concern. And when the obsessive pursuit of a love relationship is constructed on the basis of a fake online identity, we see increased incidences of catfishing taking place. Catfishing is when a person deliberately falsifies an online persona in order to lure a love target into a disingenuous online relationship. Meeting ear-to-ear is altogether contrary to such a relationship.[70]

The experience of social media seems to be less about real relationship development that qualitatively deepens human exchange and more about ways to foster self-serving wants and desires. It appears to be about accumulating recognition and visibility within a network of mediated relations, sometimes to the abandonment of common sense. This urge to be socially validated is so strong in younger generations that they have dubbed their fear of not attaining this goal as the "fear of missing out" (FOMO). This fear has taken the apparent desire for inclusion to whole new heights and drives much of our youths' constant electronic connectivity. FOMO attests not to an *other* orientation, which privileges the other over the self in a mutuality of relation, but rather to an orientation focused on self-acknowledgement. This is most keenly documented in behaviors of the younger generations, as I suggest, but probably applies in various degrees of intensity to many of us who participate.

Unfortunately, according to Williams, the designs that now undergird most social media platforms exploit our cognitive vulnerabilities and speak to the lowest parts of ourselves.[71] It is as if we are struggling all over again with understanding our very sociality and what it means—now that we are electronically interconnected in ways not even fathomable thirty years ago. We must be mindful, however, not to allow the underlying logic of social media to replace our long-standing premises about our relationality, in particular how quality human relations are co-constructed by deeper ear-to-ear communicative practices that serve to strengthen emotional bonds over sustained periods of time. We must be mindful of how our increased preferences for text- and image-based modes of sensory interaction in our new mediated environment are changing the very soundscape of our personal relations with others.

If our sounding voice in its immediacy is, indeed, the "primary publicist of each being's identity, feelings, character, and intentions,"[72] then we must be careful to preserve its sounding within our relationality, especially at a time when our information technologies seem to be muting its fullness as sensory presence. We must become more aware that the sounding of self and other within our immediacy of relation, our "social call" of humanness that I later equate as an authentic sense of enchantment, is quickly becoming an "endangered form of communication."[73] If our relationality in its immediacy of sounding experience has a "heart of its own" in its enunciation as some suggest, then it is a sensory organ of our sociality that we must attend to in our fullest capacity.[74] As we will see, the sounding voice is an aspect of our embodied existence that should not be denied, repressed, muted, or silenced. On this point, Ong was quite specific:

> Today we have often to labor to regain the awareness that the word is still always at root the spoken word. Early man had no such problem: he felt the word, even when written, as primarily an event in sound. Today there has grown out of and around the spoken word a vast network of artificially contrived media—writing, print, electronic devices . . . in which informational content is implicitly or explicitly tied in with verbal explanation far beyond the experience of early man. . . These media are a great but distracting boon. They overwhelm us and give our concept of the word special contours which can interfere with our understanding of what the word in truth is, and thus can distort the relevance of the word to ourselves.[75]

Paradoxically, while we are always *on our phones*, we risk the possibility that the sounding voice (or *phone* in Greek) will recede as a valued aspect of our existential sensorium and a means by which we establish our human relatedness. In discussing the ideas put forth by Graham Furness in his book, *Orality: The Power of the Spoken Word*, Aaron Mushengyezi reminds us, while "writing gives us the opportunity to skim, reread, jump forward, and re-experience what we read, it is an inappropriate medium for us to grasp the 'intangible elements' in the oral communicative moment in the same way we do through speaking."[76]

How does the potential of 24/7 electronic connectivity shape our existential ways of being in the world? What are the consequences of living in what many are now calling our digital age of distraction, alluded to previously by Ong back in the 1960s? What does this ever-encompassing distracting boon mean for our ongoing interpersonal relations? I take up these topics in the chapter that follows.

## NOTES

1. Joshua Meyrowitz, *No Sense of Place: The Impact of Electronic Media on Social Behavior* (New York: Oxford University Press, 1985).

2. See Edmund Husserl, *Experience and Judgement: Investigations in a Genealogy of Logic*, trans. James S. Churchill and Karl Ameriks (Evanston: Northwestern University Press, 1973); Maurice Merleau-Ponty, *Phenomenology of Perception*, trans. Colin Smith (New York: Humanities Press, [1945] 1962). These ideas are elucidated by Kestenbaum in *The Phenomenological Sense of John Dewey*.

3. Casey Schwartz, "Finding It Hard to Focus? Maybe It's Not Your Fault. The Rise of the New 'Attention Economy,'" *The New York Times*, August 14, 2018, https://www.nytimes.com/2018/08/14/style/how-can-i-focus-better.html.

4. Williams, *Stand Out of Our Light*, 19.

5. This remark comes from James Williams as quoted by *New York Times* columnist Casey Schwartz in an interview with James Williams. See Casey Schwartz, "Finding It Hard to Focus?"

6. Turkle, *Reclaiming Conversation*, 3.

7. Matthew Fanelli, "Getting Consumers' Attention Across Every Screen They Have at Home," *eMarketer*, December 1, 2017, www.emarketer.com/Article/Getting-Consumers-Attention-Across-Every-Screen-They-Have-Home/2016798.

8. Williams, *Stand Out of Our Light*, 19–20.

9. Schwartz, "Finding It Hard to Focus?"
10. Williams, *Stand Out of Our Light,* 50.
11. Ibid., 19.
12. Neil Postman, *Amusing Ourselves to Death: Public Discourse in the Age of Show Business* (New York: Penguin Books, 1985).
13. Ong, *The Presence of the Word,* 176.
14. Ong, *Orality and Literacy.*
15. In his preface to the 2000 paperback edition of Ong's *The Presence of the Word,* Thomas Farrell describes Ong's approach as phenomenological, although he specifies that he does not believe Ong is necessarily "following" the work of Edmund Husserl or others affiliated with that philosophical stance. Thomas J. Farrell, preface to the 2000 paperback edition of *The Presence of the Word,* xxiv.
16. Ong, *The Presence of the Word,* 6.
17. See, for example, Constance Classen, *Worlds of Sense: Exploring the Senses in History and Across Cultures* (New York: Routledge, 1993).
18. Immanuel Kant's philosophy is based upon exploring phenomena as the quintessential intellectual activity, thus demonstrating that by the eighteenth century the presumption held that intellection was by analogy a visual affair. On this point, see Ong, *Presence of the Word,* 74.
19. Maurice Merleau-Ponty, "The Primacy of Perception and Its Philosophical Consequences," in *The Primacy of Perception: And Other Essays on Phenomenological Psychology, the Philosophy of Art, History and Politics,* trans. James M. Edie (Evanston: Northwestern University Press, 1964).
20. Paul A. Soukup, "Looking is Not Enough: Reflections on Walter J. Ong and Media Ecology," *Proceedings of the Media Ecology Association* 6 (2005): 4.
21. Maurice Merleau-Ponty, *The Structure of Behavior,* trans. Alden L. Fisher (Boston: Beacon Press, 1963), 130.
22. Aubrey Slaughter, "Cyberspace," The Chicago School of Media Theory, accessed March 23, 2019, https://lucian.uchicago.edu/blogs/mediatheory/keywords/cyberspace/.
23. Ibid.
24. Philip W. Graham, "Space and Cyberspace: On the Enclosure of Consciousness," in *Living with Cyberspace: Technology and Society in the 21st Century,* eds. John Armitage and Joanne Roberts (London: Continuum, 2002), 156.
25. See Nicholas Carr, *The Shallows: What the Internet is Doing to our Brains* (New York: W. W. Norton & Co., 2011).
26. Walter J. Ong, "Wired for Sound: Teaching, Communications, and Technological Culture," in *The Barbarian Within: And Other Fugitive Essays and Studies* (New York: Macmillan Company, 1962), 225.
27. Refer to media theorist and political activist Sut Jhally's work *The Spectacle of Accumulation: Essays in Culture, Media, and Politics* (New York: Peter Lang, 2006). Earlier works also attest to this sensory trend. See Stuart Ewen, *All Consuming Images: The Politics of Style in Contemporary Culture* (New York: Basic Books, 1988).
28. Jacques Ellul, *The Humiliation of the Word,* trans. Joyce Main Hanks (Grand Rapids: Eerdmans, 1985), 2.
29. Ong, "Wired for Sound," 224.
30. Ihde, *Listening and Voice,* 4–5.
31. Helen Macallan and Andrew Plain claim, after all, that "in its translated graphic state as a digitized configuration of sound waves, the concept that sound possesses a spatial as well as a temporal dimension is emphasized." See Helen Macallan and Andrew Plain, "Filmic Voices," in *Voice: Vocal Aesthetics in Digital Arts and Media,* eds. Norie Neumark, Ross Gibson, and Theo Van Leeuwen (Cambridge, MA: Massachusetts Institute of Technology, 2010), 243.
32. For an overview of sound studies, see Matthew D. Thibeault, "Sound Studies and Music Education," *Journal of Aesthetic Education* 51, no. 1 (Spring 2017). See also: Jonathan Sterne, ed. *The Sound Studies Reader* (New York: Routledge, 2012).
33. Christoph Cox, "Beyond Representation and Signification: Toward a Sonic Materialism," *Journal of Visual Culture* 10, no. 2 (2011).

34. Ong, *Presence of the Word*.
35. Ibid., xxvii–xxix.
36. Vocal theorist Philip Brophy, discussing the quality of the human voice that distinguishes it from the digitalized one, says that "there is only one way in which the voice is human, and that is through its breath." Philip Brophy, "Vocalizing the Posthuman," in *Voice: Vocal Aesthetics in Digital Arts and Media*, eds. Norie Neumark, Ross Gibson, and Theo Van Leeuwen (Cambridge, MA: MIT, 2010), 362.
37. Ong, *Orality and Literacy*, 133.
38. Walter Ong, "Orality, Literacy, and Modern Media," in *Communication in History: Technology Culture, Society*, 3rd ed., eds. David Crowley and Paul Heyer (New York: Longman, 1999), 70.
39. Ong, *Orality and Literacy*, 133.
40. Ibid., 133.
41. Ibid., 134.
42. Locke, *The De-Voicing of Society*, 19.
43. Turkle, *Reclaiming Conversation*, 22.
44. Jackson, *Distracted*, 37.
45. Anton Bonev, "The Impact of the Digital Age on Human Engagement," *Medium*, July 13, 2017, https://medium.com/the-looking-glass/the-impact-of-the-digital-age-on-human-engagement-aaa42d526453.
46. Thomas de Zengotita, *Mediated: How the Media Shapes Your World and the Way You Live in It* (New York: Bloomsbury, 2005).
47. Sherry Turkle, *Alone Together: Why We Expect More from Technology and Less From Each Other* (New York: Basic Books, 2011); Turkle, *Reclaiming Conversation*.
48. See, for example, "Striking a Balance in the Age of Digital Distraction," MCW19, accessed March 4, 2019, https://www.mwcbarcelona.com/session/striking-a-balance-in-the-age-of-distraction.
49. Oscar Schwartz, "Why Beating Your Phone Addiction May Come at a Cost," *The Guardian*, March 13, 2019, https://www.theguardian.com/technology/2019/mar/13/digital-wellness-phone-addiction-tech?CMP=twt_gu.
50. As a countermeasure to the overwhelming use of cell phones for text and visually based media, in 2017, a Brooklyn-based company released a new kind of phone called the Light Phone in which its primary function is to call people. See Avery Hartmans, "This Beautiful Credit-Card-Sized Phone Just Might Cure Your Smartphone Addiction," *Business Insider*, January 10, 2017, https://www.businessinsider.com/light-phone-features-photos-2017-1.
51. Oscar Schwartz, "Why Beating Your Phone Addiction May Come at a Cost."
52. Tim O'Reilly, "Web 2.0: Compact Definition?," *Radar*, October 1, 2005, http://radar.oreilly.com/2005/10/web-20-compact-definition.html.
53. Apparently, the Google+ sociality function never really gained momentum. As of April 2019, Google+ accounts and any Google+ pages have been shut down. This measure was taken when a bug in Google+ exposed the personal data of nearly half a million users.
54. "What Is an Influencer?," Influencer Marketing Hub, accessed March 19, 2019, https://influencermarketinghub.com/what-is-an-influencer/.
55. Amanda Mull, "Talk to People on the Telephone: It's Time to Start Calling Your Friends Again," *The Atlantic*, September 16, 2019, https://www.theatlantic.com/health/archive/2019/09/ring-ring-ring/598129/.
56. Martin Buber, *I and Thou*, trans. Walter Kaufmann (New York: Touchstone, 1970).
57. Ong, *Presence of the Word*, 289.
58. Theo Van Leeuwen, "Vox Humana," in *Voice: Vocal Aesthetics in Digital Arts and Media*, eds. Norie Neumark, Ross Gibson, and Theo Van Leeuwen (Cambridge, MA: Massachusetts Institute of Technology, 2010), 14.
59. Williams, *Stand Out of Our Light*, 37.
60. Pavithra Mohan, "Google and Facebook Now Own 85 percent of Internet Ad Growth," *Fast Company*, May 31, 2017, https://www.fastcompany.com/4039263/google-and-facebook-now-own-85-of-internet-ad-growth.
61. Umberto Eco, *A Theory of Semiotics* (Bloomington: Indiana University Press, 1976).

62. "What Is an Influencer?"

63. I credit my research assistant, Sidra Veriatch, for drawing this trend to my attention.

64. Digital ad spending was projected to pass $223 billion in 2017 and to continue to grow at double-digit rates until at least 2020. See Williams, *Stand Out of Our Light,* 29.

65. Williams, *Stand Out of Our Light,* 29–30.

66. Alice E. Marwick, *Status Update: Celebrity, Publicity, and Branding in the Social Media Age* (New Haven: Yale University Press, 2013), 14.

67. Pierre Bourdieu and Loïc J. D. Wacquant, *An Invitation to Reflexive Sociology* (Chicago: University of Chicago Press, 1992).

68. As Christian Fuchs claims, these social media platforms are named, after all, Facebook, YouTube, and MySpace and not WeBook, OurTube, or OurSpace. See Christian Fuchs, *Social Media: A Critical Introduction,* 2nd ed. (Thousand Oaks: Sage, 2017).

69. The fact that cyberspace and the Internet seem to accentuate these individualistic tendencies lends further support to my argument that both are more hyper-textual/visual than oral-aural. Ong describes that it wasn't until the advent of writing and print that we became more individually focused. As he says, "the book takes the reader out of the tribe" and "he becomes more original and individual, detribalized." See Ong, *Presence of the Word,* 135.

70. I wish to thank my students in my advanced interpersonal class for informing me of this social media practice.

71. Williams, *Stand Out of Our Light,* 29.

72. Locke, *De-Voicing of Society,* 17.

73. Jane R. Thiebaud, "Effects of Technology on People: Living F2F Conversation and Social Interaction," *Proceedings of the Media Ecology Association* 11 (2010).

74. Locke, *De-Voicing of Society,* 19.

75. Ong, *Presence of the Word,* xxvii–xxiii.

76. Aaron Mushengyezi, review of *Orality: The Power of the Spoken Word* by Graham Furness, *Language in Society* 36, no. 4 (2007): 606.

*Chapter Two*

# Our Digital Age of Distraction and Our Increasing Techno-Social Dilemma

In this chapter, I discuss how the potential of 24/7 electronic connectivity is shaping our existential ways of being in the world and the techno-social dilemma we are increasingly facing. Specifically, I explicate our digital age of distraction and discuss the consequences of distraction on our conscious experience. I discuss the new attention economy such distractions manifest and outline some of the ways we seem to be struggling to maintain a healthy existence personally, socially, and professionally. I am concerned about the many cultural losses we seem to be suffering and the impending craze over social robots that helps to usher in what many are calling the post-human age. With the increase of our new intellectual technologies, we see a dispersal of focused attention to a particular object of consciousness that jeopardizes, I believe, our human relationality.

## OUR DIGITAL AGE OF DISTRACTION

An outgrowth of our highly digitalized world of connectivity is the speed and efficiency by which we can electronically connect, process bits of information, and thumb click through what the virtual world seems to offer. Given our mobile technology, this now can happen at any time and in any place. Consequently, our pace of life has dramatically increased and with it the potential for distracted ways of being in the world. Having information and connections with others at our fingertips increases the potential for a distracted or fragmented consciousness. Many news stories recount the incidents of distracted drivers or pedestrians, for example, who are focused on their cell phones—they are talking, texting, or listening to music and not paying attention to their immediate surroundings. According to the National Highway Traffic Safety Association (NHTSA), the number of distracted driving deaths has skyrocketed since 2015. In 2015, there were a total of 3,477 deaths attributed to distracted driving and 391,000 reported injuries. Additionally, fourteen percent of fatal crashes involve cell phone use. The trend is so alarming that the NHTSA began its "It Can Wait" campaign in 2015 to combat the problem.[1] Distracted walking is also a growing safety concern. The NHTSA says that over 5,000 pedestrians were killed and over 76,000 injuries were reported in 2012; these were people who were on their phones or iPods listening to music when the accidents occurred. That is approximately two deaths every hour and an injury every seven minutes in the United States.[2]

These statistics should give us pause as a society. Apparently in the summer of 2016 they did not, however. The *Pokémon Go* craze that summer did anything but dissuade such distracted behaviors. For those not familiar with *Pokémon Go*, it was an augmented reality game designed to blend the digital and real worlds. Pokémon are mythical cartoon creatures that players try to capture on their cell phones. Players walk around staring "zombie-like"[3] at their cell phone screens trying to locate aspects of the Poké-world in their actual geographical locations. The game was touted as a way to "get out and explore the 'real world,'"[4] but it ended up putting many people in danger because attention to their immediate surroundings waned. The craze revealed how psychologically ready we are to ignore our personal safety concerns in the name of electronic fun. Unfortunately, technology companies forecast that there are more such game interfaces to come, especially given the profit margins *Pokémon Go* generated.

Granted, many states in the US have acknowledged the growing problem of digital distraction by instituting bans on cell phone use while driving. The state of New Jersey is leading the way when it comes to distracted walking, being the first to ban cell phone use for pedestrians. And, while these instances certainly articulate extreme negative consequences of distraction, we also witness varying degrees of distracted behaviors every day, including people trying to multitask while on their phones—checking out at retail stores, checking in at doctor's offices, cooking dinner, or approaching a teller at a bank with a phone to the ear. Some argue that there is a strong correlation between these distracted behaviors and the rise in rates of diagnosis of ADHD (attention-deficit/hyperactivity disorder). A report published in March 2019 by the Blue Cross Blue Shield Association says that the diagnosis rates for ADHD, which is often characterized by behaviors such as difficulty paying attention, poor impulse control, and excessive activity, have risen thirty percent in the past eight years, especially in children and young adults.[5]

In our highly mediated environment, we seem increasingly susceptible to such levels of distraction, but why is a difficult question to answer. Joshua Rothman attempts to do so in his *New Yorker* article published in 2015. As he describes, one theory is based upon the work of German sociologist Georg Simmel, particularly his essay titled "The Metropolis and Mental Life." As Simmel sees it, the very materiality of our high-tech, urbanized society produces a distracted consciousness. In other words, we grow accustomed to and then begin to expect a constant barrage of stimulations that city life provides. We even crave such stimulation when we find ourselves in different, more relaxed contexts. Another theory is more spiritual in nature and harkens to the philosophies of Friedrich Nietzsche and Blaise Pascal. It is thought that we are distracted because our souls are troubled. We seek constant connections, however fleeting, because we are essentially afraid to be alone or we feel emotionally or spiritually empty.[6] Thus, in a social world that is becoming more de-vocalized as I and others have argued, we would expect to witness more troubled souls, especially if we believe that the voice is the "flesh of the soul"[7] as sound theorist Mladen Dolar suggests. Given my aim to re-enchant human communication through a recuperation of the immediate sounding voice, this latter theory, therefore, holds some explanatory power. This is especially true if we acknowledge the historical associations of the voice as the breath of the soul (a concept that is addressed in chapters that follow).

Philosopher Matthew Crawford in his book *The World Beyond Your Head: On Becoming an Individual in an Age of Distraction* offers an insightful and more contemporary alternative explanation. He contends that our current obsession with individual choice and autonomy is at the root of our distracted consciousness. Unfortunately, this obsession with choice concerning a myriad of things "serves as the central totem of consumer capitalism"[8] and so our pursuit of individual choice and autonomy, he says, are a perfect marriage in a consumer-driven culture such as our own. Crawford's ideas support those of other social theorists who are attempting to grapple philosophically with our current age of distraction, as many have taken to calling it. For most, this new age signifies a contentious new attention economy that now undergirds our social world. This is our new social landscape, where attention is quickly becoming the fundamental commodity within cyberspace and on the Internet. James Williams states that "more of our day-to-day experience stands to be mediated and guided by smaller, faster, more ubiquitous, more intelligent, and more engaging entry points into the digital attention economy."[9] Given the increased speed and voracity of our techno-social world, we are becoming "less and less able to see, hear, and comprehend what's relevant and permanent, [which is] why so many of us feel that we can barely keep our heads above water, and our days are marked by perpetual loose ends."[10] Discussing the implications of online surfing and its distracting behaviors and characteristics, Nicholas Carr contends that "the Net seizes our attention only to scatter it."[11]

Back in the 1970s, Herbert Simon insightfully pointed out that when information becomes abundant, as is now the case with the Internet and cyberspace, attention becomes a scarce resource.[12] He was right. Regrettably, the digitized forms of information and entertainment provided by our various smart devices are successfully capturing our moment-to-moment attention, pulling us away from, that is, distracting us from, our most immediate experiences. Software engineers designing such platforms and applications now readily admit that the "wonderous machines"[13] and capabilities they create are painstakingly and quite consciously designed to grab and keep our attention. As Williams points out, "the infrastructure and incentives that underlie their operation . . . are now quite mature and deeply entrenched" in the digitalized world.[14] While "gifts of information"[15] are still exchanged, of course, within the digitalized space of cyber, Williams believes the phrase "Information Age" is now relatively obsolete. For him, it does not capture adequately the essential issue at stake in contemporary society. Instead, he is convinced that we are now in the "Age of Attention," or the Age of Distraction if you prefer, where our key challenge as a society now rests in successfully resisting this electronic attention grab by technology companies and their software and digital platforms. Our freedom to pursue our own personal long-term goals and aspirations, those motivations that make life worth living in the long run, he suggests, are now being quickly sacrificed at the altar of fast and efficient technological enticements that do not serve us. Instead, he believes, they serve only temporary wants and desires that are manufactured for us in our ever-expanding consumerist orientation. So distraught about the long-term implications of this trend, Williams emphasizes that "the liberation of human attention may be the defining moral and political struggle of our time."[16] When contextualized by the fact that we seem to be always on our phones instead of relating to others in the immediacy of focused ear-to-ear encounters, his argument has a fidelity that rings true.

Maggie Jackson, author of *Distracted: The Erosion of Attention and the Coming Dark Age*, echoes Williams's sentiments about the larger contextual issues at stake in our new attention economy. She states that "the way we live is eroding our capacity for deep, sustained, perceptive attention—the building block of intimacy, wisdom, and cultural progress. Moreover, this disintegration may come at great cost to ourselves and to society."[17] Furthermore, "the erosion of attention is the key to understanding why we are on the cusp of a time of widespread cultural and social losses."[18] These words were written over ten years ago, and given the statistics cited above, this erosion of attention seems to be worsening.

The attention/distraction problematic is not a new occurrence, however, on the socio-cultural horizon. Historically, philosophers and moralists have long been interested in our lack of attention, or our susceptibility to distraction when it comes to our relationality. According to Frank Furedi, it was during the Enlightenment, in 1710, that the word *inattention* first appeared in the *Oxford English Dictionary*. And, similar to Maggie Jackson's current pronouncements, theorists back then associated inattention with indolence and moral vices. In 1770, the Scottish moral philosopher James Beattie claimed that inattention was the source of criminal habits that debase the moral faculty of men, warning that if these vices were left unchecked, social order would be severely undermined.[19] These early forecasts about distraction are certainly understandable given that in the Age of Enlightenment reason was elevated over myth and religion. Rationality and its accompaniments, logical thinking and empirically based arguments, reigned supreme. It was normally assumed that success in life required the ability to sustain focused attention. These early theorists were not too far off the mark. As we now know from neuroscience, attention is the essential knot that ties together the seemingly magical aspects of forgetting and remembering. As Maggie Jackson reminds us, St. Augustine highly valued memory, even likening it to "a great field or a spacious palace" where the muses, as offspring of Mnemosyne, offered "to humankind the threads with which to weave all creations: stories, poetry, art."[20]

So, what do we mean exactly by distraction, and how should we understand its relation to the matter of attention? To begin, I turn to philosopher and pragmatist William James who, in 1890, wrote that attention "is the taking possession by the mind, in clear and vivid form, of one out of what seem several simultaneously possible objects or trains of thought. . . . It implies withdrawal from some things in order to deal effectively with others, and is a condition which has a real opposite in the confused, dazed, scatterbrained state which in French is called *distraction*, and *Zerstreutheit* in German."[21] Moreover, James argues that for attention to occur, there must be a spreading of thought's movement, or, if you will, a holistic intentional arc of thought that directs its unified focus toward a given object to consciousness, be it person, place, or thing, at a steady rate. Attention thus manifests as a taking hold of some object to consciousness as a possession, a sign in a semiotic sense, in a "gift of undividedness."[22] Tracing attention's etymological roots to the Latin word *attendere*, we find it means giving heed to an object of consciousness or, quite literally, a sign, echoing James's understanding of it as a perceptual stretching of awareness toward an object. Distraction is often conceptualized as attention's opposite, given that it typically means to draw apart our focus and subsequent thinking. So, along these lines, we would say that distraction signifies a divided or diverted attention, a lack of thought's stretching toward its object of perception or a sign in any sustained way. Instead, thought is fragmented or broken up as an act of consciousness or intentionality, to use phenomenological theory.

Paul North gives us a more nuanced way to think about the ratio between attention and distraction. Related they most certainly are, but he argues that they are not so much opposites as they are contraries. That is, their relation is not marked so much by differences in kind or opposites but by differences in degree of perception and thought (more or less). North suggests that "the one, distraction, consists in the other, attention, to the lowest degree.... What we call distraction is attentive thought degraded until it can do nothing but clamor for a return to its ideal."[23] This discussion helps us understand our current mediated environment in which many of our distractions are moments of diverted attention—or moments in which our attention is severely impoverished as a matter of degree on one thing while giving a measure of attention to many somethings or many people at once. It is best to consider distraction as a diversion of attention, and diversion as an impoverished version of attention.[24] In any case, the fundamental attributes of attention and distraction, as well as their contribution to human experience, remain highly problematic, especially in our current media-frenzied environment.

While we are born in a certain sense to be interrupt-driven by our lower-order human capacities known as our fight-or-flight responses, our electronic devices, or interruption machines as they are sometimes called, have disrupted even that process in fundamentally new ways. Our electronic devices continuously disrupt the spreading of thought's movement toward an isolated person, place, thing, or event as a result of focused attending. Researcher Linda Stone contends that our capacity for continuous partial attention to our environment and the new habit of inattention it creates is a fundamental roadblock to our survival. As she explains, in large quantities, continuous partial attention "contributes to a stressful lifestyle, to operating in crisis management mode, and to a compromised ability to reflect, to make decisions, and to think creatively. In a 24/7, always-on world, continuous partial attention used as our dominant attention mode contributes to a feeling of overwhelm, over-stimulation and to a sense of being unfulfilled. We are so accessible, we're inaccessible."[25] It seems that Stone has hit upon the essence of this attention/distraction problematic. When we make ourselves accessible 24/7 to our host of friends, we preclude the possibility that we can be completely with another in any focused, attentive way.

Charles Sanders Peirce, James's contemporary and colleague within the American pragmatist movement in the late nineteenth century, agrees with the importance James places on the perceptual qualities of attention and distraction in human affairs. Peirce further develops the notion of attention and its contrary from a semiotic point of view, that is, from the perspective of phenomenological sign actions. We may be inclined to dismiss the notion that a distracted consciousness or fragmented attention pattern might have any real impact on human affairs. We have only to turn to Peirce's theory on this matter to see the error in our ways of thinking. Following James's train of thought, Peirce is keen on advocating for the importance of a fluency to thought's movement in all conditions of semiosis. In other words, he stipulates that continuity of thought is essential if we are to be pragmatic. As Peirce recognized, for reasonableness in thought to occur (a hallmark of pragmatist thought), a degree of fluency is required in thought's natural progression to its conclusions.[26] In other words, without a reasonableness to thought's development within sign processes, our subsequent habits and conduct are likely to be viewed as discontinuous and therefore irrational.

Thus, our growing culture of distraction or inattentiveness would greatly concern Peirce, making him question how beneficial our current modes of thinking, or multitasked thinking, are for our overall sense of self and the pragmatic well-being of communal life. A lack of fluency in thought's progression would undermine continuity and contribute, according to Peirce, to irrationality and chaotic thinking and all that entails in terms of subsequent erratic behavioral patterns. England's eighteenth-century essayist and moralist Samuel Johnson agrees. He argued that inattention or distraction was a symptom of an undetermined manner of thinking.[27] To come at this discussion specifically from a phenomenological point of view, as Peirce does in "Some Consequences of Four Incapacities,"[28] attention or the lack thereof is always a "modification of consciousness." These modifications of awareness, by inference, thus shape our habits of discourse (our expressions and perceptions), which significantly affect how we subsequently perceive, think about, and engage with the world. If we accept the premise that all states of consciousness are acquired through our interactions with signs of signification as a phenomenology of human experience, as Peirce would have us do, then attending to our current technological objects of consciousness is certainly warranted, especially given their potentialities as constant interruption machines in the sensory process of perception. It is no wonder that we see increasing patterns of attention-deficit disorders in our youth, with some theorists suggesting that we are even becoming an autistic society because of our use of electronic information technologies.[29]

Important in my quest for a re-valuing of the sounding voice and the re-enchantment of human communication, we find that attention is often described as analogous to vision. For example, technologist James Williams, following the insights of cognitive scientists, calls attention a "'spotlight' . . . or the direction of our moment-to-moment awareness within the immediate task domain."[30] He goes on to unfold the problematic of attention by naming deeper levels of attentional maladies we seem to be suffering as "starlight" and "daylight." While the spotlight is our mere superficial redirection of thought without a moment's notice, starlight is our growing frustration over attention issues that get intensified because they occur over longer periods of time. The daylight signifies, according to Williams, the "erosion of fundamental capacities necessary for navigating human life . . . [when] the ground underfoot gives way."[31] It is at this point that a deeper sense and broader experience of disruption are felt at the existential level.

His theoretical framework based upon attention as light is quite understandable given that we typically associate our perceptual experience of attention as primarily accomplished through sight. I contend, however, that attention does not entail the visual sensory capacity in isolation. As a taking hold of an object of consciousness, whether to a maximum or minimum degree, attention needs to be conceptually expanded in our lexicon so as to include other modes of perceptual experiences, such as hearing/sound. This is especially true given our concerns about the diminished value we now assign the auditory within human relationality. A taken-for-granted focus on the visual may partially explain why we do not correlate attention with the importance of sound. This is unfortunate because, as we will find in discussions that follow, sound phenomenologically penetrates our existence in far greater ways than does visual experience. This is because vision is the result of the mere refraction of light on a given surface. We learn from phenomenologists Don Ihde and Walter Ong, after all, that visual stimuli separate experiences spatially while auditory stimuli surround and saturate. By extension, we could speculate that visual dimensions of experience produce or aid in separated or distracted consciousness, while auditory dimensions of experience aid in focused attention. As we all know, the sounding voice of the other within immediate proximity is difficult to ignore completely. We may turn our bodies away from the presence of the other and remove them temporarily from sight, but we have no flaps on our ears by which we might muffle their voice. Thus, sound offers us an attentional capacity that is qualitatively distinct from sight. And because of the penetrating nature of sound as an immediate taking hold of our existential experience, we will explore later how the speaking voice as enunciation provides an especially rich medium by which to garner attendant qualities to the other and self in dialogue. Sound is unlike any other sense perception. The traditional association of attention with light is unfortunate and provides further evidence of the prominence of the visual orientation within Western thought. I address this in chapter 5.

The ramifications of our culture of distraction are enormous, especially when it comes to the aspects of human relationality that we seem to be sacrificing. According to Maggie Jackson, we are collectively losing important aspects of our culture that aided in developing a healthy sense of mutuality. One of the first collective losses we suffer is that of mutual trust. As a result, we live in a rising culture of surveillance, where the importance of the gaze has reached new heights because of our growing suspicions of one another. Citing the work of political philosopher Jeremy Bentham, who envisioned the panopticon model of surveillance for prisons, schools, hospitals, and other institutions in the 1700s, a model that Michel Foucault re-invigorated in the 1970s in his work on biopolitics, Jackson makes the compelling case for how the gaze now tethers us in our virtual worlds where we are primarily disembodied entities, a notion that I return to in subsequent chapters. Jackson suggests that "watching and tracking and monitoring provides comforting evidence—the snapshot, the print-out, the fix on a map—of 'presence' in a virtual, mobile, split-focus world."[32] So we now live in a world where surveillance cameras seem to be everywhere, even placed in our children's bedrooms. This, too, has become a cultural trend we take for granted.

Given that more and more we see a proclivity of skimming print material in our digital landscape rather than actually reading it, Jackson insists that, after trust, our second collective loss is the ability to go beneath the surface, to think deeply about things, people, and events in life. Drawing parallels between the ability to think deeply and our reading habits, she refers to an extensive 2003 study conducted by the US Department of Education called the National Assessment of Adult Literacy. This study found that nearly fifty percent of Americans do not read a single book a year. I imagine that figure may have already increased. As a "miraculous cultural invention," reading and writing, says Jackson, is "a feat so unnatural that it necessitates a painstaking rewiring of the brain to learn [and] shapes our understanding of life" in profound ways.[33] Echoing the work of Nicholas Carr on how the Internet is making us shallower thinkers and skim readers, Jackson believes this cultural loss of thinking deeply will have grave consequences for the degree to which we can handle complex personal and societal problems and issues. Education researcher Norbert Elliot agrees when he says, "If you want to have an educated citizenry, you've got to wrestle with complex ideas or you will end up with people who will only do the shallowest things."[34] This has enormous implications for social life and our immediate relationships.

The third cultural loss Jackson mentions is our "inner will and outer means to connect with one another. We risk living in solitary glass cages, *enchanted* by shadows on the wall."[35] Here she is addressing the potential loss of a certain spirit of humanity as we become gradually more fascinated by the possibility of human-machine interactions and the new forms of life we are creating through artificial intelligence (AI) and the world of virtuality. As Sherry Turkle's research accentuates, we are enthusiastically embracing the advent of social robots in all facets of our lives, even when it comes to love relationships. Disturbed by entrepreneur and computer scientist David Levy's book *Love and Sex with Robots: The Evolution of Human-Robot Relationships*, Turkle takes issue with the claim that robots will teach us to be better friends and lovers because they allow us to practice our skills on them. Perhaps even more upsetting to Turkle is the idea that the virtual world of robotic interaction will eventually replace our often messy and complex human interactions—and we will be better for it, the argument goes. After all, by engaging lovingly and sexually with robots, cheating and heartbreak will become a thing of the past. The issues of stability, dependability, and responsiveness without consequence lie at the heart of this unsettling virtual trend in interaction.

Social robots are increasingly being integrated into the emotional care of elderly patients in hospitals and the very young in home settings, both of whom often suffer from attachment or detachment issues. We now have robot dogs, cats, and the like. These robots are said to offer companionship when human interaction is waning. Turkle has spent extensive time interviewing many in various age categories about their relationships with robotic companion devices. It appears that such robots are becoming the substitutes for human-to-human emotional bonding. For example, Zora, a social robot now used in a French hospital with elderly clientele suffering dementia, is quickly becoming a popular addition to the patients' everyday experiences.[36] Zora is controlled from a laptop that remains out of sight of the client but within earshot of the unfolding conversation between the patient and it. The nurse behind the curtain types responses into the laptop, which the robot then speaks to the patient. Amazingly, the often-recognized artificiality of Zora does not seem to interfere with desired interactions and displays of affection toward it. The patients cuddle Zora, holding it in their arms tightly. Patients fuss over who will get to spend time with Zora. Proponents of such technologies argue that the rising population of older adults warrants such stop-gap measures when it comes to patient care. The logic is that if we do not have a human to interact with, a non-human will do nicely; it is the something is better than nothing relational argument.

All of these instances signal that we are moving closer to what many are calling the post-human age. In such an age, the boundaries between human and machine capabilities begin to blur dramatically—and so do the expectations we have for each when it comes to acceptable interactions. Moreover, in such instances, we move further away from our understandings of the work that human-to-human communication and relationships do for the very spirit of humanity. Our digital devices in our homes, like Amazon's artificial audio assistant, Alexa, are good examples. Most of us would declare that such devices are relatively harmless additions and quite often helpful for turning on and off lights in rooms or switching the television channels. The proliferation of such social robots on the horizon of our social experience unmistakably evidences how we are progressively primed for acceptance of more advanced machine interactions in our daily lives, at least for the lower and middle classes.

Ironically, many technologists who are complicit in the design of such enchanting electronics and those in the higher socio-economic brackets are now actually avoiding or severely limiting screen time altogether. It now appears that human contact is the next luxury good. Exposing the political aspects of our electronic culture and the power dynamics involved, we find increasingly that life for the very rich is less mediated than it is for most of us. Wealthy parents insist that their children play with modeling clay and blocks and attend private schools that are technology-free. Living without a phone, quitting social networks, or not answering emails is quickly becoming a new status symbol for the wealthy. So, "as more screens appear in the lives of the poor, screens are disappearing from the lives of the rich."[37] As chief executive of the Luxury Institute, Milton Pedraza contends that "What we are seeing [in the lives of the rich] is the luxurification of human engagement."[38] This trend lends direct support to my argument about the unintentional human sacrifices such electronic media induce.

An example of this socio-economic disparity when it comes to screen time involves an older man whose new best friend is a cat named Sox who *lives* on an electronic tablet. The man apparently knows that Sox is completely artificial, but he does not seem to mind. Even though Sox "is operated by workers around the world who are watching, listening and typing out her responses, which sound slow and robotic . . . her consistent voice in his life has returned him to his faith."[39] An even more dramatic example of the direction in which we seem to be heading is the recent case of a medical doctor in California who believed that it was quite acceptable to tell a patient he had not long to live via a hyperlink on a robotic video screen rolled into the patient's hospital room. The patient died the next day. We can easily speculate that the de-humanized act of telling could have been related to his quick demise.[40]

Given the growing trend toward adopting these types of devices as human interaction substitutes, we know we have entered a radically different social space (a post-human space?) for understanding what constitutes healthy relationality. The downside of our apparent burgeoning social robot craze is, of course, that we can embrace the machine not as a tool but as part of us and as one of us in their artificiality, which many of these examples seem to indicate. When we do so, we begin to sacrifice essential qualities of our authentic humanness that necessarily emerge through the spiritual, aesthetic, or human connection we make with other human beings in the immediacy of voiced relations. Potentially more unsettling, we can easily begin to perceive ourselves as similarly artificial and shallow as the machines we come to admire.

Within our highly mediated age of distraction, our sensible world flattens, that is, the richness of being human begins to dissipate into the world of the virtual in all of its abstractions and potentialities. Thus, our sensible world takes on the figurative meaning of the word *flat*, that is, wanting in spirit.[41] Maggie Jackson interrogates this situation:

> For efficiency's sake, do we split focus so finely that we thrust ourselves in a culture of lost threads? Untethered, have we detached from not only the soil but the *sensual* richness of our physical selves? Smitten with the virtual, split-split, and nomadic, we are corroding the three pillars of our attention: focus (orienting), judgment (executive function), and awareness (alerting). The costs are [indeed] steep.[42]

More and more, we seem to not only surf on the Internet but through our everyday lives, much like our newly adopted behavior of skim reading. As writer Nicholas Carr admits about his own struggles with concentration and contemplation within the digital age of distraction, "once I was a scuba diver in the sea of words. Now I zip along the surface like a guy on a Jet Ski."[43] His chief concern should begin to echo in all of our hearts and minds: How is all of this electronic connectivity that promotes merely skimming through life restructuring our brains and, consequently, how we interpret the world? Studies examining the effects of different information mediums on brain function reveal that

> the possibility that critical analysis, empathy and other deep reading processes could become the unintended 'collateral damage' of our digital culture is not a simple binary issue about print vs digital reading. It is about how we all have begun to read on any medium and how that changes not only what we read, but also the purposes for why we read. . . . [This type of skim reading] affects our ability to navigate a constant bombardment of information. It incentivizes a retreat to the most familiar silos of unchecked information, which require and receive no analysis, leaving us susceptible to false information and demagoguery.[44]

As Carr discusses in *The Shallows: What the Internet is Doing to Our Brains*, cognitive science informs us that the brain has neuroplasticity. What that means is that the changing stimuli from our outside environment definitely restructure the vital paths of brain circuitry created through the neuron/synapse interfaces. The neural pathways so constructed (both phenomenologically and semiotically) thus become our habits of being in the world—the ways we perceive, think, and orient ourselves toward it. So, our brain circuitry continually adapts and changes according to our changing social environmental influences.

The significance of these changes to the brain and to our ways of perceiving the world are enormous, especially considering the degree to which we now rely on electronic modes of connectivity, or what Carr calls our new media: "intellectual technologies." Our use of such intellectual technologies, such as all of our smart devices, is re-mapping our brains through the acquisition of new habits and not always in positive ways, as suggested previously. As Carr states, "the Net's cacophony of stimuli short-circuits both conscious and unconscious thought, preventing our minds from thinking either deeply or creatively. Our brains turn into simple signal-processing units, quickly shepherding information into consciousness and then back out again,"[45] and "it becomes harder to distinguish relevant information from irrelevant information, signal from noise. We become mindless consumers of data."[46] Especially important to my concerns is the fact that every kind of technological development, Carr reminds us, "embodies an *intellectual ethic*, a set of assumptions about how the human mind works or should work,"[47] although it often goes unnoticed or recognized by its inventors and its users. In addition, Carr claims that an invention's intellectual ethic is what significantly influences our ways of thinking and living our lives. When it comes to our electronic forms of connectivity on the Internet and within cyberspace, Carr thereby questions the ethic that it entails, given that both have produced a "juggler's brain,"[48] in which sustained connectivity of any sort, including ear-to-ear interactions with human others, is at a premium. Our use of such information technologies is thus impacting our ethical ways of being in the world, a point I return to later.

The long-term consequences of such living must not be ignored; otherwise, we create the conditions for a forgetfulness of what is of real value in life, especially when it comes to our human relationships. Former technologist James Williams speaks to this very issue when he declares that our attention deficits are not merely surface quality annoyances that we typically experience in frantic times in our lives. For Williams, the concept of distraction and the juggler's brain needs a more thorough hermeneutic. For, as he says, too often we think of distraction at a more superficial level, as "mere annoyance" or as mere "surface-level static" that has become a routine part of our everyday lives.[49] While definitely designed to maximize our engagement with its various forms, the technology industry has drained words such as *engagement* of their deeper meanings. For example, the technology industry defines engagement, which is their primary user goal, as clicking, tapping, or scrolling as much as possible across multi-various platforms. Williams reminds us that such "engagement goals"[50] are not ones we have for ourselves but ones that technology designers have made for us. He makes an insightful point when he declares that "no one wakes up in the morning and asks, 'How much time can I possibly spend using social media today?'"[51] As a result, the "lives of flesh-and-blood humans" are being purposely driven by intricate navigational systems that often do not serve our long-term goals for living but the short-term goals that technology companies have set for us.[52] The technologist's meaning of engagement is a far cry from what our dialogic philosophers such as Martin Buber or Maurice Friedman had in mind when they carefully theorized the contours of social engagement as an "I-Thou." For these philosophers of communication, engagement means speaking and listening to one another in our immediacy in such a way as to maximize our relationality with one another as unique beings.

So, in his own experience as a technology user, Williams admits eventually feeling a level of disruption at a deeper, more existential level of being that disturbed him greatly and eventually led him to leave the tech industry:

> For too long, we've minimized the threats of this intelligent adversarial persuasion [of the digital age of distraction] as mere "distraction," or minor annoyance. In the short term, these challenges can indeed frustrate our ability to do the things we want to do. In the longer term, however, they can make it harder for us to live the lives we want to live, or, even worse, undermine the fundamental capacities such as reflection and self-regulation, making it harder, in the words of philosopher Harry Frankfurt, to "want what we want to want." Seen in this light, these new attentional adversaries [our interruption machines] threaten not only the success but even the integrity of the human will, at both individual and collective levels.[53]

These conditions are best understood as our new techno-social dilemma.

## OUR TECHNO-SOCIAL DILEMMA[54]

In extending the work of his mentor, Neil Postman, in *Amazing Ourselves to Death: Neil Postman's Brave New World Revisited*, Lance Strate brings the media ecology perspective to bear on our full-fledged electronic age.[55] When Postman wrote his compelling book *Amusing Ourselves to Death: Public Discourse in the Age of Show Business* in the 1980s, we had yet to witness the atmospheric rise of the Internet, the web, social media, and various mobile devices as integral aspects of our everyday existence. Strate extends Postman's ideas by addressing Aldous Huxley's prophetic argument in his novel *Brave New World*, published in 1932. Huxley warns about a future in which our obsessive pursuit of entertainment or fun replaces our higher and nobler ambitions and aspirations as human beings.[56] In many respects, as a culture, we seem to be quite satisfied with these new forms of play or frivolity that our electronic devices provide. We have only to consider the popularity of video games to support such an assertion.[57] And while philosopher Friedrich Schiller informed us in the 1700s that the sensuous, or "play impulse," was an integral component of our humanity that necessarily offered balance to the material, or "formal," impulse of reason, nevertheless, if left unchecked, the play impulse would prove detrimental to our overall well-being. I will speak to this point most directly in chapter 3. In any case, Schiller goes on to say that culture must assume the task of "watch[ing] over these two impulses, and . . . secur[ing] for each its boundaries."[58] I am not convinced that we, as a culture, are currently being reflective enough about these very boundaries. This is unfortunate, given that our confusion about the consequences of our new habits of discourse can have detrimental effects in the long run when it comes to our relationality. More often than not, we are too amazed by our smart technologies most of the time to even care about the long term.

Huxley lamented that with the rise of technological progress, we run the risk of loving our new forms of obsessions, as he defined them. In other words, we come "to adore the technologies that undo [our] capacities to think."[59] Huxley foresaw a future in which (a) no one would want to read a book anymore; (b) we would become passive and egotistical consumers of goods and services; (c) truth would be "drowned in a sea of irrelevance";[60] and (d) we would become a culture based on trivial concerns, precipitated by an emotivism that was altogether self-serving.[61] If we realistically assess our current socio-cultural landscape, we must admit that we seem, in many respects, to be living the very future Huxley predicted.

As Strate and others have implied in their writings, we appear to be quite fascinated with our evolving electronic technologies, often at the expense of our human relationships, indicating a growing imbalance between the two. There is a reason why Strate identifies our fascinations with electronic technologies as "fatal amusements."[62] They are wondrous miraculous machines, so it is no surprise that we are thoroughly amazed or stupefied by their digital displays, functionality, sound enhancements, and social escape features. The mechanical workings of high-definition visuals, for example, are mysteries to most of us, and because of these very qualities, they fascinate us even more. Or, with one or two clicks, we have instantaneous access to a wealth of information that the house of Google has provided, quite literally, at our fingertips.

What consequences are we seeing within cultural life that can be traced to these new electronic patterns of relating that are transpiring at the boundaries of human-machine interactions? It appears that our current techno-social dilemma is exacerbating the problem of determining the difference between what is actual communication in the way I have described it and what is merely attractive artifice—electronic connection disguised as real communication. How do we distinguish between the abundance of electronic enhancements that powerfully compel us toward satisfaction with information-only message transmissions and the deeper levels of communicative engagement that function to ultimately sustain our well-being? Drawing from the writings of dialogic philosopher Martin Buber, for example, Walter Ong understands this information versus communication distinction well when he claims that communication is "not simply new gimmicks enabling man to 'contact' his fellows but, more completely, the person's means of entering into the life and consciousness of others and thereby into his own life."[63]

As the discussion on the growing interest in social robots suggests, the boundary between human qualities and machine capabilities is rapidly blurring—and with it our clear understanding of the value of actual human communication. With this blurring comes a hermeneutical predicament unlike any we have historically faced. How do we recognize, interpret, and enact healthy forms of relationality, given our newly found ways of connecting electronically? As we develop more intimate and emotional connections with intelligent machines, some even calling these new hybrid psychological connections "electronic emotions,"[64] we must ask who we are becoming as thinking and feeling beings in the process.[65] Given the array of electronic intelligent devices we now use on a daily basis, we must not forget that "not only does the technology extend human body and sensory systems [as McLuhan suggests] . . . but it is also being *incorporated* into the human body"[66] at the interface between us and our technological inventions. What does this technological integration mean for our ongoing status as sensuous human beings and for our relationships with one another? Donna Haraway, who writes about the technologizing of the human body within what many are calling our post-human phase of cultural evolution, insists that such blurred boundaries greatly increase our sense of identification and connection with the very tools we use.[67] I think she is right. We now hear many theorists claim that we are turning into *homo technologicus*,[68] and they are not referring to our fascination with new types of ballpoint pens.

My growing concern is this: The more we treat machines as people—given their sophisticated simulations of human emotion and intelligence within interaction—the more we may be inclined to begin to treat people as machines.[69] Treating people as machines means appealing to them during our interactions in ways that simulate simple robotic expressions and perceptions, thereby signifying the most rudimentary of human sharing capabilities along with the attendant elementary expectations, motivations, experiences, and understandings. Hopefully, we will not arrive at the point in our human relationality where a simulation of conversation and human companionship with an intelligent machine becomes good enough for us, a concern Turkle expresses quite adamantly in her work. Given the current social landscape reviewed in this chapter and in the previous one, the prognosis, however, is not good. Even social robot developers are quite aware that they do not have to build a very sophisticated robot to get us to treat it as if it were an actual pet or another human being.[70] Furthermore, and lending support to my contention that the voice is a salient aspect within human relations, robotic developers often emphasize the importance of the artificial voice as a key factor in duping us into believing the robot is human-like. This is understandable because, as I develop herein, the actual voice as sound activates the boundary of relationality in very distinct and powerful ways unlike other forms of sensory experience. AI pioneer Marvin Minsky expressed these same concerns in the 1980s. From the outset of the AI movement, he was afraid that we were remaking ourselves to be companions of our intelligent machines, and not the other way around.[71] So, as we grow into our psychological attachments with the inanimate, our understanding of ourselves as humans is being re-engineered along with the artificial intelligence we are creating.

A growing body of research now addresses this essential problematic: How is humanity in the process of being re-engineered as we move into the so-called post-human world? It appears that this is happening at the cognitive as well as embodied level of experience. For example, Nicholas Carr documents the ways in which our brains are changing due to our new modes of electronic connectivity. As a reminder, Carr contends that our new electronic forms of connectivity are making us more shallow perceivers of the world and, in turn, more shallow thinkers. Given the now-widespread adoption of brain neuroplasticity in the field of neuropsychology, that is, the brain's capacity to change neuropathways based upon environmental factors that impact perception and expression, we must now seriously reflect upon how these changes impact the ways we view the world, self, and others. Neuroplasticity of the brain is a marvelous process that evidences our powerful human adaptive capacities when it comes to the myriad of environmental interfaces we encounter. However, we must thoroughly acknowledge that the changes we are witnessing in human thought and action are a direct result of our pervasive new techno-social environment.

Brett Frischmann and Evan Selinger in *Re-Engineering Humanity* explain how insidiously this re-engineering is taking place, especially at the embodied level, even in social circumstances that on the surface appear to be quite banal. In their discussion of Alexa, Amazon's digital voice-activated assistant, Frischmann and Selinger, for example, describe how Alexa is actually programmed to program us. The anthropomorphic features of Alexa and many digital speaker assistants like it give the illusion of humanity, and yet they claim such devices are highly manipulative. Frischmann and Selinger echo the sentiments of former technologist James Williams when they declare that technology companies "use smart technologies to gain control over us by framing our choices and nudging us towards programmed lives of convenience and cheap bliss."[72] Frischmann and Selinger are also quick to underscore the fact that we become readily complicit in such manipulations. While personal agency and choice are vital aspects of our being that have prompted numerous wars over the centuries, it appears we have actually chosen to "leash"[73] ourselves to these smart devices. Frischmann and Selinger remark that "as we feed on incremental satisfactions, curiosities, updates, and attention [provided by these smart devices], we treat ourselves as grazing sheep and make ourselves more susceptible to conditioning."[74] Such ways of subjugating our own freedoms of choice sound eerily similar to hegemonic mechanisms of oppression that have subjugated people in a number of social contexts throughout history. As we know from critical theory, hegemonic forces often work insidiously by convincing the oppressed that oppressors have their best interests at heart, be they economic, political, or personal.

Recognizing such forces provides a beginning countermove in our pursuit of a re-enchantment of human communication as a salient aspect of our relationality. For we know that when the ways of subjugation are normalized within a culture, as is the case with our growing fascinations with social robots and other electronic devices, the first step back to personal freedom is always through reflection and realization. By realizing that we are becoming complicit in maintaining the very norms that may not serve our own best interests as humans, we provide the foundation for change. Turkle is convinced that it is not too late to make the necessary psychological adjustments that are needed to forestall this techno-social dilemma. I agree but also believe that a re-enchantment of human communication is now warranted, one that is premised upon an acknowledgment of the semiotic and phenomenological auditory composition of relational experience.

While we must admit that the process of techno-social engineering has transpired since the dawn of ancient civilizations,[75] nevertheless we appear to be at an existential tipping point when it comes to our human relationality, particularly given the strong enchanting effects of our new smart devices as connecting mechanisms. As the virtual world of digitalized representations proliferates in cyberspace and on the Internet, the more the actual world of immediate existence with others seems to recede into the shadows. It is time to heed the insightful remarks of semiotician Jean Baudrillard, who warns that in a world of mere simulation, like the one in which we increasingly live, these simulations easily become accepted as second nature, as the hyperreal.[76] Unfortunately, such views move us closer to a more complete derealization of experience. We must not forget, therefore, that the word *virtual*, with its Medieval Latin etymological roots, is derived from *virtus*, meaning strength or power.[77] We must remain vigilant when it comes to safeguarding the aspects of our humanity that serve our goals of intimacy and deep relational satisfaction, especially as we move into the virtual world of symbolic representations, abstractions, and simulated experiences offered every day by our new smart technologies. Given that so much of our lives is now spent within electronic interactions, we must begin to realize that "the resonance of voice, wind, material objects, bodies . . . has been exiled to places without people, while discourse and debate now travel the currents of social media, confined to brief snippets of text and thirty-second sound bites, while the populace, ears plugged, dwells within the confines of soundproofed and acoustically regulated walls,"[78] we have arrived at a very different sense of social life and the role voice plays in it. When the post-human condition can be described very simply as "all that has ever been described, proscribed, and inscribed as being indelibly human [becomes] erased,"[79] then the human voice can easily become co-opted in service to the universalizing demands of a shallow consumerist culture. As a result, we leave behind one of the essential qualities that makes us human to begin with.

Given this, I contend that it is useful for us to begin to view our current amazements with the digitalized world through the sensory trope of *enchantment*. Here, the notion of trope accentuates the way in which enchantments powerfully "turn our thinking" and perceptions of the world. The concept of enchantment is gaining momentum in the diverse contemporary fields of literary criticism, business, philosophy, anthropology, and media studies, to name just a few. The trope of enchantment offers a particularly rich framework in which to interrogate our current challenges and possible forms of redress, particularly as they relate to a productive and pragmatic human relationality. The notion of enchantment helps us explicate how technology functions, the power it yields over our lives, and the consequences it presents to the continued nurturance of the human aesthetic sense of spirit that enriches us as conscious beings. To be enchanted, in part, means to be temporarily fastened to a perceptual, aesthetic object of consciousness in an intense and often emotional way. As mentioned, software developers are quite aware of this enchanting propensity of electronic technology and try to capitalize on its effects as much as possible in their sophisticated designs. Technology's enchanting characteristics signify the degree to which developers have successfully captured our attention and engaged us as a user, as technologist Williams informs us.[80]

I will argue in the next chapter that these forms of enchantment are mostly fleeting infatuations with our devices' amazing interfaces. It is as if we are truly under their spell, exemplifying the traditional negative connotations associated with enchantment. I believe our new electronic fascinations increasingly reveal disingenuous motivations on our parts that require focused, honest interrogation. Such a stance echoes many social theorists before me concerned about the degree to which our electronic enchantments undermine deeper levels of intimacy and human relationality. As a preview of what is to come, I will identify these kinds of electronic enchantments in the predominantly video-centric and logo-centric world of the Internet and cyberspace as *inauthentic*. My designation of inauthentic is informed by philosopher Maurice Merleau-Ponty's theory of existential ambiguity and its correlation to our modes of authentic and inauthentic being and relating. It is to an explication of the experience of enchantment as a phenomenological sign process that I now turn.

## NOTES

1. Bridget Clerkin, "Death by Text Message? Stats Show How Technology Is Killing Us," *DMV.org*, April 28, 2017, https://www.dmv.org/articles/death-by-text-message-stats-show-how-technology-is-killing-us/.

2. "Distracted Walking a Major Pedestrian Safety Concern," *Safety.com*, April 15, 2019, https://www.safety.com/distracted-walking-a-major-pedestrian-safety-concern/.

3. Caitlin Dewey, "What the Heck Is Pokémon Go? An Explainer for the Out-of-Touch And/Or Old," *The Washington Post*, July 11, 2016, https://www.washingtonpost.com/news/the-intersect/wp/2016/07/11/what-the-heck-is-pokemon-go-an-explainer-for-the-out-of-touch-andor-old/?utm_term=.18997aedc819.

4. Ibid.

5. Abbie Kopf, "A New Report Shows That Diagnosis Rates for ADHD Have Risen 30 percent in 8 Years," *USA Today*, March 29, 2019, https://www.usatoday.com/story/sponsor-story/blue-cross-blue-shield-association/2019/03/29/new-report-shows-diagnosis-rates-adhd-have-risen-30-8-years/3309871002/.

6. Joshua Rothman, "A New Theory of Distraction," *The New Yorker*, June 16, 2015, https://www.newyorker.com/culture/cultural-comment/a-new-theory-of-distraction.

7. Dolar, *A Voice and Nothing More*, 71.

8. Matthew B. Crawford, *The World Beyond Your Head: On Becoming an Individual in an Age of Distraction* (New York: Farrar, Straus and Giroux, 2015), 76.

9. Williams, *Stand Out of Our Light*, 90.

10. Jackson, *Distracted*, 14.

11. Carr, *The Shallows*, 118.

12. Williams, *Stand Out of Our Light*, 13.

13. Williams, *Stand Out of Our Light*, xi.

14. Ibid., xii.

15. Ibid., xi.

16. Ibid., xi.

17. Jackson, *Distracted*, 13.

18. Ibid., 15.

19. Frank Furedi, "The Ages of Distraction," *Aeon*, April 1, 2016, https://aeon.co/essays/busy-and-distracted-everybody-has-been-since-at-least-1710.

20. Jackson, *Distracted*, 215–6.

21. William James, *The Principles of Psychology, Vol. 1*, ed. Frederick Burkhardt (Cambridge: Harvard University Press, [1890] 1981), 1:381–2.

22. Paul North, *The Problem of Distraction* (Stanford: Stanford University Press, 2012), 3.

23. Ibid., 5.

24. Semiotician Charles Sanders Peirce helps us see that attention is the result of activating continuity within sign relations while distraction is the hallmark of discontinuity.

25. "Continuous Partial Attention," The Attention Project, accessed August, 10, 2019, https://lindastone.net/qa/continuous-partial-attention/.

26. This is what Peirce identifies as the principle of continuity and it occurs as a result of thought's movement through the three existential sign categories of firstness, secondness, and thirdness in any becoming of a sign in its generality. On the importance on a fluency to thought's movement, see Peirce, *The Collected Papers*, 6.143.

27. Frank Furedi, "The Ages of Distraction."

28. *The Essential Peirce: Selected Philosophical Writings*, eds. Nathan Houser and Christian Kloesel, vol. 1, *1867–1893* (Bloomington: Indiana University Press, 1992), 47.

29. See Locke, *The De-Voicing of Society*.

30. Williams, *Stand Out of Our Light*, 45.

31. Ibid., x.

32. Jackson, *Distracted*, 129.

33. Ibid., 159.

34. Ibid., 165.

35. Ibid., 186; emphasis added.

36. Adam Satariano, Elian Peltier, and Dmitry Kostyukov, "Meet Zora, the Robot Caregiver," *The New York Times,* November 23, 2018, https://www.nytimes.com/interactive/2018/11/23/technology/robot-nurse-zora.html.

37. Nellie Bowles, "Human Contact Is Now a Luxury Good," *The New York Times*, March 23, 2019, https://www.nytimes.com/2019/03/23/sunday-review/human-contact-luxury-screens.html.

38. Quoted in Nellie Bowles, "Human Contact is Now a Luxury Good."

39. Bowles, "Human Contact Is Now a Luxury Good."

40. Dakin Androne and Artemis Moshtaghian, "A Doctor in California Appeared via Video Link to Tell a Patient He Was Going to Die. The Man's Family Is Upset," *CNN*, March 11, 2019, https://www.cnn.com/2019/03/10/health/patient-dies-robot-doctor.
41. See Classen, *Worlds of Sense*, 66.
42. Jackson, *Distracted*, 215; emphasis added.
43. Carr, *Shallows*, 7.
44. Maryanne Wolf, "Skim Reading Is the New Normal: The Effect on Society Is Profound," *The Guardian*, August 25, 2018, https://www.theguardian.com/commentisfree/2018/aug/25/skim-reading-new-normal-maryanne-wolf.
45. Carr, *Shallows*, 119.
46. Ibid., 125.
47. Ibid., 45; emphasis added.
48. Ibid., 115.
49. Williams, *Stand Out of Our Light*, 7.
50. Ibid., 8.
51. Ibid., 8.
52. Ibid., 10.
53. Ibid., xi–xii.
54. This designation of the techno-social dilemma I credit to Brett Frischmann and Evan Selinger, *Re-Engineering Humanity* (Cambridge: Cambridge University Press, 2018).
55. Lance Strate, *Amazing Ourselves to Death: Neil Postman's Brave New World Revisited* (New York: Peter Lang, 2014).
56. Ibid., xii.
57. As of 2017, the monthly number of video game console users in the United States averaged 85.7 million. See "Monthly Number of Game Console Users in the United States from 2nd Quarter 2012 to 2nd Quarter 2017 (In Millions)," *Statista*, accessed May, 15, 2019, https://www.statista.com/statistics/320315/number-users-game-consoles-usa/.
58. Friedrich Schiller, *On the Aesthetic Education of Man* (Mineola: Dover Publications, [1795] 2004), 68.
59. Neil Postman, *Amusing Ourselves to Death*, vii.
60. Ibid., vii.
61. Alasdair MacIntyre takes up this issue of emotivism and its detrimental effects on a society's moral compass in his 1981 book, *After Virtue: A Study in Moral Theory* (Notre Dame: University of Notre Dame Press).
62. Strate, *Amazing Ourselves to Death*, 3.
63. Ong, *The Presence of the Word*, 15.
64. Jane Vincent and Leopoldina Fortunati, *Electronic Emotion: The Mediation of Emotion via Information and Communication Technologies*, eds. (Oxford: Peter Lang, 2009).
65. Rosalind W. Picard, *Affective Computing* (Cambridge: MIT Press, 1997).
66. Satomi Sugiyama and Jane Vincent, "Social Robots and Emotion: Transcending the Boundary Between Humans and ICTs," *intervalla* 1, no. 1 (2013): 2; emphasis added.
67. Donna Haraway, "A Cyborg Manifesto: Science, Technology, and Socialist-Feminism in the Late Twentieth Century," in *Philosophy of Technology: The Technological Condition: An Anthology*, eds. Robert C. Scharff and Val Dusek (Malden: Blackwell Publishing, 2003).
68. Giuseppe O. Longo, "Body and Technology: Continuity or Discontinuity?," in *Mediating the Human Body: Technology, Communication, and Fashion*, eds. Leopoldina Fortunati, James E. Katz, and Raimonda Riccini (Mahwah: Lawrence Erlbaum Associates, 2003), 23–29.
69. This is, of course, one of Sherry Turkle's main concerns.
70. See David Gelernter, "The Danger Is Not Machines Becoming Humans, but Humans Becoming Machines," Big Think, December 13, 2013, https://bigthink.com/in-their-own-words/the-danger-is-not-machines-becoming-humans-but-humans-becoming-machines.
71. Referenced in Turkle, *Reclaiming Conversation*, 338.
72. Frischmann and Selinger, *Re-Engineering Humanity*, 3.
73. Ibid., 10.
74. Ibid., 10.

75. Lewis Mumford, *The Myth of the Machine: Technics and Human Development* (New York: Mariner, 1971).

76. Jean Baudrillard, *Simulations*, trans. Paul Beitchman, Paul Foss, and Paul Patton (New York: Semiotext[e], 1983).

77. Pierre Levy, *Becoming Virtual: Reality in the Digital Age*, trans. Robert Bononno (New York: Plenum Press, 1998).

78. Frances Dyson, *The Tone of Our Times: Sound, Sense, Economy, and Ecology* (Cambridge, MA: Massachusetts Institute of Technology, 2014), 2.

79. Philip Brophy, "Vocalizing the Posthuman," 381.

80. See, for example, Mórna Ní Chonchúir and John McCarthy, "The Enchanting Potential of Technology: A Dialogical Case Study of Enchantment and the Internet," *Personal and Ubiquitous Computing* 12, no. 5 (June 2008).

*Chapter Three*

# Enchantments and Their Inauthenticity

*The Play of Amusements*

In the preceding chapter, we explored some of the consequences of always being *on the phone* in our digital age of distraction, which herald the techno-social dilemma we are currently facing. For an insightful entry point into this socio-cultural condition, I turn to the sensory trope of enchantment.

The trope of enchantment provides us with a means by which to turn our thinking, examine our assumptions, and critically reflect upon where we are socially and personally as we move further into the electronic post-human age. The trope of enchantment, with its primary auditory entailment as a call or summons, announces the aesthetic ways in which our voices as sounding media are losing some of their essential material qualities as salient aspects of our lived experience. Moreover, with the trope of enchantment, we begin to appreciate the aesthetic value our sounding voices have as we seek to nourish productive human relations in a fast-paced digitalized world. My hope is that through this investigation we may re-enchant human communication by way of our immediate ear-to-ear relations and begin to respect more fully the real value it has in our lives.

A closer look at enchantment from my human science perspective of communicology is now warranted. In what follows, I begin by interpreting how all enchantments are best understood as semiotic phenomenologies of the speaking/listening person. In general, they are expressions of our perceptions of the life world and vice versa. I then offer a hermeneutic of authenticity/inauthenticity by referring to the insights of Maurice Merleau-Ponty, especially his understanding of our lived, existential ambiguity. Both of these discussions provide the theoretical grounding for my analysis of our techno-social dilemma and our enchantments with electronic connectivity. Within the world of cyber, we find a pervasive tendency to enact what I identify as inauthentic enchantments, which offer only an existential playground for mere amusements. While amusements are not inherently immoral or bad, unfortunately, such enactments habitualize, more often than not, inauthentic modes of being and relating. Our propensities for mere amusement within our chaotic, ambiguous, fast-paced digital world of distraction forestall the contrary acts of critical yet imaginative thinking described by Peirce as the *play of musement*. It is the play of musement, we will find, that nourishes and possibilizes more productive communicative patterns between interlocutors.

## ENCHANTMENT AS A PHENOMENOLOGICAL SIGN PROCESS

Taking a communicological perspective on enchantment means viewing it phenomenologically as an embodied experience and as a reflexive consequence of sign actions or semiosis.[1] I follow Peirce and his phenomenological understanding of the triadic nature of all sign actions as a way to unpack the aesthetic sign condition of enchantment.[2] According to Peirce, anything we encounter in our experience can become a sign if we perceive it as representing something else, for example—an idea, a feeling, an action or behavior.[3] Thus, all signs have referential functions. Peirce offers us a theoretical way to understand how signs, including the signs of enchantment, are based upon phenomenological and semiotic recursive mediations of conscious experience and the experience of consciousness in the production of meaning. Drawing from Peirce, I am able to flesh out the very contours of our mediated experiences of enchantment as a communicology.

How do we arrive at meaning an interpretation of enchantment as a unique sensory experience? For Peirce, in general meaning or signification is always a mediated consequence of embodied sign actions or relations that are actualized reflexively and recursively within lived experience. He envisions these relations within a triadic categorical scheme he identifies as firstness, secondness, and thirdness.[4] Embodied sign conditions are constituted as a result of these triadic relations within every sign's creation. Meaning evolves, in other words, as an interpreter (perceiving subject) recursively moves from the experience of firstness as a sign relation, which is our spontaneous yet immediate *sensory* encounter with a sign, to secondness as a sign relation, which he calls the object level or the point at which we experience the brute oppositions of experience. At secondness, we begin to interpret the sign based upon making distinctions and differences within our perceptual field of experience or our sensorium, as Ong suggests. For the most part, however, both relations of firstness and secondness are at the pre-conscious level of phenomenological intentionality. In the recursive becoming of the sign to conscious awareness, we come to the thirdness of sign relation, which is the interpretive level. At this point, the full significant effect of the sign (or meaning) is experienced as a result of the recursive mediation of firstness and secondness by thirdness as constituting sign relations. He calls this effect of sign actions at this point the *interpretant*.

In general, Peirce associates the sign relation of firstness with affect, pure possibility, and tone. Firstness is the iconic function of signs. Sign processes and their constitution, in other words, begin by way of an imaginative, sensory attunement or unity of experience with people, places, things, and events in the world. As I will argue later, the aesthetic affectual experience of enchantment, especially in what I will call its authentic configurations, accentuates the sonorous or tonal aspects of lived experience as specifically a sign relation of firstness.[5] This is especially because of authentic enchantment's intense tonal manifestations as sound phenomena, but also because they amplify the important aesthetic dimensions of experience more generally.[6] I will have more to say about this idea of tone in another chapter. In any case, Peirce is quick to remind us that the experience of firstness is not conceptual. This is because the "qualitative immediacy [of firstness] falls outside the reach of conceptual articulation."[7] Firstness is thus an elusive category of experience, paradoxically ineffable in its qualitative distinctiveness as a unity of experience.

The sign relation of secondness is the object level of conscious experience and functions indexically to produce an evolving *token* of mediated experience. That is, the distinctions of objects to consciousness begin to make a difference in our perceptual field of experience. Quite simply, we recognize a person as opposed to an electronic tablet, and a smartphone as opposed to a sunset, although those differences have yet to be articulated in language at the level of thirdness. Important to keep in mind is the fact that these distinctions are shaped by the particular objects to consciousness that are captured in a given space and time within our perceptual field or in our sensorium. As Peirce reminds us, and as Ong's work echoes, visual as well as auditory objects to consciousness thus are integral in shaping the eventual significant effect of a given sign relation and its ultimate meaning. In terms of our dialogic relations with others as an event of discourse, this second step in the evolutionary potential of a sign's development is highly significant. For we need to distinguish the face of the other, as Emmanuel Levinas would say, or the voice of the other, as I contend, in order to establish any subsequent ground for ethical relations within discourse.

At thirdness we arrive at the symbolic or linguistic level of sign relations, given that any interpretation of the world, including any experience of enchantment, is figured as a *type* from the available socio-cultural codes or *langue*, as semiotician Saussure describes it.[8] In other words, we name or map the pre-existing territory of conscious experience, and this results in what Peirce calls an interpretant. We claim, for example, "What a marvelous sunset." In doing so, the coded sign relation meets with our embodied experiences of firstness and secondness in this ultimate production of meaning. At this level of sign relation, we thus appeal to the signifying order or linguistic cultural codes at our disposal that have been previously learned so as to articulate the sign's meaning for us.

Furthermore, as Peirce describes, the interpretant of a sign always inaugurates the production of another sign (firstness) as we think and act in the world in naturally reflexive and recursive ways. He identifies this infinite, recursive process of mediation of signs as firstness and secondness by thirdness as *semiosis*. The important thing to keep in mind is that these aspects of the triad are all phenomenological sign *relations* that interrelate with one another in the process of signification. Thus, semiosis is an inherent aspect of our evolving experience at any given moment in time as we perceive and interpret the world around us. Given that signs are mediated by embodied subjects through consciousness, Peirce consequently honors the tenets of phenomenology, calling it in his initial writings "phaneroscopy."[9] With Peirce, we appreciate that such a semiotic process emphasizes to varying degrees the sensory nature of objects of consciousness. We understand that we are active participants in any sign relation's ultimate constitution and meaning as a phenomenology.[10]

Therefore, enchantments are best understood as *mediated* experiences or phenomena indicative of all acts of semiosis. They are, however, particular interpretants recursively co-constituted between a perceiving subject and an object present to consciousness at a particular moment. It is especially important to this discussion to think of our mediated experiences as transpiring along a semiotic continuum. That is, while all experience is mediated semiotically and phenomenologically (including speaking with and listening to the voice), this mediation can occur at higher and higher orders of abstractions or what Peirce calls translations,[11] signifying greater degrees of distantiation from the immediacy of embodied experience. We call such higher-order abstractions *disembodied experiences* because they plunge us deeper and deeper into the symbolic world of representation and signification and further away from rudimentary or concrete sensory experience. Thus, the further we move into the symbolic relation of thirdness in our discourse and actions, the world of representation and translation, the less we are aware that our phenomenological experiences are shaped by the effects of embodied semiosis. Instead, our experience becomes more disembodied from its actuality, and we remain immersed within the world of the symbolic, the world of signs, in spheres of second-, third-, or even fourth-order significations. In such instances, we say that our experiences are highly mediated, where the symbolic aspects of semiosis seem to override the phenomenological or embodied awareness of the world as immediate sensory experience at the level of firstness and secondness.

Acknowledging that semiosis is a dialectical process of communication, that is, expression and perception of the world have their significant roles to play, semiotician Susan Petrilli argues that we can think of any interpretant as ultimately a "response" or expression to signs we perceive in the process of actively constructing the knowable world. The value of her work rests in highlighting the fact that all signs, including those of enchantment, inherently function communicatively, what she likes to call the dialogical nature of signs.[12] That is, signs entail both perceptions and expressions of a sign user. As Petrilli indicates, "the meaning of a sign is a response, an interpretant that calls for another response, another interpretant . . . [which] implies the dialogic nature of the sign and semiosis"[13] in the process of constituting human interpretation.

In the case of enchantment regardless of its context, it is easy for us perhaps to acknowledge the experience as a perceptual one, whether it is through sight, sound, smell, taste, or touch—making the experience seem only a passive action of semiosis. For example, we often say we are enchanted by something, as if we are acted upon by some object or event in the outside world with very little active semiotic and phenomenological involvement on our part. However, from a communicological perspective, we can hear that enchantment is constituted very much within an active, expressive phenomenological and semiotic moment by a perceiving subject. We are actively involved through our perceptions and expressions in constituting the kind and degree of enchantments we experience. We need to remember that "perception is already expression as human beings are aware not of identities but of patterns and relations. *Signifying* is dynamic and characterized by fluidity: Firstness, Secondness and Thirdness seep into each other."[14]

Important to note is the fact that we develop subsequent habits of perception and expression that possibilize different experiences of enchantment. Our experiences of enchantment in whatever form they take are dependent, therefore, upon how our sign actions evolve at specific times and places and the sensory or phenomenological aspects of our being that are activated—sight, sound, taste, touch, or smell. Thus, with his notion of the sensorium, Ong well understood that these sensory components are fundamental existential media that dramatically shape our conscious experience. The sensory aspects of objects to consciousness, such as the sight of light on the surface of a stream or the sound of an owl, are integral in the process of shaping thought and action and operating recursively, our thoughts and actions impact our subsequent interactions with signs as sensory media. While Ong did not frame his discussions on the sensorium through the lens of semiotics, he appreciates how our aesthetic sensibilities are often hierarchically constituted communicatively, given the varying ways the objects present to consciousness through our process of phenomenological mediation. For example, sight or the visual can take precedence over sound or the auditory based upon the unique qualities of the object present to consciousness that we value. Value preferences such as these become habits of perceiving and expressing within semiotic phenomenological relations, a point made earlier using the works of both Dewey and Peirce. This explains why a given culture's sensibilities are informed by the different value preferences the people of that culture hold in common. The discipline of anthropology understands this variance well. Over the last few decades, a growing body of research interrogates what is called the anthropology of the senses.[15]

Semiotician Petrilli is also concerned about our active responses, expressions, or interpretants within sign processes, given the inherent axiological nature they entail. Taking her lead from semiotician Thomas Sebeok, who initiated a movement in global semiotics,[16] Petrilli understands that all sign actions, whether at the interface of humans and nature or at the level of dialogic encounters with others, carry a response-bility with them to honor the productive, pragmatic future evolution of both poles of experience (subject and object). Petrilli's holistic way of thinking provides a foundation for her semio-ethical perspective, which I shall appeal to and describe in more detail later. Following this line of thinking, we can readily see that affectual or aesthetic experience (as firstness) and ethics (as secondness) are inherently intertwined within all events of phenomenological semiosis at the level of thirdness. Phenomenologist and semiotician Merleau-Ponty concurs and names the consequence of this process at the level of thirdness the aesthetic *logos*. He wants us to be aware that perception is more than a mere gathering of sense data. Perception, he argues, is inherently axiological, imbued with an affectual aesthetic as we stylize our world. So, by the time we reach awareness at the level of signification or thirdness, the *logos* is always already aesthetically constituted. As Colapietro reminds us, regrettably these "affective dimensions of human life have still not been fully given their due"[17] in philosophical discourse. My aim in this book is to address this issue.

Now, what is particularly interesting about enchantment as a sensory experience is that it typically carries a unique phenomenological flow. This quality informs my subsequent discussions, particularly as it relates to the distinction I draw between inauthentic and authentic enchantments. Suffice it to say at this point that this flow of experience is understandable given enchantment's historical association with sound, which manifests in and through time. As we learn from Ong, "None of the other senses [other than sound] gives us the insistent impression that what it registers is something necessarily progressing through time. . . . Sound implies movement and thus change."[18] This is in sharp contrast with sight or the visual, which manifests in and through space. To elaborate further, Ong states, "Sight can follow motion through time [as in a video or film] but it seeks [ultimately] to fix its objects" in space.[19] Thus sound is highly dynamic as opposed to the visual, which has to pair itself with the auditory to make it so.[20] Enchantment's etymology as sound, that is, as oral chanting, thus stresses the importance of the *tonal* quality of experience, thereby linking it with the dynamical aspects of sensory experience and its attendant temporality. Enchantments, therefore, play with our temporal experience, either "slowing down or speeding up the tempo of"[21] an object to consciousness. I make the argument later on that it is this temporal flow of enchantment as auditory experience that is particularly relevant when it comes to distinguishing between its authentic and inauthentic entailments.

Because of their dynamical quality, enchantments also serve integrative functions both personally and socially. The power of enchantment has been historically recognized in cultures around the world for centuries. Repetitious sounds, for example, represented by the enactment of chanting, are highly ritualistic in many cultures. From anthropological research, we know that rituals serve integrative functions[22] within a given community; that is, they bring people together so as to announce and enact commonly held beliefs and customs. The experience of enchantment in its ritualized form is no different, regardless of the source of sensory input—sound or image. However, I aim to show that auditory enchantments often produce the most significant effects, especially within the context of dialogic relations.

An enchantment interpretant is a phenomenological sign condition that, through its activation of wonder and awe, fastens us to lived experience in often intense, affectual, and aesthetic ways. Enchantment produces a bodily sensory awareness that powerfully connects us to one another and the world in a mutually reciprocal relation of fleeting interdependence. Enchantment is often described as a state of interactive fascination or wonder with an object present to consciousness, and given my above discussion of a dialogic sign condition, we can now understand why. Regardless of the sensory form it emphasizes (sound or sight), enchantment is much more than a passive perceptual experience. Enchantment is also a semiotic and phenomenological aesthetic *expression of attachment* to a given object to consciousness, be it a person, place, thing, or event. It represents a temporary *attunement* and an acknowledgement of something greater than or outside of our typical *sense* of ourselves that calls us to respond through our continuing expressions and/or perceptions. Paradoxically, enchantment draws us out of ourselves and into the world at the same time that it integrates or unites us with things or ideas greater than ourselves. As we will see in the chapters to follow, this is an altogether healthy process when it comes to establishing deeper and more satisfying dialogic relations with others. Enchantment's power is most traditionally recognized, however, in a negative way; that is, to be enchanted is to be deluded. I will have more to say about this later.

As in all conscious experiences of signs understood phenomenologically, enchantment evolves through the semiotic and phenomenological modes of experience Peirce identifies as firstness, secondness, and thirdness, as previously explained. However, enchantment as an interpretant appears to emphasize different aspects of these relational modes of being, depending upon which aspect of sensory experience within semiosis is activated at a given point in time. It is now appropriate to describe my use of the terms *authentic* and its counterpart, the *inauthentic*, as they relate to the conscious experience of enchantment. Here I draw heavily from continental philosophy and particularly the writings of semiotic phenomenologist Maurice Merleau-Ponty. Known as the philosopher of ambiguity,[23] Merleau-Ponty reminds us of the implicature of existential ambiguity and the forms of authenticity within human affairs. We find that existential ambiguity conditions the very possibility of authenticity and inauthenticity as communicative experience. A review of his writings on this subject will prove helpful.

## THE COMMUNICATIVE IMPLICATURE OF EXISTENTIAL AMBIGUITY AND AUTHENTICITY

Merleau-Ponty theorizes that the embodied synthesis we experience at the boundaries of consciousness (semiotic structures) and experience (phenomenological acts) is always comprised of "open inexhaustible" horizons of experience that make our fundamental relations to the world inherently ambiguous.[24] In other words, between person and sign, body and culture, experience and consciousness exists an inescapable existential *tension* he describes as a lived ambiguity. At the boundary of the sign of person and the person that is signed is a contest of conscious experience and the experience of consciousness that enables the condition of this lived ambiguity. Every person-to-person meeting activates this condition of lived ambiguity to varying degrees as do our interactions with places and things. Merleau-Ponty believes that our *être au monde* (presence-in-the-world) involves an inherent degree of risk because of this ambiguity. It is operative as an existential boundary condition that implicates us in the discourse of others.

Merleau-Ponty theorizes that both the problem and potentiality of authenticity inheres within this lived ambiguity. Said differently, between the world of signs and the embodiment of signs lies the essential problematic of authenticity as an implicature of ambiguity. This is because our lived ambiguity as a being in the world with others necessitates choice making (a developing axiology) as we are immediately confronted with value choices and ethical issues and concerns as a relational being. How we respond to our existential ambiguity instantiates either an authentic or inauthentic orientation toward and enactment in the world. As he claims, "I know myself only in my inherence in time and in the world, that is, I know myself only in ambiguity."[25] According to Merleau-Ponty, the tension of lived ambiguity comes in two forms, depending upon the semiotic and phenomenological conditions of its constitution and enactment by a speaking/listening body-subject. We perceive and express our lived ambiguity in two ways depending upon how we semiotically interpret and phenomenologically respond to our life-world. These two forms he names "positive and negative ambiguity."[26]

For Merleau-Ponty, the quest for certainty or knowledge in its most rigid forms is the consequence of interpreting our lived ambiguity in a negative way. Instead, he believes that we must remain "open" to further questioning of our experiences moving back and forth "from knowledge to ignorance, from ignorance to knowledge."[27] Unfortunately, our typical "flight from ambiguity,"[28] or a focus on reducing the uncertainty of lived experience at all costs, becomes a common response to our existential ambiguity interpreted as negative. Under such semiotic and phenomenological conditions, we habitually appeal to an apparent pre-existent fixed-world of representational meaning that semiotically over-determines our phenomenological modes of being and relating that might otherwise produce more iterative enactments. Why we appeal to pre-existent meanings is quite understandable; we perceive there is less psychological and social risk involved if we use established means of discourse. There is a degree of existential comfort, in other words, when we draw from sedimented or taken-for-granted ways of interpreting and responding to the world. Under such conditions, we appeal to highly codified ways of speaking/listening and are fully immersed in discourse as *parole parlée* (speech merely spoken).[29] In such cases, our perceptions and expressions of the world have been reified by these pre-existing code conditions. It is a convenient method of interpreting the world but highly restrictive in terms of creative thinking. We might argue that in such cases life is lived as merely a readerly text, as semiotician Roland Barthes would say, that is, produced by evidentiary factums and which often leads to relativistic thinking.[30] This condition is merely a life lived within a predetermined web of representational meaning similar to Heidegger's notion of the "everydayness," which results in becoming merely a *they-self*, one of many in anonymity.

In contrast, positive ambiguity is constituted when we recognize the salient function of expressions and perceptions as self-evidentiary components of the dialectic of consciousness and experience. Under such conditions, we find a spontaneity that offers the possibility of speaking and listening imaginatively, poetically, yet with integrity. Rather than a re-iteration of established code conditions, as exemplified in negative ambiguity responses we demonstrate, instead there is an appreciation for the iteration of originary speech in its particularity. This approach to our lived ambiguity functions to create a life lived as a writerly text, as Barthes describes it. This type of text or life relies not solely on representational modes of discourse but also "self-signifies,"[31] although not in a narcissistic way. Instead, this is a life lived in a way that fosters a "poetry of human relations,"[32] a semiotic and phenomenological condition that Merleau-Ponty believes lies at the very heart of a healthy or pragmatic way of being in the world with others. In such instances, we live with a personal sense of freedom, integrity, and self-fulfillment that does not promote self-indulgence or eclipse the well-being of self and others in their relationality. Thus, acknowledging our lived ambiguity as positive results from an adherence to *parole parlante*, or speaking speech in its originary iterations.[33] It is a life lived with distinction, in the true sense of the term as a stylized particularity, and not merely repeating discursive patterns with a sense of redundancy. Furthermore, the ability to move reflexively between knowledge and ignorance of the world as positive ambiguity reveals the "mystery of the world and of reason," so Merleau-Ponty contends.[34] As I submit elsewhere,[35] approaching the tensive moments of lived experience as a positive ambiguity also requires approaching relationality as an abductive logic, as Peirce describes it. Merleau-Ponty is appreciative of this logic when he theorizes that while inductive and deductive logics are typical methods of verification of truth claims in the world and so have their parts to play, they do not speak adequately to the "positive steps of thinking or its most valid accomplishments,"[36] which abductive logic allows. Induction and deduction do not, in other words, adequately interrogate an issue like positive ambiguity and, by implication, the question of authenticity in human relationality.

With Merleau-Ponty, we come to understand that our conditions of ambiguity actually problematize and yet make possible our authentic enactments in speech and discourse. When we respond to the world and our lived ambiguity from a negative perspective, we have a tendency to adopt inauthentic modes of being and relating. In effect, we equate perception and expression only with its "sedimented characteristics,"[37] that is, with their ability to represent or recollect "a pre-established sign"[38] that may not fit the particularity of experience at a given point in time with a particular person. Especially in light of our postmodern state of fragmentation and multiplicity, everyday life can take on a banality as we find ourselves within a perceived repetition of differences that because of their frequency become merely more of the same. This produces, unfortunately, a presencing of many others (persons, texts, events) as a redundancy of cultural consciousness that exacerbates the problem of being authentic.

In contrast, when we approach the communicative situation as the accomplishment of an aesthetic *logos*, as Merleau-Ponty suggests, we actualize more "authentic speech," that is, speech that is "primordial, creative, and expressive of existential meaning"[39] and that appreciates the particularity of a given discursive event. This authentic approach to our life-world reveals a "movement of disclosure . . . that strives to inhabit the everyday in a way that enables the intensification of the questionable-ness, uncanniness, openness . . . alterity, and, it is hoped, possibilities for things to become otherwise."[40] Therefore, to demonstrate an authentic orientation toward the world of events and people requires us to acknowledge and appreciate the particular instances of discourse for their potential in developing a sense of self and other relations and to recognize those relationships as integral to the process of constituting a meaningful authentic existence in the first place.

However, as philosopher Charles Taylor warns, when taken to extreme the "self-signification" aspect of authenticity can produce what he calls a "culture of authenticity."[41] Such a culture overall is viewed as egoistic in nature given that everyone is struggling for possible freedoms from the tyranny of sociopolitical institutions that over-determine personal experience. Many would argue that such a culture of authenticity is a necessary consequence of postmodern life with its fragmentation and celebration of difference. In any case, as Merleau-Ponty suggests, there is a delicate balance in determining authentic forms of discourse and action. This determination resides in the particularity of experience rather than appealing to a cultural consciousness that refers primarily to some "reality beyond itself."[42] Understanding the authentic/inauthentic dialectic as a consequence of our response to lived ambiguity lends further insight into this existential dynamic. On this point, Taylor's interpretation of authenticity is helpful:

> Authenticity (A) involves (i) creation and construction as well as discovery, (ii) originality, and frequently (iii) opposition to the rules of society and even potentially to what we recognize as morality. But it is also true . . . that it (B) requires (i) openness to the horizons of significance (for otherwise the creation loses the background that can save it from insignificance) and (ii) a self-definition in dialogue. That these demands may be in tension has to be allowed.[43]

Thus, for Merleau-Ponty, the dialectic of authenticity and inauthenticity and its enactment always returns to the specific ways we deal with the lived tension of our existential ambiguity. Do we merely repeat the cultural codes of discourse we have learned (*parole parlée*)? Or, through discourse, do we abductively possibilize new iterations of meaning (*parole parlante*)? While Martin Heidegger's sense of authenticity is actualized through our "resoluteness" to finitude,[44] we see that Merleau-Ponty's authentic being struggles against the apparent finitude of the sign or signification. Ironically, he recognizes, however, that the authentic being also needs the function of signs within discourse with others to phenomenologically instantiate productive dialogic relations.

It is now time to classify our experiences of enchantments in a general way according to their semiotic and phenomenological entailments, using Peirce's triadic categories of experience. Drawing from the insights of Merleau-Ponty and the discussion above, we can now begin to understand our experiences of enchantment as manifesting authentic or inauthentic responses to the world.

## AUTHENTIC AND INAUTHENTIC ENCHANTMENTS

At least in its authentic entailments, as I discuss in more detail in chapter 7, enchantment seems to herald the sign relation of firstness. That is, these forms of enchantment are thematized more by their qualities of pure possibility, affect, and the aesthetic tonality or resonance found in life itself. As we shall see, in authentic experiences of enchantment, particularly as they relate to the sounding voices of self and other, thirdness, or the symbolic level of sign relations, is weakened or lessened. This is understandable given the above discussion on how authentic and inauthentic modes of being are instantiated. Constituted as they are within the symbolic signifying order of language, our rational beliefs and inferences are temporarily suspended to allow for the experience of authentic attunement with the world of people, places, things, and events as a particularity. This is activated at the aesthetic level of firstness. My interpretation makes sense if we consider how our symbolic naming or mapping of the territory of authentic enchantments often proves challenging. We have a difficult time fully describing the experience of authentic enchantment using the available codes of discourse at our disposal. This is equally true when we experience amazing encounters with nature's wonders, such as a beautiful sunset or waterfall, as it is when we are enchanted by a deeply felt relation with another human being. This quality of feeling is what gives authentic enchantment its powerful, mysterious, ineffable nature as a sign relation of firstness. Authentic enchantments also signify precious moments of existential irruption within our taken-for-granted experiential world. This irruption proves to be highly beneficial for human relationality, especially when we want to break repetitive unproductive habits of discourse and action and instead enact moments of *parole parlante* (speaking speech).[45] It is as if the immediacy of firstness overrides the mediation of experience as a consequence of thirdness. We experience a "sense of" or "feel for" these authentic forms of enchantment that produce what Peirce describes as vague "habits of feeling."[46]

In contrast, inauthentic enchantments are dominated by the sign relation of thirdness, not firstness. That is, the immediacy (or firstness) indicative of vague qualities of feeling are over-ridden by the mediation of thirdness. I explore these sign relations in more detail below. In general, we find that our appeals to electronic connectivity often promote more inauthentic encounters with the world. This is because our sensory interfaces are shaped heavily by the typical video-centric and logo-centric ways of electronically connecting, as previously reviewed. The rich auditory qualities of these forms of enchantment are reduced or faded altogether, too often awash within the noise of socio-cultural electronic buzz, a felt redundancy to lived experience. Although not directly referencing electronic devices, George Ritzer calls similar forms of enchantments disenchanting because they prove disappointing in the long run.[47] I will have more to say about this later.

The aesthetic qualities of enchantments' sensory experiences and their traditional links with the sacred cannot be overstated, especially when it comes to their authentic entailments. In their work on the epistemology of the sacred, Gregory Bateson and his daughter, Mary Catherine Bateson,[48] acknowledge that the aesthetic dimension of experience, which often leads to enchantment, is an integral aspect of what we identify as the sacred. Bateson and Bateson, of course, argue that the aesthetic quality of sensory experience is a healthy and necessary part of an ecology of mind.[49] That is, Gregory Bateson contends that an adequate understanding of the ecological links between mind and nature and person and culture is premised upon an aesthetic awareness or consciousness. Looking at enchantment from the perspective of media ecology, we see the significant effects that enchantments as aesthetic awareness produce for an individual or a group.

We also begin to appreciate how enchantments are shaped by the prior contexts and current patterns of thinking that pre-dispose interpreters to particular responses—be they aesthetic, ethical, political, or otherwise. These responses are the analogue aspects of experience that so enrich our understanding of enchantment and our own relationality. As Bateson scholar Morris Berman contends in his 1984 book, *The Re-Enchantment of the World*, enchantment is a central metaphor of Bateson's evolving epistemology of the sacred. Berman claims that Bateson's "pattern which connects," or what he calls the "sacred," is amplified by the existential concept of enchantment. This is especially apparent if we consider Bateson's insistence upon conceptualizing mind and nature as a unity of affectual experience and interpretation, an aesthetic. Bent on counteracting the unproductive modern dualisms that separate intellect from the heart, Bateson thought both should be enveloped within an aesthetic frame that more adequately captures their salient qualities in communicative experience. As most Bateson scholars know, Bateson was quite fond of quoting Pascal who claims that "the heart has its reasons of which reason knows nothing." In many ways, Bateson's approach to the ecology of mind seen through the lens of aesthetics is similar to John Dewey's aesthetic project when it comes to human relations. For both honor the integral role aesthetic experience plays in constituting and shaping discourse and action.

Gregory and Mary Catherine Bateson's work on the sacred as a way of knowing was not, however, an effort to extend its original meaning associated with a transcendent deity. Rather, they sought to outline a secular and more immediate way to understand the all-important aesthetic patterns of existential connection between culture and nature. For Bateson, these connective patterns constituted what we hold as sacred or dear to our hearts to begin with. I follow their lead on this point in the discussions that follow. As we shall see, the sensory trope of enchantment provides us with a qualitatively rich hermeneutic tool by which to understand both the sacrality inherent in immediate voiced relations with another as an experience of enchantment (discussed in chapters 6–8) and the profane dimensions of experience that inauthentic enchantments often articulate. I now turn specifically to the world of cyberspace and our tendency to constitute more inauthentic enchantments therein.

## CYBERSPACE AND INAUTHENTIC ENCHANTMENTS

It behooves us to explore the cultural conditions from which we currently manifest enchantments, especially given the heavy influence of our fast-paced, electronically mediated environment. Our new media form a significant ecological web of enchanting relational experiences that radically shape the ways we interpret the world and the communicative practices or habits of discourse that we subsequently enact. Software developers fully acknowledge that the experience of enchantment in human-computer interaction is now an integral component in their design strategies. As they indicate, given the discretionary nature of user interactions with the Internet, cell phones, cyber-communities, or computer games, designing for enchantment becomes a most pragmatic endeavor.[50] These electronic mediated forms of enchantment, however, have a tendency to produce inauthentic experiences. Inauthentic enchantments will be described as particular phenomenological sign processes, in light of the above discussions. The aesthetic dimensions of the auditory elements at the sign relation of firstness are increasingly muted in inauthentic enactments by the hyper-textual/visual elements of the symbolic. These conditions produce significant effects and often lock us into discursive practices that merely echo *parole parlée* (speech spoken). The silencing of the auditory dimensions of such enchantments exemplify the dominance of relational thirdness. They also represent our responses to our lived ambiguity from a negative standpoint. This sign condition calls for a closer look. I begin with an overview of the semiotic qualities of these particular enchanting relations.

As I mentioned previously, our fascination with smartphones and other electronic devices appears to, more often than not, keep our responses to the world at the symbolic level of Peirce's thirdness. This is the mode most closely associated with the intelligible—more than the ineffable—aspects of being. At this level, our experiences are semiotically rooted in a continuity of meaning that has been derived symbolically as a relation of thirdness. That is, these forms of enchantment are ways of perceiving and expressing in which the shared signs, symbols, and socio-cultural codes within a given linguistic system reign supreme in our experiences and interpretations of meaning. Given the predominance of the visual/textual modes in cyberspace and on the Internet, as outlined in previous chapters, it is not surprising that this semiotic relation is heavily shaped by instances of semiotic closure. Semiotic closure transpires in thirdness and tends to fixate meaning, giving signification its static sense within acts of symbolic representation (*parole parlée*). This fixation is indicative more of the very feature of the binary, digital aspects inherent to language—displaying the presence/absence functions of signification more generally. These features thus signify the dominance of the visual/textual over the auditory in cyberspace and often produce enchantment in its diminished or inauthentic form. This is partially because the call or summons such enchantments evoke is not immediately voiced as an auditory aspect of being as a sign relation of firstness. Instead, these calls of enchantment are articulated more in the hyper-textual/visual world of representation and mediation, where the acousmatic voice, as we will see in chapter 4, stands in close symbiotic relation. As a reminder, the auditory nature of cyberspace and the Internet is highly mediated electronically, exhibiting voices that are mainly disembodied articulations that serve a pre-existent *logos*.

Our experiences of surfing the web are quickly normalized in everyday life, so much so that they seem only rational or logical. Our new operating assumptions thus propel us toward more ways to electronically connect, creating a redundancy to experience. Following Peirce, we know that the logical, at least in its traditional sense as *logos*, is a sign relation of thirdness. These enchanting experiences seem so logical that nowadays when we meet someone who does not live in the cyber world of lived abstractions and the symbolic we tend to find them suspect. We are not being irrational, we conclude, when we spend several hours clicking through news feeds or playing video games; we are being quite rational in the world in which we now live.

One of the prizes we seek on the Internet or in the space of cyber is codified information—in whatever form it comes—because we are enchanted by the symbolic power it seems to hold. We have not dubbed our new electronic age the "age of information" for nothing. This is because we believe we have the world of information and knowledge at our fingertips as long as we continue surfing the web or connecting on social media platforms. The concept of vagueness is anathema to the web. Whatever uncertainty we have can be quickly alleviated by swiping and clicking—and with it perhaps a feeling of negative existential ambiguity. What typically evolves in the space of cyber is, as Gregory Bateson would say, only pattern and redundancy in thought and action.[51] Perhaps that is why we become obsessed with surfing the web or thumbing through our applications on our smart devices. While felt redundancy certainly produces a sense of stability to lived experience and reduces a degree of uncertainty and minimizes psychological risk, it also prompts us to seek further information to break the psychological monotony. Our constant thumbing through our various feeds thus counteracts the banality this typical barrage of intelligibility (as information) creates as a phenomenology.[52] A vicious cycle of stimulation and redundancy ensues. Some students of mine have admitted they can spend five to seven hours a day in this vicious electronic cycle. Unfortunately, these behaviors oftentimes display the acquisition of "false needs" or "repressive satisfactions." According to Bartky,

> Repressive satisfaction fastens us to the established order of domination, for the same system which produces false needs also controls the conditions under which such needs can be satisfied. "False needs" . . . are needs which are produced through indoctrination. . . . They are needs whose possession and satisfaction benefit not the subject who has them but a social order whose interest lies in domination.[53]

The consequence of this sign condition of inauthentic enchantment is that the symbolic aspect of human experience tends to over-determine the phenomenological or the uniquely embodied felt-presence of existence at the level of firstness. Or, said differently, our cognitive functions over-ride a fuller sense of the actual affectual or aesthetic qualities, grounded as it is within the immediacy of speaking and listening as a particular embodied experience. These conditions are not surprising given that they appear to reflect a position toward our existential nature as a bad ambiguity, as Merleau-Ponty describes.

This is not to say, however, that an aesthetic is not a vital aspect of many of our cyber or virtual experiences. There is an aesthetic that is realized, but it is one that is pre-existent and based upon strategic marketability. My point here is to call attention to the fact that the aesthetic within digitalized experiences is qualitatively different than the aesthetic felt within the immediacy of speaking and listening with another. The digitalized aesthetic is a pre-fabricated one that is constituted to appeal to the masses. It appears, however, that we have quickly adapted to the aesthetic of the artificial or virtual instead of the actual, the aesthetic that, according to Merleau-Ponty, substantially nourishes the developing *logos*. This is why in sign conditions of inauthentic enchantment we often confuse the representative map of the world offered by the symbolic space of cyber for the actual territory of our lives that is lived as an aesthetic condition. In such cases, our life-world is fully embodied in the virtual and not the actual. Hence, these enchantments and their symbolic products begin to repress their originary form in the immediate experience of sign relations of firstness. The forms of the symbolic—fleeting images, textual excerpts, and soundbites—may quickly become conflated with the actual. We become existentially confused, and this confusion turns easily into mere psychological acquiescence. Under such conditions, we find a hollowing out or flattening of embodied aesthetic experience, given that such a world can easily become a sea of signifiers with too few signifieds or substantial meaning. The artificiality of the aesthetic that accompanies virtuality is quite stimulating, perhaps even intoxicating, but it does not last and it is not our own.

Another way of understanding the inauthentic forms of enchantment concerns the mythical elements we so often associate with enchantment. Bruno Bettelheim's seminal work on fairy tales as forms of enchantment is a good case in point. Bettelheim claims that the mythical aspects of fairy tales are prime examples of putting enchantment to good use.[54] Important distinctions should be made between originary *mythic* consciousness and its symbolic and quite reductive counterpart, *mythologies*. Following the work of philosopher Ernst Cassirer on myth, we see that myth or *mythos* lies at the very root of all human experience and thereby undergirds our imaginative capabilities in profound existential ways. As described by Cassirer scholar Peter Savodnik, "Myth or mythical consciousness provides our first apprehension of the world and forms the basis for other levels of consciousness to follow.... The mythical conception of the world is always reflected in an interconnectedness and concreteness."[55] Because of this, he says, "there is no distinction between the sensuous image," in this case, the sound and what is taken to be real "... and so the mythical image [sound] stands before us as the concrete incarnation of the meaning it represents. It is so woven into our intuition of reality as to be indistinguishable from it."[56] Thus, mythical consciousness always reflects a sign relation of firstness, as Peirce understands it. This imbues consciousness heavily with its originary aesthetic qualities.

In inauthentic enchantment, the mythic elements of experience are present, but they have become *mythologized* by their symbolic grounding in semiotic thirdness (logic). In other words, in inauthentic enchantment, the originary *mythos* of authentic enchantment has been perverted into a highly codified, sedimented system of representation that subsequently takes on a life of its own. Mythical consciousness is over-determined by the symbolic. In cases of inauthentic enchantment, we convert the imaginative and abductive thrust of mythic consciousness into what semiotician Roland Barthes would call a secondary order of signification, a symbolic discourse, a mythology.[57] This discourse then easily appropriates any original phenomenological *mythos* through a proliferation of possible signifiers, as Barthes contends. Consequently, narratives we share in cyberspace about ourselves and others often quickly get out of hand in our acts of spinning—like fairy tales, which represent highly codified sign systems. This partially explains the appeal of the Internet and the space of cyber for those who are psychologically adrift or without a firm sense of self. We can easily try to re-authorize a different identity or persona by appealing to the highly codified forms already in symbolic circulation. The world of electronic connectivity capitalizes on our desires for these originary elements of *mythos* that have been with us practically since the dawn of time. Their imaginative potential is part of the web's powerful appeal. It becomes difficult to recognize that they are merely re-circulated mythologies produced for mass consumption and re-circulation. Again, these actions reflect an interpretation of our existential ambiguity as negative and the digital world as a remedy.

The mythologies of semiotic thirdness in inauthentic enchantments are highly motivated, that is, they are not innocent or authentic speech.[58] Our inauthentic enchantments with electronic connectivity compel us to interpret them in very specific ways that often serve interests other than our own, as I suggested previously. One example of this is Apple's marketing strategy and their famous icon—the apple with a bite taken out of it. This is an appropriation of a highly symbolic, and, in this case, religious, myth from the Bible concerning Adam and Eve's experiences in the Garden of Eden. In addition to appropriating a highly religious sacred mythology that implies its opposite—the profane—the icon is used to create a sense of identification with the product by literally showing how tempting it must be to consume from the tree of knowledge the icon represents. Therefore, instances of inauthentic enchantment are often constituted by the over-determination of thirdness or the symbolic *logos*, especially when it comes to converting mythic consciousness as its servant. It is no wonder that the mythical dimensions of the sign condition of inauthentic enchantment often contain a surplus of significations; like a bad painting, our experience is too complete—too filled out semiotically, as Barthes remarks.[59] This aids in producing its redundancy. While we may be initially attracted by its mythical elements and the tales we can tell about ourselves and others, in the end we are often left disappointed and unsatisfied emotionally. The experience becomes like any other sedimented inauthentic experience—its originary uniqueness is erased, and we perpetuate a negative view of our existential ambiguity as a condition that must be overcome.

I cannot help but think of the success of the Disney company with its "Wonderful World of Disney" TV programming as a good example of how the literal incorporation of the mythic is accomplished on a grand scale and fed back to us in ready-made symbolic systems of meaning. A good many Americans, both children and adults alike, are quite enchanted by Disney's array of animated characters in their movies and television shows. The popularity of Disney is only surpassed by the degree to which its audience is righteously devoted to the stories it tells. I experience this first-hand when I teach a media literacy class. Students are extremely upset when we apply the critical tools of analysis to Disney characters and plotlines. It is as though critiquing Disney as a system of representation is sacrilegious. This is because Disney has successfully created a social imaginary based upon a reproduction of highly codified historical mythologies and served them up as the main course. These mythologies subsequently replace any originary mythical consciousness we might have had.[60] It is not surprising that many educators and parents are claiming that our young children are at risk psychologically because they appear to increasingly lack the ability to engage in imaginative play that leads to creativity and learning.[61] With so many children growing up with Disney representations, this condition becomes easier to understand. Disney now supplies its widespread audience with ready-made mythologies so we no longer have to create our own. Perhaps the Disney company understood historically that tapping into the uses of enchantment in this way would be a key factor in developing their power and fame as worldwide storytellers. If so, they took to heart Bettelheim's claims. Unfortunately, these forms of enchantment evidence the ways in which enchantments are traditionally associated with an ability to cast a spell or delude us.[62] Their powerful representations conjure the mystical, magical, or imaginary components of existence that seem to overpower us. When our originary mythical consciousness is deluded by unwitting acceptance of a prescribed set of mythologies, we find enchantment in its negative form—as inauthentic. Our abductive capabilities are diminished.

Another way to understand our fascination with our electronic forms of connectivity and the allure of information is to frame them philosophically using the work of phenomenologist Martin Heidegger, particularly his writings about the power of the call of technology. As explained by Michael Hyde, for Heidegger, technology does not call us back to our originary sense of being, or *Dasein*. Instead, Heidegger says that technology calls us out into the world of *know-how*. The world of know-how eclipses the mysterious and ineffable qualities of life that we associate most closely with authentic enchantments. Consequently, our experiences with technology are often dominated by a desire for the intelligible and an artificial yet highly appealing aesthetic. Technology, in other words, calls us to the reality of answers that can be easily searched on our computers and smart devices, dispelling any uncertainty we may possess. To characterize this process semiotically, our enchantments with technology are dominated by thirdness—where the interpretant is thoroughly grounded by the instantiation of the symbolic realm. Consequently, our experience becomes sedimented or fixed.

Like other forms of inauthentic enchantment we have been discussing, our responses to the call of technology too often suppress our return to the original, affectual, aesthetic, and phenomenological qualities found most prominently in the sign relation of firstness to secondness. It is in that relation that we feel more fully the unique effect of others and the world in a more immediate or direct aesthetic way as a positive ambiguity. This is especially true in the case of sounding voices, given that within cyberspace voices are represented in highly mediated, digitalized forms. It is not surprising that we learn from Heidegger that the call of technology is a *delusion* of sorts—where the call is perverted by what he calls the *they-self*, the group of anonymous others. We should interpret the *they-self* as the symbolic realm of mediation—the realm of codified, sedimented discourse that we all speak as cultural beings. The *they-self* represents a mere echo by the repetitious sounding of all the previous voices of a group within a given epoch.

Our response to the call of technology perverts our experience of enchantment, given its predominate video- and logo-centric configurations in cyberspace—producing a tendency for more inauthentic experiences and ways of being and relating. This explains why many theorists are concerned about our socio-cultural welfare, given the emotional emptiness and repressive satisfactions such delusions eventually create.[63] Inauthentic enchantment experiences produce what Bateson would describe as only pattern and redundancy—a display of the relation of thirdness—constituted by the digital codes of language in which we are immersed. Paradoxically, we feel empowered by our ensuing intelligibility at this level of experience, our ability to reduce our uncertainty in the world. When it comes to our interpersonal relationships, we run the risk of accepting the idea that we no longer need to uphold the mystery of the other or hear their auditory call to being in the immediacy of experience as ear-to-ear relations. Instead, we just text or send an email. At the very least, we might assume we have already found the mystery of the other within the symbolic realm of codified information and electronic connectivity. We know all there is to know about a person by what we glimpse in his or her texts and emails. The other becomes only a representative of the *they-self*, presumably already known all too well.

Turning from the work of Heidegger back to Peirce, we recognize that inauthentic enchantments also have a diminished capacity for the production of abductive moments in thought. Merleau-Ponty finds abduction to be an integral aspect of living positively with our existential ambiguity and possibilizing an authentic existence in the world. For Peirce, abduction or the hypothesis generating logic "is the only logical operation which introduces any new idea; for induction does nothing but determine a value, and deduction merely evolves the necessary consequences of a pure hypothesis."[64] Abduction, for both Peirce and Merleau-Ponty, is not only the basic logic that we use to differentiate figure and ground within immediate experience as a gestalt, but it ignites the very spark of ingenuity and creativity that makes life aesthetically pleasing.

Abduction often transpires through acts of what Peirce calls the *play of musement*,[65] an important concept for Peirce in his pragmatic understanding of thought's evolution toward continuity. Peirce develops his notion of the play of musement after studying Friedrich Schiller's concept of play in *On the Aesthetic Education of Man*, written in 1795.[66] Peirce characterizes the play of musement as "a certain agreeable occupation of mind. . . . The particular occupation I mean . . . may take either the form of aesthetic contemplation, or that of distant castle-building . . . or that of considering some wonder."[67] We see less and less of the play of musement within our online habits of discourse. In such cases of inauthentic enchantments, therefore, the play of musement, or pragmatic thinking, as Peirce would say, is significantly diminished. In other words, the theoretical aptitude or critical reflection inherent in the play of musement is eclipsed by its counterpart, the mere play form of *amusement*.[68] In *Dialectic of Enlightenment*, philosophers Max Horkheimer and Theodor Adorno claim that amusement disables systemic thinking. Amusement, they say, "is possible only by insulation from the totality of the social process, by desensitization . . . [to] the . . . claim of every work . . . to reflect the whole."[69] Unfortunately, in such instances of amusement, a banality to existence often manifests since the production of more abductive or creative moments of thinking are thwarted by the bombardment of the symbolic in repetition. We sometimes sacrifice actual thinking or musement about important topics and issues in the world in order to seek amusement, as media ecologist Postman declared some time ago concerning our fascination with television. Horkheimer and Adorno warn us about the allure of the commodified consumerist system of entertainment, what they call the "culture industry"[70] as it relates to the theater of amusements. As they say, "The culture industry can pride itself on having energetically executed the previously clumsy transposition of art into the sphere of consumption."[71]

Because of its richness as an interpretive lens in understanding our electronic fascinations, a more detailed description of the concept of play is in order. As I suggest elsewhere and following Gadamer's hermeneutical understanding of play, viewing inauthentic enchantments through the lens of play allows us to understand how these forms are constituted as unique sign actions grounded phenomenologically primarily in amusement.[72] Living with existential ambiguity prompts many forms of response (expressions and perceptions), and when such conditions are viewed negatively, it appears that the play of amusement is an especially enticing type of response.

## THE PLAY OF AMUSEMENT AND ITS INAUTHENTICITY

Inauthentic enchantments as amusement are primarily about satisfying the experience of *sensory* enjoyment by appealing to the realm of the highly codified world of the symbolic in its hyper-textual/visual form. This sensory enjoyment is dominated by the visual/textual composition of cyberspace and the Internet, as I explained earlier. Social critic Bernard Stiegler agrees with my designation when he calls our current fascination with digital technology fleeting "strokes of enchantment."[73] Amusements in this sense are aesthetic experiences of the symbolic that are marked by fascination with things in the world (like our new digital devices) that are often used as means to ensure self-gratification primarily through consumption disguised as entertainment. In his analysis of the McDonaldization of American culture, George Ritzer proclaims that we have seen an unfortunate increase in the "rationalization" of such forms of indiscriminate consumption disguised as mere leisure.[74]

At the extreme, the play of amusement within cyberspace looks very much like a distracted consciousness. This is because, ironically, a distracted consciousness is the result of being attracted to or attached to too many phenomena at once. As previewed earlier, it is best to conceptualize distraction as a contrary of attention, rather than its opposite. The current onslaught of intelligibility through playful amusements on the Internet and within cyberspace creates a non-fluent character to thought's movement within semiosis. As detailed in chapter 2, this is because the aesthetic quality to thought's natural unfolding as a continuity, as Peirce and William James have described it, has been eclipsed or truncated by symbolic interruptions and quick fixations of signification.

Peirce helps us understand the sign conditions of amusements with his concept of perceptual judgments, a key factor in particular sign actions. When we engage in mere perceptual judgments, it appears that the proper evaluation process of incoming information or stimuli is disrupted. Under such sign conditions, our desire is merely to be *sensually* stimulated predominantly through entertainment. In other words, our ability to habituate ourselves in such a manner so as to make *good* observations of the world—observations paired with reflection/deliberation activated through what Peirce describes as self-control are over-ruled or thwarted.[75] Lacking the needed focus and attention that careful or thoughtful deliberation requires, our observations of the world (perceptual judgments) become shallow and subject to the demands of the fast-paced mediated environment with their constant appeals to our fleeting desires. Because of this, we seem to rely on pure sense perceptions or perceptual judgments (as Peirce would say is indicative of artists), which stand outside the bounds of rational criticism and self-control. As Peirce indicates, artists are "those for whom the chief thing is the qualities of feeling."[76] So, by appealing more and more to the play of inauthentic enchantments as amusement through commodified forms of leisure, as our electronic fascinations suggest, we are becoming less able to make critical distinctions and see differences that make a difference in the phenomenal world of cyberspace. It is not that symbolic artistry itself is bad, for that would reflect a lack of appreciation for an aesthetic. As a matter of fact, after working out his category of firstness as an aesthetic sense of feeling, Peirce realizes the value the aesthetic has in shaping ethical relations (secondness) and logical arguments (thirdness).[77] With the concept of perceptual judgments, Peirce is merely trying to signal a potential ecological imbalance in our thinking when we *only* appeal to feeling and its attendant desires as ways of interpreting and responding to the world. Our judgments need to be balanced, Peirce thinks, with self-control (an aspect of thinking that begins to enter into the semiotic process at secondness), which undergirds all rational thinking through careful consideration.

When we look closely at amusements from the standpoint of imagination and our abductive capabilities, we see a decrease in the reasonableness of our attractions, or what we find admirable. Peirce believes this is a consequence of interpreting the world through perceptual judgments alone. For example, things that are deemed admirable within cyberspace are increasingly based upon arguments of feeling and sensibility, characteristics of artists' abductions, according to Peirce, rather than arguments of reason that are characteristic of rational/scientific thinkers.[78] Increasingly, we see political commentators and social critics denounce the irrational trend in public discourse. Peirce's concept of perceptual judgments helps us explain why. This habit of unreasonableness or irrationality can occur, Peirce theorizes, when perceptual judgments over-determine the rational or reasonable. So, our quick thinking/judgments, like those of the artist, have become more habitually detached from the concrete reasonableness of experience—and tied more to what we might call the primary *sensuality* of experience that is wrought with feelings and their attendant desires. This habit of perception is paradoxical, given that with inauthentic amusements we seek such sensuality not in the world of immediate experience but in the world of digitized representations and abstractions. In explaining Horkheimer and Adorno's insightful analysis of the consequences of repeated exposure to the culture industry, Jane Bennett declares that "every increase in the sharpness of video cuts or the peppiness of hit songs issues in a decrease in the critical faculties of its audience. Mass entertainment is replete with images of novelty and surprise, but the upbeat 'tempo and dynamics' are carefully calibrated to preclude the exercise of mental effort and independent thinking. The result is a passive, consumptive audience."[79] I think this trend also helps to partially explain why our culture appears to be, at least in its popular renditions, so focused on the body/sensuality as opposed to the "sensuousness of thought," which Peirce suggests evolves through rational modes of thinking.[80] Stiegler also describes this cultural trend with its focus on the objectified body as the creation of a "libidinal economy," represented most prominently in current popular culture by advertising and tabloid magazines. He claims that it is an outgrowth of capitalism and a consumerist-oriented culture. As Stiegler argues, the organization and production of *desire* is the telos of such an economy.[81] Peirce would find this overwhelming desire threatening to the very nature of pragmatic thought, in line with what Horkheimer and Adorno claim.

Using Peirce's discussion of artistic abductions, in particular, we can understand this trend in terms of our heightened desires for entertainment. He says that artistic creativity/abduction has as its purpose "to seek"—an existential striving to embody the phenomena of life through representational means; an intense desire, in other words, propels all aesthetic action.[82] Our instances of inauthentic enchantment as the play of amusement, especially as they relate to consumer goods, services, and the marketing of the self and others, appear to provide the scaffolding for the maintenance of this type of social economy and the insatiable desires that it creates and upholds. The rise of the play of enchantment in its inauthentic form as amusement could be a consequence of our increasingly widespread use of artistic abductive processes in our interpretations of and responses to the world. Perhaps Donald Trump is the premier representative example of artistic abductions, given his often-contrary statements of supposed falsehoods that appear seemingly out of nowhere. This trend could also explain, to some extent, the cultural landscape of our postmodern times, which is often characterized as one of pure play—or the carnival.[83] The amusing aspects of inauthentic enchantments, especially our electronic media, are particularly significant given the ways in which they shape our discourse and action.

The final area of interpretation I want to explore speaks directly to the phenomenological and semiotic relations with others that inauthentic enchantments typically instantiate. This area is particularly relevant in terms of our relationality and the degree to which an ethical generosity toward the other in discourse is even possible. As Bateson and his Palo Alto colleagues outlined,[84] relations between entities, be they people or countries, can be categorized as complementary or symmetrical, depending on whether they are constituted on the basis of perceived differences or similarities, respectively. Important to remember is that each relation is a consequence of sign actions, that is, the semiotic and phenomenological perceptions/expressions of participants. Each relation also produces a subsequent effect, an interpretant, on ensuing dialogic relations that recursively shape our thinking.

Our electronic forms of connectivity and the motivations that drive our pursuits are often based on a desire to establish symmetrical relations. Symmetrical relations are grounded in similarity and perceived equality. While this initially sounds positive, symmetrical relations do not always foster cooperation. Instead, they typically instantiate competition between those involved. Because there is a perceived similarity between two entities, we may strive for separation or distinction. This semiotic condition helps us understand why the world of cyberspace and the Internet fuels our narcissistic tendencies and perhaps fosters the "culture of authenticity" that Taylor alludes to. Of course, the political ramifications of this symmetrical condition often produce relational discord. In the case of our enchantments with our new mediated electronic devices and our life online, our responses become a "one-upmanship" where our means of dealing with our felt negative ambiguity locks us into a never-ending game. We think we need the latest, fastest capacities and the most iconic *likes* on our social media platforms, rather than actually focusing on the uniqueness of the other. This tendency is also pronounced when we are determined to master the latest technology so it does not get the upper hand on our daily experiences. It appears that the pursuit of information and its overload has only exacerbated our existential ambiguity perceived as negative. Symmetrical relationships can easily go into what Bateson describes as runaway or schismogenesis[85]—where our purpose going forward is lost to the demands of the immediate game of relation in which we are engaged. As a result, we lose awareness of the complexity and recursive nature of relations and, instead, become reductive in a focused, self-serving manner. These unfortunate social conditions were outlined in chapters 1 and 2.

Such relations, Bateson says, are based on trying to maximize our position, which never serves the greater good or whole within relational experiences but is typically self-serving.[86] Thus, symmetrical relations are often highly entropic where disintegration of the system/environment interface ensues—in this case, the very human relations themselves. The maximization of personal gain runs contrary, of course, to an open, ethical stance toward the other. Often our responses to new media technologies through inauthentic enchantments only produce more self-serving behaviors and prevent us from authentically approaching the other or even knowing how, as Turkle's research suggests. Ironically, in our distinct mastery of technology with its latest applications and platforms, we become like everyone else, a new version of Heidegger's notion of *they-self*. With our ability to electronically connect, the realization of the *they-self* only increases exponentially. At the very least, we think we must have the latest smart devices everyone has, a marketing ploy I described earlier that technology companies know too well. Under such circumstances, narcissism easily takes hold as the concern for self-maximization overrides our concern with optimizing healthier self and other relations. Our enchantments with technology and their potential for electronic connectivity are often based upon symmetrical relations that do not promote open, authentic encounters with others based upon a commitment to the greater good. Instead, they create the intrapersonal bubbles of individual experience we witness every day on people's personal web pages or blog posts. Inauthentic enchantments seem to further divide us from one another as our existential desire for the other in his or her uniqueness can become severely reduced over time. In sum, these inauthentic enchantments do not nourish a deep level of relationality that is born from a sense of our positive ambiguity in the world.

It is now time to explore more specifically how our inauthentic enchantments with technology problematize our ongoing understanding and appreciation of the sounding voice within human relationships. For as Norie Neumark suggests, the specter of authenticity haunts digital media when it comes to the voice. Although the voices of self and other are still expressed and heard within our electronic forms of connectivity, they are relegated, I argue, to the parameters of our social, mediated forms of discursive practices. Hence the digitalized voice produces not authenticity but an "authenticity effect."[87] While their aesthetic value in regard to our relationality is significantly reduced by the dominance of hyper-textual/visual components within cyberspace, we seem to be content with those insufficient sign relations just the same. It is to the acousmatic voice and its echoes within cyberspace that we now turn.

## NOTES

1. For a review of communicology as a human science, see Richard L. Lanigan, *Phenomenology of Communication: Merleau-Ponty's Thematics in Communicology and Semiology* (Pittsburgh, PA: Duquesne University Press, 1988); *The Human Science of Communicology* (Pittsburgh, PA: Duquesne University Press, 1992); "The Self in Semiotic Phenomenology: Consciousness as the Conjunction of Perception and Expression in the Science of Communicology," *The American Journal of Semiotics* 15–16, no. 1–4 (2000). See also Isaac E. Catt and Deborah Eicher-Catt, "Communicology: A Reflexive Human Science," in *Communicology: The New Science of Embodied Discourse*, eds. Deborah Eicher-Catt and Isaac E. Catt (Madison: Fairleigh Dickinson University Press, 2010).

2. Charles Sanders Peirce, "The Categories Defended," *Essential Peirce: Selected Philosophical Writings,* Vol. 2, 1893–1913, ed. The Peirce Edition Project (Bloomington: Indiana University Press, 1998).

3. Charles Sanders Peirce. "Logic as Semiotic: The Theory of Signs," in *Philosophical Writings of Peirce,* ed. Justus Buchler (New York: Dover Publications, 1940).

4. As Peircean scholar Vincent Colapietro reminds us, Peirce's "doctrine of firstness, secondness, and thirdness was one of the principal tools by which he opened and cultivated semeiotic as a *field* of inquiry." He goes on to stipulate that "the Peircean categories are put forth not as a static taxonomic but rather as a dynamic interrogative framework . . . Being signs, they have an inherent vitality and, thus, an inherent dynamism: they exert an agency of their own." See Colapietro, "A Lantern for the Feet of Inquirers: The Heuristic Function of the Peircean Categories," *Semiotica* 136, no. 1 (2001), 202.

5. This designation corresponds to Peirce's category of firstness described as a felt qualitative immediacy. This point becomes increasingly important in my subsequent discussions on the voice of enunciation (chapters 6–8). For reference on immediacy as a sign relation of firstness see Vincent Colapietro, "Qualitative Immediacy and Mediating Qualities: Reflections on Firstness as More Than a Category," *Semiotics 2018*, doi: 10.5840/cpsem201813.

6. Interestingly, Colapietro claims in addition to Peirce's association of tone with firstness, it is feasible to conceive each category within his heuristic framework as exemplifying a

different tonal quality. In attempting to characterize his categories Peirce asserts that, "Perhaps it is not right to call these categories conceptions; they are so intangible that they are rather tones or tints upon conceptions." Colapietro contends that even though Peirce recognizes the possible tonal aspects of his categories, "the principal media" he uses to characterize the functioning of the categories in relation to one another is by way of "visual signs." Colapietro states, "It is, thus, quite natural that he was disposed to use the metaphor of light to characterize various aspects of one of his principal philosophical concerns, the articulation of a doctrine of categories." On these points see, Charles Sanders Peirce, *The Collected Papers,* 1.353, quoted in Colapietro, "A Lantern," 201, 203.

7. Colapietro, "A Lantern," 203. The idea that firstness exists outside of its conceptual *articulation* becomes highly relevant in my subsequent distinction between the voice of articulation and the voice of enunciation, explicated in chapters 5–8.

8. Ferdinand de Saussure, *Course in General Linguistics,* trans. Wade Baskin (New York: McGraw Hill, 1959).

9. Peirce, "Principles of Phenomenology," 74–97. As he asserts, a *phaneron* is "the collective total of all that is in any way or in any sense present to mind, regardless of whether it corresponds to any real thing or not," Peirce, *The Collected Papers,* 1.284.

10. Peirce's semiotics is *realist* in the sense that he acknowledges that objects to consciousness exist in the external world and yet they are not made relevant or meaningful to us without our semiotic interaction with them. He thus insightfully bridges the theoretical gap between subject and object or knower and known that is the hallmark of phenomenological inquiry and honored by its basic tenet known as *intentionality.*

11. Peirce, *The Collected Papers,* 5.594. Translations are movements to greater levels of abstraction or generality.

12. Here Petrilli is extending the work of Peirce who also theorizes that "all thought takes the form of dialogue and [who] repeatedly confessed that his own thinking manifestly assumed that form," Colapietro, "A Lantern," 201. See Peirce, *The Collected Papers,* 6.481.

13. Susan Petrilli, *Sign Crossroads in Global Perspective: Semioethics and Responsibility,* ed. John Deely (New Brunswick: Transaction Publishers, 2010), 53.

14. Deborah Eicher-Catt and Isaac E. Catt, "Peirce and Cassirer, 'Life' and 'Spirit': A Communicology of Religion," *Journal of Communication and Religion* 36, no. 2 (2013), 82.

15. See, for example, the work of David Howes, "Introduction to Sensory Museology," *The Senses and Society* 9, no. 3 (2014).

16. Thomas A. Sebeok, *Global Semiotics* (Bloomington: Indiana University Press, 2001).

17. Vincent Colapietro, "Emersonian Moods, Peircean Sentiments, and Ellingtonian Tones," *The Journal of Speculative Philosophy* 33, no. 2 (2019), 180.

18. Ong, *The Presence of the Word,* 41–42.

19. Ibid., 41.

20. While the visual does not always pair itself with the auditory, here Ong is specifying that if the visual intent is to be dynamic, then it has to pair itself with the auditory (given that the visual as space is inherently static).

21. Bennett, *The Enchantment of Modern Life,* 127.

22. Victor Turner, *Dramas, Fields, and Metaphors: Symbolic Action in Human Society* (Ithaca: Cornell University Press, 1974).

23. Alphonse de Waelhens, "A Philosophy of the Ambiguous," in *The Structure of Behavior,* by Maurice Merleau-Ponty, trans. Alden. L. Fisher (Boston: Beacon Press, [1951] 1963).

24. Maurice Merleau-Ponty, "An Unpublished Text by Maurice Merleau-Ponty: A Prospectus of His Work," in *The Primacy of Perception,* ed. James. Edie (Evanston: Northwestern University Press, 1964), 5. This writing is touted as one of the few texts in which he articulates his position on ambiguity. This argument is put forth by Herbert Spiegelberg in his book *The Phenomenological Movement: A Historical Introduction* (The Hague: Martinus Nijhoff, 1971). For more insight on this topic, I refer you to the article by Deborah Eicher-Catt, "The Authenticity in Ambiguity: Appreciating Maurice Merleau-Ponty's Abductive Logic as Communicative Praxis," *Atlantic Journal of Communication* 13, no. 2 (2005).

25. Maurice Merleau-Ponty, *Phenomenology of Perception,* trans. Colin Smith (New York: Humanities Press, [1945] 1962), 345.

26. Merleau-Ponty, "An Unpublished Text," 3–11.
27. Maurice Merleau-Ponty, *In Praise of Philosophy and Other Essays*, trans. John Wild, James Edie, and John O'Neill (Evanston: Northwestern University Press, [1953] 1963), 5.
28. Donald N. Levine, *The Flight from Ambiguity: Essays in Social and Cultural Theory* (Chicago: University of Chicago Press, 1985).
29. Saussure, *Course in General Linguistics*.
30. Roland Barthes, *S/Z*, trans. Richard Miller (New York: Noonday, (1970) 1974).
31. Richard L. Lanigan, *Semiotic Phenomenology of Rhetoric: Eidetic Practice in Henry Grattan's Discourse on Tolerance* (Washington: University Press of America, 1984), 14.
32. Merleau-Ponty, "An Unpublished Text," 9.
33. Saussure, *Course in General Linguistics*.
34. Merleau-Ponty, *Phenomenology of Perception*, xxi.
35. Eicher-Catt, "Authenticity in Ambiguity."
36. Merleau-Ponty, "An Unpublished Text," 3.
37. Merleau-Ponty, *Phenomenology of Perception*, 190.
38. Ibid., 184.
39. Lanigan, *Semiotic Phenomenology*, 14.
40. Daniel L. Smith, "Intensifying Phronesis: Heidegger, Aristotle, and Rhetorical Culture," *Philosophy and Rhetoric* 36, no. 1 (2003), 101.
41. Charles Taylor, *The Ethics of Authenticity* (Cambridge: Harvard University Press, 1991).
42. Terence Hawkes, *Structuralism and Semiotics* (Berkeley: University of California Press, 1977), 114.
43. Taylor, *Ethics of Authenticity*, 66.
44. Michael E. Zimmerman, *Eclipse of Self: The Development of Heidegger's Concept of Authenticity* (Athens: Ohio University Press, 1981).
45. While not addressing the topic of enchantment per se, philosopher and communication theorist Michael Hyde speaks to the positive impulse such existential irruptions have and relates these moments to our ongoing health and moral orientation toward others. He advocates that we need to recognize the "irruptions that we are," given that such irruptions potentialize our very existence. For more on this fascinating argument see Michael Hyde, *The Interruption That We Are: The Health of the Lived Body, Narrative, and Public Moral Argument* (Columbia: University of South Carolina Press, 2018).
46. Colapietro, "Qualitative Immediacy," 176.
47. Ritzer, *Enchanting a Disenchanted World*.
48. Bateson and Bateson, *Angels Fear*.
49. Gregory Bateson, *Steps to an Ecology of Mind* (New York: Ballantine Books, 1972).
50. John McCarthy, Peter Wright, Jayne Wallace, and Andy Dearden, "The Experience of Enchantment in Human–Computer Interaction," *Pers Ubiquit Comput* 10, no. 6 (2006).
51. Gregory Bateson, *Mind and Nature: A Necessary Unity* (New York: E. P. Dutton, 1979).
52. In common nomenclature, we call this experience information overload.
53. Sandra Lee Bartky, *Femininity and Domination: Studies in the Phenomenology of Oppression,* (New York: Routledge, 1990), 42.
54. Bruno Bettelheim, *The Uses of Enchantment: The Meaning and Importance of Fairy Tales* (New York: Vintage Books, 1976). Bettelheim applies Freudian psychoanalysis to his study of fairy tales. While space does not allow a thorough unpacking of this approach, suffice it to say that he well understood the power of the mythical to appeal to the psyche.
55. Eicher-Catt and Catt, "Peirce and Cassirer," 89.
56. S. G. Lofts, *Ernst Cassirer: A "Repetition" of Modernity* (Albany: State University of New York Press, 2000), 92.
57. Roland Barthes, *Mythologies*, trans. Annette Lavers (New York: Hill and Wang, 1972).
58. For an insightful description of authentic and inauthentic speech, see Lanigan, *Phenomenology of Communication*.
59. Barthes, *Mythologies*, 127.

60. For a discussion on the political dimensions of Disney's manufactured mythologies see: Henry A. Giroux and Grace Pollock, *The Mouse that Roared: Disney and the End of Innocence* (Lanham, MD: Rowman & Littlefield, 2010).

61. See, for example, Kyung Hee Kim, "The Creativity Crisis: The Decrease in Creative Thinking Scores on the Torrance Tests of Creative Thinking," *Creativity Research Journal* 23, no 4 (2011).

62. Refer to Saler, "Modernity, Disenchantment."

63. See, for example, Turkle, *Alone Together.*

64. Gérard Deledalle, *Charles S. Peirce's Philosophy of Signs: Essays in Comparative Semiotics* (Bloomington: Indiana University Press, 2000), 8.

65. Thomas A. Sebeok produced an insightful collection of essays in honor of Peirce's development of the play of musement. See Thomas A. Sebeok, *The Play of Musement* (Bloomington: Indiana University Press, 1981).

66. Schiller, *On the Aesthetic Education of Man.*

67. Charles Sanders Peirce, "A Neglected Argument for the Reality of God," in *The Essential Peirce: Selected Philosophical Writings*, ed. Peirce Edition Project, vol. 2, *1893–1913* (Bloomington: Indiana University Press, 1998), 436.

68. See Deborah Eicher-Catt, "Enchantment and the Serious Play of A(musement)," *Language and Semiotic Studies* 4, no. 2 (2018).

69. Horkheimer and Adorno, *Dialectic of Enlightenment*, 144.

70. Ibid.

71. Ibid., 134–35.

72. Eicher-Catt, "Enchantment."

73. Bernard Stiegler, *The Re-Enchantment of the World: The Value of Spirit Against Industrial Populism*, trans. Trevor Arthur (New York: Bloomsbury, 2014), 5.

74. Ritzer, *Enchanting a Disenchanted World.*

75. Peirce, *The Collected Papers*, 5.442.

76. Ibid., 1.43.

77. This is akin to Merleau-Ponty's sense of the aesthetic *logos*. As explained by Jeffrey Barnouw, for Peirce "action and thought depend on acquired patterns of feelings which come under the purview of aesthetics." See Barnouw, "'Aesthetic' for Schiller and Peirce: A Neglected Origin of Pragmatism," *Journal of the History of Ideas* 49, no. 4 (1988), 627. See also: Isaac E. Catt, "Charles Sanders Peirce," in *Encyclopedia of Communication Ethics: Goods in Contention*, eds. Ronald C. Arnett, Annette M. Holba, and Susan Mancino (New York: Peter Lang, 2018).

78. On this point, see David Niose, "Political Discourse is Getting Dangerously Anti-Intellectual," *Psychology Today*, December 30, 2015, https://www.psychologytoday.com/us/blog/our-humanity-naturally/201512/political-discourse-is-getting-dangerously-anti-intellectual.

79. Bennett, *The Enchantment of Modern Life,* 122.

80. Douglas R. Anderson, *Creativity and the Philosophy of C. S. Peirce* (Boston: Martinus Nijhoff Publishers, 1987).

81. Bernard Stiegler, *Symbolic Misery,* trans. Barnaby Norman, vol. 1, *The Hyper-Industrial Epoch* (Cambridge: Polity, 2014).

82. Anderson, *Creativity.*

83. In regard to this, see Kenneth J. Gergen, *The Saturated Self: Dilemmas of Identity in Contemporary Life* (New York: Basic Books, 1991).

84. Paul Watzlawick, Janet Beavin Bavelas, and Don D. Jackson, *Pragmatics of Human Communication: A Study of Interactional Patterns, Pathologies, and Paradoxes* (New York: W. W. Norton & Company, 1967).

85. Gregory Bateson, "The Cybernetics of 'Self': A Theory of Alcoholism," In *Steps to an Ecology of Mind* (New York: Ballantine Books, 1972).

86. For more, refer to Morris Berman, *The Re-Enchantment of the World* (Ithaca: Cornell University Press, 1981).

87. Norie Neumark, "Doing Things with Voices: Performativity and Voice," in *Voice: Vocal Aesthetics in Digital Arts and Media,* Norie Neumark, Ross Gibson, and Theo Van Leeuwen, eds. (Cambridge, MA: Massachusetts Institute of Technology, 2010), 95.

*Chapter Four*

# Echoes of the Acousmatic Voice in Cyberspace

*The Impersonal Self*

The auditory dimensions of our sensorium impact how we perceive and express our relationality. Because of this, it is time to look closely at the structural elements of the voices we hear within cyberspace and on the Internet. In particular, I review the ever-present *acousmatic* voice, a designation by sound theorist Michel Chion that I find useful.[1] These are disembodied impersonal voices of self and other that echo through cyberspace. Impersonal voices play a major role in ultimately forming our long-term disenchanted enchantments with electronic connectivity and the reduced relationality it provides. This is especially true when we normalize their auditory characteristics and heed their call instead of the call from the immediate auditory experience with another in ear-to-ear relations. The mediated impersonal voices sounding through cyberspace call us reflexively toward impersonal relations. As a result, these voices play a primary role in the constitution of what I call the *impersonal self*. We discover that the impersonal self is not a beneficial sign condition to uphold, especially if we want to enhance a healthy sense of self and other relations at a more intimate level of experience. As a result, the voices we hear in cyberspace, the voices that accompany images in mainstream media such as film and television, or the voices we hear over the telephone or the Internet (such as a podcast), are disembodied representations of a person who speaks.

# THE ACOUSMATIC VOICE AND OUR AUDITORY CONTENTMENTS

As I previously noted, we are developing a tendency to use more logo-centric ways of electronically connecting to others within cyberspace. We email or text friends, loved ones, and associates rather than calling them on the telephone. We are quickly becoming a culture that would rather "text than talk,"[2] as Turkle's research indicates. The de-voicing of society has radical implications for how we view relationality and its satisfying enactment. And yet, because cyberspace and the Internet are also video-centric, as I have previously argued, we know that this connectivity is also augmented by sound. It is not uncommon to hear the typical sounds of our life-worlds represented through digitalized means, and this includes the speaking voice. However, the full temporal qualities of sound are being eclipsed by the over-riding spatialized elements that digitalization requires.

As our voices are lifted from the flesh of our bodies and propelled into the space of cyber through mediated electronic forms, their auditory potential as signifiers of time severely fades. This is unfortunate. This is because, like the sounding word that is fixed by the spatialized form of writing or print, these voices are spatialized as well in their digitalization. As Thomas Levin suggests, "the computer is becoming a site of telephony, a sending of the voice as data. But for your voice to be sent, it must be translated into a form that can be stored, transported and reproduced; it too must, in other words, become writing."[3] This process of translating the voice into spatialized representations emphasizes the blurring of the very distinction made by media theorists between the temporality of the spoken word and the spatiality of the written word. Recall from earlier discussions that sound is typically associated with time, given its inherent dynamic flow as an event or happening. Ong's work in particular stresses this important aspect of sound. Sound exhibits endurance in time. Sight or the visual/textual, on the other hand, is linked with space, primarily because it tends to, through the process of abstraction, fixate its objects to consciousness within relational points of reference. As a derivative of speaking, the written word fastens the spoken word in its temporal diachronic endurance to a fixed synchronic presentation. This tendency is important given that each (sight or sound) represents different axiological judgments as perception. Sound is thought to lend its enduring qualities to present existence in a profound way unlike the spatial configurations of sight. The visual transforms the word as written and makes it "motionless [and] 'objective' . . . *impersonal*, and out of time."[4] And while our concern here is not with the written word but the spoken word as voiced in its immediacy, I contend that the same spatializing process holds true when it comes to the voice. Voicing in the space of cyber and on the Internet necessarily digitalizes and spatializes its sounding and diminishes its temporal effect. Sound theorist R. Murray Schafer emphasizes this fact, when in 1980 he coined the terms "schizophonia" and "schizochronic"[5] to designate the "splitting of a sound from its natural source by the means of recording technology. Such a technology ... splits a sound from its time; in the case of the voice, a recording splits it from the time of its utterance."[6] The ramifications of this process when it comes to the value of the human voice in its immediate sounding between two people are enormous. For as we know from Ong and others, the spatializing of the voice will automatically shift our senses of it as a matter of kind and degree. In other words, the voice becomes less temporal as it takes on the qualities of the spatial, and this sensory shift dramatically changes our experiences of it.

As a result, our voices as unique particularities are weakened and, more importantly, subordinated to acts of abstraction and representation within the space of cyber. This process of mediation, abstraction, and representation is inherent within all voiced relations to some extent.[7] However, the voices of cyberspace exhibit this mediation and abstraction to an extreme degree. In cyberspace, the voice's association with its originary temporal components is easily co-opted by the dominant spatiality of the visual/textual media. This is especially true when we view the voice as merely a tool in service to a linguistic order, a dominant ideology that currently holds sway on our assessment of the voice. Following voice theorist Mladen Dolar, I discuss in the next chapter how our perception of the voice as a servant to the linguistic order participates in the actual murder of the *phone*, understood as an aesthetic enactment of our particularity. However, as Dolar rightly suggests, while the voice in service to the signifying or linguistic matrix mutes or silences the voice, it also produces a remainder.[8] It is this remainder or excess, this aspect of the voice, that I pursue in this work, for I am convinced that it provides the key to an aesthetic re-enchantment of human communication in our immediate ear-to-ear relations.[9]

In our highly mediated electronic environments, sounding voices from the human body are synthesized, enhanced, dubbed, and otherwise vacated from the body that originally spoke in the full immediate act of expressivity.[10] In the last chapter, I argued that our enchantments with electronic media risk an inauthentic way of being in the world. Our perceptions of the voice within this context substantially contribute to this risk. We must remember that these forms of enchantment are called forth through ever-increasing symbolic acts of abstraction and mediation in which the originary auditory components of the voice have been severely weakened even as they are electronically enhanced for clarity and intensity. Above all, these voices have been activated in service to their spatial counterparts, the visuals. The less mediated or more direct sources of voice that call us to engage with the other in significantly different ways have been disconnected from their human moorings. This process regrettably dilutes the bones, flesh, and blood of the voice and establishes it as a mere semiotic entailment.[11] In terms of these highly mediated voices, we distinguish them from one another, in other words, based upon the differences in semiotic relations operative at a given moment in time.

It is important to note that the calls from the kinds of enchantments that are so voiced in cyberspace are altogether artificial and inauthentic or run the great risk of being so. This is primarily because these voices now emanate from reproduced forms of mediation and representation that are disembodied and semiotically constrained by the dictates of a signifying system outside of our control. More likely than not, these voices merely signify *parole parlée* (speech spoken). Put succinctly by sound artist Brandon LaBelle, "with the advent of computer technologies, the synthetic voice brings a twist to the poetical by introducing a voice that has no origin in a given body: the disembodied, radiophonic, and electronically manipulated voice is emptied of psychology, spirit, or granularity with the synthetic voice. Leaving both life and death behind, the synthetic voice is a digital shadow."[12] Unfortunately, the mediated voice in such circumstances becomes easily an interpellated voice within cyberspace, one with political implications, according to Dolar.[13] The interpellated voice is a voice that primarily sustains the social order and the status quo of our Internet craze—it upholds the signifying "order of things" in its articulation.[14]

The political voice to which Dolar refers is now easily available for appropriation by others given its widespread circulation within cyberspace.[15] It is a voice in service to the signifying or symbolic order that is quite beyond any immediate hearing or anyone's complete control and interpretation. As much as we may struggle to signify *parole parlante*, or speaking speech, within the cyberworld, the fact remains that the sheer volume and proliferation of signs too often encourages only their continued appropriation within a highly semiotic world. French philosopher Michel Serres, in his discussions on sound and sense warns us, according to Frances Dyson, that by attending only to the din of these mediated voices, we can "become deaf to the sounds of the earth, and as a consequence now lack the ability to sense, and this is pivotal to the sustenance of common sense. All that we hear, all we can listen to, is the racket of our own voices—arguing, legislating, pronouncing, warring, and transferring power."[16] The result is, unfortunately, that "the common has been appropriated and destroyed, and the driving force has been the production and circulation of . . . high frequency buzz."[17]

Michel Chion's concept of the *acousmatic voice* helps us understand the consequences of the extensive mediation of the human voice in the vast noise or racket of cyberspace. According to Chion, the acousmatic voice is "simply a voice whose source one cannot see, a voice whose origin cannot be identified, a voice one cannot place. It is a voice in search of an origin, in search of a body, but even when it finds its body, it turns out that this doesn't quite work, the voice doesn't stick to the body, it is an excrescence which doesn't match the body."[18] Apparently Chion borrowed the word *acousmatic* from Pierre Schaeffer, who refers to it in his 1966 writings on music. As Dolar explains, this word refers to a sound or noise of which we cannot immediately pinpoint the cause.[19] Drawing from the ancient disciples of Pythagoras, the Acousmatics, as they were called, followed his teachings even though his presence was concealed by a curtain and they were unable to see him for many years.[20] They only heard and followed his voice. It is this sense of concealment of its source that lies at the heart of the acousmatic voice.

Chion informs us that we experience the acousmatic voice most readily in cinema and television especially in the form of voiceover commentary or narration. In addition, Dolar makes the case that we first experienced the acousmatic voice in everyday life in any sustained way with the advent of new media in the modern era, such as the radio, the gramophone, the tape recorder, and the telephone. Today, the acousmatic voice resounds within our highly digitized environments of electronic connectivity, the world of virtuality, where the actual sources of the voice are merely presumed or occluded altogether. The sources of voice are most often lost in a sea of digitalized sound enhancements designed to capture our immediate attention and fascinate us with their synthesized re-productive qualities. In these cases, a technical appliance (an electronic device, such as a computer, electronic tablet, smartphone, or television sound bar, for example) becomes a substitute for the invisible absent source and we more often than not do not question its viability as such.[21]

Especially important to my interrogation of healthy human relationality is the fact that, according to Dolar, when a voice is detached from the immediacy of a body (such as the voices within cyberspace and on the Internet), it becomes inherently *uncanny*. It takes on a mysterious quality because of the immediate concealment of its source. Because of this, it becomes highly appealing to most of us—at the very least an intriguing specimen of sound—and takes its place alongside our fascination with the hyper-textual/visual elements offered within cyberspace. As Dolar indicates, such a voice seems to be everywhere given its detachment from a specified body and this detachment gives the voice an aura and authority that it would not otherwise have.[22] A good example here is the acousmatic voice represented in the film *The Wizard of Oz*, an adaptation of L. Frank Baum's now-famous novel of the same name. As long as the source of the wizard's voice is concealed, it resonates power and authority.[23]

It may be tempting for us, at this point, to consider that the acousmatic voice represents an authentic voice, in the way I discussed authenticity in the previous chapter. Recall that authentic speech is speech that "self-signifies" and, more importantly, "enables the intensification of the questionable-ness, uncanniness, open-ness . . . alterity"[24] of the situation and the other. While the acousmatic voice may manifest an uncanniness in the process of its representation, its disembodied nature forestalls interpreting it as authentic. Even personal vlogs (video blogs) on YouTube, suggests Neumark, may appear to be personal and authentic, but these designations "are not quite what they seem in networked culture."[25] We must remember that authentic speech exhibits primordial, creative, existential meaning, which implies that it must directly emanate from a recognizable body-subject by another. Moreover, the mysterious elements conjured by the acousmatic voice within cyberspace seem to correlate with a negative interpretation of our existential ambiguity. This is because its uncanniness may actually amplify our uncertainty in the world. There is a haunting quality, after all, to their sounding. To alleviate this negative ambiguity, we may obsessively pursue information within the virtual as a way to reduce uncertainty. The prevalence of acousmatic voices in cyberspace, I submit, thus enhances an overall sense of negative ambiguity. This does not bode well for us culturally.

The disembodied nature of the acousmatic voice does entice us, however. For it lends an air of mystery and wonder, given that it is detached from its original sources of enunciation. Because of this, it can quickly become enchanting, although I believe this form of enchantment deludes in the end rather than delights in any positive way. In general, the presence of acousmatic voices within cyberspace partially explains the enchanting effects of electronic media. Acousmatic voices can quickly take on amplified significance in our highly technologized world. This is because they appeal to our insatiable desire for enhanced experiences, analogous to our enthrallment with high-definition visuals that bring us the grandeur of the world in surreal forms of digital display. As Macallan and Plain contend, "the highly treated, hyper-real voice has rapidly been absorbed, not just into obvious genres such as science fiction and the horror, but into mainstream cinema and television in general."[26] Furthermore, the form of enthrallment these hyper-real voices produce is insidiously manipulative, according to Horkheimer and Adorno. Through their appeals to the sensory or affectual dimensions of experience, as a result of these activations, our senses are both stimulated and dulled through repeated exposure.

From a semiotic perspective, another way to think about acousmatic voices is as "floating signifiers" with no real signifieds—given that their sources of production remain hidden and unknown. These voices merely echo within the space of cyber and thus contribute most readily to inauthentic discourse. Regrettably, cyberspace functions as an echo chamber and a powerful one at that. We quickly become part of the culture industry that virtuality promotes without much thought. Explaining the relationship between personal affect and external manipulative forces of the culture industry, Bennett declares that "as a result [of being enlisted in this interchange] we are enlisted in our own commercialization; we voluntarily exercise our imagination in ways that stunt it while enjoying pleasurable feelings of activeness or vitality."[27]

When we succeed in voice disacousmatization, or the process of actually identifying the source of the voice as a signified relation, we consequently reduce the voice's mystery, and the voice loses most of its charismatic elements.[28] Once the curtain is pulled opened by the dog Toto in *The Wizard of Oz*, the wizard's power and magic dissipate quickly. The mysterious aura of the voice ceases.[29] The voice becomes banal. Using a visual analogy to illustrate this banality, the actual experience of a beautiful ocean may find us visually wanting if we try to match it with its virtual, high-definition, simulated representation we see on television or on our computers. Macallan and Plain put it rather simply when they insist that,

> Now . . . the voice only mediated by the microphone and left untreated [electronically] may transmit as "bad" or "poor," or even—in an ironic turn—as simply "unreal." And the inability of even sound designers to always be able to discern the difference between a fabricated and an untreated voice indicates that sound has arrived at the same ambiguous position that William J. Mitchell noted of electronic photography in 1992, when he argued that the digital image "shakes our faith" in the truth of the image.[30]

While the process of disacousmatization of the voice is never complete, according to Chion, we still try to locate or presume to know the source regardless. This testifies to the fact that the acousmatic voice is a powerful one and resists being neutralized by the visible.[31] Here we see a perfect combinatory semiotic and phenomenological process in which both the visual and auditory dimensions work together to contribute to the enchanting effects of the voice within the space of cyber.

Furthermore, if we accept the idea that acousmatic voices become banal when bodily sources are identified or presumed, then what impact might that phenomenological process have when we turn our attention back to actual life? In other words, what happens when our ear-to-ear relations are enacted within visible and auditory contexts of recognizable addressers and addressees? If we have become too enthralled and enchanted by the acousmatic voices within cyberspace and on the Internet, how do they now compare to the real-life voices of others in the immediacy of ear-to-ear relations? It seems to me that the already normalized articulations of the acousmatic voice within cyberspace and on the Internet help to partially explain why we are becoming a more de-vocalized or de-voiced society. I suspect that the more we become accustomed to and enchanted by the acousmatic, disembodied voice of the other (with its apparent mystical, uncanny elements) and normalize its representation within our everyday lives, the more the actual sounding voice of the other within immediate ear-to-ear relations becomes disenchanting. At the very least, the immediate voice seems banal or may become an unwelcome intrusion within a now-preferred experience of virtuality. We desire to hear the potentiality of the voice in its virtuality without appreciating its actual characteristics as a lived bodily phenomenon.

This perceptual trend is already evident in our younger populations. For them, the human voice within immediate encounters feels like an unwelcome interruption in their daily efforts to connect electronically with others.[32] They would rather text than talk, sometimes at all costs. The flight from conversation that Turkle addresses in her work appears to pivot around the silencing of the immediate sounding voices of self and other. Or, if we do hear the voice in its immediacy, we are left existentially wanting as a result of our contentment with the enhanced voices that now resound and echo in cyberspace. Or, it is as though the negative ambiguity ushered in by the prevalence of acousmatic voices has now become fully associated with the immediacy of voices in general. As Turkle's millennials admit, there is an uncomfortableness that now inheres within ear-to-ear dialogic relations that they try to avoid. Digital conversations are valued because they present little risk, and voiced encounters feel like an uneasy interruption in their electronic flow of interaction. It seems we may be losing an aesthetic appreciation of that when we speak with our voice in the presence of the other, we speak with "every fiber of our being."[33] I submit that those fibers represent important heartstrings that should be repeatedly strummed interpersonally in immediate ear-to-ear relations and not left to be simulated by a sophisticated sound machine. As Dolar testifies, a mechanically produced voice is very much an *impersonal voice* and unfortunately, the one that in today's culture we are more often than not listening to.[34]

Although the voices of self and other are still heard within our electronic forms of connectivity, their immediate sounding potential is increasingly relegated to the margins of our discursive practices. Although their aesthetic value to our relationality is significantly reduced by the dominance of hypertextual/visual components within cyberspace, we seem to be becoming more contented with those voiced sign relations just the same. What effects do these sign conditions produce, especially in terms of our relationality? It is to this question that I now turn.

## THE IMPERSONAL SELF

Because mediated voices are detached voices from a lived-body, they easily become *impersonal* articulations of who we are, who we want to become, and what we want to really share. These voices also become interpellated, that is, in service to the complex, digitalized webs of cultural meaning to which they adhere. This is unfortunate and has serious implications for the ways we perceive and interact with one another because it intensifies what I call the constitution of the *impersonal self*. Let us look closely at how this sign condition of the self materializes.

If we adhere to the symbolic interactionist perspective (founded by social psychologist and pragmatist George Herbert Mead), we assume that our very sense of self, who we are and the significance we hold in others' lives, is primarily formed through our symbolic/semiotic enactments with others. Our interactions with others thus take on additional import. This means that we must remain vigilant in reflecting upon the ways in which we attempt to establish connections with others since those connections shape our sense of identity. Mead's perspective is in sharp contrast to a purely psychological stance that identifies the self as an isolated interiority that somehow forms as a result of internal cognitive mechanisms and processes quite separate from the influence of a self's socio-cultural environment. With Mead, we understand that our semiotic and phenomenological interactions with others, either ear-to-ear or by electronically mediated means, establish the very basis of how we know ourselves—our human subjectivity, our sense of existential agency and human purpose. The pragmatic theories of Peirce and Mead suggest that our subjectivities are dialogic products of our sociality, given our embeddedness within a complex semiotic network of relations that allows us to engage in discourse in the first place.

So, it is best for us to acknowledge at the outset that we are ever-changing *interpretants* for one another within an infinite and often unstable flux of social semiosis, as semiotician and pragmatist philosopher Vincent Colapietro contends.[35] As Peirce declares, the self is, indeed, a sign, understood only through a network of semiotic and phenomenological relations that are constituted over time and in particular locations between interlocutors. Our personal positionality within the space of cyber and the voices we articulate and hear thus bear consequentially on our sense of self. We are now significantly mediated by ever-expanding artificial forms of intelligence and the auditory allure of acousmatic voices. How do these new mediated forms affect the kinds of interactions we have and the kinds of selves we co-construct together?

Chapters 1 and 2 discussed at length the forms of electronic connections we are using and the degree to which they are now integrated into our daily lives. In this chapter, we also learned that the acousmatic voice is a primary electronic form that echoes throughout cyberspace and on the Internet. We have yet to address the changes in discursive content we are producing by using such mediated forms of connectivity. For if we follow a media ecology perspective, we know that forms of media drastically impact the content that is shared or exchanged.[36] In this way, we understand that both the form and the content of our interactions bear directly on our sense of self.

Looking critically at social media platforms, we find that, by their very nature, they lend themselves to abbreviated content. Twitter limits a given post to 280 characters. The kinds of interactions we are having through our tweets, Facebook posts and Messenger exchanges, texts, and so forth are comprised of mostly cryptic messages or kernels of information that are shared primarily for the sake of expressive efficiency. Overall, we are seeing an escalation in abbreviated discourses. Regrettably, such abbreviated discourses are superficial in nature and thus also abbreviate the relationality so established. If both the form and content of our electronic messages are abbreviated, in other words so too is our relationality. It follows that such abbreviations also impact our evolving sense of self.

Consequently, the content of what we are sharing often takes on more *impersonal tones*, that is, messages that are premised upon immediate instrumental goals and not ones that are focused on the personal or unique thoughts and feelings of those involved. Messages are shared, but increasingly their content is mostly superficial, echoing their form. Carr's research on how the Internet is making us shallow perceivers and thinkers supports this idea about the reflexivity involved between the personal and the social. When we perceive the other and the circumstance of our sociality at only a superficial, fleeting level of relationality, then we begin to habitualize these perceptions into our forms of expression. Because of their highly codified nature, these shallow forms of expression are often filled with clichés, acronyms, and literal abbreviations. Such forms of expression require very little personal or psychological involvement from the speaker or listener as interpretive agents. So, we may have increased our degree of electronic connectedness with the use of texts, tweets, and emails, but, by doing so, we also alter the quality and depth of our relations with one another. This is especially disheartening if we begin to substitute these virtual ways of relating for the actual lived practice of speaking and listening in immediate ear-to-ear contexts.

Philosopher Martin Buber, in his famous writings on dialogue, describes these types of shallow interactions as "I-It" relations, where the other and the self are perceived as merely interchangeable objects of consciousness. In other words, we perceive that our interlocutor is just another human being among the many we might encounter in a day, even if that human being is a loved one. In essence, we do not look beyond the surface level and often judge one another based on fleeting visual impressions and glances. A defining feature of such relations is the psychological distance they endorse. Given that these types of relations are often premised only on what we see of the other, they definitely exemplify a visualist orientation toward the world. It is disturbing to learn that our younger generations (millennials and Gen Z'ers) provide the most direct example of this "I-It" discursive trend, although I suspect that many of us are increasingly making such discursive choices as well, based upon these shallow perceptions.

Sherry Turkle is quick to point out that our electronic texts, online posts, emails, and photos from family, loved ones, and friends—our online interactions—serve as only *reminders* of intimacy, a sense of psychological closeness previously co-constructed by spending quality time in the ear-to-ear presence of others. As she says, these textual reminders of intimacy can, quite possibly, "lead us away from intimacy itself" if they become the predominant means of interaction.[37] In such cases, we mistake the map of relations for the territory—the actual relation. Her research participants claim that one of the advantages of such forms of electronic relating is that they provide a way of being connected while still keeping others at a comfortable psychological and often physical distance. Again, this should not be surprising given that print/text is a visual, spatial medium. It functions as it should. These new forms of discourse are thus highly regulatory both personally and socially, as our appeals to them continue to increase and they become presumed habits of discourse.

In regard to our content in our electronic forms of connectivity, Turkle found that millennials in particular prefer texting because they can edit their texts before sending and select the appropriate emoji to convey their sentiments—something that oral-aural modes of interaction do not offer. This way of relating gives us a feeling of being more in control of our message production and increases our sense of efficiency, the gold standard of electronic connectivity. This is not the first time the issue of personal control has surfaced in our discussions on technology in our "Age of Attention." Recall from chapter 2 that technologist James Williams claims that, in our current age of attention, control over our kinds and degrees of electronic connectivity is the defining problematic of our times. It stands to reason that our habits of self-control learned as a result of our distracted consciousness could easily spill over unwittingly into our ear-to-ear human relations, even though their application in this latter context is most problematic and disturbing.

Uncertainty reduction seen through the lens of control also begins to explain the underlying negative ambiguity that seems to motivate such actions. Turkle's research participants admit that the spontaneity and unpredictability of immediate ear-to-ear relations is most disconcerting. They do not like the fact that they cannot take back and edit something they have said in traditional speaking/listening contexts. It appears that in the age of attention/distraction, controlling the flow of information exchange has come to dominate and shape all of our attempts to communicate. Ironically, while such attempts at control are intrinsic to information exchange, they run counter to the very nature of communication, as I described. Communication requires a spontaneity in speaking and listening, an ability to adjust to another's perceptions and expressions in the momentary flow of interaction. Our attempts at information control, therefore, speak volumes about the lived ambiguity of experience and our interpretations of that ambiguity as negative. We may be getting better at controlling and sharing information but not necessarily at accomplishing communication.

Further emphasizing the issue of control within electronic connectivity, millennials and Gen Z'ers in particular obsessively experience what they describe as a "fear of missing out" (FOMO). Again, depending upon how much we check our phones, we all might display this type of behavior. We might assume that FOMO behaviors (which involve constant checking of our phones to see what has been uploaded to our various feeds) signify an appreciation on our part of a deeper sense of belonging to a group. In other words, we might assume that it signifies the definitive nature of actually being connected. I think an alternative and less positive explanation is in the offing, especially if we look closely at Turkle's research on millennials.

During her interviews, Turkle discovers that the content of their personal interactions when together as a group of friends is often dictated by what they are currently searching for and reading on their ready-to-hand mobile devices. In other words, the device actually constrains the topics discussed. If we consider what is more often than not circulating on the web in their various feeds, we find that this is mostly superficial, information-only material, much of which is mere entertainment-related content in one form or another. My students may not know the current secretary of state in the U.S. government, for example, but they know the latest boyfriend of one of the Kardashian women. As my students explain (and echoing the millennial participants in Turkle's research), FOMO does not refer to a fear of not being connected to others, but rather a fear of missing out on media *content* that will give them something to respond to on these social media platforms—such as which celebrities recently had a fight or which basketball team is making it to the Final Four. So, the social media obsession and anxiety disorder[38] that many now say this age group is experiencing is not about being disconnected as much as it is about not having anything to say once they are connected. Given that the content of their discourse is now almost completely centered around what content they are viewing or listening to on the web and in cyberspace, their fear actually signals an anxiety about not having enough information to share at a moment's notice. As Turkle interprets this, and as I concur, this means they are not sharing or discussing their personal thoughts and feelings about the world but simply the bits of information that are literally fed to them by their smart devices. This is the ultimate example of an impersonal encounter in both form and content. Drawing from the work of Peirce, we see that impersonal encounters such as these transpire on the basis of semiotically and phenomenologically perceiving the other and self as only generalities within the discursive world. Consequently, we express and perceive in the most mundane and general of ways. Serres addresses this best when he claims that by appealing to the endless reverberations of the electronic voice, "Eloquence . . . collapses into gibberish and boredom."[39]

Perhaps more disturbing is the possibility (or fact?) that these shortened forms of texts, tweets, and social media messages and posts and the abbreviated discourses they reflect could now be echoed in our daily oral-aural immediate discourses with one another. So, both the form and the content of what we say to one another when ear-to-ear run the risk of also being diminished or flattened, given these new electronic habits of discourse. These abbreviated forms of discourse reflect, more often than not, an instrumental focus to the exclusion of deeper, more personal ways of being and relating with one another. Our discourse, even with family and friends who are dear to us, can take on these impersonal tones. This is where the real threat to everyday conversation and communication is most keenly felt. Employers frequently lament the inability of their younger recruits to carry on a normal conversation with clients. Teachers are disappointed that their students do not seem to know how to ask questions and respond orally in class in a regular dialogic fashion. Youngsters are sitting in a circle with their electronic tablets rather than talking and being with one another at playtime. Comedian Stephen Colbert joked with Turkle about these discursive practices when she was a guest on his show. Discussing her concerns about our current flight from conversation, he remarked, "Don't all these little tweets, these little sips of online connection, add up to one big gulp of real conversation?"[40] We have to conclude emphatically "no." We must be mindful that connections (information sharing) do not necessarily constitute genuine communication, which is always based upon a richer sense of human mutuality in its unpredictable unfolding during the course of a conversation.

Our concerns about our current status of relationality should escalate when we also consider our increased proclivity to desire social robots or similar devices instead of the companionship of flesh-and-blood human beings. As Sherry Turkle explains,

> we have built machines that speak, and, in speaking to them, we cannot help but attribute human nature to objects that have none. . . . *At a first, we speak through machines* and forget how essential face-to-face conversation is to our relationships, our creativity, and our capacity for empathy. *At a second, we take a further step and speak not just through machines but to machines.* This is a turning point. When we consider conversations with machines about our most human predicaments, we face a moment of reckoning that can bring us to the end of our forgetting.[41]

Although the sharing of immediate information with our family and friends by texts or tweets may be helpful and even warranted at times, we do need to acknowledge that such discursive habits produce very different forms of interaction. Consequently, in our retreat from voice to short snippets of text, we necessarily learn different things about ourselves and others. These discursive habits produce different kinds of information that are shared. In addition, given their overall shallowness in terms of content and characteristics, the degree of what we learn about the other is also reduced. In turn, we are also apt to learn much less about who we are and who we might become as social beings.

Under these artificial social conditions, we risk becoming shallow selves, selves who lack substance, character, a sense of integrity, empathy, and a general concern for the well-being of others. It is not that we cannot express deeply held sentiments in an electronic text, such as "I love and miss you"—this is definitely the case. But because of the asynchronous nature of such an interaction and the lack of voiced elements, we do not automatically establish a dialogic encounter with the other, as Buber advocates. Because we are not listening to the other in the true auditory sense of the word in such text-based modes of interaction, we also miss the qualities of feeling that the sonorous voice represents within the speaking and listening dialectic. Electronic messages within impersonal interactions are, therefore, disembodied, and the potential for shared meaning is reduced. As a result, we diminish the opportunity to manifest what I identify later as genuine *interper-sónal* self and other relations. These are types of relations co-constructed within *sonic* dimensions enunciated through acts of immediate speaking and listening within ear-to-ear contexts of discourse. Following phenomenologist Alfred Schutz, we will come to understand that these sonic relations help to constitute "the mutual tuning-in relationship upon which all communication is founded . . . by which the 'I' and 'Thou' are experienced by both participants as a 'We' in vivid presence."[42]

By privileging electronic connectivity with its abbreviated forms and content of interaction, we run the risk of becoming an impersonal self, one that is as shallow as the forms of connectivity it uses. The other becomes equally impersonal. The constitution of the impersonal self is reflected in and exacerbated by our inauthentic enchantments within cyberspace, prompted by the amplification of acousmatic voices, voices disembodied from their speaker in which interpellation is also intensified. The impersonal self is a diminished self, one who has lost touch with a deeper sense of and appreciation for humanity. It is a self that can easily be battered about by the waves of hyperconnectivity and our fast-paced society with its 24/7 electronic web of alluring significations.[43] The impersonal self is left feeling untethered, anxious and depressed, unable to cope productively with the onslaught of information and amusements it has helped to create. Perhaps this is because our culture industry colonizes "genuine personal emotion."[44] In any case, the lived negative ambiguity that undergirds such a self is perpetuated through a dynamic process of semiosis.

## OUR DISENCHANTED ENCHANTMENTS

We have long lamented the rising tide of depression in America—especially among the young. According to the World Health Organization, almost 300 million people suffer from depression worldwide.[45] In the United States, 17.3 million adults report experiencing a major depressive episode in the past year, and nearly 50 percent of all people diagnosed with depression are also diagnosed with an anxiety disorder. Even more disturbing is the fact that the prevalence of adults with major depressive episodes is highest among individuals aged from 18 to 25 years, making depression the second leading cause of suicide among 15- to 19-year-olds.[46] Teenagers are now readily admitting that depression and anxiety are major issues among their peers, with 70 percent of them saying so. Some psychologists are pointing to increased social media use, academic pressures, and frightening events like terror attacks and school shootings as possible causes.[47] A new report compiled by Blue Cross Blue Shield (BCBS) reports that depression is skyrocketing in America, with rates of depression reported by BCBS members rising by 33 percent from 2013 through 2016 and the incidence of depression climbing the fastest among adolescents (up by 63 percent) and millennials (up by 47 percent).[48]

Equally troubling is the rise of anxiety in America, which, an American College Health Association study found, is quickly overtaking depression as the most common reason that college students seek counseling services. In 2016, 62 percent of undergraduates reported feeling "overwhelming anxiety" in the previous year, compared to 50 percent in 2011.[49] According to a national survey by the American Psychological Association released in May 2018, Americans' anxiety levels overall experienced a sharp increase in the past year, with almost 40 percent of respondents saying they felt more anxious than they did a year ago (this increase also jumped by 36 percent between 2016 and 2017).[50] While health, safety, and politics were among the key areas of anxiety reported, almost half (48 percent) of those surveyed also reported feeling anxiety about their immediate *relationships* with family, friends, and co-workers. These increased levels of anxiety were common to both men and women and seen across people of different races, ethnicities, and ages. While millennials and the younger generations are more anxious than older people, baby boomers saw the biggest age-related spike in anxiety. A study reported in *Mental Health* found that teenagers' reports of feeling anxious, depressed, and hopeless rose sharply around 2012, the period in which smartphones became popular.[51] It comes as no surprise that many cultural theorists, medical professionals, and psychologists are declaring that our information age has now been thoroughly realized as the *age of anxiety*. It seems that it is not only adolescents who are experiencing FOMO, or the fear of missing out, given the onslaught of ready-to-hand information at our fingertips. Instead, all of us in one way or another are sensing an urgency of being that pervades daily existence and that is qualitatively distinct from other historical moments.

It appears that we are increasingly experiencing a disappointment with life or an overall sense of psychological dissatisfaction as we move deeper into the twenty-first century and the age of distraction. Interestingly, this disappointment coincides with our appeals to inauthentic electronic enchantments as mere amusements. Although no empirical evidence exists that supports a direct cause-and-effect relationship between our increased use of electronic media and the rise of anxiety and depression in America, a strong correlation between the two is nevertheless suggested.

This is especially true if we dismiss the bio-medical model that advocates that anxiety and depression are caused by chemical imbalances in the brain.[52] As it stands, "the prevailing cultural view," as David Karp suggests, "is that a healthy revision of self is best accomplished through a revision of one's biochemistry."[53] This is interesting given the fact that drug company websites do not explicitly state that the causes of depression are known. As an example, many allege that "Depression is a serious medical condition that can hold you back from what you enjoy. And while no one knows for certain what causes it, experts believe that depression results when certain chemicals in the brain are out of balance."[54] Adopting the scientific community's own criteria for judgment, we have to say that this theory is not conclusive. An alternative explanation to the bio-medical model is now gaining support in wider circles of psychiatry and brain research.[55] Philosopher and psychiatrist Thomas Fuchs evidences this trend when he says that "the brain is only the biological condition for realizing conscious and intentional acts of life, not their cause."[56] Rather than looking at depression and anxiety as medical diseases for which prescription drugs are the only rational remedy, for example, it is more productive to see them as psychological illnesses constituted within the depleted soil of human relations.[57] Reversing the dominant perspective that attributes psychological maladies to the brain, a cultural discourse that has now unfortunately successfully codified our thinking, we come to a fuller appreciation of the mind as constructed communicatively within human relations.

The mind understood as thoroughly social is seen clearly as the progenitor of our psychological troubles and not pre-existing chemical imbalances in the brain. The voices of others we attend to and the relations that ensue have a significant impact on our psychological well-being. With the growing appeal and acceptance of acousmatic voices within cyberspace as our voices of communication, we are radically changing the qualitative nature of this social mind. Disembodied acousmatic voices moderate how we articulate our very being to one another. Our sense of self radically shifts and becomes diminished and fragmented as well. Potentially, the rich aesthetics of being through our immediate voices are co-opted by the symbolic, and we are transformed into mere commodities for mass consumption within cyberspace. As a result, our minds become as profane as the disintegrating mechanisms that structure them.

As Stiegler argues in his book *The Re-Enchantment of the World: The Value of Spirit Against Industrial Populism*, many of our forms of enchantment nowadays (especially those created through digital technologies that I identified as tending toward the inauthentic) are increasingly ending with personal or psychological disappointment. We have entered, Stiegler says, a new era of *symbolic misery* induced by our hyper-industrial epoch in which the technologies of marketing and consumerism have assaulted our aesthetic sensibilities too much. Too often we are left with a sense of loss when it comes to appreciating any actual experiences of the aesthetic in life. Because these electronic enchantments resound as inauthentic calls to our being, as I argued, they leave us feeling existentially hollow—spiritually adrift in a sea of consumerist capitalism fueled often by our ever-increasing narcissistic tendencies toward continual self-gratification.

Extending my sensory trope of enchantment, it appears that many of us are now experiencing an overall *existential dissonance*, rather than a felt harmony or *resonance* among self, other, and our world. The 24/7 clutter of messages and information translates after a while to only existential noise.[58] Here the Latin etymology of the word *noise* adds clarity; we feel existentially nauseous. We become easily immersed within a techno-social dilemma where distinguishing what is real from artificial connections becomes difficult to determine. While there are certainly economic, political, and other health factors that may exacerbate this felt dissonance, we must reflect carefully upon the current ways in which we are negotiating our relationships in life, especially since they provide the existential resilience we so ardently need. Essential questions remain: What are we being mindful of in the space of cyber and on the Internet? Do these ideas and things nourish the better aspects of ourselves or appeal to the lowest parts of who we are? What modes of being are we mindlessly adopting? In what ways is our sensorium changing because of the voices to which we now increasingly attend?

Too often we find communicative practices framed within impersonal, abbreviated information-message exchange structure (for example, texting, tweeting, emailing, and the like), which diminish the duration and quality of the relationships we create with others. Too often we become too receptive to ready-made ideas—easily adopting others' ideas instead of thinking critically on issues and deliberating for ourselves. As I discussed, our tendency to enact inauthentic enchantments seldom nourishes more rational ways of thinking. Instead, our inauthentic enchantments condone further perceptual judgments based upon mere qualities of feeling rooted in the symbolic that too often reflect unbridled imaginations, as Peirce describes. Unbridled imaginations lead to generalizations that are not always grounded in the facts of experience. These forms of imagination then exhibit an irrationality or non-rationality to the actions performed from them.[59] Regrettably, such unbridled assumptions create cultural discourses that resemble mere *echolalia*, as media ecologists have claimed.[60] These discourses are produced by the endless repetition of established cultural codes that have come to dominate our social landscape. The rise of acousmatic voices and their echoes within cyberspace are examples of the very drone of senseless noise that echolalia produces. The disembodied acousmatic voices are easily appropriated by others in service to their needs, not our own. I call our fascinations inauthentic partially because they manifest within highly mediated sound environments where the pure auditory voices of self and other have been lost in their experiential immediacy as material sign relations of firstness. In their place, we hear the abstracted voices of articulation, upholding the established symbolic order and reflecting the sign relations of thirdness and mediation.[61] When we become a society with an insatiable desire for new information and amusements, we risk devolving into a culture that no longer knows how to think and interact successfully with others.

These kind of discourses and practices severely diminish a healthier and fuller sense of the self that normally comes from a fully nourished body and mind. Muting the immediacy of voices that promote fundamental social connections in favor of listening to acousmatic voices within social media leaves us fundamentally deprived as human beings. Given their construction within the realm of the virtual, the selves who listen only to the acousmatic voices and their echoes are selves whose sense of who they are and what they bring to the common table of human relationality is diminished. We are left with impersonal selves. We face an experience of *disenchantment* with the world created by a diminished social economy of our own making. It appears that our inauthentic enchantments with electronic connectivity are, indeed, disenchanting enchantments.[62] Ironically, the more we are *on our phones*, the more our actual embodied voices are silenced or muted and we become separated from one another in significant aesthetically rich and immediate ways.

How did we arrive at such a place of existential anxiety, depression, and disenchantment? In the next chapter, I make the case that our soundscape within human relations has dramatically changed as a result of our unwitting acceptance of the actual murder of the *phone* (voice), understood as an aesthetic embodied element of discourse and action. If the immediacy of voice is, indeed, a metaphor for the articulate heart as John L. Locke suggests,[63] then those heart strings are no longer vibrating to their fullest potential. A closer look at why is in order. We are reminded that, "For twenty-five centuries Western knowledge has tried to look upon the world. It has failed to understand that the world is not for beholding. It is for hearing . . . . Now we must learn to judge society by its noise."⁶⁴

## NOTES

1. Chion, *The Voice in Cinema*.
2. Turkle, *Reclaiming Conversation*, 22.
3. Thomas Y. Levin, "Before the Beep," in *Voices: Vocal Aesthetics in Digital Arts and Media*, Norie Neumark, Ross Gibson, and Theo Van Leeuwen, eds. (Cambridge, MA: Massachusetts Institute of Technology, 2010), 18.
4. Ong, *The Presence of the Word*, 34; emphasis added.
5. R. Murray Schafer, *The Tuning of the World*, 90.
6. Virginia Madsen and John Potts, "Voice-Cast: The Distribution of the Voice via Podcasting," in *Voices: Vocal Aesthetics in Digital Arts and Media*, Norie Neumark, Ross Gibson, and Theo Van Leeuwen, eds. (Cambridge, MA: Massachusetts Institute of Technology, 2010), 41.
7. Recall that the human voice as embodied is first mediated by the breath and then mediated by culture given that our expressions and perceptions of it are, most certainly, a semiotic process. As Norie Neumark suggests, "embodied voices are always already mediated by culture; they are inherently modified by sex, gender, ethnicity, race, history, and so on." See Neumark, "Doing Things," 97. These mediations of the voice are the semiotic codes of culture that impact how we express and perceive.
8. Dolar, *A Voice and Nothing More*, 20.
9. I interpret Dolar's designation of "remainder" as a negative, while "excess" implies its opposite. Subsequently, I refer to this aspect of the voice as "excess."
10. It is important to note that the fundamental nature of the voice even within immediate ear-to-ear relations is a reflexive act of embodiment and disembodiment. As vocal theorist Steven Connor reminds us, "to say that my voice comes from me is also to say that it departs from me." Steven Connor, *Dumbstruck: A Cultural History of Ventriloquism* (New York: Oxford University Press, 2000), 4–5.
11. Ibid., 19.
12. Brandon LaBelle, "Raw Orality: Sound Poetry and Live Bodies," in *Voices: Vocal Aesthetics in Digital Arts and Media*, Norie Neumark, Ross Gibson, and Theo Van Leeuwen, eds. (Cambridge, MA: Massachusetts Institute of Technology, 2010), 161.
13. Dolar, *A Voice and Nothing More*, 122.
14. This expression comes from Michel Foucault's work, *The Order of Things: An Archeology of the Human Sciences* (New York: Vintage Books, 1973).
15. I think the highly textual/visual elements of cyberspace are easily interpellated as well.
16. Dyson, *The Tone of Our Times*, 14.
17. Ibid., 14.
18. Dolar, *A Voice and Nothing More*, 60.
19. Ibid., 61.
20. Ibid., 61.
21. Ibid., 63.
22. Ibid., 62.
23. Ibid., 62.
24. Smith, "Intensifying Phronesis," 101.
25. Neumark, "Doing Things," 101.
26. Macallan and Plain, "Filmic Voices," 252.
27. Bennett, *The Enchantment of Modern Life*, 124.
28. Dolar, *A Voice and Nothing More*, 67.
29. Ibid., 67.
30. Macallan and Plain, "Filmic Voices," 253.
31. Dolar, *A Voice and Nothing More.*, 79.

32. Turkle, *Reclaiming Conversation*, 45.
33. This phrase comes from physician and communication researcher James Lynch. See: http://sfhelp.org/cx/skills/listen_lynch.htm.
34. Dolar, *A Voice and Nothing More*, 22.
35. Vincent M. Colapietro, *Peirce's Approach to the Self: A Semiotic Perspective on Human Subjectivity* (Albany: State University of New York Press, 1989).
36. Postman, *Amusing Ourselves to Death*.
37. Turkle, *Reclaiming Conversation*, 12.
38. This is now being named an official anxiety disorder. See Sarah Fader, "Social Media Obsession and Anxiety," Anxiety and Depression Association of America, November 2018, https://adaa.org/social-media-obsession-and-anxiety.
39. Michel Serres, *The Five Senses: A Philosophy of Mingled Bodies,* trans. Margaret Sankey and Peter Cowley (London: Continuum, 2008), 22.
40. Turkle, *Reclaiming Conversation*, 19.
41. Ibid., 16–17.
42. Alfred Schutz, *Making Music Together, Collected Papers II: Studies in Social Theory,* ed. and introduction Arvid Brodersen (The Hage: Martinus Nijhoff, 1964).
43. For an interesting discussion on our current 24/7 online culture, see Jonathan Crary, *24/7: Late Capitalism and the Ends of Sleep* (New York: Verso, 2014).
44. Horkheimer and Adorno, *Dialectic of Enlightenment,* 144.
45. World Health Organization, August 30, 2019, https://www.who.int/news-room/fact-sheets/detail/depression/.
46. Amy Morin, "Depression Statistics Everyone Should Know," Verywell, July 26, 2019, https://www.verywellmind.com/depression-statistics-everyone-should-know-4159056.
47. Karen Zraick, "Teenagers Say Depression and Anxiety Are Major Issues Among Their Peers," *The New York Times*, February 20, 2019, https://www.nytimes.com/2019/02/20/health/teenage-depression-statistics.html.
48. Bill Hoffmann, "Report: Depression is Skyrocketing in America," *Newsmax*, May 10, 2018, https://www.newsmax.com/newsfront/survey-depression-surge-america.
49. Benoit Denizet-Lewis. "Why Are More American Teenagers Than Ever Suffering From Severe Anxiety?" *The New York Times*, October 11, 2017, https://www.nytimes.com/2017/10/11/magazine/why-are-more-american-teenagers-than-ever-suffering-from-severe-anxiety.html.
50. Peter Dockrill. "America Really is in the Midst of a Rising Anxiety Epidemic," May 9, 2018, https://www.sciencealert.com/americans-are-in-the-midst-of-an-anxiety-epidemic-stress-increase.
51. Amy Ellis Nutt, "Why Kids and Teens May Face Far More Anxiety These Days," May 10, 2018, https://www.washingtonpost.com/news/to-your-health/wp/2018/05/10/why-kids-and-teens-may-face-far-more-anxiety-these-days/?noredirect=on.
52. I thank Isaac E. Catt for bringing this cultural trend to my attention. For a thorough critique of the bio-medical model, see Isaac E. Catt, "Communicology and the Ethics of Selfhood Under the Regime of Antidepressant Medicine," in *Philosophy of Communication Ethics: Alterity and the Other*, eds. Ronald C. Arnett and Pat Arneson (Madison: Fairleigh Dickinson University Press; Lanham: Rowman & Littlefield, 2014).
53. David A. Karp, *Speaking of Sadness: Depression, Disconnection, and the Meanings of Illness* (New York: Oxford University Press, 1996), 81.
54. Pristiq, "Frequently Asked Questions," August 30, 2019, https://www.pristiq.com/faqs.
55. See, for example, Gary Greenberg, *Manufacturing Depression: The Secret History of a Modern Disease* (New York: Simon & Schuster, 2010); Irving Kirsch, *The Emperor's New Drugs: Exploding the Antidepressant Myth* (New York: Basic Books, 2010); Joanna Moncrieff, *The Myth of the Chemical Cure: A Critique of Psychiatric Drug Treatment* (Houndmills: Palgrave MacMillan, 2008); Loren Mosher, "Are Psychiatrists Betraying Their Patients?," *Psychology Today*, September 1, 1999, https://www.psychologytoday.com/articles1999909/are-psychiatrists-betraying-their-patients?page=5; Elliot Valenstein, *Blaming the Brain: The Truth About Drugs and Mental Health* (New York: Free Press, 1998); Robert Whitaker, *Anatomy of an Epidemic: Magic Bullets, Psychiatric Drugs, and the Astonishing Rise of Mental Illness in America* (New York: Crown Publishers, 2010).

56. Thomas Fuchs, *Ecology of the Brain* (Oxford: Oxford University Press, 2018).
57. I credit this distinction to Catt, "Communicology and the Ethics of Selfhood."
58. See Crary, *24/7*.
59. Alfred Korzybski, *Science and Sanity: An Introduction to Non-Aristotelian Systems and General Semantics* (Fort Worth: Institute of General Semantics, [1933] 1994).
60. Strate, *Echoes and Reflections*.
61. Alfred Korzybski, founder of General Semantics, would say that our increasing appeals to the mediating effects of the symbolic exhibit an intensional orientation toward the world which leads to psychological misevaluations and maladjustment. According to Korzybski, when the verbal or intensional aspects tend to dominate, then sanity is threatened. For Korzybski, we need extensional methods of evaluation to determine how the facts of experience fit with their verbal representations. The argument I am making here is that the world of cyberspace and the Internet (the world of virtuality) makes those successful determinations much more problematic. For more on Korzybski's theory, see *Science and Sanity: An Introduction to Non-Aristotelian Systems and General Semantics* (Fort Worth: Institute of General Semantics [1933], 1994.
62. Ritzer, *Enchanting a Disenchanted World*.
63. Locke, *The De-Voicing of Society*.
64. Michael Bull and Les Back, eds. *The Auditory Culture Reader* (Oxford & New York: Berg, 2003), 1.

*Chapter Five*

# The Murder of the *Phone* in Plain Sight

*The Voice of Articulation*

Why are we seeing such a widespread increase in existential dissonance and disenchantment in our everyday life-worlds, as evidenced in the preceding chapter? How did we arrive at a stage of cultural evolution where the acousmatic voice instead of the voice of immediacy is awarded such prestige and power within discursive relations? Why has it apparently become so easy for us to culturally dismiss the voice of immediacy and its value within ear-to-ear relations and, instead, appeal to text/visual-based elements of information exchange through electronic mediation? Why do we seem willing to run the risk of de-voicing society through our paradoxical electronic habits of text-based discourse *on the phone*? In general, why did the auditory aspects of our sensorium shift so dramatically to the visual when it comes to our relationality, even when theorists such as Ong and others were convinced that with the advent of our electronic revolution, we would enter a stage of full-fledged secondary orality? These questions prompt my ongoing analysis.

As this chapter describes, the murder of the *phone*,[1] understood as the aesthetic voice in excess of the symbolic, transpired historically in Western culture as we moved deeper into an ocular-centrism. This is evidenced by our progressive focus on language in the forms of writing and print. As we witness the continued dominance of the visual over the auditory in contemporary culture, in addition we must also note a silencing of what I will call the voice of enunciation (explicated in chapters 6 and 7) in favor of the voice of articulation.[2] When we grasp the magnitude of this shift in our sensorium along with our taken-for-granted understanding of the voice from the narrow perspective of linguistics, it comes as little surprise that the voice was not taken up as a major philosophical topic until both Derrida and Jacques Lacan did so in the 1960s, although from very different perspectives.³ I will be addressing both of their ideas on this topic in the present chapter.

By way of a preview, I begin with a historical account of sense experience according to Constance Classen, who interrogates the senses from an anthropological perspective.⁴ She offers a hermeneutic of the senses by looking closely at their historical representations and specifically underscores the importance of sight and sound as the primary senses. Here, we return to the ancient Greeks and the depictions of sight and sound through their iconic mythological representations, Apollo and Dionysus, respectively. The works of Ong, phenomenologist Don Ihde, and others help explicate the salient distinctions of sight and sound found in more contemporary scholarship, especially through the lens of semiotics and phenomenology. We discover why the diminished value accorded the auditory voice of speaking resides in a long Western philosophical tradition of neglect as we moved further into a visualist orientation toward the world. The writing of Italian philosopher Adriana Cavarero further aids in clarifying how the actual murder of the *phone* transpired as a consequence of the "devocalization of logos."⁵ Following her theoretical lead, I engage Jacques Derrida's critique of the metaphysics of presence. He describes a fundamental phonocentrism within Western scholarship and advances an alternative in grammatology. Unfortunately, Derrida contributes to the occlusion of the speaking voice and unwittingly propels us even further into the text-based world we witness today. Derrida's eventual claim that "there is nothing outside of the text,"⁶ supports the overall linguistic turn in philosophy. While contributing significantly to our understanding of the power of language and discourse to shape our sense of reality, he also further devalues the speaking or sonorous voice in excess of sedimented meanings. Lacanian scholar and sound theorist Mladen Dolar approaches the actual murder of the *phone* as an embodied uniqueness of sound through his critical examination of linguistics and particularly phonology. I review his discussions and end with an explication of what I call the voice of articulation, the talking corpse of the *phone* that, as predominantly a semantic phenomenon, is merely in service to a given signifying order of things. This voice represents Foucault's notion of the *voiceless name*, explicated herein.

## A HISTORICAL ACCOUNT OF THE HIERARCHY OF THE SENSES

Ong and others have argued that we have progressively adopted a visualist orientation toward the world. We have steadily allowed the visual dimensions of experience (with all their attendant aesthetic qualities) to eclipse the auditory, in particular the spoken word. How has this bias for the visual as a cultural experience come to pass?

According to Ong and following his mentor Marshall McLuhan, our visualist orientation is primarily a result of the invention of the first alphabet by the Sumerians around the end of the fourth millennium BC and the subsequent advent of the phonetic alphabet developed by the Greeks around 750 BC.[7] It is the Greek alphabet, of course, that became the model for most Western cultures, including its refinement as the Roman alphabet that we follow today. Ong suggests that it was at this point in history that a major shift in our intellectual capabilities occurred as we moved from primarily an oral-aural culture, with its focus on knowledge attainment through speaking or orality, to a print and eventually a typography culture, in which literacy or the ability to read and write took hold. The invention of the alphabet and writing produced a significant shift in our existential sensorium as our axiological preferences for sight over sound changed. Even though Ong prophesized that our electronic revolution would become an age of secondary orality that would reverse or, at the very least, mitigate the rise of this visualist trend, that has not been the case. Given his celebration of sound as the spoken word, his prediction is understandable and perhaps merely a hopeful gesture. As I previously evidenced, however, we are entering a time of *secondary literacy*,[8] with media literacy becoming the hallmark of behavioral competency in today's world. We have moved culturally, in other words, deeper into the realm of the visual, exhibited by the hyper-textual/image-based space of cyber and the Internet that increasingly captivates our everyday lives. The dominance of the visual is due in part to our highly consumerist culture. We are "surrounded by television and magazine advertisements, billboards, company logos and store window displays . . . [and now the world of cyber] . . . consum[ing] the products and socio-economic values of our society above all through our eyes."[9] In such contexts, the auditory always appears merely to serve the visual.

The ranking of sight over sound and our underlying assumptions about the five senses actually have their roots in ancient Greece.[10] As anthropologist Constance Classen explains, it was Aristotle who deemed that there should be five main senses to begin with, each corresponding to the known natural elements—earth, air, fire, water, and the quintessence.[11] Although the first four are quite familiar, the addition of quintessence is probably not. Understood as soul, heart, or personification, quintessence fuels what later becomes identified in the Middle Ages as essentially a spiritual sense. Classen points out that this notion of a spiritual sense "persisted up until the Enlightenment, during which period the mental faculties and the sensory faculties came to be defined as fundamentally different in nature: the conception which dominates today."[12] This is understandable given the rise of secularization in such a developing age of scientific inquiry. It is important to note that even the ancients "were apt to think of the senses more as media of communication than as passive recipients of data."[13] In contemporary culture, however, we seem to have forgotten this crucial point.

A view of the senses as fundamental media radically shifted historically as the physical sciences took hold in the Age of Enlightenment and beyond. Philosopher René Descartes had a lot to do with solidifying this theoretical shift. Descartes regarded the senses as deceptive and demarcated the world of the senses and the world of mind. His proclamation of "I think, therefore I am" was bent on grounding existence solely as a function of mental capacities, ironically conceived as insight. He thereby relegated the senses in general to obscurity. Classen indicates that while philosopher John Locke at least acknowledged that "ideas enter the mind *through* sensory experience,"[14] both Descartes and Locke viewed the senses as "purely physical mechanisms."[15] In discussing the views of Descartes and Locke on the senses, Classen goes on to say that

> hearing is not the Pegasus which carries us to heaven, smell is not the "high priest of the microcosm," but they are simply different modalities for conveying information about the physical world to the mind. For Descartes this information was not essential for mental activity, for Locke it was, but in either case sensory perception is regarded as a natural, rather than a spiritual or cultural, function. This "scientific" understanding of sensory perception has remained with us to the present time.[16]

Classen believes that the Enlightenment of the eighteenth century was an "eye-minded philosophy"[17] perpetuated in part by both Locke's and Descartes's work "with its emphasis on the visual basis of mental activity . . . [which] in turn increased the importance of sight in other spheres of life as well."[18]

As Classen makes clear in her historical overview, the identification of the senses and their rankings were not constant throughout history. Aristotle is credited with entrenching the standard ranking we use today, "with sight occupying the highest position followed by hearing, smell, taste, then touch."[19] Our philosophical and scientific shift to the visual as the preferred mode of understanding the world is not surprising given sound's primary association with the invisible, that is, more evanescent or ineffable aspects of human existence. This may be one of the reasons sound played such a major role in earlier oral-aural cultures when religion and myth were primary arbitrators of knowledge and truth. Even in medieval Europe, sight was typically ranked first among the senses. Interestingly, the reference to the Dark Ages semiotically implies the importance of its opposite.[20] However, Classen makes clear that Thomas Aquinas attempted to displace this ranking with his emphasis on the salient aspects of the spoken word of God.

Classen applauds the efforts of McLuhan and Ong for exploring "the relationship between the sensory order of culture and its social and cognitive order."[21] These media ecologists, as I discussed, understand well that the shifts in our ways of thinking, being, and relating correspond to "transformations in the ratio of the senses resulting from the introduction of new media of communication."[22] In acknowledging the impact of the invention of the alphabet and the "transformation from a hearing-dominated to a sight-dominated culture,"[23] Classen asserts that vision's role in the acquisition of knowledge quickly replaced what had previously been speech or the spoken word. As the printing press came to dominate cultural media, knowledge was enhanced through an increase in literacy, which quickly became the gold standard for a person's social development. Ong claims that our contemporary preference for the objectivist orientation of observational science is a direct outcome of the dominance of the visualist orientation. He explains that "writing and print . . . brought the scientific mentality into being."[24] In speaking about the influences these visual sensory shifts had on our thinking, Classen states the following:

> McLuhan, along with others, such as Walter Ong, argues that this transformation of the sensory order had a range of profound social and intellectual effects. On the cognitive level, the increased visualism produced by writing led to a dominantly objective, linear, analytic and fragmented mode of thought. On a social level, it led to de-personalization, individualism and the division of labour.[25]

If it is a truism that "the way a society senses is the way it understands,"[26] then our current axiological preferences in terms of sensory experience should be carefully examined. We need to understand and appreciate the distinctions between sight and sound as they play out within human relationality. Given the fact that philosophical thought has long "indicated a preference for the visual and . . . it has harbored from its classic times a suspicion of the *voice*, particularly the sonorous voice,"[27] we must interrogate this continuing preference.

One of the consequences of the domination of the visual is the reductive way in which sound and voice as essential media are typically characterized. I now take a closer look at the dichotomous aesthetic qualities of our two most dominant senses, sight and sound.

## THE DICHOTOMOUS AESTHETICS OF SIGHT AND SOUND

As the two most dominant senses, both sight and sound present a dichotomy of experience. That is, they have very different aesthetic characteristics and represent very different orientations toward the world that are often in opposition. This dichotomy is as old as Western civilization itself and can be traced back to their representations in ancient Greek mythologies. This is the dichotomy dramatized by the Greek gods Apollo and Dionysus. Philosopher Friedrich Nietzsche is credited with elaborating this distinction in *The Birth of Tragedy*. Arguing for the distinctive qualities of music (sound) versus art (visual) as an aesthetic he says that "unlike all those who seek to infer the arts from a single principle, the necessary spring of life for every work of art, I shall fix my gaze on those two artistic deities of the Greeks, Apollo and Dionysus. For me they are the vivid and concrete representations of two worlds of art, utterly different in their deepest essence and their highest aims."[28] Apollo represents our love of light (the visual, or what Nietzsche describes as the plastic arts), while Dionysus depicts our love of sound and music. Philosopher Gordon Graham further explicates Nietzsche on this important opposition:

> The visual and plastic arts manufacture images whose purpose is to catch our attention and invite our contemplation. This contemplation, however, is passive. Other than the direction of attention itself, it involves no practical activity on our part. In contrast, to be moved by the spirit of Dionysus is to go beyond mere contemplation, because Dionysus is a spirit that takes possession of us and impels us into action.[29]

Hence, our love of light as represented by the icon Apollo is contrasted with a fundamental suspicion of sound and voice, primarily because they have the potential to move us to action in both productive and unproductive ways. Dionysus is typically represented as the dark, furious, pulsating spirit of sound that can overwhelm us through its festive, musical qualities. These qualities are thought to easily disrupt our taken-for-granted ways of being and relating as supposed rational archetypes of the dominant *logos*. Although Derrida critiques what he defines as the metaphysical history of presence as phonocentrism (as I discuss below), I find sound theorist Mladen Dolar's counterargument about the voice quite compelling. In his extensions of Lacan's writings on the voice, Dolar contends that in our historical consideration of the voice, we should not consider it as a safeguard of presence,[30] as Derrida asserts. Instead, the voice should be heard as potentially dangerous, threatening, and possibly ruinous, exemplifying its historical association with the iconic Dionysus. While these characteristics sound quite negative, in fact they point to the power of the voice to irrupt taken-for-granted modes of discourse. It is this aspect of the voice that Dolar believes testifies to the disruptive nature of the voice that counters a supposed metaphysics of presence.[31] As an example of the historical suspicion that has surrounded the voice, Dolar cites the orientation toward music in ancient cultures, both occidental and western. As he suggests,

> The main concerns, which will recur throughout history with astonishing obstinacy, are already there in a nutshell: music, and in particular the voice, should not stray away from words which endow it with sense; as soon as it departs from its textual anchorage, the voice becomes senseless and threatening—all the more so because of its seductive and intoxicating powers. Furthermore, the voice beyond sense is self-evidently equated with femininity, whereas the text, the instance of signification, is in this simple paradigmatic opposition on the side of masculinity. . . . The dichotomy of voice and *logos* is already in place.[32]

It is no wonder that the feminine Muses as patrons of the old world of voice and sound (from which our word *music* is derived) exemplify the role that sound played in earlier oral-aural cultures. As historical accounts confirm, in these earlier oral-aural cultures, sound represents a call for active celebration or play in the pursuit of relationality, insight, creativity, and knowledge. Importantly, in oral-aural cultures, this active call is perceived positively. As Cavarero notes, the songs of the Muses, unlike the Sirens of Homer, did not kill. Instead, they act "to inspire verses to poets who, strictly speaking, no longer sing."[33] Peirce seems to appreciate these ancient connotations about sound as represented in oral-aural cultures when he explores the play of musement (described earlier) as a creative and pragmatic process of semiosis. As an aesthetic of experience marked by a freedom of movement within contemplation, the play of musement highlights, for Peirce, the imaginary potential within productive, that is, logical, sign actions. And while he does not characterize this process as a medium of sound in particular, he does envision it as a semiotic, which includes the possibility of sound initiating this freedom of movement as a quality of firstness. I have more to say about this later.[34]

With the advent of writing and print, however, the once-positive valence of sound and music in oral-aural cultures shifted dramatically. Plato specifies that music in particular can unsettle the "fundamental political and social conventions"[35] and fray the social fabric of everyday life. Plato was convinced that "the music and the rhythm must follow the speech."[36] The *logos* meant thinking not speaking; more importantly, for Plato, thought preceded speech. It is interesting to note that both Plato and Aristotle argued for dispensing with the flute, banning it because, as a wind instrument, it easily substituted for the voice of speech.[37] As Dolar explains, it should not be surprising, therefore, that Dionysus chose the flute as his instrument and Apollo chose the lyre.[38] It is in these historical associations that we find the dichotomy of sight and sound keenly pronounced—with sound placed firmly under suspicion.

According to Ong, the distinction between a visual and auditory orientation to the word is also exhibited in our ancient Western religious traditions. Referencing the distinction between the visual preference Christianity gives as a "revealed religion"[39] and the earlier Hebrew tradition, Ong indicates that the Hebrews equated the spoken word, in particular, to an action or event—an association that represents a Dionysian grasp of reality. As Ong states, "The [spoken] word is something that happens, an event in the world of sound through which the mind is enabled to relate actuality to itself."[40] He continues, "As events, [spoken] words are more celebrations and less tools than in literate cultures. Only with the invention of writing and the isolation of the individual from the tribe will verbal learning and understanding itself become 'work' as distinct from play."[41] Thus, the spoken word implies different referential dimensions than the written word. With its visual form, our engagement with the written word is thought to be more passive. Continental philosopher Jean-Luc Nancy concurs. When comparing the written word as visual form and the sonorous qualities of speaking, Nancy argues that the "sonorous . . . outweighs form." He goes on to say that the sonorous "does not dissolve [visual form], but rather enlarges it; it gives it an amplitude, a density, and a vibration. . . . The visual persists until its disappearance; the sonorous appears and fades away into its permanence."[42]

Understood as an event or happening, we can hear sound's semiotic entailments as speaking and easily recognize that they are less temporally *deferred* than in written texts in a Derridean sense. That is, speaking/listening (as auditory enactments) accentuate presence and immediacy in the way Buber characterizes them. As Ong indicates, "for oral-aural man, utterance remains always of a piece with his life situation. It is never remote"[43] or distant. This is unlike the written word (as visual), which allows for separation between writer and reader through its typical asynchronistic, spatial qualities. Writing always implies an absent reader. This helps to explain why sound, or the auditory, is most often associated existentially with time unlike the spatial association of sight.[44] Thus, unlike the printed word, speaking and listening as auditory components, amplify the existential dimension of time—calling us to more readily attend to the natural flow of time within a given speaking/listening event. As Ong claims, while "sight can follow motion through time [as in a video or film]. . . . It seeks to fix its objects," unlike sound.[45] This leads Ong to claim that, unlike vision, "sound is more real or existential than other sense objects, despite the fact that it is also more evanescent."[46] Nancy agrees. As he explains, "it is perhaps in the sonorous register that our feeling-oneself feel is most obviously manifest."[47] Here, Nancy is equating feeling-oneself feel with the very notion of *sense*. These qualities of sound as temporal dimensions of experience prompt Ong to declare that "none of the other senses [other than sound] gives us the insistent impression that what it registers is something necessarily progressing through time. . . . Sound implies movement and thus implies change."[48] Sound theorist Julian Henriques agrees when he claims that, unlike the visual, "the sonic suggests an understanding that is based on connection, combination and synthesis, rather than division, separation or analysis alone."[49] Unlike vision, which fixates objects in space, sound is inherently time-expressive and dynamical, which corresponds to the god Dionysus. It seems as though the visual dimensions of experience have to pair themselves with the auditory in order to make them dynamic. John Shepard, who interrogates the social dimensions of music, also supports these interpretations on the association of sound and time when he asserts that

> sound is more symptomatic of the flow of time than any other phenomena. . . . Although all other phenomena occur with a stream of time, the fact that they may be generally isolated and examined at leisure demonstrates that, as far as their influence on the arrangement of people's sensoria is concerned, they are not so inexorably tied to that stream as sound is.[50]

Furthermore, we know that with the visual, we never get beyond surfaces. Sight functions as reflected light on the surfaces of things. As Ong explains, sight "can never get to an interior as an interior, but must always treat it as somehow an exterior."[51] As Ong scholar Reid Locklin claims, "the interiority of sound, for Ong, draws together several dimensions of the experience of hearing. Sight renders space an empty medium between the eye and a particular object; sound renders space a vast interior, a living reality, continuously inhabited by voices, music and noises of various kinds. Sight isolates and dissects, while sound incorporates and unifies."[52] So, unlike vision, sound (like its medium of air) surrounds us and penetrates our awareness and being—sometimes to the point of uncomfortableness. With its Latin etymology, the word *noise* translates as nausea or seasickness, indicating how sound can be dramatically disturbing and even painful.[53] This condition gives rise to the old adage that we can close our eyes to block out visual elements in experience, but we have no flaps on our ears. Sound theorist R. Murray Schafer agrees when he declares that "we have no ear lids. We are condemned to listen."[54] So, our experience of sound is much more penetrating existentially. Nancy asserts that "sound . . . penetrates through the ear [and] propagates throughout the entire body something of its effects, which could not be said to occur in the same way with the visual signal."[55] There is an imminence to sound that seems to surround us, and given its intense materiality, sound is often likened to a "sense of touch that connects us with our bodies and the world with the 'thisness' of experience."[56] Because of their penetrating qualities, auditory objects to consciousness offer more resistance to our will and place more demands on us existentially.[57] This uncontrollable aspect of the sounding of the other within the inter-mediacy of ear-to-ear relations may explain some of our current avoidance behaviors noted earlier, especially when it comes to interacting in today's text-based communication climate. Less feeling of self-other control in voiced relations is accompanied by more lived ambiguity within experience, too often interpreted as negative. This appears to be the case, especially for the younger generations (as described previously) but manifests across our population more generally.

Given the distinctive qualities of both sound and sight, we must now begin to ask why our present culture continues the long tradition of Western philosophical thought when it comes to neglecting the aesthetic dimensions of sound and voice and accentuating instead the textual/visual. Why has secondary literacy in its hyper-textual/visual representations taken hold, as increasingly evidenced in the world of cyberspace and the Internet? If Ihde is correct when he declares that "without voice the *per-sona* recedes, and there is the possibility of 'depersonalization,'"[58] a declaration made also by Ong, we must question why we are so willing to move into these potential shallow spaces of relationality and find our existential home there. Perhaps we might argue that depersonalization is now warranted in an electronic mass mediated culture in which the boundaries between the private and public are readily blurred. Perhaps it is our new taken-for-granted way of being in the world. Or, do the aesthetic qualities of the voice just reviewed somehow prompt a relational backlash, given our proclivity for more devocalized ways of relating? In terms of temporality, are we now more comfortable making our discursive practices more static and asynchronous—which our text-based modes of interaction do? Do we want, at all personal and social costs, to reduce the unpredictability and perceived negative ambiguity that speaking/listening entail within the free-flow of inter-mediate ear-to-ear experience? Are we living in such an era—with its constant barrage of incoming messages that prompts us to want to fixate our objects to consciousness in their spatiality more so than in the past? Given the remoteness our text-based modes of interaction now present *on our phones*, are we becoming less desirous of presence and inter-mediacy within human relations that the dialogic philosophers declared are potentially the most fulfilling for us? Have our electronic modes of superficial interactions already primed us to be less inclined to want deeper levels of intimacy, or worse, have we already forgotten how to create them when we do so desire them?[59]

Classen prompts us to ask this question: What modes of consciousness are created by treating sight versus sound as a fundamental way of knowing?[60] In addition, we should ask this: What modes of consciousness are we creating by further diminishing the value accorded the immediate voice of speaking as a fundamental way of relating? We have reviewed the historical and cultural contexts that set the stage for our murder of the *phone*. We discovered that the initial murder weapons were axiological, value preferences for the visual over the auditory throughout history that are only accelerated by our current mass mediated electronic environment. But there are other murder weapons as well, in particular theoretical ideas about the role of language and discourse in speaking and listening. These too have contributed to the eventual demise of the *phone* in excess of sedimented meaning. It is to these ideas that I now turn.

## PHILOSOPHY CLOSES ITS EARS

Adriana Cavarero in her book *For More Than One Voice: Toward a Philosophy of Vocal Expression* provides a backdrop for dramatizing the murder of the *phone*. She aims to rethink the role of voice in human relationality as a way to invigorate an anti-metaphysical ontology of the voice that runs counter to Derrida's critique. For Cavarero, this new ontology must be grounded not in thinking or abstract ideas as ideation (in the Kantian sense) but in an embodied and contextual relationality produced by sonorous voices. Her project is inherently communicological, although she does not specify it as such. She turns to the voice in its "singularity" so as "to 'return' speech to the body—that is, in order to reverse the philosophical tendency to subordinate speech (as in the semantic destiny of the term *logos* itself) to a mute, immaterial order of signification . . . to . . . rescue both the voice and the body from the figuration to which they have been subjected by the politico-philosophical tradition of the west."[61] For Cavarero, the unfortunate relegation of the voice in service to the semantic sense of the *logos* must be rectified.[62] Such a theoretical move requires an extensive hermeneutic of the *logos* as sonorous speaking, as an auditory phenomenon that, to her way of thinking, does not broadcast its supposed animalistic or mere bodily qualities or its semantic entailments. As she indicates, her aim "is to free logos from its visual substance, and to finally mean it as sonorous speech—in order to listen, in speech itself, for the plurality of singular voices that convoke one other in a relation that is not simply sound, but above all resonance."[63] When understood as thinking as in Plato's sense, she contends that the *logos* "loses its phonic component and consists in a pure chain of signifieds. . . . The voice thus becomes the limit of speech—its imperfection, its dead weight."[64]

Cavarero relies on the work of Hannah Arendt, especially given Cavarero's underlying feminist pursuit of the political dimensions of voice. Cavarero insightfully points out how the androcentric positionality of Western thought has historically relegated the voice of singularity to a secondary status given its traditional association with the body. As she says, "Symptomatically, the symbolic patriarchal order that identifies the masculine with reason and the feminine with the body is precisely an order that privileges the semantic with respect to the vocal."[65] Hence, the voice that comes from "the vibration of a throat of flesh"[66] has become historically suspect because of its supposed feminine natural entailments. Dating back to Homer's early depictions of the Sirens as seductive and dangerous in his ancient Greek myth, these beliefs about how women's voices are powerful and devilish remain with us today.⁶⁷ In this regard, Cavarero echoes Dolar's reading of the feminization of the voice discussed earlier. As she indicates, in formulaic fashion Western philosophy upholds the idea that "woman sings, man thinks."⁶⁸ I am fully aware of this theoretical stance as I assert the need for a re-enchantment of human communication as a woman writer and theorist. There might be a tendency for my readers to easily associate enchantment's auditory entailments (as indicative of repetitious chants or singing) with a strictly feminine issue, enactment, or concern. Such a theoretical position merely echoes the bias of Western philosophy and a patriarchal order of discourse. Such a stance precludes a more insightful understanding of the nature and function of human communication as a combinatory logic of nature (body) and culture (sign) as communicology.

Cavarero's ambitious project to prevent philosophy from continuing to "close its ears"⁶⁹ to the sonorous value of the speaking voice is a daunting task, she admits. For while she acknowledges that over the last many decades we have seen the vocal sphere being analyzed from a number of perspectives, philosophy overall has remained fairly silent on the issue of voice.⁷⁰ In her review of the literature on voice and vocality, she acknowledges the psychoanalytic treatment of voice, especially as advanced by Jacques Lacan in the 1960s. Lacan was one of the few theorists who saw "the need for a theory of the voice, the object voice, the voice as one of the paramount 'embodiments' of what [he] called *object petit a*."⁷¹ It was Lacan who specified that the sonorous voice should not be turned into a mere object of aesthetic pleasure, which isolates it from its social entailments and reduces the voice to a fetish object. Nor should the voice be conceived solely as a vehicle for meaning, in service to what he describes as signification.⁷² Instead, Lacan pursued the object voice, "which does not go up in smoke in the conveyance of meaning, and does not solidify in an object of fetish reverence, but . . . functions as a blind spot in the call"⁷³ from the other as sonorous speaking. From Lacan's semiotic perspective, this blind spot is best understood as the non-sonorous object voice that, while inaudible, still implicates the voice's materiality in its desire for the sonorous. Cavarero believes that although such treatments within psychoanalysis entail a recognition of the relationship between voice and body as an economy of drives, they still miss the mark at interrogating the unique aspects of the voice as an originary sonorous excess. As she claims, within the psychoanalytic sphere there is "nevertheless . . . a tendency to 'rediscover,' in a positive sense, the musical and seductive power of the voice that the metaphysical tradition—starting from Plato's famous hostility toward Homer—has constantly tried to neutralize."⁷⁴ While her point is well taken about the treatments of psychoanalysts and particularly Lacan when it comes to the voice, the extension of the psychoanalytic perspective offered by Dolar comes closer to an appreciation for the audible voice of excess in its originality that she is actually pursuing. Dolar extends the ideas of Lacan and insists, as we will see, that voice is not merely a leftover from linguistic speech understood as *logos*. Instead, Lacan's object or pure voice, according to Dolar, is indicative of an originary excess of the *logos*, which opens "a zone of undecidability"[75] in discourse as a dialectical movement of sound and silence. This zone of undecidability, we will find, possibilizes what Merleau-Ponty identifies as a positive ambiguity in conscious experience. I shall have more to say about this in the chapters to come.

In addition, Cavarero acknowledges the influential reflections on vocality and textuality of semiotician Roland Barthes. In Barthes's writings, we find an appreciation for what he describes as the *grain* or timbre of the voice, that aspect of voice that enunciates "the materiality of the body that springs from the throat, there where the phonic metal is forged."[76] According to Paul Filmer and his application of sound studies to choral performance, Barthes attempts to expose the distinction between the grain of the voice as a *geno-song* and the aspect of the voice he calls *pheno-song*. Filmer explains: The *pheno-song* is "the features which belong to the structure of the language being sung . . . [while] *geno-song* . . . is . . . the generative sense of singing itself which is beneath *pheno-song* and which makes it possible."[77] It becomes apparent that with his notion of the grain of the voice as a *geno-song*, Barthes is trying to tease away the immanent vocal aspect of singing as a bodily phenomenon from the role the voice plays in signifying practices as speech. While Barthes at least recognizes the value of the voice as "a pivotal joint between body and speech,"[78] Cavarero believes that in Barthes's work, both voice and body and their interrelationship are described in terms that are still too general. Her project is meant to articulate the uniqueness of voice in its originality as speaking that extends Barthes's notion of the grain. Yet, as we will see, Dolar appeals to the very timbre of the voice that Barthes describes as the grain to recover the individuality of the voice he is also pursuing. He likens the timbre to a "fingerprint" and declares that this aspect of the voice does not contribute to meaning and by not doing so, becomes linguistically irrelevant yet interpersonally significant.[79]

Finally, in her literature review on the discipline of speech and communication, Cavarero declares "that even those philosophies that value 'dialogue' and 'communication' remain imprisoned in a linguistic register that ignores the relationality already put in action by the simple reciprocal communication of voices."[80] Consequently, she claims that even the discipline of speech and communication ignores the uniqueness of the voice in its originality as an event of speaking. I think she has a point. While sonorous speech as a form and function of discourse is most certainly recognized in our traditional conception of orality within public contexts (and explored to some extent within rhetorical studies), this is not the case when it comes to the interpersonal level of discursive practices. Interrogations on the nature and function of the speaking voice within relational contexts is sorely lacking. For example, in searching the online communication databases, I found just several publications that address the issue of the speaking voice within the communication discipline.

In order of appearance by date, interpersonal scholar John W. Lannamann wrote a book chapter titled "The Politics of Voice in Interpersonal Communication" in 1995.[81] In this piece, Lannamann argues that the study of the social environment has to recover an appreciation for the voice, especially given the highly commercialized age of digital consumption. The politics of the voice is certainly a key factor within interpersonal relations, and yet his call for further research was seemingly ignored. In 2004, communication and media theorist John Durham Peters published a piece called "The Voice and Modern Media" in which he offers a brief overview of the ways in which the voice has been conceptualized throughout modernity.[82] He is particularly interested in the current status of the voice given the rise of new media platforms. Acknowledging the disembodied voice that modern media promote in their broadcasting, Peters questions if we can now sufficiently distinguish between real sociability and surrogate sociability, given the increase in text-based forms of electronic communication. However, he concludes that the voice is still a prized medium in the digital age, basing this claim on the fact that Americans are buying digital phones at an alarming rate. While these buying patterns are certainly true, the presumption that we are using these telephones for voice calling is erroneous, as I evidenced. The third publication in communication most directly supports the arguments I make. In the *Proceedings of the Media Ecology Association* in 2010, Jane R. Thiebaud "focuses on the decline of living f2f conversation and social interaction" as a result of the rise of the "technologized word."[83] Drawing from Ong as I do, Thiebaud raises serious issues with and concerns about the nature and quality of our current interactions. Obviously, three publications over almost a 20-year period do not sufficiently interrogate the nature and value of the speaking voice within interpersonal relations. We do, however, find treatments of the voice and its role in relationality within the work of Merleau-Ponty and Michel Foucault, as I discuss later. Regrettably, aside from a communicological treatment of the voice published in 2010, referencing the work of anthropological linguist Edward Sapir,[84] mainstream communication scholars have yet to adequately take up the issue of voice in any sustained way.[85]

Phenomenologist Don Ihde is one of the few contemporary scholars who tried to rectify this theoretical lack when it comes to the voice, particularly in *Listening and Voice: Phenomenologies of Sound.*[86] Ong is, of course, another, especially in *The Presence of the Word*. It appears that, for the most part, the discipline of communication has merely conceptualized the voice as a tool in service to linguisticality, evidenced historically by the elocutionary movement. As medieval scholar Paul Zumthor indicates, this is precisely because vocality and orality are typically conflated in the historical literature on the subject. He believes it is strange that "among all our institutional disciplines, there does not yet exist a science of the voice."[87] He distinguishes between vocality and orality, according to Cavarero, by specifying that orality focuses on the voice as the bearer of language. Vocality, on the other hand, specifies the full range of activities and values of the voice that are independent of language. Cavarero agrees with Zumthor's assessment and insists, therefore, that the study of vocality must emphasize the salient bond between voice and speech. She goes on to say that "voice is sound, not speech. . . . Speech constitutes its essential destination."[88] This destination, we have found in previous discussions, is Peirce's semiotic phenomenological category of thirdness, where the accomplishment of signification is achieved within the symbolic functions of language and discourse. Underscoring the extent to which philosophy in particular has neglected the treatment of the voice, Cavarero remarks that philosophy "stands out among the disciplines for the force with which it renders the voice insignificant."[89]

The historical narrative of the voice did not begin that way, however. As we know from the study of orality, "voice is a central theme for a kind of knowledge that is inaugurated in Greece as the self-clarification of logos."[90] Rhetoric (*rhetorice* or *rhetorica*) with its root in *erō* or *ereō*, meaning "I speak," signifies the study of public speaking understood as a verb, an action.[91] In spite of this, as we historically became a writing and print culture with a focus on "grammar" as the study of the written rather than the spoken word,[92] the traditional sense of *logos* as the dialectical enactment of speaking speech (*parole parlante*) and speech spoken (*parole parlée*) as outlined by Merleau-Ponty becomes unfortunately associated primarily with language and thought and not vocality per se. Jonathan Sterne agrees when he contends that the "vast literature of sound studies [that] has developed over the past 20 years . . . has provided more robust conceptions of sonic culture [and the voice] than orality."[93]

This occlusion of the speaking voice by the grammarians is evidenced if we consider the word *verbal* as conceptualized within our current lexicon. In tracing its etymology, we find that the word *verbal* derives from IE *wer*, which means "to speak" and is associated with the aspect of "predicate," which comes from the Latin *praedicāre*, meaning "to cry out, preach."[94] As such, the very act of verbalizing originally meant to speak as an auditory gesture rather than the broader contemporary association it now has with language and semantics in general. Verbal now primarily emphasizes the use of language, and voice is translated more broadly to include both speaking and writing. Consequently, the speaking voice of *logos* and the verbal are seamlessly eclipsed and instead put in service to language, thought, and meaning. Philosophy as a discipline, Cavarero asserts, follows suit and "avoids getting caught up in the very question of the voice."[95] Instead, the *logos* is associated progressively not with the voice per se but with thought, as Plato outlined it. This philosophical neglect of the uniqueness of the voice drives Cavarero's project as she aims to rectify the "devocalization of logos."[96]

One of her chief philosophical adversaries is Jacques Derrida, the philosopher and semiotician who criticized what he identified as phonocentrism of Western thought.[97] Cavarero's critique of Derrida is understandable, given her project to resurrect an appreciation for the speaking voice. Her critique is certainly required because of his philosophical position on the *phone* in regard to language and speech. Given his interest in the spoken word and orality more generally, Ong also addresses Derrida's textualism and finds it wanting. As he views it, Derrida missed the fact that "there is no text apart from sound."[98] In any case, in Derrida's philosophy, we find another essential weapon in the historical murder of the *phone*. How does Derrida's philosophical project contribute to the *phone*'s demise? A closer look is in order.

## DERRIDA'S CRITIQUE OF THE METAPHYSICS OF PRESENCE AS PHONOCENTRISM

To Derrida's way of thinking, the speaking voice in its conceptualization as a singularity and originary excess of sedimented or symbolic speech enforces a metaphysics of presence. This metaphysics, according to Derrida, has historically sustained an erroneous perspective on knowledge acquisition and certitude by upholding an originary sense of their constitution by means of self-consciousness. Derrida contends that this metaphysics of presence has dominated our thinking and understanding of the functions of language and discourse over centuries. His "war against metaphysics"[99] is waged collectively in *Speech and Phenomena,*[100] *Writing and Difference,*[101] and *Of Grammatology.*[102] As I see it, his general project is threefold: Critique the metaphysics of presence, do so by attacking what he perceives as the phonocentrism of Western thought that supports it, and advance grammatology or writing as the destabilizing force in this metaphysics that diminishes the value placed on the sonorous voice.

Derrida interprets the metaphysics of presence as a philosophical orientation where "the concept of a pure and immediate presence functions in metaphysics as the guarantee of an evident and necessary truth, and thus [our Western] concept of presence is 'foundational.'"[103] Said differently, this metaphysics not only acknowledges a self-consciousness and/or self-presence but views consciousness as pure, foundational, or transcendental. As Derrida remarks, this modern metaphysics of presence "defines the very element of philosophical thought, it is evidence itself, conscious thought itself, it governs every possible concept of truth and sense."[104] He reinforces his critique of this metaphysics through a semiotic lens. That is, he contends, especially as presented in the linguistic writings of Ferdinand de Saussure, that the signifier/signified relation merely upholds this metaphysics of presence. This is because it is based upon a typical binary and hierarchical system that opposes intelligibility to sensibility. Thus, sensibility, in this case the phonic sign, is subordinated to intelligibility or the concept. In such a configuration, Derrida contends that the signified or concept is presumed to exude presence (understood foundationally), while the signifier or phonic sign functions merely to re-present it in its pre-given state. Thus, there is a pretense, as Derrida sees it, that the signified "lies at the origin of the sign."[105] Derrida believes that there is no origin, fixed point, or stable pre-existent presence within the operation of signs. In the unfortunate theoretical configuration of Saussure as Derrida views it, the graphic sign (with which he is most concerned) unfortunately becomes merely a sign of a sign or the sign of a phonic sign.[106] It is this very derivative view of writing that Derrida seeks to reverse in his semiotic critique. His notion of *differance* as the play of signifiers in discourse where there is no foundational sense of meaning is his corrective. He seeks to erase the value placed upon Saussure's notion of the signified as a foundational category because it supports a supposed metaphysics of presence. There are no origins of meaning for Derrida, only the operations of *differance* within signifying practices.

Regarding his second theoretical maneuver, why does Derrida attack the voice per se and identify Western thought as phonocentric? For Derrida, "the voice becomes precisely the metaphysical feature par excellence, the very thing that metaphysics privileges, over and against writing, in order to construct itself as a system of presence."[107] Derrida believes that the very notion of presence privileges a phonocentrism because it is premised upon a conception of the sonorous voice as the originary source of discourse. In other words, the voice is conceived as presentation and not representation. The presence Derrida is trying to subvert "is an effect of the metaphysical privileging of the voice."[108] In order to advance his argument about writing as non-derivative and non-essentialist, he must attack the sonorous voice perceived as its opposite. According to Derrida, in our traditional interrogations of orality, we have privileged the voice as a pre-existent presence and forgotten that meaning is always derivative of signs as a play of *differance*. As Thomas Farrell remarks, in his critique of the voice as a metaphysics of presence, Derrida is "reminding us of the structural limitations of language."[109]

Derrida proffers writing and in particular his deconstruction project as a way to "destabilize" the perceived phonocentric order of metaphysics. In his reading of Derrida, Ong finds it ironic that Derrida characterizes writing as the destabilizing force—lending to writing the auditory characteristics indicative of Dionysus.[110] Nevertheless, Derrida's philosophical treatment of metaphysics of presence advances a deconstruction project that is bent on unveiling "a rather different notion of the sign—namely, the sign, or trace."[111] In doing so, he interprets Plato as condemning writing and thereby appeals to the system of presence as phonocentrism. We need to understand Derrida's interpretation of Plato as a strategic theoretical move; it allows him to advance his phonocentric position on metaphysics. Bent on showing that the signified and signifier relationship is fictitious as an unfolding metaphysical presence, Derrida's attack on the metaphysic of phonocentrism comes to its full force. Here he develops his now famous philosophy of *differance*. Cavarero elaborates:

> What matters to him, what orients his deconstructive labor, is the philosophy of *différance*—or a theory on the interminable deferral of a trace, understood as the movement of signs, whose concept basically coincides with writing. Writing, generally understood, is in fact the privileged realm of the movement of a trace that, not by chance, acquires the name of *arche-écriture* in Derrida's lexicon. Derrida's interest in the *phone*, his discovery of the theme of the voice, emerges precisely from this prejudicial interest in a writing conceived "as a texture of differential traces, as an open system of deferrals and deviations, which do not allow access to any presence." In other words, it is the speculation on writing as *différance* that orients the theoretical axis in which Derrida places the theme of the voice, making it play a metaphysical role in opposition to the antimetaphysical valance of writing. He can thus read the ancient platonic condemnation of written discourse as a demonstration of this thesis, or as a symptom of the system of presence.[112]

For Cavarero, therefore, the contemporary philosophy of Derrida contributes to the devocalization of the *logos*. This is the *logos* understood as *phone semantike* as Aristotle defines it. By counter-posing his notion of *differance* that transpires within the proliferation of signs and signifying systems viewed as non-essentialist, Derrida seeks to destabilize (quite successfully, I might add) the pure voice of speaking in the immediacy of discursive experience. As Cavarero reads Derrida, he is not attacking a system constructed on the metaphor of voice or the voice of consciousness or inner voice, but on the physically sonorous voice. For Derrida defines the voice "as relating to the speech of a self-referential subject who basically speaks to himself."[113] While denouncing a metaphysics of presence understood as "a desire to affirm certainty or certitude in the metaphysical propositions we set forth in language,"[114] Derrida devalues the material, sonorous voice altogether.

As significant as Derrida's contributions are to our understanding of language and discourse and especially to the discipline of semiotics, they also uphold a visual/spatial orientation toward discourse and action rather than an auditory one. He clearly associates the written, visual sign with spatiality, making clear that "unlike the voice, writing, trace par excellence—spacing, movement, genuine play of signs—cannot generate an effect of presence."[115] As I previously reviewed, writing and print are spatial and thereby visually dominant as signifying systems. Derrida believes that writing is subversive "because its spatial organization undermines the absolute identification of signifier and signified that voice seems to present."[116] The sonorous voice on the other hand, as Derrida sees it, is correlated with time and, as such, "is represented as an acoustic signifier that is more or less collapsed with the signified, hence giving the illusion of presence."[117] This auditory view of the metaphysics of presence is exemplified in his writings in the 1960s. According to Derrida, the auditory nature of the *logos* is suspect unlike the spatiality provided by writing. And yet as Cavarero indicates, in his later writings Derrida ironically acknowledges the fundamental role of the eye in the construction of a metaphysics of presence. This leads Cavarero to conclude that in Derrida's theory we find the traces of a logocentric videocentrism that contradicts his earlier ardent critique of phonocentrism.[118] Regardless, his earlier theories on the suspicious auditory nature of speaking as presence seem to have carried the most philosophical weight in the scholarship that followed. Derrida's postmodern philosophical project of deconstruction solidifies in many ways the historical value placed on the visual over the auditory throughout Western thought. It elevates the text over the auditory activity of speaking.[119] As Farrell concludes about Derrida's project, "Derrida uses the term *ecriture* (writing) to make sweeping claims about spoken words, even though spoken words cannot be seen, as writing can be, he stands in the visualist tradition of philosophic thought exemplified by Plato and Aristotle."[120]

We see evidence of Derrida's residual influence on the matter of the temporality of voice and its apparent opposition to writing as spatiality in philosopher and feminist scholar Judith Butler's work. As Annette Schlichter contends, Butler (particularly in *Gender Trouble*[121]) relies too heavily on Derrida and his critique of phonocentrism to outline her theory of gender performativity. She insists that Butler's "theory of gender performativity and the consecutive deliberations about the matter of bodies do not account for voice as sound. . . . Not only does Butler miss out on theorizing the voice, she eventually presents us with voiceless bodies."[122] Schlichter's rather harsh critique of Butler rests on what she sees as a tendency in her work to emphasize the body and corporeality within a logic of the visual and not the auditory or vocal. This is ironic given that Butler professes to be engaging and highlighting the *materiality* of existence as a semiotic and phenomenological project.[123] Schlichter even goes so far as to claim that Butler exhibits "a form of phonophobia that emerges from her specific situatedness as a feminist philosopher engaged in deconstruction."[124] According to Schlichter, in "*Gender Trouble* [Butler] develops a critique of feminist phonocentrism (even if Butler herself does not use the term), from which the theory of gender performativity emerges, and it inherits some of the problems of Derrida's reading of the treatment of the sonic."[125]

Above all, and echoing Derrida's attempts to do away with essential origins and presence, Butler contends that nothing pre-exists prior to representation. Yet, as we will see, Cavarero, Dolar, and Schlichter all agree that "vocality cannot be fully contained within the economy of language or the symbolic. Rather, voice functions as a medium of intelligible speech but as material object also transgresses its boundaries"[126] as an ineffability. Although Derrida critiques the Saussurean theory of semiotics for its supposed essentialist orientation as previously described, Alexander Weheliye believes Derrida upholds its major essentialist premises just the same. As Weheliye stipulates, Derrida elevates "the linguistic as the *prima facie* spot from which to think and imagine all vocal utterances."[127] Of course, Derrida's work greatly influences academic scholarship and the important linguistic turn within a number of disciplines. This is understandable given his clear pronouncement that "there is nothing outside of the text."[128] This philosophical turn bent on interrogating the power and function of language and discourse primarily from within a spatial or textual frame of reference is itself ironic. For we must remember, as Ong suggests, that the term linguistics was "formed by reference to the Latin *lingua*, [meaning] tongue, with the explicit suggestion of sound."[129] As we will see, even though the discipline of linguistics originates in pursuit of the *phone* through the study of the phoneme (and here Roman Jakobson's work comes readily to mind), linguistics does not pay much attention to the sonorous voice of excess just the same. The slow but steady murder of the *phone* continues.

## THE MURDER OF THE *PHONE*

So far, I have explicated a number of murder weapons or ideologies when it comes to our understanding of human relationality, particularly in terms of silencing the sonorous voice in speaking and listening. This silencing is due in part to the hierarchal placement of sight over sound throughout Western history. As Ihde indicates, this hierarchy does not specify "so much in a purposeful reduction of experience to the visual as in the glory of vision that already lay at the center of the Greek experience of reality."[130] Noting Greek scholar Theodor Thass-Thienemann, Ihde admits that "The Greek thinking was conceived in the world of light, in the Apollonian visual world."[131] Dionysus, as the dark and unpredictable deity of sound and festival, becomes easily suspect under such a theoretical rubric. The rift between sight and sound was permanently forged when Aristotle said, "Above all we value sight . . . because sight is the principle source of knowledge and reveals many differences between one object and another."[132] This idea lays the groundwork for defining vision most directly as the objective sense and gives rise to its continued dominance well into the Enlightenment and beyond. To be objective means to distance oneself so as to get a clearer picture of the matters at hand.

Thus, Western philosophy becomes increasingly deaf to the importance of sound and voice as it orients almost exclusively to sight in its worldview (pun intended), neglecting the sonorous qualities of the voice for their inherent value in discourse and action. As we have seen, Plato's suspicion of sound and music does not help. Derrida's interpretations of the ancients, in particular Plato, only exacerbates the neglect. Contextualizing his phonocentric critique as a counter to Plato's critique of writing, Derrida announces a philosophical problem that must be reckoned with. Advancing his project of deconstruction through grammatology, Derrida pounds another nail in the coffin of the sonorous voice, that is, the "bones, flesh, and blood"[133] of the voice, as a salient aspect of our corporeality. As Dolar theorizes it, however, the final nail in the coffin of the sonorous voice is driven in by the discipline of linguistics and, in particular, the new science of phonology as it appeared on the scene. A closer look is in order.

According to Dolar, linguistics and particularly the semiology of Saussure had a lot to do with the further devaluing of the voice. In order to initiate a new science of language (as the semiology of Saussure was meant to do), the voice as an originary source of discourse has to be reckoned with as an integral element. Saussure solves the problem of the voice by effacing its apparent positivity as a signifier, since his semiology dictates that there are no positive units of discourse within a given semiotic system. The voice as signifier can only be fixed within the web of semiotic differences or differential oppositions.[134] This means that the materiality of the voice and its particular qualities have to become irrelevant in order to accomplish signification. Dolar explains this theoretical shift rather clearly, saying that

> if we are to take seriously the negative nature of the linguistic sign, its purely differential and oppositive value, then the voice—as the supposedly natural soil of speech, its seemingly positive substance—has to be put into question. It has to be carefully discarded as the source of an imaginary blinding that has hitherto prevented linguistics from discovering the structural determinations which enable the tricky transubstantiation of voices into linguistic signs. The voice is the impeding element that we have to be rid of in order to initiate a new science of language.[135]

This new science of language must leave behind the discipline known as "traditional phonetics," focused as it was on studying the sounds of language, including their production and physiological properties.[136] In its place, according to Dolar, the new linguistics discovered the *phoneme*, the "fleshless and boneless entity defined purely by its function—the silent sound, the soundless voice."[137] This new linguistics known as phonology does not pursue questions about sound productions; these questions are considered obsolete. Instead, the focus is on differential oppositions of phonemes and their relational natures, what Roman Jakobson describes as distinctive features.[138] Sounds of speaking thus become isolated and become accordingly "just senseless quasi-algebraic elements in a formal matrix of combinations."[139] This is a rather scathing assessment of phonology by Dolar when it comes to the sonorous voice. Although the rendition of semiology provided by Saussure was significantly enhanced, critiqued, and refined by Jakobson, it nevertheless provided a cornerstone in the development of structural linguistics.

Dolar concludes that relegating sound to its structural parameters within a given signifying system results in the *phone*'s murder. He stipulates that

> having dismantled the sounds into mere bundles of differential oppositions, phonology could then also account for the surplus that is necessarily added to purely phonemic distinctive features—the prosody, the intonation and the accent..... Bones, flesh, and blood of the voice were diluted without remainder into a web of structural traits, a checklist of presences and absences. The inaugural gesture of phonology was thus the total reduction of the voice as the substance of language. Phonology, true to its apocryphal etymology, was after killing the voice—its name is, of course, derived from the Greek *phone*, voice, but in it one can also quite appropriately hear *phonos*, murder. Phonology stabs the voice with the signifying dagger; it does away with its living presence, with its flesh and blood.[140]

Accordingly, in such a signifying matrix the voice is seen as only a vehicle of meaning and as a "vanishing mediator,"[141] between structural elements in a given signifying system; it disappears in its service to meaning. Dolar concludes that there is no linguistics to the voice per se, only phonology. In her treatment of the voice, Cavarero's ideas resonate with Dolar's when she specifies quite succinctly that

> the voice thus gets thematized as the voice in general, a sonorous emission that neglects the vocal uniqueness of the one who emits it. In this way, the voice in general turns into the phonetic component of language as a system of signification. In this semantic and depersonalized form, the voice becomes the specific object of a discipline that—while it takes the modern name *linguistics*—actually goes back at least as far as Plato's *Cratylus*.[142]

It is the voice of excess of signification as articulated by Lacan that Dolar is pursuing as he tries to re-invigorate our understanding of the sonorous voice. This is the audible object voice or the voice with "side effects" other than linguistic that must be appreciated for the part it plays in our relationality, apart from its codified symbolic entailments. Peirce helps us find this voice within his triadic semiotic theory as a relational element of firstness and secondness. I have more to say about this in chapter 6.

## THE VOICE OF ARTICULATION

The murder of the *phone* leads to an acceptance of the *phone* as only a mediator of linguistic phenomena, that is, as a mediator of meaning through the symbolic. This is what I call the voice of articulation. In its spoken version, it is simply a talking corpse that initiates and accomplishes language and thought. Unfortunately, this conception of the voice pervades our everyday existence, especially as we move deeper into electronic modes of interaction that are heavily text and image based. This is the voice in service to signification, or what is commonly referred to as a para-linguistic phenomenon and yet defined by the linguistic just the same. By accepting this articulation of the voice as the voice par excellence, the voice that exists outside of symbolic meaning is deemed unintelligible and therefore illegitimate. Exterior to the *logos* understood as mere language and thought, this latter aspect of the voice is rendered mute or silent by our pursuit of signification and meaning. Throughout history, we have seen that the alternative voice in excess of signification in its audible form is suspect, given that it represents a lawless or untamed quality to our existence and is aligned with nature and the feminine. The voice of articulation I have so named because in its role as mediator of meaning, its prime duty is pronouncement of ideas constituted within a given system of signification. This voice is thus constrained in many ways (although we do not recognize it), tamed by the symbolic parameters in which it speaks.

It is a fully conventionalized voice, bound to the rules specified by particular contexts of discourse. As such, it is judged by its competency, by performing according to a given set of logical rules dictated by a particular discursive context. The voice of articulation thus strives for a competent performance of language that is often prescribed for it by the context. In its spoken version, its urgent desire is to show competence in its originary association with skills that improve diction, pronunciation, and so forth. This is the voice that was championed by the elocutionary movement and its derivatives. So, the voice of articulation is a voice bent on competent linguisticality within the symbolic world of discourse and action. As a result, its discursive freedom is constrained. If we interpret competency as an achievement of our discursive goals, then Peirce's sense of articulation as translation lends insight here. As Vincent Colapietro explains, "translation [is] one of Peirce's tropes for the process of articulation."[143] Peirce recognizes the necessary flow of thought in the direction of incessant new and higher levels of translations or abstractions. And yet, as Colapietro indicates, thought's translation or articulation may be necessary but "is not sufficient. For . . . [in] ascending to levels of generality [thought] seems to be floating in a limitless vacuity," as described by Peirce.[144] In other words, the more competent we become using the voice of articulation the more general and abstract our ideas also become.

The voice of articulation is the voice that speaks and responds most often in our daily lives, especially when we take the sonorous qualities of the voice for granted or overlook them altogether. This is also the voice, in its acousmatic rendition, that often echoes throughout cyberspace and on the Internet. Ultimately, it is the voice in service to signification and the symbolic order of things. One thing the voice of articulation does not possibilize is a sense of wonder or an appreciation for the mystery and positive ambiguity of life pronounced quite readily by its sonorous counterpart as excess. In this sense, appealing only to the voice of articulation contributes to our experience of existential dissonance and disenchantment. This is because the voice of articulation that we listen to orients us toward a depersonalization of experience as Ong describes it. As Farrell elaborates,

> When Ong refers to the depersonalization of the word, he is referring to situations in which we no longer advert to a person or are aware that someone is speaking—we do not advert to the person behind the word, so to speak, the human voice from which such an utterance might come, because the written or printed texts with words seem to detach them from a person.[145]

This voice of articulation is the voice whose auditory sense of fullness has been muted in favor of intelligibility. This is the voice celebrated by Aristotle as the *phone semantike*, the signifying voice that illustrates Aristotle's animal rationale. Thus, its enchanting effects when they do materialize are inauthentic, as I described. The voice of articulation promotes inauthentic enchantments.

In regard to how this voice functions within the immediacy of relations, I turn to communication theory and particularly to Gregory Bateson and his Palo Alto colleagues. Western thought thrives on binary oppositions, and when it comes to our understanding of the actual messages we share with one another, we find few exceptions to this rule. As Bateson and his colleagues affirmed in the 1960s when they were working on the communicative dimensions of schizophrenic experience, every message we send and receive has two essential components: the content dimension and the relational dimension.[146] The content of what we say is, of course, the informational aspects of a given message. Information is the result of linguistic codification. This aspect of a given message is thought to be the most important by the typical interlocutor. It's "what you say to me as content" that supposedly counts in the construction of meaning. The content of what we say to one another is news of difference, Bateson suggests this difference makes a difference in our subsequent expressions and perceptions of the world. News of difference is coded information, particular to a given cultural context. Information acquisition is correlated with uncertainty reduction, and, as we have seen in previous discussions, such a reduction becomes an all-consuming goal in today's electronic climate. I submit that this content element of a message is not possible without the voice of articulation, whether in its written or oral form. It is the voice that is the vehicle of information—information shared in linguistic form—either written or spoken. The voice of articulation is thus the vehicle for our statements and their string of signifiers.[147]

Unfortunately, the voice of articulation can quickly digress into mere *babble* (especially in cyberspace and on the Internet) as the act of voicing itself overrides the content of what is shared or the sharing of content overrides relationality. In Merleau-Ponty's treatment of the psychological development of language in the child, he discusses the vocal practice of babbling by the infant. He argues that infants seem to imitate the "gutterals [or sounds] which cannot be seen on the lips of the person speaking. If there is any influence from the environment, it is hearing and not vision that evokes the imitation."[148] Thus, the more we hear the acousmatic voice and the voice of articulation in cyberspace, the more we may try to imitate it and produce mere babble. Merleau-Ponty goes on to claim that "even before speaking, the child appropriates the rhythm and stress [*accentuation*] of his own language."[149] Applying this to the voices of cyberspace, we hear how powerful these voices are in shaping our own modes of discourse. The significance of Merleau-Ponty's insights rests with the notion that babbling for infants is a repetitive vocal practice that is entirely meaningless. It signals a desire to participate in vocality and yet does not contribute to a more nuanced co-constitution of meaning between participants. Highly mediated voices thus create a reverberation in the enclosed space of cyber which "obliterates foreground and background—all sound, all thought, blends into noise. [In such circumstances] it is impossible for a voice to have resonance in this space, and without resonance, the voice has no meaning—no rhythm, no tone, no sense," according to Frances Dyson.[150]

When it comes to this babbling in the space of cyber, the voice of articulation can display such meaningless vocality. The voice may easily articulate mere soliloquies of expression derived from an egocentric position in the world. Or we may share information or content for its own sake because of the value we place in knowing we are contributors to the signifying matrix—to the supposed conversation. In severe cases of appealing to only the voice of articulation within cyberspace, paradoxically we can actually regress toward the infantile (*in-fans*, the one who can't speak). By constantly surfing the Internet and participating in cyberspace, we can simply become creatures much like infants who, in their solipsistic world of babbling, become motivated by the desire to participate in the communicative matrix.[151] Even though our babbling may not be directed toward a definite interlocutor and may not always make sense in the logical world, our discourse is still caught within a structure of address and therefore caught within redundant discursive practices.[152] Heidegger, of course, refers to this form of discourse as idle talk or *gerede,* although he concedes that in its everydayness it is a necessary function of discursive practices.[153] However, some critics would go so far as to argue that this tendency toward our solipsistic babbling with its focus only on the content dimension of messages (exacerbated by cyberspace and the Internet) contributes to the increasing infantilization of the postmodern adult, producing an infantilist ethos. As described, this ethos is one of "induced childishness: an infantilization that is closely tied to the demands of consumer capitalism in a global market economy."[154] It appears that our media-frenzied environment with its consumerist orientation merely exacerbates this regrettable tendency of discourse.

The second component of a message is said to be the relational component. The relational dimension of a message is that aspect that holds clues about the relationality of the interlocutors, the status they hold in relation to one another. While the content aspect is theorized as primarily verbal (defined in our contemporary lexicon as linguistic), the relational dimensions are considered non-verbal or non-linguistic, that is, outside the bounds of language. This also includes the para-linguistic, considered as aspects of the sonorous voice or oral. The relational dimension is thus how something is said rather than what is said. Research in communication has repeatedly found that it is the relational dimension of a message that carries the most weight when it comes to discussants arriving at meaning, not necessarily the content. Interlocutors seem to pay more attention (although mostly unwittingly) to how something is said (whether it is written or spoken) than what is said. Ironically, this is the element of a message that is most compromised in our electronic forms of connectivity, given that non-verbal cues (both visual and auditory) are mostly absent. If we wanted to make de-codification complex by eliminating or severely diminishing the relational elements of messages, we seem to have succeeded with our use of electronic forms of information exchange.

Even though the relational elements most assuredly take account of the orality of voice in immediate ear-to-ear encounters, we still find that the relational elements of voice are primarily thought of in terms of their service to meaning. As Dolar contends, even the typical aspects of the voice known as accent and intonation (those aspects we often characterize as para-linguistic) can be understood by way of codification. Regrettably, in the discipline of communication, these traditional ways of thinking about the binary aspect of messages primarily uphold a view of the voice in its limited capacity—as only articulation. Far too often, even the voice of excess heard within the relational elements of a given message is ultimately co-opted in service to meaning.

In our consideration of the voice, we find that the traditional designations of content and relational elements of a message, while heuristic in many respects, severely limit the full appreciation of the voice as a phenomenological and semiotic medium as I am advancing it. Content and relational seem to function in opposition, with the content portion accentuating intelligibility as the symbolic, while the relational can be correlated with making distinctions and differences as sense experience. I insist that insight is to be gained by interpreting message production as a triadic endeavor of semiosis. Appealing to the triadic structure of a sign advanced by Peirce, we can see how our conception of messages needs to be theoretically re-configured. This requires a more nuanced interpretation of message components and how they function as sign actions.

This theoretical move thus necessitates an important extension of the work of Bateson and his Palo Alto colleagues. Instead of characterizing messages in terms of their content and relational components only, we must add a third component. As we discover, between the voice as a vehicle of meaning (as a thirdness) and the voice appreciated for its relational components (as a secondness), we must additionally hear the aesthetic voice as excess of symbolicity—the voice in excess of mere articulation. This is the voice that functions at the level of Peirce's category of firstness as distinct *qualia* of sensory experience and is aesthetically *sensed* as a sign relation of secondness. As we shall see in the chapters that follow, this theoretical move also aligns with Merleau-Ponty's and Peirce's triadic conception of the aesthetic *logos* and Foucault's understanding of the nameless voice.

Above all, the voice as articulation is speaking/listening where their enactment is over-determined by a signifying system or code system. Hence, the voice of articulation is the voice of discourse and does not possibilize a discourse of the voice. The articulating voice is most often merely a gesture of *parole parlée* (speech spoken), which comes in both written and spoken forms. Because of this quality, the voice of articulation diminishes our relationality, producing a flattened experience. This is due in part to the fact that the sensory richness of the auditory is not fully appreciated. In its pursuit of redundancy (indicative of babbling or idle talk), this voice ignores the qualities of uniqueness and individuality. Thus, our sensible world takes on the figurative meaning of the word *flat*, that is, wanting in spirit.[155] The voice of articulation most certainly can enchant, but it calls us to listen and respond in highly codified and prescribed ways. It deludes rather than delights, given that its enchanting qualities are derived from codes of discourse that are not our own. In this sense, this voice articulates fictions, and our enchantments with it produce inauthentic modes of relating. As a result, speaking with and listening to the voice of articulation affords relationality only a superficial quality and thereby exacerbates our techno-social dilemma outlined earlier.

To listen to this voice only results in not fully *sensing* the other, reducing the impact the auditory nature of being requires.[156] In this sense, the symbolic is truly standing in the place of the full semiotic function of signs. The result is that we are too often deceived by the power of language that it promotes. This is because "symbols are by definition ontological lies, mispresentations, because symbols are precisely re-presentations and not sign presentations."[157] Given the predominance of this voice within the space of cyber and the Internet, its qualities and the impact it carries are disconcerting. This is a dangerous acoustic space to occupy as a listening subject.

## The Voiceless Name

Michel Foucault's conceptualization of the *voiceless name* adds insight as we seek to understand the nature and scope of the voice of articulation. These ideas are expressed by Foucault in a small volume entitled *La Pensée du Dehors* (The Thought from Outside).[158] As Lanigan describes it, Foucault's concept of the voiceless name serves to exemplify the Law of Representation and articulates the very problematic of language.[159] In other words, when we speak with the voice of articulation, the naming of experience within signifying practices takes precedence over the actual auditory event of speaking (which Foucault identifies as the Law of Communication). The Law of Representation articulates the problematic of language because it calls our attention to the ways in which language uses us. When we unreflectively operate according to the Law of Representation, it rules our conscious experience in profound ways.

Given what I have outlined in preceding chapters, it appears that this Law of Representation is fully functional in cyberspace and on the Internet. When operating according to the Law of Representation, we naturally assume that language and other symbolic mechanisms of communication merely function positively to reference pre-existent socio-cultural meanings. As a result, our ritualized behaviors in cyberspace and on the Internet are not questioned for their functionality, even though these habits of discourse often relegate us to an unknown status as a "deictic ghost."[160] In other words, we only speak the *langue* of our culture and thereby lose some of our agential qualities as human beings; we speak, in a sense, in an existential vacuum with a voice that is not our own. In the process, as auditory speakers, we become mere "disguised objects"[161] of discourse rather than subjects exercising a full sense of existential agency and volition. Under such conditions, we risk becoming transformed into objectified things. On Foucault's rendering of the Law of Representation Lanigan stipulates,

> The person [under the Law of Representation] is reified as the object of study in the positive regard of the neo-modern social sciences . . . so in the social sciences "individuals" become anonymous analytic objects to which the practice of discourse points but which we do not and cannot understand in our lived-world of existential choice and practice.[162]

Under the Law of Representation, individual personalities are eclipsed by the representational status of the word or *logos*—by our own acts of objectively naming the things in the world we encounter. This seriously threatens our evolving sense of self and our very humanity. Our subjectivities are easily co-opted by the inter-subjective nature of daily life. Operating only under the Law of Representation constitutes self and other as the same voice in language.[163] As a result, we experience a monotony of being self as cultural sameness, that is, the potential vitality of the individual subject becomes subsumed by the authorial name or culturally defined *logos*. In such cases, symbolic markers dominate our existence. We find ourselves unwittingly participating "within the cultural flow of accommodation,"[164] as we seek instrumental gains within symbolic deductive and reductive views of person and culture. This is Heidegger's concern that articulating such habitual, highly codified behaviors would turn us merely into a *they-self*. This is Ong's concern that by approaching speaking as merely an act of *logos*, we become de-personalized beings, distant from the existential rootedness of our very being. This is Foucault's concern that we can easily become voiceless names in the process of abiding by the Law of Representation.

Foucault admonishes that when we become voiceless names, we lose our agential voice and our symbolic expressions are heavily shaped by the mere act of naming or representing our experiences. We continue to speak, obviously, but we become voiceless—our voices are disembodied. Foucault was quick to always indicate that once language "names," actual discourse ends.[165] It is the appreciation of discourse that drives his pursuits. Once we become locked psychologically into the codified world of the symbolic, our chances of semiotically co-constituting originary and meaningful discourse with another are diminished. Assuming this is true, we must question how much actual discourse transpires in cyberspace and on the Internet these days, given the redundancy of the voices of articulation. Or is it best to see our interactions within them as propagating only language games, in which we celebrate our functionality as language users and supposed knowledge producers? Foucault's famous aphorism, "I lie/I speak" is meant to highlight how only following the Law of Representation ("I lie") results in articulating a subject signified, one that cannot actually "speak" in any originary way. The Law of Representation and the voice that articulates it thus deludes conscious experience, given that this voice is grounded in deception, a deception that exists at the very heart of the process of re-presentation itself.[166]

Even though the voice of articulation upholds the Law of Representation, it is important to acknowledge that this voice is an integral aspect of our discursive selves. As Foucault conceives it, *parole parlée* (speech spoken—"I lie") is the reflexive counterpart to *parole parlante* (speaking speech—"I speak") in which the tropic logic of discourse unfolds. Dolar agrees about the important role the voice of articulation serves when he claims that this aspect of the voice, while properly pacified and tamed, is necessary to complement the letter or *logos*.[167] The voice that I am pursuing alongside Dolar and Cavarero resembles, therefore, the sounding voice of *parole parlante* ("I speak") that is too often covered up by "articulated speech."[168] Even as I pursue this alternative function of the voice, I am reminded that "articulation in itself is not necessarily a violent, disfiguring, impoverishing, or in some other way untoward response to being."[169] The voice that articulates is a necessary function in human experience, given that all sensory experience is mediated through language or the symbolic. My point is that our quest for meaning that the voice of articulation enables often over-rides fully acknowledging "our more arresting and disruptive experiences, the ones most insistently driving toward expression"[170] that have yet to be articulated. These kinds of vocal experiences, what Foucault calls *énoncé*,[171] most certainly fit the category of enchantments. They will prove in the end to be highly beneficial when it comes to co-constituting a healthy sense of relationality. As Foucault's work insightfully confirms, we exist as speaking subjects/subjects of speech at the very interstices of the tropic logic that plays out as "I lie/I speak."

Following Dolar, Cavarero, and Foucault on the issue of voice, I find that it is the timbre of the voice (Barthes's grain) that initially helps in formulating an alternative to the voice of articulation. I identify this alternative as the voice of enunciation, in part to acknowledge Foucault's identification of *énoncé* as speaking speech. It is the inarticulate voice, if you will, framed in apposition to the voice of articulation just described. Ong also helps in this regard by offering a recuperative moment concerning the "presence of the word" as spoken. He seeks not to uphold a metaphysic of presence as it is typically conceived but aims to re-enchant our understanding of the speaking voice. He emphasizes the salient qualities of the sonorous voice that "calls up a person" in the inter-mediate presence of the other as a possibility of genuine or authentic dialogue.[172] I follow Dolar's suggestion: As we struggle to hear an alternative voice, "we have to make our way in the opposite direction, as it were: to make a descent from the height of meaning back to what appeared to be mere means; to catch the voice as a blind spot of making sense, or as a cast-off of sense."[173] If we accept the premise that a healthier relationality depends equally upon the speaking voice as well as the voice of language, as I am suggesting, then we must accept that it is the voice that enacts our very being at the axis of the personal and the social.[174] Our beginning discussion on this alternative auditory understanding of voice is addressed in the next chapter.

## NOTES

1. This phrase comes from Dolar, *A Voice and Nothing More*, 19.

2. While Dolar does not label these two voices in the manner I do, my labels are primarily derived from his discussions in which he seeks to distinguish between a voice in service to meaning and "a voice and nothing more." My designation of enunciation is also drawn from French theorists such as Michel Foucault, Maurice Merleau-Ponty, and Julia Kristeva. Their writings emphasize the important reflexive relationship between speech spoken (*parole parlée*) and speaking speech (*parole parlante*). The latter comes closest to aligning with my designation of the voice of enunciation and the former with what I am calling the voice of articulation. The word *énoncé* in French (from which enunciation is derived) means "to state or express, i.e., to utter." The sense in which I am using enunciation also is specified in the works of Husserl and Benveniste, according to Kristeva. For an explication of these terms, I refer my readers to Julia Kristeva, *Revolution in Poetic Language*, trans. Margaret Waller (New York: Columbia University Press, 1984); Lanigan, *The Human Science of Communicology*.

3. Dolar, *A Voice and Nothing More*, back cover.

4. Classen, *Worlds of Sense*.

5. Cavarero, *For More Than One Voice*, 33.

6. Jacques Derrida, *Of Grammatology*, trans. Gayatri Spivak (Baltimore: Johns Hopkins University Press, [1967] 1976), 158.

7. See Marshall McLuhan, *The Gutenberg Galaxy: The Making of Typographic Man* (Toronto: University of Toronto Press, 1962).

8. I venture that the meaning of this literacy is altogether different than the one inaugurated by writing and print. We now talk about *media literacy* and with it the deterioration of language use in all its original elements: semantics, grammar, and pragmatics. Everyday language use and competency appears to be waning as the drive for new media competencies are on the rise.

9. Classen, *Worlds of Sense*, 6.

10. Classen is quick to note that through recent scientific developments, the traditional assumption that there are only five senses is being challenged. As she explains, "touch has been broken down into a multitude of specialized senses including kinaesthesia—the sense of movement—perception of temperature and perception of pain." See Classen, *Worlds of Sense*, 5.

11. As Classen explains, Aristotle "condensed different sensations of temperature, hardness, and wetness into one sense of touch" and ordered the five senses with sight, hearing, taste, and touch constituting the basic four, with smell placed "in the middle, linking sight and hearing with taste and touch." See Classen, *Worlds of Sense*, 2.

12. Ibid., 3.
13. Ibid., 2.
14. Ibid., 4; italics in original.
15. Ibid., 4.
16. Ibid., 4.
17. Ibid., 27.
18. Ibid., 27–28.
19. Ibid., 3.

20. The elevation of sight over sound persists even though more contemporary research indicates that "hearing is often the last mode of perception to shut down in the process of death." This would indicate that hearing may be more primary than sight. See Alexa Hagerty, "Speak Softly to the Dead: The Uses of Enchantment in American Home Funerals," *Social Anthropology* 22, no. 4 (2014).

21. Classen, *Worlds of Sense*, 5.
22. Ibid., 5.
23. Ibid., 5.
24. Ong, *The Presence of the Word*, 66.
25. Classen, *Worlds of Sense*, 5–6.
26. Ibid., 136.
27. Ihde, *Listening and Voice*, 14.
28. Friedrich Nietzsche, *The Birth of Tragedy*, ed. Michael Tanner, trans. Shaun Whiteside (London: Penguin Books, [1886] 1993), 76.
29. Gordon Graham, *The Re-Enchantment of the World: Art Versus Religion* (Cambridge: Oxford University Press, 2007), 106.

30. Dolar, *A Voice and Nothing More*, 43.
31. Ibid., 43.
32. Ibid., 43.
33. Caverero, *For More Than One Voice*, 106.
34. It is interesting to note that Peirce's rendition of the play of musement appreciates, perhaps unwittingly, the combinatory logic of masculine thinking and feminine voicing. As I reviewed in chapter 3, Peirce does associate tone with firstness (along with its visual counterpart, tint).
35. Plato, *Republic IV* 424c-3.
36. Plato, *Republic III* 398d, 400d.
37. Dolar, *A Voice and Nothing More*, 45.
38. Ibid., 46.
39. Ong, *Presence of the Word*, 10.
40. Ibid., 22.
41. Ibid., 30.
42. Jean-Luc Nancy, *Listening*, trans. Charlotte Mandell (New York: Fordham University Press, 2007), 2.
43. Ong, *Presence of the Word*, 33.
44. In one of his few references to the auditory, Peirce refers to the distinction between the visual as spatial and the auditory as time in his discussion on the algebraic formulation of any sign. See Peirce, *The Collected Papers*, 2.418.
45. Ong, *Presence of the Word*, 41.
46. Ibid., 111.
47. Nancy, *Listening*, 8.
48. Ong, *Presence of the Word*, 41–42.
49. Julian F. Henriques, "Sonic Dominance and the Reggae Sound System Session," in *The Auditory Culture Reader*, eds. Michael Bull and Les Back (New York: Berg, 2003), 453.
50. John Shepherd, *Music as Social Text* (Cambridge: Polity, 1991), 20.
51. Ong, *Presence of the Word*, 74.
52. Reid B. Locklin, "Sacred Orality, Sacred Dialogue: Walter J. Ong and the Practice of Hindu-Christian Studies," *Journal of Hindu-Christian Studies* 26 (2013), 83.
53. Classen, *Worlds of Sense*, 70.
54. Murray Schafer, "Open Ears," in *The Auditory Culture Reader*, eds. Michael Bull and Les Back (New York: Berg, 2003), 25.
55. Nancy, *Listening*, 14.
56. Henriques, "Sonic Dominance," 461.
57. Lenore Langsdorf, "The Primacy of Listening: Toward a Metaphysics of Communicative Interaction," in *Postphenomenology: A Critical Companion to Ihde,* ed. Evan Selinger (Albany: State University of New York Press, 2006), 41.
58. Ihde, *Listening and Voice*, 153.
59. As Graham Furness notes in his book, *Orality: The Power of the Spoken Word,* the dichotomy of sight and sound can be misleading because our senses collaborate in the constitution of our overall sense experience in the world. While that perceptual process is definitely true as a phenomenology, socio-cultural preferences for one sense over the other is proven repeatedly in the anthropological literature and supported by Ong's interrogations. On this, see Furness, *Orality: The Power of the Spoken Word* (New York: Palgrave Macmillian, 2004).
60. Classen, *Worlds of Sense*, 1.
61. Paul A. Kottman, translator's introduction to *For More Than One Voice: Toward a Philosophy of Vocal Expression*, by Adriana Cavarero, trans. Paul A. Kottman (Stanford: Stanford University Press, 2005), xxii.
62. Here Cavarero is referring to Aristotle's definition of the *logos* as *phone semantike*. At least, Cavarero contends, Aristotle understands *logos* as speech. This is in contrast to Plato's use of the word, which for him means thinking. For more on this distinction see Cavarero, *For More Than One Voice*, 183, 42.
63. Ibid., xxiii.
64. Ibid., 42.

65. Ibid., 6.
66. Italo Calvino, *Under the Jaguar Sun*, trans. William Weaver (New York: Harcourt Brace, 1988), 33–64, quoted in Cavarero, *For More Than One Voice*, 3.
67. JR Thorpe of *Bustle* magazine offers a short but interesting summary on the suspicion of women's voices throughout history. One example from ancient Greece is the role women played at funerals. They weren't allowed to talk but were hired to sing the *naeniae*—the funeral songs. Thorpe notes that from the sixth century BC on, however, laws were passed to restrict women's mourning rituals and singing because they were deemed too powerful in their control of honoring the dead. See JR Thorpe, "7 Bizarre Historical Beliefs About Women's Voices," *Bustle*, October 27, 2016, https://bustle.com/articles/191686-7-bizarre-historical-beliefs-about-women's-voices.
68. Cavarero, *For More Than One Voice*, 6.
69. Ibid., 7.
70. In making this claim, Cavarero is aware of disciplines that study orality that honor the qualities of the speaking voice on which she is focused. She cites oral poetry within the discipline of literature as a good case in point.
71. Dolar, *A Voice and Nothing More*, 11.
72. Lacan's understanding of signification is extended and developed by Julia Kristeva. Lacan's signification is understood primarily from the perspective of the symbolic. Kristeva distinguishes between the semiotic and the symbolic. For Kristeva, the semiotic is the action of signs (viewed as feminine), whereas the symbolic is associated with the law, the father (masculine). For more, see Kristeva, *Revolution in Poetic Language*.
73. Dolar, *A Voice and Nothing More*, 4.
74. Cavarero, *For More Than One Voice*, 11.
75. Dolar, *A Voice and Nothing More*, 13.
76. Roland Barthes (in collaboration with Roland Havas), "Ascolto," in *Enciclopedia Einaudi* (Turn: Einaudi, 1977), 1:247 quoted in Cavarero, *For More Than One Voice*, 15.
77. Filmer, "Songtime: Sound Culture, Rhythm and Sociality," in *The Auditory Culture Reader*, edited by Michael Bull and Les Back (New York: Berg, 2003), 98.
78. Cavarero, *For More Than One Voice*, 15.
79. Dolar, *A Voice and Nothing More*, 22.
80. Cavarero, *For More Than One Voice*, 16.
81. Lannamann, "The Politics of Voice," 114–31.
82. John Durham Peters, "The Voice and Modern Media," in *Kunst-Stimmen*, eds. Doris Kolesch and Jenny Schrödl (Berlin: Theater der Zeit, 2004), 21.
83. Thiebaud, "Effects of Technology," 117.
84. Deborah Eicher-Catt, "Recovering the Voice of Embodied Dialogue: Edward Sapir's Contribution to Communicology," *International Journal of Communication* 20, no 1–2 (2010).
85. As I address later on in this discussion, we do find many references in the literature to the non-verbal/oral dimension of messages, what we call the paralinguistic aspect of messages that focus our attention on vocal tone, inflections, accent, and the like. The non-verbal aspect of the voice is explored within other disciplines than just communication such as the natural sciences, social psychology, and theater studies. However, in most all of these cases the voice is discussed in relation to its primary role in service to meaning and not the enhancement of relationality per se as an auditory phenomenon. For examples, see: Maniui Tiwari and Maneesha Tiwari, "Voice—How Humans Communicate?" *Journal of Natural Science, Biology, and Medicine* 3, no. 1 (2012); Mark G. Frank, Darrin J. Griffin, Elena Svetieva, and Andreas Maroulis, "Nonverbal Elements of the Voice," in *The Social Psychology of Nonverbal Communication*, eds. Aleksandra Kostic and David Chadee (London: Palgrave Macmillan, 2015); Andrew McComb Kimbrough, "The Sound of Meaning: Theories of Voice in Twentieth century Thought and Performance." Dissertation, Louisiana State University, 2002.
86. Ihde, *Listening and Voice*.
87. Paul Zumthor, *Oral Poetry: An Introduction*, trans. Kathryn Murphy-Judy (Minneapolis: University of Minnesota Press, 1990), 44.
88. Cavarero, *For More Than One Voice*, 12.
89. Ibid., 8.

90. Ibid., 9.

91. Walter Ong, "Grammar Today: 'Structure' in a Vocal World," *Quarterly Journal of Speech* 43, no. 4 (1957): 401. As Ong notes, the term *grammar* comes from the same stem as the Greek word *graphein*, which means to write.

92. Ong, "Grammar Today."

93. Jonathan Sterne, "The Theology of Sound: A Critique of Orality," *Canadian Journal of Communication* 36 (2011): 222.

94. Stephen A. Tyler, "The Vision Quest in the West, or What the Mind's Eye Sees," *Journal of Anthropological Research* 40, no. 1 (Spring 1984): 26.

95. Cavarero, *For More Than One Voice*, 9.

96. Ibid., 33.

97. Admittedly, in his critique of phonocentrism, Derrida acknowledges the importance of the etymological heritage of the words *logos* and *verbal*, as explained above. However, since the linguistic turn in philosophy, both words are typically associated solely with language as writing and speaking and not with speaking as a sonorous activity per se.

98. Walter Ong, review of *Saving the Text: Literature/Derrida/Philosophy*, by Geoffrey H. Hartman, *Philosophy and Rhetoric* 15, no. 4 (October 1982): 277.

99. Cavarero, *For More Than One Voice*, 215.

100. Jacques Derrida, *Speech and Phenomena*, trans. David B. Allison (Evanston: Northwestern University Press, 1973).

101. Jacques Derrida, *Writing and Difference*, trans. Alan Bass (Chicago: University of Chicago Press, 1967).

102. Derrida, *Of Grammatology*.

103. Cavarero, *For More Than One Voice*, 216.

104. Derrida, *Speech and Phenomena*, 62–63.

105. Cavarero, *For More Than One Voice*, 217.

106. These ideas are explicated by Derrida in *Of Grammatology*, 27–73.

107. Cavarero, *For More Than One Voice*, 213.

108. Ibid., 218.

109. Thomas J. Farrell, preface to the 2000 paperback edition of *The Presence of the Word: Prolegomena for Cultural and Religious History*, by Walter Ong (Binghamton: Global Publications State University of New York, [1967] 2000), xvii. Ironically, it is the very limitations of language that the sonorous voice announces.

110. Ong, review of *Saving the Text*, 274–77.

111. Cavarero, *For More Than One Voice*, 217.

112. Ibid., 220.

113. Ibid., 224.

114. Farrell, preface to *Presence of the Word*, xviii.

115. Caveraro, *For More Than One Voice*, 222.

116. Annette Schlichter, "Do Voices Matter? Vocality, Materiality, Gender Performativity," *Body and Society* 17, no. 1 (2011): 37.

117. Ibid., 37.

118. Caveraro, *For More Than One Voice*, 222–23.

119. Ong says that in a graphic culture (such as ours), the degradation of sound is a regular byproduct of unreflectively understanding the role of sound or the sonorous voice. Reducing sound to the "fixity of space," as Derrida's grammatology does, underestimates the value of the speaking voice.

120. Farrell, preface to *Presence of the Word*, xx–xxi.

121. Judith Butler, *Gender Trouble: Feminism and the Subversion of Identity* (New York: Routledge, 1990).

122. Schlichter, "Do Voices Matter?," 32.

123. Schlichter admits that Butler's 1997 book *Excitable Speech* "gestures toward the vocal through her insistence on the status of speech as bodily act . . . [but Schlichter contends that] Butler's theory does not manage to capture the voice since her greatest concern remains the body's legibility, which is . . . a form of (logocentric) visualization." See Schlichter, "Do

Voices Matter?," 42. For more on these points, see Judith Butler, *Excitable Speech: A Politics of the Performative* (New York: Routledge, 1997).

124. Schlichter, "Do Voices Matter?," 36.
125. Ibid., 37.
126. Ibid., 39–40.
127. Alexander G. Weheliye, *Phonographies: Grooves in Sonic Afro-Modernity* (Durham: Duke University Press, 2005), 34.
128. Derrida, *Of Grammatology*, 158.
129. Ong, "Grammar Today," 401.
130. Ihde, *Listening and Voice*, 6.
131. Theodor Thass-Thienemann, *Symbolic Behavior* (New York: Washington Square Press, 1968), 147 quoted in Ihde, *Listening and Voice*, 6.
132. Aristotle, *Metaphysics*, trans. John Warrington (London: J. M. Dent and Sons, 1956), 51.
133. This phrase is referenced in Dolar, *A Voice and Nothing More*, 17. Here, Dolar is alluding to a phrase apparently used by Roman Jakobson when discussing its opposite, that is, the soundless voice.
134. Dolar, *A Voice and Nothing More*, 17.
135. Ibid., 17.
136. Roman Jakobson's early work was devoted to phonetics, the study of sounds. See Roman Jakobson, *Six Lectures on Sound and Meaning* (Boston: Institute of Technology Press, 1942).
137. Dolar, *A Voice and Nothing More*, 17.
138. Ibid., 18.
139. Ibid., 18.
140. Ibid., 19.
141. Ibid., 15.
142. Cavarero, *For More Than One Voice*, 9.
143. Colapietro, "A Lantern," 204.
144. Peirce, *The Collected Papers*, 5.595.
145. Farrell, preface to *Presence of the Word*, xix.
146. These aspects of messages are summarized by the Palo Alto group: Paul Watzlawick, Janet Beavin Bavelas, and Don D. Jackson, *Pragmatics of Human Communication: A Study of Interactional Patterns, Pathologies, and Paradoxes* (New York: W. W. Norton & Company, 1967).
147. Dolar, *A Voice and Nothing More*, 23.
148. Maurice Merleau-Ponty, *Consciousness and the Acquisition of Language*, trans. Hugh J. Silverman (Evanston: Northwestern University Press, 1973), 14.
149. Ibid., 15; brackets in original.
150. Frances Dyson, *The Tone of Our Times*, 110.
151. Dolar, *A Voice and Nothing More*, 26.
152. Given this discussion, it is interesting to note that social critics claim that we are currently witnessing an infantalization of our culture. Even famed French anthropologist Claude Levi-Strauss observed back in 1946 an immaturity in American cultural habits and customs. For an interesting read, see Elantseva Marina, "The Infantilization of Western Culture," Accessed August 30, 2019. http://theconversation.com/the-infantilization-of-western-culture-99556
153. Martin Heidegger, *Being and Time*, trans. John Macquarrie and Edward S. Robinson (Oxford: Blackwell, 1962), 167–170.
154. Jacopo Bernardino, "The Role of Marketing in the Infantilization of the Postmodern Adult," *Fast Capitalism*, October 1, 2013, https://www.uta.edu/huma/agger/fastcapitalism/10_1/bernardini10_1.html.
155. See Classen, *Worlds of Sense*, 66.
156. On this point, see Bodie, Graham D. and Nathan Crick, "Listening, Hearing, Sensing: Three Modes of Being and the Phenomenology of Charles Sanders Peirce," *Communication Theory* 24, no. 2 (May 2014).
157. See Richard L. Lanigan, "The Voiceless Name and the Nameless Voice: Foucault's Phenomenology of Discourse," in *The Human Science of Communicology: A Phenomenology*

*of Discourse in Foucault and Merleau-Ponty* (Pittsburgh: Duquesne University Press, 1992), 162.

158. This is according to Lanigan, "Voiceless Name."

159. Ibid.

160. Richard L. Lanigan, "Somebody Is Nowhere: Michel Foucault on Rhetoric and the Discourse of Subjectivity in the Human Sciences," in *The Human Science of Communicology: A Phenomenology of Discourse in Foucault and Merleau-Ponty* (Pittsburgh: Duquesne University Press, 1992), 84.

161. Lanigan, "Somebody Is Nowhere," 83.

162. Ibid., 83.

163. Lanigan, "Voiceless Name," 169.

164. Edward Sapir, *Culture, Language and Personality: Selected Essays* (Berkeley: University of California Press, 1966), 159.

165. Foucault, *The Order of Things*, 118.

166. It is deception in terms of both self and other because, with the Law of Representation, too often we forget that the representational *maps* we use can never thoroughly or directly articulate the territory, a concept we learn from General Semantics. See, Alfred Korzbyski, *Science and Sanity,* fifth edition (Englewood, NJ: Institute of General Semantics, [1933] 1994).

167. Dolar, *A Voice and Nothing More*, 113.

168. Ivan Capeller, "Sounds, Signs and Hearing: Towards a Semiotics of the Audible Field," *Athens Journal of Philology* 5, no. 1 (2018): 18.

169. Vincent Colapietro, "Striving to Speak in a Human Voice: A Peircean Contribution to Metaphysical Discourse," *The Review of Metaphysics* 58, no. 2 (2004): 373–74. In this passage, Colapietro is drawing ideas from John E. Smith, "Being, Immediacy, and Articulation," *The Review of Metaphysics* 24, no. 4 (June 1971), 594.

170. Colapietro, "Striving to Speak," 375.

171. See Richard L. Lanigan, "Foucault's Chinese Encyclopedia: *Le Même et L'Autre*," in *The Human Science of Communicology: A Phenomenology of Discourse in Foucault and Merleau-Ponty* (Pittsburgh: Duquesne University Press, 1992), 145.

172. As Thomas Farrell indicates in his preface to the 2000 paperback edition of *The Presence of the Word,* Ong's use of the term *presence* follows dialogic philosopher Martin Buber's sense of the term and not Martin Heidegger's. For Ong, presence means a calling forth of otherness within dialogic relations in their immediacy of experience. This is the sense of presence that I use throughout this project. See Farrell, preface to *Presence of the Word*, xviii.

173. Dolar, *A Voice and Nothing More*, 16.

174. Ibid., 14.

*Chapter Six*

# The Enchanting *Phone* as Phenomenological Event

*The Voice of Enunciation*

How do we get beyond only speaking with and listening to the voice of articulation, as described in the preceding chapters? Foremost, it requires a theoretical shift in the way we conceptualize the voice. It involves a more thorough interrogation of the voice in excess of the signifying practices that too often define it, as Lacan and others suggest. Above all, it means focusing on our sense of vocality as a bodily practice—in other words, as a phenomenological event rather than primarily a symbolic process of discourse. Such a theoretical move offers an appropriate counterbalance to the voices of articulation that resound so consistently within cyberspace and on the Internet in their typical visual and spatial configurations—whether written or reproduced audibly in digitalized form. Connor finds the phenomenological event of speaking and listening of primary importance when he suggests,

> My voice is not something I merely have, or even something that I, if only in part, am. Rather, it is something that I do. A voice is not a condition, nor yet an attribute, but an event. It is less something that exists than something which occurs. . . . For Merleau-Ponty, phonetic gesture is not a form of representation, or mimicry of pre-existing thoughts, but a way of bringing the speaker's world into being.[1]

The alternative voice I wish to offer in this regard is the voice of enunciation, the voice whose qualities are pursued explicitly by Lacan, Ong, Dolar, and Cavarero and implicitly by Merleau-Ponty and his student Foucault. This is the voice that we speak and hear in excess of the symbolic functions of discourse that try to dominate it. The temporal voice of enunciation in its sounding disrupts the spatiality of written discourse and temporarily destabilizes sedimented meaning systems. This is the voice that is celebrated by sound poets who desire to counter the order of speech and its linguistic coding. It announces why "man in the age of writing is relatively unhappy, having renounced a part of his libido in order to subject himself to a series of restrictions which deprive him of the pleasure connected with the vocal act"[2] in its very performativity. For Merleau-Ponty, this is the voice enunciated most readily in *parole parlante*, speaking speech as opposed to *parole parlée*, speech spoken. For Foucault, this voice is reflected in the one that speaks, most easily heard as the reflexive counterpart of his aphorism "I lie/I speak." As we shall see, it represents not the voiceless name, as Foucault's discourse of language outlines, but the presentation of the nameless voice. The voice that we revive from the talking corpse of articulation brings us back to the inherent temporality of its sounding as a phenomenological event in all its richness as an auditory medium of profound materiality and endurance. Viewed from a phenomenological perspective, it is the voice of the pre-logical and serves as a prelude to the voice of signifying practices. This voice is the salient embodied or phenomenological action that inaugurates a speaking to and listening, which is highly aesthetic. As such, it nourishes a deeper level of relationality than what is offered by the voice of articulation.

Although Lacan claims that the voice as an *object petit a* or pure voice of excess is one of the paramount embodiments of the subject, so far in our discussion we have seen that the voice and the potential it carries for a fuller sense of experience and being has received very little attention in the philosophical literature. As Cavarero remarks in regard to philosophy's tendency to ignore the uniqueness of the sonorous voice, in philosophical circles "the voice thus gets thematized as the voice in general, a sonorous emission that neglects the vocal uniqueness of the one who emits it."[3] If it is not ignored outright, the voice comes under attack. We have seen this by way of Derrida's critique of the supposed phonocentric nature of Western ontology and Dolar's assessment of phonology as yielding the signifying dagger to the voice I wish to revive. Or, perhaps worse yet, this voice is altogether eclipsed or muted, perceived only as a taken-for-granted property of discursive practices. As a result, our vocality has been traditionally conceptualized in two primary narrow ways: (a) as a vehicle of meaning (as demonstrated by the voice of articulation) or (b) reduced to a fetish object admired for only the aesthetic pleasure it can provide. This is the voice that concerns Plato in his admonishment of music and song conceived as mere distractions to the rationality of the *logos*. This is the voice he heard emanating from the bards that had to be silenced. It is also the voice that if not pleasurable is thought to be dangerous, given its supposed intoxicating allure as exemplified in Homer's myth of the Sirens.

However, in addition to these two conceptual levels of the voice, we discover an important third. Drawing from Lacan's notion of the non-sonorous voice as *object a* or the pure voice in excess of signification, I acknowledge à la Dolar, the appositional voice of sonority in its uniqueness. Don Ihde pursues some of these qualities of the voice in his insightful book *Listening and Voice: Phenomenologies of Sound*, and philosopher Vincent Colapietro addresses aspects of this voice as well in his article "Striving to Speak in a Human Voice: A Peircean Contribution to Metaphysical Discourse," published in *The Review of Metaphysics*. In addition to Merleau-Ponty's and Foucault's insights on the phenomenological event of speaking, I appeal to Peirce's triadic categories of human existence to find an alternative third conceptual level from which to explicate the voice. The alternative voice, I submit, is enunciated within the semiotic and phenomenological relation of firstness and secondness, a semiotic aspect of the voice that has yet to be adequately theorized. This is the voice I am calling enunciation.

In addition to the scholars mentioned above, I draw from the works of both Dolar and Cavarero for an explication of this alternative voice. These scholars help flesh out the qualities and functions of the voice of enunciation as a fundamental medium of human experience in its own right. By designating the pure voice as an excess of signification, Lacan is attempting to mark the void of silence that the non-sonorous voice of *object a* creates. Dolar is bent on extending the work of his mentor on the topic of voice by accentuating the reflexive sonorous qualities that arise from their oppositional relation to silence. In this sense, Dolar stresses this voice's phenomenological characteristics by teasing it away from its typical association with the symbolic generation of meaning, as merely a cultural or symbolic phenomenon. I applaud these writers' efforts to emphasize the form and function of this aspect of the voice as a phenomenology at the pre-logical level and intend to feature these aspects of the voice in my subsequent discussions. The point I wish to make clear is that the sonorous voice we are pursuing along with Dolar and others, in its phenomenological enunciation, is by no means non-semiotic. As an object to consciousness like any other sign condition, this voice *is* mediated in experience, as Peirce's ideas about all sign constitution suggest. But its mediation is significantly less than what we find in the voices of articulation. In other words, there is a concreteness that is given within its qualitative immediacy that is unlike the voice of articulation.[4] This distinction makes a substantial difference in terms of understanding the voice's ultimate nature and function within human relations.

I shall be careful to explicate this voice while not reducing it to a mere lack in relation to signifying practices—in other words, as merely empty, a remainder or leftover that has no value of its own. To reduce our understanding of voice in this way is a vice of logocentrism, according to Cavarero. Here, Merleau-Ponty's work is useful. He reminds us that to free meaning from the event of speaking, as we aim to do, requires that we appreciate the "background of silence which does not cease to surround it and without which it would say nothing."[5] Silence and speaking are thus reflexive relations, a point Lacan well understood. As a way to contextualize the reflexive process of speaking, Merleau-Ponty goes on to stipulate that "speech always comes into play against a background of speech; it is always only a fold in the immense fabric of language."[6] His first reference to "speech" implies the event of speaking, while the second reference to "speech" refers to the process of signification. In both statements, Merleau-Ponty is acknowledging speaking as a semiotic process that phenomenologically mediates between the voices of silence and signifying practices. As my reader will hear, my subsequent arguments are heavily shaped by these fundamental ideas. Although speaking as an auditory phenomenon presents a fold in discourse, it is nonetheless an important one, particularly if we want to attest to the voice's originary nature and function as a fully embodied *natural* materiality at the pre-logical level of existence. For we will find that this originary nature of the voice powerfully calls us toward one another so as to actualize an aesthetic co-presence within speaking and listening. While the voice I am pursuing can easily be dismissed as a mere bodily or quasi-animal emission, I aim to argue, unlike Cavarero, that these natural or *wild* attributes of the voice of enunciation need to be theoretically embraced. Essentially, like Cavarero and Dolar, I seek to understand speaking "from the perspective of the voice instead of from the perspective of language."[7] By "fully investing in the auditory as a means to split the subject from a totalizing semantics . . . [we] lac[e] speech through the erotic potentiality of sound and amplify . . . the *tension* at the heart of what it means to speak (and to be spoken to)."[8]

In this regard, Peirce's triadic theory of signs helps extend our conceptualization of the voice by specifying the accompanying semiotic qualities it possesses as a phenomenology of human experience. This requires making an important theoretical distinction between signification as an accomplishment of meaning and the process of a sign's evolutionary development in conscious experience through the triadic relations of firstness, secondness, and thirdness. By assuming this corrective theoretical position, the qualities and functions of the voice of enunciation are adequately theorized from both a phenomenological and a semiotic perspective. Hence, we come to a fuller sense of the voice of enunciation as inherently an important communicological medium. Furthermore, we find that this voice is ironically inarticulate in its pre-logical status. Yet this voice resounds most powerfully just the same in its aesthetic naturalness or wildness. It is the perception and expression of this voice that ultimately offers us the possibility of recuperating the positive aspects of enchantment as the auditory existential call of the wild that beckons us to the uniqueness of alterity itself—within oneself and another.

## THE VOICE OF ENUNCIATION, ITS
## CHARACTERISTICS AND FUNCTIONS

By selecting the word *enunciate*, I aim to focus attention on the sonorous, auditory emissions of speech aside from the signified relation that is ultimately its final destination in discourse. With the use of this designation, I pay homage to the French term *énoncé,* which means "to utter or state." My use of *enunciate* is deliberately chosen so as to oppose it to the voice of articulation and to Lacan's sense of the voice as *object a* in its silence. As I reviewed in the last chapter, I use the term *articulation* to highlight speaking and listening in which our main concern is to participate competently in the various prescribed language games and meaning systems we confront each day as discursive beings. Unfortunately, the voices of articulation that we speak with and listen to often keep us grounded in sedimented discourse, marked culturally by the process of signification that moves us to higher levels of abstraction or translation, as Peirce suggests.

Given that currently the hyper-textual forms of electronic connectivity are steadily de-voicing our interactions, we could conclude that these voices of articulation are actually keeping our discourse at the *dumb* level. That is, our discourse seems to be increasingly soundless or dumb, drawing from the original sense of the word. This is because within such electronic visually dominated mediated environments we have speech that progressively doesn't make any sound. This devocalization trend, as I reviewed, ultimately increases the depersonalization of self and other relations. Even so, our participation in the chorus of voices that our articulations generate is most certainly a cultural demand; lived experience without such a chorus, however soundless, would be incomprehensible as both Merleau-Ponty and Foucault suggest. The voices of articulation are, therefore, necessary but not sufficient conditions for maintaining discursive practices.

In contrast, by *enunciate* I mean to accentuate the inaugural moments of speaking and listening as pure auditory phenomena or gestures, in a Merleau-Ponty sense of the word. It is the voice that shares affinities with *parole parlante* (speaking speech). It is the voice that prompts Foucault's pronouncement of "I speak" as a performative. This is unlike articulation, which accentuates our competent performance of language and discourse within various contexts of interaction. To enunciate thereby acknowledges the originary potential that speaking and listening have as contributors to relational experiences of uniqueness; it is not tied to a universality of discourse, although it may contribute to its eventual constitution. This voice represents Dolar's pure sonorous voice of excess, as he extends the work of Lacan. Dolar alludes to this voice of enunciation that I am proposing in the following; as he stipulates, the excess voice coincides with the very process of enunciation: it epitomizes something that cannot be found anywhere in the statement, in the spoken speech and its string of signifiers, nor can it be identified with their material support. In this sense the voice as the agent of enunciation sustains the signifiers and constitutes the string, as it were, that holds them together, although it is invisible because of the beads concealing it. If signifiers form a chain, then the voice may well be what fastens them into a signifying chain. And if the process of enunciation points at the locus of subjectivity in language, then voice also sustains an intimate link with the very notion of the subject.[9]

The voice of enunciation is best understood as an originary insertion into the otherwise mundane flow of cultural experience; it inaugurates the becoming of the sign to conscious experience at the pre-logical level and as a natural event of human speaking and listening. As such, this voice hails the sign relation of firstness and secondness, with firstness sounding its aesthetic capabilities and secondness stressing its dynamic nature to break the flow of experience as we encounter object relations in the world. The voice of enunciation re-introduces us to the important embodied or phenomenological *action* of the sonic voice as a salient event that transpires in time. Barthes informs us that aspects of this voice are best understood as "the grain of the throat, the patina of consonants, the voluptuousness of vowels, a whole carnal stereophony . . . [from] the body, of the tongue, not that of meaning, of language."[10] Because it accentuates our natural corporeality, the voice of enunciation can subvert the order of language and politics.[11]

Dolar insists that the voice implies its affinity with time by the fact that it fades at the moment it is sounded.[12] On the important relationship between the sounding voice and time, Ong also reminds us that sound in general and the spoken word in particular were understood by oral-aural cultures as foremost events or happenings. He believes that while we are no longer primarily an oral-aural culture, the characterization of sound as an event or happening is an "abiding truth."[13] He goes on to say that "sound is more real or existential than other sense objects, despite the fact that it is also more evanescent. Sound itself is related to present actuality rather than to past or future."[14] As such, the spoken word is much more powerful in its effect than the written word, given that it is inseparable from the immediate action that produced it. Ong refers to the Hebrew use of the word *dabar* to illustrate, given that *dabar* means both word and event.[15] He concludes that sound indicates a here-and-now sense of activity, and, therefore, the spoken word is "more real and more really a word than the word sensed, through writing."[16] In its capacity to create or initiate an event of experience, the voice thus hails the semiotic relation of secondness. In addition, as an event or happening sound as the spoken word provides, Ong suggests a "special sensory key to interiority."[17] I take this to suggest the phenomenological or existential level of experience that Merleau-Ponty and others sought to interrogate. Cavarero agrees when she states that "the voice is the way in which the exquisitely human uniqueness emits its essence."[18] Here, Cavarero is acknowledging its qualitative features in its firstness as immediacy. Ong appreciates the sonic voice in a similar fashion as Lacan and others, attempting to clarify its relation to originary experience in its iteration as a naturally embodied, aesthetic act rather than a re-iteration of cultural, sedimented discourse.

Important to our discussion of relationality, Ong characterizes sound and the speaking voice as transpiring in time, emphasizing the temporal flow of immediate experience within sounding events. He contrasts the spoken word that stresses time from the written word, which honors spatial configurations. As he indicates,

> Speech itself as sound is irrevocably committed to time. It leaves no discernible direct effect in space, where the letters of the alphabet have their existence. Words come into being through time and exist only so long as they are going out of existence. . . . A moving object in a visual field can be arrested. It is, however, impossible to arrest sound and have it still present. . . . Sound is psychologically always something going on, something active, a kind of evanescent effluvium which exists only so long as something or someone is actively producing it.[19]

He is explicating, in other words, the temporal flow of our very being that the experience of sound articulates. These ideas are akin to Heidegger's sense of the temporality of our essential existence in his work *Being and Time*. Sound lends continuity to experience. While Ong is not approaching the topics of sound and voice from a perspective concerned specifically with signification, like Lacan, Dolar, and others, he is attempting to foreground the phenomenological or embodied dimensions that sound announces within human affairs in its immediate auditory emissions. In discussing sound more broadly, Ong stipulates that

> although something of what happens when a sound occurs can be thus represented, sound itself in its full existential actuality cannot. These representations in space suggest inevitably a quiescence and fixity which is unrealizable in actual sound. . . . Strange though it seems to us, sound in its own actuality cannot be measured. Its reality eludes diagrammatic representation. This is a hard truth for technological man to accept.[20]

Thus, the voice of enunciation shares close affinities with the heightened sense of sound that Ong articulates in these passages. Ong is attempting to stipulate the phenomenological qualities of sound and the spoken word in their relation of firstness to secondness that are in excess of a meaning system that they may ultimately serve (thirdness). In this way, he aligns with Lacan and others whose theoretical trajectories advocate for an appreciation of the voice in excess of signification. Ong instructs us that the spoken word as voice must be theorized as an event of discourse that happens in time, as a salient and powerful irruption into the signifying order of things. Ultimately, this voice hails the trope of enchantment in all its auditory fullness as a summons or call, given the inherent power it exudes as a salient event of speaking and listening.

While the phenomenological qualities of the voice of enunciation may be relatively easy to comprehend, its semiotic characteristics may be more allusive. In reference to its semiotic aspects, the voice of enunciation heralds the semiotic relation of firstness and secondness as Peirce describes it. Exemplifying the category of firstness, the voice of enunciation is thereby *qualia*. It is an initial quality of experience as a felt embodied phenomenology—a visceral response to the world that, because of its auditory nature, is particularly intense and bodily penetrating for both self and others. This bodily response constitutes the sign as a semiotic process of meaning making, as I reviewed earlier. Peirce scholar Douglas Anderson stipulates that firstness specifically entails the qualities of (a) spontaneity, (b) initiation, and (c) originality/novelty.[21] Spontaneity implies discontinuities or gaps in conscious experience. This is the very irruption of the semiotic into the phenomenological and focuses our attention on the movement of experience from firstness to secondness. Initiation refers to the abductive process itself, initiating inquiry (understood broadly) that potentializes new ideas as the flow of thought unfolds in experience to its ultimate destination in thirdness. Originality/novelty speaks to the freshness attached to our experience of firstness, although originality and novelty will always be tempered by previous experiences of thirdness as contextual elements.

It is important to keep in mind then that this insertion or irruption into the temporal flow of experience by the voice of enunciation at the level of firstness is a recursive embodied movement of semiosis as it moves us through the categories of secondness and thirdness. The sounding voice may be naturally originary as I am claiming, but it is ultimately not an *origin* in the sense of a static fixed point within a presumed transcendental consciousness. In other words, Peirce's triadic framework reminds us that the thirdness of symbolic accomplishment or intelligibility is always only a temporary stasis of meaning in the ongoing evolution of semiosis as existential boundary conditions flux and change in acts of expression and perception through relations of firstness and secondness. Thirdness, or the codified meanings of previous experience as culturally derived, quickly move back to the immediacy of firstness when the phenomenological subject perceives another potential sign within experience that must be expressed. My point is that, although *all* signs irrupt the temporal flow of experience in their constitutive acts in the movement of thirdness to firstness and secondness, the sounding voice as enunciation irrupts in a more intense and powerful way than other sensory stimuli we might encounter. Because of this, the voice of enunciation has the natural capacity to temporarily suspend the domination of the cultural markers of experience at given moments in time. It thereby instantiates the self and other dynamic in its association with secondness.

Paradoxically, as Peirce argues, the experience of semiotic firstness is also a temporary felt sense of *unification* with the world of objects to consciousness. Here Peirce is acknowledging the intentional arc of consciousness of which phenomenology speaks: the arc that initially connects us to the world as a consciousness of things at their pre-logical or pre-conscious level. Subsequently, firstness, in general, is always a sensory experience of some kind that can be prompted by any of the five senses.[22] However, drawing from Ong's work on the phenomenology of sound, we now recognize that sound in particular binds us to the world of experience in powerful and penetrating ways. This is dissimilar to visual experience, which he believes has a tendency to create more separation and distance because of its spatial qualities. It is the binding quality of sound in its temporal flow that prompts Ong to claim that sound and voice as the spoken word is the very foundation of relation that ultimately builds unification, a sense of communion or community over time. Unlike the written or printed word, which distances us from one another through layers of abstraction and mediation, the immediate sounding of voices transgresses the visual and the symbolic, if only temporarily.

The sounding nature of voices within immediate ear-to-ear relations can offer, therefore, an effective counter to our distracted and increasingly fragmented existence in our electronic media-frenzied environments. Speaking with and listening to the voice of enunciation has different physical and psychological effects for both self and other than speaking or listening to the voice of articulation. In any case, Peirce encourages us to realize that all objects to consciousness at the pre-conscious level of firstness are sensory interfaces of intentionality. However, the activation of sound binds us more immediately than other sense perceptions. Because of the penetrating nature of sound as an immediate taking hold of our existential experience, the speaking voice of enunciation provides an especially rich medium by which to manifest attendant qualities to the other and self in dialogue, especially in immediate ear-to-ear contexts as we move into the semiotic relation of secondness. Thus, the sounding voice of enunciation offers us an attentional capacity that is qualitatively distinct from sight. This important point should no longer be ignored in the philosophical literature on sound and the voice, particularly as they relate to human relations. The voice of enunciation can mitigate the distracting tendencies we seem to be developing within our digital age. It can assuage the de-voicing by spatiality that is occurring in our textual electronic forms of interaction. This is a crucial sensory distinction that carries import when it comes to constituting productive forms of relationality. With this voice, we may transcend the mere superficiality such electronic connections typically entail.

## The Aesthetics of the Sounding Voice

Important to my explication of a healthy relationality, Peirce believes that firstness is always imbued with and experienced as an aesthetic. This is because firstness is grounded in sensory experience as affect in a powerful phenomenological way. For Peirce, aesthetic deals with what is "'objectively admirable without any ulterior reason' . . . with 'objects simply in their presentation' . . . and with 'things whose ends are to embody qualities of feeling.'"[23] Although admittedly the lesser developed of his work on the normative sciences (the others being ethics and logic), aesthetics are nevertheless associated by Peirce with his category of firstness. In his later works especially, Peirce acknowledges the necessary relationship aesthetics has with ethics (which he associates with secondness) and logic (which he associates with thirdness).[24] I have more to say about the ethical implications of the voice in the next chapter.

In any case, Peirce views aesthetics from a phenomenological perspective—that is, as a thoroughly embodied experience that fuels evolving sign relations.[25] Peirce believes that the aesthetic sensibility of firstness synthesizes feeling or affect with the artful creativity of imaginative thinking and reasoning, which emerge in thought in its mediation by thirdness. Accordingly, all accomplished thought at the level of thirdness (*logos*) is aesthetically derived to some extent from its relation to firstness. On this point, Peirce is in full agreement with Merleau-Ponty's sense of an aesthetic *logos*, as discussed earlier. The logical or intelligible (arrived at the level of thirdness) is infused with its pre-logical counterpart as an aesthetic in all acts of semiosis.[26] The degree and kind of aesthetic that functions within semiosis is therefore salient in the eventual sign condition that is produced and its significant effects. This is especially important as it relates to dialogic relations, as we will see.

For those familiar with Hans-Georg Gadamer's work, especially *The Relevance of the Beautiful*, it is easy to identify theoretical affinities with Peirce on the understanding of the importance of aesthetics to ontological and epistemological issues and concerns. Gadamer seeks to improve the way we theorize aesthetics, given the typical abstract nature in which art or the aesthetic in general is described. He offers a theoretical framework bent on uniting the aesthetic with the everyday world, arguing for the relevance of the beautiful in our understanding of everyday life as an artful unfolding of experience. Gadamer's distinction between *erfahrung* and *erlebnis*, terms he borrows from Hegel, is most telling.[27] Each form of aesthetic produces very different effects, as I now explain.

When we reify or idealize art or the aesthetic by focusing on its mere pleasurable capacities or valences, Gadamer calls this *erlebnis*. This interpretation of the aesthetic merely reflects its abilities to entertain or amuse.

Earlier I made the claim that our inauthentic enchantments within the hypertextual world of cyberspace and on the Internet generate and proliferate this kind of aesthetic, given their predominantly textual/visual form. I argue that their effects are often superficial and inauthentic when it comes to our enchantments. This is because the world of cyberspace and the Internet foster an orientation toward the world through primarily the play of amusement. This kind of aesthetic configuration feeds "merely subjective validity."[28] It is self-serving, in other words. As Gadamer indicates, this perspective on the aesthetic makes no claim on us as existential beings in relation to historical knowledge or the social world. It is the idealized version of the aesthetic—in whatever forms it takes as a sign condition. This characterization of the aesthetic when applied to the voice can quickly convert the voice to merely a fetish object, as Lacan claims.

*Erfahrung*, on the other hand, is an aesthetic that makes an existential claim on us, according to Gadamer. It is an aesthetic sensibility that calls us outward into the real world of history and tradition at the same time that it possibilizes productive knowledge through social action that can be utilized pragmatically in the future. This is the aesthetic that calls for a response in the real world of human affairs by a social agent. For Gadamer, "the ontological function of the beautiful is to bridge the chasm between the ideal and the real."[29] As we shall see, this kind of aesthetic as *erfahrung* is pronounced within the voice of enunciation whose qualities I am describing. This type of aesthetic resounds in the play of musement, rather than mere amusement, and thereby potentializes an authentic position toward others. I will have more to say about this in the next chapter.

Peirce's and Gadamer's views on the aesthetic share much in common. Like Peirce, Gadamer views the aesthetic as serving a "quasi-religious function"[30] in that the aesthetic, especially defined as *erfahrung*, tends to be unifying even as it is ineffable, or perhaps because of it. This aesthetic has a spiritual component, and both scholars define the meaning of spirit rather broadly. They see the spiritual as a vital principle in life or, in other words, as an animating force of all life. This aesthetic evokes the mysterious or ineffable aspects of existence, the immaterial that moves our conscious experience beyond its mere cultural dimensions. For both Peirce and Gadamer, this aesthetic also produces sensuous knowledge, a form of knowledge that for Peirce reflects a reasonableness in thought, the *summum bonum* of his philosophy. Gadamer and Peirce agree with the founder of philosophical aesthetics, Alexander Baumgarten, who asserts that an appreciation of the aesthetic leads to the "art of thinking beautifully."[31] In addition, both Gadamer and Peirce acknowledge the important fact that the aesthetic disposition assumed by the subject is also culturally derived, given that the operative valence system is learned. Peirce's understanding of the recursive nature of semiosis (moving from thirdness to firstness and secondness and back again) speaks to that fact most directly, indicating how prior meaning systems or habits employed will shape ongoing interpretive acts within semiosis. In a similar fashion, Gadamer understands that what is deemed beautiful or aesthetic is historically learned. In the end, both scholars concede that it is impossible to divorce the affective nature of aesthetics as phenomenological experience from its ethical entailments in semiosis, a point that leads Peirce to conclude that "aesthetics is the least important [of the normative sciences, to his way of thinking] but [the] most necessary"[32] in any process of inquiry, scientific or otherwise. Although pragmatism promotes self-reflection and self-control given our fallibility as human beings, the aesthetic also encourages inquiry, curiosity, and continued questioning. According to Peirce, therefore, the aesthetic has a pragmatic trajectory. Like Schiller before him, Peirce is convinced that "there is no other way of making sensuous man rational except by first making him aesthetic."[33]

Other theorists concur on this important point—Jane Bennett, for example. Bennett speaks most directly to the inherent nature of the aesthetic in shaping ethical conduct. Following earlier attempts by both Schiller and Foucault to outline the aestheticization of ethics, Bennett advocates an affective model of ethics that does not reduce ethics to a narcissistic practice of self-gratification.[34] Nor does she advocate a Kantian notion of morality that detaches it from the senses and houses it solely in the rational. Instead, she is convinced that an aesthetics such as exemplified in particular kinds of enchantment (understood in what I describe as its authentic entailments) can enable a positive, ethical generosity toward the other. Bennett recognizes that "ethics entails both a moral code (which condenses moral ideals and metaphysical assumptions into rational principles and reasonable rules) *and* an embodied sensibility (which organizes affects into a style and generates the impetus to enact the code)."[35]

And finally, on the similarities between Gadamer and Peirce on the relationship between aesthetic and ethics, both understand that there is an insufficiency to ethics when we appeal only to the intellect as a way of activating it. When we do so, we fail to recognize ethic's important aesthetic or sensible components as a phenomenology.[36] Both scholars assert that there must be an acknowledgment of the natural freedom to thought's unfolding (Schiller's, Peirce's, and Gadamer's sense of play) that imbues it with its ineffable or affectual qualities and functions. According to Bennett, the aesthetic disposition that Schiller offers these later theorists is "a particular inflection of an inherent human impulse to play."[37] What form play takes is dependent upon the aesthetic sensibility that a particular object to consciousness motivates.

Given Peirce's understanding that firstness is experienced as a sensory aesthetic, at this point, it might be easy to presume that the sonorous voice as an aspect of firstness would cohere with the aesthetic pure voice mentioned earlier, especially as detailed by Lacan. Recall this is the voice that is recognized for purely its aesthetic value in song and music, the aspect of the voice that so troubled Plato. Recall as well that this manner of thinking about the voice is one of the typical ways in which voice is narrowly theorized. Both of these conceptualizations of the voice share similarities with the aesthetic voice of enunciation we are pursuing. For example, both the aesthetic voice of enunciation and the pure aesthetic voice are related ultimately to secondness and mediated by thirdness in their natural unfolding. As a result, they both nourish our evolving thought processes. We only have to imagine being taken away from immediate experience by that favorite song to understand this point. The visceral feelings instigated by the voice of enunciation and the pure aesthetic voice at the level of firstness are necessary as we aesthetically order conscious experience and move through the thinking process. Additionally, both renditions of the voice accentuate it as an important medium of the body that imbues the body with aesthetic qualities and affectual sensibilities.

While the voice of enunciation and this pure voice share these aesthetic qualities, that is where their similarity ends. On the ground of dialogue, their functionality and depth of influence are quite different. I will give an example. Drawing from my discussion above, the pure aesthetic voice of song and music is appreciated and valued in its own right. Its main function is to please the ear, to evoke affectual responses perhaps but nothing more. This voice stresses the mere aesthetic for its own sake. This voice, whose qualities are pleasurable or painful perhaps, enchants us just the same by calling us back to ourselves, most often in reverie (as in the case of pleasure) or avoidance (as in the case of annoyance). This voice's constitution as pleasure or annoyance is its act of signification. As such, we make what Peirce describes as perceptual judgments on the aesthetics of this voice (as appealing or annoying, for example), but most often we absorb their impact at the pre-conscious level of sensory reactions. We can also consider an interlocutor's voice in this shallow manner as well, focusing only on its pure aesthetic qualities. When we do, we often neglect the content and the relational components within a given exchange. These examples reflect the voice that resounds the aesthetic of *erlebnis*, as Gadamer suggests. In her discussion on the sonorous quality of enchantment as an aesthetic, Bennett is quick to point out the potential "dangerously amoral character of aesthetic pleasure"[38] when experienced alone, apart from any moral precept.

The voice of enunciation we are seeking is an aesthetic of *erfahrung* that is in service to strengthening relational or communicative bonds between self and other. The enunciative voice is spoken in ear-to-ear dialogic contexts and thus serves as the "primary publicist of each being's identity, feelings, character, and intentions"[39] in acts of immediate sharing. Its aim is to provoke the furthering of active ear-to-ear discursive speaking and not just passive listening or listening to the voice of the other for pleasure or annoyance. Through its natural affective power at the level of firstness, it aesthetically irrupts rather than pacifies sensory experience and so demonstrates its relation of secondness. Akin to the qualities associated with *erfahrung*, this voice is potentially transformative existentially.

So, the voice of enunciation enchants as well but in a radically different way. It naturally calls us out into the inter-subjective world we constitute with others (into the relation of secondness and thirdness), invoking the possibility of finding a deeply felt mutuality in discourse. The voice of enunciation activates the boundary of relation in distinct and powerful ways, unlike our experiences with writing/print or the visual as an aesthetic experience. Consequently, the voice of enunciation aids in creating an aesthetic sensibility toward self and others (a display of the sign relation of firstness and secondness) when it comes to discursive practices that can prove to be more productive and pragmatic in the long run. Listening attentively to and speaking the voice of enunciation hails imaginative thinking. It also fosters, according to Bennett, an ethical generosity toward others, as I detail in discussions to come. While both kinds of voices resound aesthetically as bodily comportment, they do so in different ways, with different aims and with different ends. The one voice takes us back to ourselves, the other indicates the importance of the self and other relation.

## Recovering the Lost Art of Conversation

The aesthetic qualities of the voice of enunciation are vital phenomenological elements of messages that have yet to be adequately theorized in the communication literature. In addition to the traditional content and relational elements of messages outlined by Gregory Bateson and the Palo Alto group, a third needs to be added: the phenomenological aesthetic as a vital sensory element in discourse in its natural unfolding. Peirce's triadic nature of signs and Gadamer's hermeneutics of aesthetics help us see that every message includes these three elements working in relation to one another in phenomenological acts of mediation.

The content, or *what* is said, is grounded in symbolic thirdness. This is the accomplishment of signification and meaning that interlocutors hope to achieve together. The relational component, or *how* something is said, is also important, as we know in offering cues regarding how to interpret the content. This aspect of any message as sign is acknowledged in the communication literature as primarily non-verbal or oral components. So, at a minimum, the oral aspects of the voice are recognized in the relational component in the context of speaking and listening in our current theorizing. However, the natural aesthetic qualities of the voice as a phenomenological auditory emission are too often perceptually co-opted in mere service to the semantic (which is thirdness). In other words, the communication discipline recognizes the vocal as only *phone semantike*, as Aristotle outlined so long ago.

This is the voice in service to speech. Additionally, the relational or status element of a message, whether verbal/oral or non-verbal, is primarily derived from making comparisons, distinctions, or differences between interlocutors as to their positionality with one another. This element most closely corresponds to secondness, as Peirce defines it, not firstness. Secondness functions indexically to point to and distinguish between objects to consciousness in the evolution of a sign's constitution.

To these two elements just described we must add a third, the *who* that is speaking as an aesthetic pronouncement of phenomenological uniqueness. We must attend to the aesthetic sensibility operating within the wholeness of the self-other relation as an object to consciousness, indicative of the emotive and vocative functions of firstness, whether we are talking about vocal or written discourse. It also highlights the semiotic impact of secondness on discourse. This theoretical move acknowledges Roman Jakobson's model of communication more explicitly by recapturing the importance of the emotive and vocative functions of discourse enunciated within the addresser and addressee relation.[40] Of course, the power the aesthetic sensibilitites of self and other display in discourse are dependent upon whether the voices take written or vocal forms. We find that the voice of enunciation within discursive practices as the particularity of the one who speaks within ear-to-ear relations is particularly salient in inaugurating the possibility of communication by unique interlocutors in the first place. Such a theoretical move accomplishes two things: (a) It highlights the importance of the aesthetic of firstness, and (b) it acknowledges the relation of firstness and secondness in shaping discourse. Accordingly, the phenomenological component of speaking and listening shares the stage with the developing semiotic of secondness and thirdness.

Such a conceptualization gives new meaning to our long-held commonsense view that there is, indeed, an *art* to conversation and discourse. That art is sufficiently acknowledged when we take into consideration the degree and kind of aesthetic sensibility that nourishes every communicative exchange. If that sensibility is over-shadowed by the symbolic functions of thirdness (as I have argued is the case in inauthentic moments of enchantment), then our discourse could be rendered banal, dominated by the exchange of mere information. We develop "I-It" relations as Buber claimed, where the optimization of self and other as unique particularities is left dormant. It is no wonder that currently, in our heightened electronic age of distraction, the lost art of conversation is a growing concern. It appears that our new electronic habits of discourse contribute to the very diminishment of our aesthetic sensibilities toward the other at the same time that a new kind of consumerist aesthetic (a digitally enhanced visual one) reigns supreme.

If every *sign*, that is, every *message* functions within triadic relations of mediation, then the aesthetic sensibility emitted by the one who speaks and listens must be included as part of the semiotic process and phenomenological event of speaking and listening. This theoretical shift hails two salient aspects about the interrelationship of communication and particularly the voice that have yet to be adequately interrogated in the communication literature: (a) This shift re-invigorates our appreciation for the vocality within social affairs as an important phenomenological ingredient in our lived experience of relationality as an unfolding aesthetic within immediate ear-to-ear relations, and (b) it inverts the sedimented hierarchy of intelligibility over sensibility that structuralists like Saussure established some time ago.

On the first point, by reviving an appreciation for the vocality of discourse as a phenomenology, we begin to honor once again the aesthetic qualities of sounding voices as integral aspects and eventual effects of discourse. In our culture of distraction and the attendant techno-social dilemma we now face, re-orienting our ears to the other as the one who speaks and listens rather than focusing on what is before our eyes invigorates the aesthetics of discourse in profound and productive ways, as I will discuss further in the chapters to follow. Recognizing this vocal ability infuses discourse with quite literally a sense of the *naturalness* of phenomenological experience. It acknowledges the important role an aesthetic consciousness serves in unifying the perceptions and expressions of self and other within discursive practices.

On the second point, Derrida's critique of Saussure regarding this hierarchy has merit. Focused as it is on the signified/signifier relation in that order, Saussure's structure of the semiotic process privileges the former (defined as intelligibility) over the latter (seen as sensory or the sensible). This is because, to Saussure's way of thinking, the signified is necessary and evident, that "functions as the origin of the latter and therefore subordinates it."[41] The signified becomes the "foundational valence"[42] for defining intelligibility in relation to the signifier, theorized as sensory experience.

As I have argued, Peircean semiotics possibilizes an inversion of this hierarchy. This is because Peirce associates sensory experience as pure affect or feeling with firstness (as a phenomenology) and intelligibility as the final but temporary accomplishment of meaning at thirdness as a semiotic process. Of course, the actual experience of sign constitution may not be ordered in just that way, given that firstness, secondness, and thirdness are ultimately mediated relations in constant recursion, both phenomenologically and semiotically. Nevertheless, Peirce's triadic structure of consciousness and experience at least allows for the possibility that sensibility to the aesthetic (in the way I am using it herein) infuses the semiotic process in such a way as to thwart, if sufficiently recognized, any prescribed semantic markers of intelligibility that predictably over-determine discursive practices.

Theoretically, Peirce allows us to signal the possibility of joining, not separating, our understanding of cultural practices (the domain of signification, representation, and meaning) with nature (the noumenal domain of materiality understood as an affectual and aesthetic sensibility). His triadic structure of semiosis helps to account for the process of signification as a discursive construct of semiosis at the same time that it highlights our sensory engagement with the world as a phenomenology in a non-essentialist way. As I have argued elsewhere, Peirce's understanding of semiosis demonstrates the very trajectory of Gregory Bateson's life work in this regard. Bent on resolving the destructive dualist interpretations of mind and body, culture and nature (with the former over-determining our understanding of the latter in increasing ways in our digital age of distraction), Bateson proposed that we start recognizing their "sacred unity."[43] With Bateson, we discover the logic of the sacred in Peirce's writings as a triadic relation, which includes mental process as an aesthetic sensibility within cultural practices.[44]

In the end, we find in Peirce's theory a framework that provides us with a way to renew our appreciation for the saliency of the aesthetic voice of sound in shaping all human affairs in its natural entailments as a phenomenology. With these ideas, we recover a sense of the lost art of conversation. And while my focus here is on the auditory component of the aesthetic in discourse, in general Peirce's theory aids in reviving the inter-subjective *who* that is always speaking and listening as an integral aesthetic aspect of message or sign production as a phenomenology, whether auditory, visual, or otherwise.

## THE *WHO* THAT SPEAKS:
## LEVINAS AND THE DISCOURSE OF VOICE

I turn to Emmanuel Levinas, a prominent twentieth-century thinker who seeks to articulate the importance of understanding speech aside from its mere signified relation. Levinas challenges the logocentric view of metaphysics by outlining an elaborate philosophical interpretation of discourse. One of his primary concerns entails a perceived neglect in Western thought concerning the nature and function of the *action* of discourse. Instead, he believes we have favored the *logos*, perceived quite narrowly as merely logic or reason. He clearly states that "*logos* as discourse is completely confused with *logos* as reason."[45] As a response to this neglect, Levinas details his philosophy of the "Saying" and the "Said." By doing so, Levinas attempts to provide a hermeneutic of the action of discourse, the Saying, and, in the process, endeavors to reinstate the saliency of the *who* that speaks as an inimitable singularity or uniqueness. Levinas conceives of the Said as the *what* of discourse, which puts it squarely in the realm of language and signification. He is convinced that philosophy has for too long focused on the Said and not the Saying. In detailing this dichotomy, Levinas thinks that the Said is too often "assumed as an autonomous reality, independent of the proximity of the interlocutors in the event of Saying. Philosophy's exclusive interest in the Said corresponds to the central role of a *logos* understood as an intelligible order that represents, expresses, signifies, designates, duplicates, and organizes the objective order of beings."[46] Underlying Levinas's entire philosophical project on the distinction between the Saying and the Said and their reciprocal relation is the desire to advance understanding of ethics as a "radical responsibility for the other"[47] that is activated in discourse by the unique presentation of the other's face in proximal acts of speaking or Saying.

Levinas gives us much in the way of theoretical insights when it comes to teasing away the Saying or speaking from the Said. He helps us appreciate speaking and listening in their own right as actions and functions of the *logos*. Like Ong and other phenomenologists, Levinas believes that the act of Saying or speaking is best viewed as an embodied event in which we speak to each other in time aside from the particular contents of what is being expressed. It is to this event of discourse as Saying that Levinas seeks to philosophically return so as to reveal the originary giveness of unique speakers in their oral emissions to each other as a function of discourse. His writing is as provocative as it is instructive. It seems as though he is bent on returning us to the very aesthetic action of discourse as described above, although he does not explicitly state that. In his notion of the Saying, he attempts to capture the *who* that speaks by dispelling the idea that acts of speaking are somehow separated, disembodied functions of interlocutors. As Cavarero interprets Levinas, "every act of speaking is thus from the start the relation of unique beings that address themselves to one another. They reciprocally expose themselves to one another, in proximity; they invoke one another."[48] His theoretical trajectory brings Levinas to focus on the faces of self and other as the initial prompts of relationality, given that the mouth of Saying is one of its abiding features.

For Levinas, the face of the other, therefore, exposes the radical alterity of otherness as it emphasizes the existential grounding of the Saying. From the semiotic perspective of Peirce, we can easily see that Levinas is pursuing the action of firstness as Peirce describes it, before the unique identity of the who that speaks devolves into the universality of the Said (secondness and thirdness). Yet Levinas is quick to indicate, as is Peirce in his relational ontology, that in no way should the who that speaks be identified as a completely autonomous *I*. This is because identity is only formed by meeting difference and alterity within the proximal relations formed within self and other relations.[49] Given that no two people have identical faces, this radical alterity and ground of relation for Levinas is thus best conceptualized or visualized, if you will, by the presence of the face that for Levinas prompts discourse and a sense of ethical obligation.

While I appreciate his philosophical project and the influence his work has had on our understanding of speaking aside from its metaphysical trappings as signification, it is surprising to note that Levinas did not thematize the Saying by way of the voice per se. Given the heavy influence of the Hebrew tradition on his thinking, his theoretical turn to the face and mouth instead of the voice is a bit troubling. Cavarero agrees and states, "For as the Hebrew tradition itself teaches, the voice in fact maintains a relation—of distinction, anteriority, and excess—with speech, in a way that seems perfectly adapted to the role that Levinas calls on Saying to express."[50] While his recognition of the importance of the materiality of bodily sensations as functions of the recognition of the face of the other are apparent in his writings, the saliency of the vocal or auditory dimensions of these sensory experiences are not.

Cavarero believes, and I concur, that Levinas comes closest to the theme of the voice in his notion of the Saying by focusing on acts of respiration. It is through the reciprocal exposure to the breath within close proximity of one another, he theorizes, that we immediately experience the potential of actual communion. This phenomenon of indivisibleness produced by the breath he calls *pneumatism*. *Pneuma* is the Greek translation of the Hebrew word *ruah*, which means breath. Of course, since ancient times, "the center of word is in breath and sound, in listening and speaking. In the ancient mythologies, the word for soul was often related to the word for breath."[51] On this point, it is interesting to note that the Hebrews, in addition to understanding God's power as expressed in breath, or *ruah*, also acknowledged the role of the voice, or *qol*, in the Bible.[52] And yet Levinas does not. Instead he turns more directly to the breath as an emission of the face as Saying. In this way, "Levinas does not focus on the acoustic aspect of breathing [as Saying], but rather on the fact that breathing alludes to a reciprocal contamination that opens everyone to the other in the vital act of respiration itself."[53]

It is here, Cavarero says, that Levinas encounters directly the problem of distinguishing between the breath as Saying for the human and the reciprocity of breath or Saying shared by animals. This separation of the human and animal was long ago pronounced by Aristotle in specifying that human's Saying is *phone semantike*, a signifying voice, which is radically distinct from that of animals. Of course, Levinas's answer to this problematic was to specify that the animals' respiration was short of soul, unlike that of humans. In this way, Levinas upholds the traditional philosophical distinction between animal and human life that subordinates the former to the latter. It is interesting to note here that Derrida in his posthumous book, *The Animal That Therefore I Am*, critiques this very hierarchy and versions of it in thinkers such as Levinas, Descartes, Kant, and Heidegger. I shall return to this theme in the discussion that follows.

Although Levinas moves us further away from a presumed understanding of speaking as only articulation (the Said), which is a worthy philosophical enterprise, I submit that his characterization of the Saying still falls short theoretically in helping us understand the natural *auditory nature* of Saying in phenomenological experience as fully an aesthetic. This is especially true if our objective is to appreciate the felt sense of obligation another's presence in proximity demands of us, a felt sense prompted, as we have learned, more intensely by sound than sight. With its focus on being in front of the other as a visual, albeit sensual, regarding of each other's uniqueness (a sign condition of secondness), Levinas's theoretical framework still upholds the long-standing visualist orientation of Western philosophy that we are trying to leave behind. Unfortunately, his horizon of ethics is therefore visual. I harmonize with Cavarero who states, "His radical ethics, which postulates the responsibility of each one for the other, is an ethics based on vision—the ordinary, material, unavoidable vision of the other's face."[54] As she continues, it is important for anyone who desires to recover the auditory dimensions of communicative action as Saying to recognize "the surprising tendency of Levinas to proceed from the question of speech not to the voice, but to resolve speech in the face."[55]

With Levinas, we do begin to understand the important distinction of the Saying and the Said as a counter-theoretical move that overturns the dominant logocentrism typical of Western philosophy. This is altogether a good theoretical step when it comes to understanding discursive practices in a more nuanced way—that is, from a communicological standpoint. Levinas does not take us far enough in hearing the salient and quite natural auditory components of the Saying as aesthetic vocal emissions. We are reminded once again that

> images require the distance of vision that separates subject from object. By contrast, sound is immersive and proximal, surrounding and passing through the body. And while . . . images involve the spatial juxtaposition of elements, the sonic . . . involve[s] a temporal flux in which elements interpenetrate one another. In Henri Bergson's terms . . . images present us with 'discrete multiplicities' while, in the sonic . . . we encounter 'continuous multiplicities.'[56]

Unfortunately, Levinas institutes a digital logic of relationality with the Saying and the Said all the while searching for the analogical, the both/and, most prominently manifest through the experience of sound. Therefore, I disagree with Emmanuel Levinas's position that the "face of the other" is the primary phenomenological and semiotic ground from which we encounter the other in his/her full alterity. It is by way of speaking with and listening to the voice of enunciation that alterity is most pronounced. Here, Connor's insights are instructive. As he states, "Nothing else about me defines me so intimately as my voice, precisely because there is no other feature of myself whose nature it is thus to move from me to the world, and to move me into the world. If my voice is mine because it comes from me, it can only be known as mine because it also goes from me."[57]

Following Peirce and the preceding discussion of Levinas, we must conclude that the *who* that speaks in discourse is existentially enunciated by way of relationality itself. It is not a self-transcendent *I* that is an autonomous being, but an existent that arrives on the scene of discourse most prominently in its auditory irruption as a relational phenomenology and through the process of developing semiosis (moving from firstness to secondness). With Peirce, we understand that the "auto-affection" that Derrida dismisses in *Of Grammatology*, or the "illusory idea that the human voice confers self-transparency of expression, presence and a bedrock against the supplementarity and immateriality of signification,"[58] can be accounted for within Peirce's relational, triadic ontology without aligning affect necessarily with a transcendent *I*. Affect is altogether a relational phenomenon that is aesthetically induced as a given sign condition of firstness is related to secondness and mediated by thirdness. Most importantly, with Peirce, we can hear the *who* that speaks in our theoretical interrogations of discourse without losing completely its auditory, affective qualities to the gestures of the visual, as Derrida proposes.

This brings us to the last quality and function of the voice of enunciation that I want to underscore. The phenomenological aesthetic that I hope to revive allows for nature to once again share center stage with culture.

## THE CALL OF THE WILD

The last quality of the voice of enunciation to address is its unconventional or untamed nature in its momentary event of irruption. Because this voice resonates at the pre-logical level of firstness as I described, it has yet to be fully co-opted or tamed in service to the signifying order of things. This is the "lawless voice," as Dolar describes, the voice that exists beyond the logos.[59] Because of its momentary untamed nature, there is an element of chance and chaos that resounds within this voice in its irruption, given that Peirce conceives of firstness as freedom and spontaneity.[60] This voice is therefore endowed with an unpredictability in its initial speaking that sounds its lawlessness. Perhaps it is this very quality of the voice of enunciation that stalls more immediate ear-to-ear discourse for the many people who are uncomfortable with its potential chaotic flow. Speaking anxiety, whether in public or smaller social contexts, could be a result of experiencing this very unpredictability. Peirce says that firstness reflects a momentary rational discontinuity,[61] and this discontinuity and unpredictability resound within its register. It is exactly its quality as an excess of signification that enables the voice of enunciation to disrupt discursive practices, so as to potentialize different habits of speaking and listening.

The voice of enunciation is the voice that has strayed from its linguistic or cultural components in its sounding, if only temporarily. Because of this, it resonates with the *wild*, as I insist, in its qualitative distinctiveness as a *natural* phenomenological element of discourse. In its absolute pure representation in literature, it is the voice of the Siren in Homer's myth, because it resounds outside the bounds of cultural dominance (associated with the masculine) and is, therefore, suspect and perhaps dangerous. There is risk in attending to this voice, but under normal circumstances, as we shall see, the reward outweighs any initial existential costs when it comes to manifesting a deeper accomplishment of inter-subjective experience.

The voice of enunciation represents an iteration of the wild in its naturalness and speechlessness,[62] given its temporary lack of immediate determination in thirdness. In her discussions on the relationship between nature and forms of enchantment, Bennett claims that the auditory call of nature in general is speechless or wild. Nonetheless, she argues, it whispers to us. Perhaps this auditory faintness of the natural call of the wild explains why we listen less and less to it, given the buzz and noise of our digitalized electronic environments.[63] Or why when we do hear its faint materiality, we are enchanted even more by the reminder of that which will speak or that which is yet to unfold in discourse. This same quality of the wild inheres within the human voice of enunciation, resounding the phenomenological aesthetic elements of discourse and the authentic enchantments that I argue may ensue.

Given our current digital age and our proclivity as a culture to distance ourselves from an appreciation of nature in its unfolding naturalness, I am convinced that the life and writings of Henry David Thoreau can offer us alternative insights about the auditory nature of communicative experience and our subsequent enchantments. His exhortations help us attend more readily to the natural elements within human experience that irrupt into our banal sense of everydayness, our cultural webs of meaning that too often dominate our existence. Important to my project is the fact that Thoreau explicitly problematizes the notion of enchantment in his writings, according to several literary scholars.[64] Bennett says it most directly when she asserts that "Thoreau courts the Wild so that he might experience the charm/disruption that I call enchantment."[65] The elements he attends to in nature thus prompt his willful determination to negotiate carefully the complex boundary between the natural and cultural worlds and, more importantly, see them as an analogue logic. Bennett agrees when she says, "Indeed, on my reading, Thoreau is a master of the nature/culture finesse; the world he describes is full of admixtures of the raw and the cooked."[66]

As many scholars have indicated, Thoreau is bent on enacting a form of ethical engagement with the world by using nature and the wild as vehicles for "fashioning" these more desirable aspects of his character.[67] This is not surprising, given that Thoreau went to Walden to recapture a sense of the wild as a means of refuting the civilized world that was, for him, becoming exceedingly shallow and banal. Thoreau yearned for wildness, a sense of the untamed. According to Bennett, he wishes

> to cultivate a kind of sensibility, one subtle enough to discern the fascinating specificity of a thing. This sensibility, crafted by means of a special relationship to the wild and surprising elements in experience is, Thoreau believes, indispensable to *activate* his will to resist the lure of social conformity. He will use the Wild to educate his sense-perception, and he will use the bodily excitement generated by sense to propel a life lived deliberately.[68]

Thoreau's use of the term *wild* is meant to signify a magical or ineffable catalyst that he believes invigorates musement or contemplation, in a Peircean sense. His insightful writings on human experience are testimony to the value of this very catalyst.[69] Yet, Thoreau understood that invoking a sense of the wild was also risky for the natural "provokes and invigorates"[70] in unpredictable ways. In any case, his ruminations about nature and the wild assist us in appreciating more fully what it means to listen to and speak with the voices of enunciation as a mutual call of the wild.

He is not the only American philosopher who appreciates a sense of the wild. According to Linda Simon, Thoreau's pursuit of the wild resonates with the philosophy of pragmatist William James. The universe that most intrigued James was one imbued with "wild facts." Simon declares, "The universe that James celebrated was discontinuous, prismatic, chaotic; a universe in which life was 'always off its balance,' a universe that heralded uniqueness and idiosyncrasy."[71] Interestingly, we hear the influence of his fellow pragmatist Peirce on his thinking, taking into account Peirce's conceptualization of firstness. Both James and Thoreau focus on the miraculous and astonishing aspects of human experience and use that focus as an essential strategy for understanding the complexities of lived experience. James's philosophy in particular focuses on the necessity of contingency, what he described as the "if" of experience that a sense of wildness reflected. Simon explains,

> The feeling of 'if' characterizes the essence of James's psychology, focused as it is on the fluid encounters between self and external world, and the complicity of the individual in creating that world; and of his philosophy of pragmatism and pluralism, terms for a process of knowing a universe that can, and does, and inevitably must change—continually unpredictably, wildly.[72]

Both philosophers, it seems, understand, like their contemporary Peirce, that we can never completely know the universe. Furthermore, what knowledge we have accumulated must be continually questioned, leading to further inquiry and wonder about the world. As Peirce always claimed, the unfolding of thought begins with a sufficient dose of doubt, an irritation that prompts reflection and thinking. Hence, for all three philosophers, there is an inherent fallibility in human experience itself that must not be denied but embraced for the qualities it productively and pragmatically brings to thought's table.

Like Thoreau, a sense of wildness was itself a source of enchantment for James. As a self-proclaimed enthusiast of nature and the sublime, Thoreau experiences what he later describes in his essays and journals as enchantments in the natural world. According to Bennett, at the heart of Thoreau's philosophy is this appreciation of enchantment as a powerful experience he discovers in nature, especially in relation to its sounds. He writes about how these occasions of enchantment radically affect his sense of connection with something beyond himself and predispose him to particular reflective moods about relationality in general. As he remarks, the crickets' sound is a voice that "has set me thinking—philosophizing—moralizing at once."[73] Rather than describe these enchantments as mere delusions (which reflects their typical negative association as spells), Thoreau is quick to assert that such experiences, especially in their auditory forms, such as the sounds of crickets, are a fact of existence, even though they coalesce as moments of surprise that always escape our will to contrive them.[74] So, while we cannot cultivate a sense of enchantment per se, Thoreau believes we can cultivate a disciplined attention to an aesthetic sensibility toward the world through listening to the sounds of the wild that ultimately attune us to the world in a more ethical way. The sense of attunement of which he speaks, of course, emphasizes a sense of embodiment and materiality that we have been pursuing in our quest for the phenomenological elements of voice. Thoreau understands that, paradoxically, the sounds of nature in their materiality focus our attention on the unique and immaterial qualities of lived experience.[75] These very qualities endow the experience of enchantment with its sense of mystery and instantiate a condition of existential ambiguity.

Zebuhr, in writing about Thoreau and his appreciation of the sounds of the wild as forms of enchantment, reminds us that Simone de Beauvoir also interconnects the importance of our lived sense of ambiguity and sounds. Beauvoir also relates our auditory enchantments with our developing ethical comportment in the world. Like her contemporary Merleau-Ponty, who is often deemed the philosopher of ambiguity, Beauvoir insists that in the history of philosophy we have tried to escape ambiguity in our almost obsessive pursuit of certainty. Zebuhr explains that Beauvoir appeals to sounds throughout her writings, "specifically echoes and echoing, to figure moments of ambiguity in her fiction."[76] With her colleague, Alexandra Morrison, Zebuhr stresses how sound prompts the very sign condition of ambiguity for Beauvoir.[77] Zebuhr goes on to make important connections between the experience of ambiguity and enchantment—as a temporary felt sense of surprise and wonder.

Ambiguity is, therefore, one of the natural consequences of the irruption of sound into lived experience in general, imbuing it, if you will, with a sense of the wild, the spontaneous. Within such resounding moments, we enter into an existential condition of momentary surprise and wonder, a condition of enchantment as our experience is mediated by the relation of firstness and secondness. When it comes to furthering our appreciation of the auditory nature of the actual voice of enunciation as a call of the wild, we can begin to hear the resonance this voice shares with enchantment and an auditory sense of *bewilderment*. Simon informs us that

> wildness lies at the heart of bewilderment. Etymologically, wild derives from roots meaning willed or willful, uncontrolled and, indeed, uncontrollable. If bewilderment means disorientation and confusion, it also means liberation from the merely rational and material. The bewildered give themselves permission to reject the notion that nothing exists except matter.[78]

To be bewildered, in the way Simon is using the term, means rejecting the notion of only a materialism within lived experience, a sense of certainty provided by the rational order of things. To be bewildered means moving beyond the taken-for-granted concreteness of everyday experience and opening existentially to an encounter with the immaterial or ineffable aspects of life.

As mentioned, Thoreau experiences his sense of bewilderment or enchantment through the sounds of nature, in particular. It is not mere coincidence, therefore, that he refers in his writings to the *sounds of nature* as enchantments, signaling his comprehension of enchantment's etymological auditory roots.[79] Thoreau is more interested in hearing nature than seeing it.[80] Scholars have remarked about his repeated references to sound in his works, especially in *Walden* in the chapters titled "Sounds" and "Solitude," although Zebuhr also notes that his journals are filled with descriptions about the experience of hearing.[81] So focused is he on the sounds of the nature or the wild that he equates the enchantment of the visuals of nature more so with *false playing* and contrasts the visuals with enchantments that are more auditory as *true playing*. According to Thoreau, visual enchantments can be beautiful and dazzling. However, visual enchantments too often entail being under the spell of enchantment, referring to enchantment's negative connotation as illusive or delusionary. My discussion of our enchantments with our hyper-textual/visual electronic information technologies as inauthentic enchantments are consonant with Thoreau's descriptions of the visual dimensions of nature.

Comparing his experiences of auditory with visual enchantments, he declares, "I was inclined to think that the truest beauty was that which surrounded us—but which we failed to discern."[82] Here the penetrating nature of the auditory is favored aesthetically over the visual. As Zebuhr attests, for Thoreau, "true beauty [as enchantment] does not suggest to us that it exists for our viewing pleasure. Rather, what truly enchants is that which we do not see, or more precisely, as he says, what we 'fail to discern.' . . . What enchants is what we cannot separate out [in its visual configuration], what we cannot decide upon, recognize, or willfully detect."[83] Thoreau firmly holds that it is the auditory forms of enchantment in which the fullness of our attunement with the world of others comes to the fore; in such experiences, we may learn to cultivate an aesthetic sensibility or disciplined attentiveness that is qualitatively distinct from a visual one. This leads Bennett to claim, with Thoreau, that it is through our most profound experiences of enchantment at the crossing of nature and culture that we learn to cultivate an "ethical generosity" toward the world.[84]

I submit that the pure auditory voice in its *naturalness* as an aesthetic sensibility must be appreciated, therefore, for the part it plays in our ultimate constitution of conscious experience as semiotic process and phenomenological event of discourse. Such a theoretical move requires that we allow for nature and a sense of the wild to re-invigorate our understanding of what transpires when two people talk and listen to each other in immediate ear-to-ear contexts. It means honoring the aesthetic sounding voice of humans in its physiological manifestations, which temporally exist outside of speech, outside the intelligible, tying the human voice to its animal or wild nature. Although Aristotle seeks to set us apart from the animal by determining we are the "speaking or rational animal" who speaks with a voice that is soulful, I contend that we must now embrace the qualities of the wild that resonate within our soulful voices.[85]

Philosopher Helmuth Plessner, in his accounts of our expressivity from an existential perspective, stipulates that we most certainly have pre-linguistic auditory emissions that move us closer toward our animal natures. For him, the vocal experiences of laughing and crying serve, in part, to testify to this fact. They are examples of our expressivity being employed in excess of signifying practices per se. Like the voice in particular, laughing and crying also become quickly signified, however, in their perception. In their case, they prompt signification, given the inherent question of meaning they immediately provoke. We learn from Plessner to think of the eruptions of laughing and crying as tied to affect, yet they are separate from emotional expressiveness in their movement in discourse. As insightful as he is about the nature of our expressivity, it is unfortunate that in his discussions of laughing and crying he indicates that the face "takes the lead" in representing the body expression as the "mirror of the soul."[86] In this way, Plessner maintains a visualist orientation to expressivity as philosophy has repeatedly done, in a similar manner to Levinas.

Thinking with Plessner, we begin to understand that the voice as an integral component of our expressivity is an aspect of our being, an interior soulful quality similar to Ong's account and the one I am advancing, at the same time that we have a voice, a relation that we use in mediation with the outside world. Plessner reserves some theoretical room for an appreciation of the natural, or what I am calling the wildness of being, in our expressive acts. Our existential problematic when it comes to understanding our vocality or expressivity, as Plessner says, rests with continually finding the existential balance between our interior expressive qualities and exterior bodily comportment. For Plessner, this problematic is at the very heart of our existence as human beings.

Plessner concludes that our difference from animals is the "relation we have to our body."[87] When we emit pre-linguistic vocalizations, such as with the emissions of laughing and crying, we are conscious of our bodies as expressive and perceptive points of mediation with the world, even though these emissions in the moment of irruption are mostly involuntary. This is unlike the sounds animals make in their signaling processes. They do not have the distinct ability to create a "double distance"[88] or detachment from their points of contact with the world through consciousness of their means of emission: barks, tweets, and the like. Plessner contends, therefore, that we hold an "eccentric" position to ourselves that displays this inherent equivocality to relations. We are a body and we have a body; furthermore, we are consciously aware of both conditions as they play out simultaneously in experience.[89] His notion of our eccentric position is based upon three primary dialectics of expressivity: (a) the natural versus the artificial, (b) the immediate versus the mediated, and (c) a rootedness versus a groundlessness.[90] According to Plessner, all of these dialectics are operative within our lived experience and imbue it with a lived sense of ambiguity as we confront life's everyday challenges.

Animals, on the other hand, hold a "centric" position to the world and themselves. They do not have a consciousness of their being as such and, because of this, experience no equivocation in the world. They merely act from a center of existence, responding to the world of stimuli in developed patterns of action. The essential difference between the eccentric and centric positionality of humans and animals thus rests upon a recognition that expressivity as an action or performative irrupts the taken-for-granted of everyday existence—it offers a break in our way of being, if only temporarily. For Plessner, laughing and crying are thus unique expressions of the breakdown of the eccentric position, given that in such circumstances we are taken over by a more primal yet human means of expression.

Even in this brief description of Plessner, we find support for several points we have been exploring. First, Plessner's philosophy reinforces a return to an appreciation for the animal qualities of our existence, specifically at the vocal level. While he does not address the voice in particular, he does acknowledge the body and implicitly the voice as "primal sounding boards of expression."[91] Secondly, he endorses an interpretation of the voice of enunciation as indicative of the wild or natural elements of human existence, although he insists that to remain natural, that is, to speak and behave spontaneously, is difficult for us because our existence is so bound to the artificial.[92] By this, I interpret him to reference the cultural or symbolic. Third, his philosophy recognizes the existential ambiguity that humans experience, induced by their phenomenological and semiotic capabilities. This echoes the theme of ambiguity voiced in the works of Merleau-Ponty, Beauvoir, and others. As he theorizes, laughing and crying are the paramount exemplars for understanding how expressivity in general functions as an index of the many crises we experience, precipitated by confronting the fact that our relations with our own bodies are equivocal; we are a body and we have a body. Fourth, Plessner's work helps us understand how our expressivity in general, and our vocality in particular, function as pivotal points of mediation between the cultural aspects of our existence and the natural or more primal ones.

## THE VOICE OF ENUNCIATION AS A NATURAL SUMMONS TO CULTURAL EXPERIENCE

I submit that we must take into account the voice of enunciation as a call of the wild and an essential component of speaking and listening. Unlike Seth Kim-Cohen in his recent book *In the Blink of an Ear: Toward a Non-Cochlear Sound Art*, I do not think that the auditory in general must be theorized, ironically, through the lens of discursivity understood narrowly as textual linguisticality alone. Indicative perhaps of any critic who might argue against thinking of sound as a material substance in excess of signification, as I purport to do, Kim-Cohen asserts,

> The suggestion of an unadulterated, untainted purity of experience prior to linguistic capture seeks a return to a never-present, Romanticized, pre-Enlightenment darkness. . . . If some stimuli actually convey an experiential affect that precedes linguistic processing, what are we to do with such experiences? . . . If there is such a strata of experience, we must accept it mutely. It finds no voice in thought or discourse. Since there is nothing we can do with it, it seems wise to put it aside and concern ourselves with that of which we can speak.[93]

And yet, as we learned from the above discussions grounded in a semiotic phenomenology, Kim-Cohen could not be more misguided when it comes to theorizing sound and, in particular, our vocality. I am not advocating from a nostalgic position, harkening us back to an idealized or romanticized version of the voice with my offer of the voice of enunciation. Following Peirce's realism quite closely on this point, I believe the time has come in the communication discipline to begin to adequately theorize speech in its vocality and not through the lens of only language. The natural or wild qualities of our voice as a salient sonority of aesthetic experience must be acknowledged as an integral component of our lived relationality in its qualitative distinctiveness as an aspect of firstness. Given its affiliation with time and its inherent flow, the sounding voice of enunciation offers us an appropriate counterbalance to the mediated voice within cyberspace in its visual and spatial configurations—the voice of articulation.

As I have shown, the lawless voice that resounds momentarily outside the bounds of signification is altogether a consequence of semiotic processes and phenomenological events of discourse. With its ultimate destination in signification, it resounds nonetheless in its natural gestures of speaking and listening with an aim to penetrate, more deeply, self and other relations. The voice of excess thus announces our radical alterity through creating a semiotic and phenomenological irruption in the dominant, symbolic systems of meaning as a felt event. When this happens, this voice penetrates the semiotic relation of secondness. The voice that enunciates within immediate ear-to-ear relations potentializes Merleau-Ponty's sense of *parole parlée* (speaking speech). He tells us that speaking speech is possibilized when "language speaks peremptorily when it gives up trying to express the thing itself . . . [when] true speech . . . signifies . . . [and] does not go so far as to become a common name."[94] Following his mentor, Foucault later calls this sign action the nameless voice.

This voice re-invigorates our communicative relations with what I call a sense of the wild, that is, the untamed yet semiotic aspect of our pure potentiality. Within such irruptions, therefore, we discover our semiotic potentiality as phenomenological beings as we simultaneously confront the existential ambiguity such an irruption necessarily entails. By exploring the voice of enunciation, we have successfully revived the trope of enchantment, enunciating the important role *phone* as an aesthetic plays in our human relationality. The sonic voice of enunciation thus acts as an existential call or summons to hear relationality in its most immediate offering of presence.

It is at this juncture, having explored the qualities and some of the functions of the voice of enunciation, that we need to address specifically the consequences this voice presents for our relationality. We find that its pivotal nature better serves a relationality shaped by authenticity. It is here that we begin to evoke a re-enchantment of human communication through what I identify as *interper-sónal* relations. These themes are addressed in chapter 7.

## NOTES

1. Connor, *Dumbstruck*, 4.
2. Renato Barilli, liner notes to *Futura: Poesia Sonora* (Milano: Cramps Records, 1989), 4 quoted in Brandon LaBelle, "Raw Orality," 151.
3. Cavarero, *For More Than One Voice*, 9.
4. See Colapietro, "Striving to Speak," 384. Also, Colapietro, "Qualitative Immediacy."
5. Maurice Merleau-Ponty, "Indirect Language and the Voices of Silence," in *Signs*, trans. Richard C. McCleary (Chicago: Northwestern University Press, 1964), 46.
6. Ibid., 42.
7. Cavarero, *For More Than One Voice*, 14.
8. LaBelle, "Raw Orality," 167, emphasis added.
9. Dolar, *A Voice and Nothing More*, 23.
10. Roland Barthes, *The Pleasure of the Text*, trans. Richard Miller (New York: Noonday Press, 1975), 66–67.
11. Cavarero argues that Barthes, especially in *The Pleasure of the Text*, is actually upholding the aesthetic voice as a fetish object that Lacan contests. Although we may judge his assessments accordingly, he serves to at least identify the aesthetic dimensions of the voice as a bodily practice of discourse. Barthes understands the subversive nature of this voice.
12. Dolar, *A Voice and Nothing More*, 59.
13. Ong, *The Presence of the Word*, 111.
14. Ibid., 112.
15. Ibid., 113.
16. Ibid., 114.
17. Ibid., 117.
18. Cavarero, *For More Than One Voice*, 240.
19. Ong, *Presence of the Word*, 40–42.
20. Ibid., 44.
21. Anderson, *Creativity and the Philosophy*, 44.
22. Illustrating the dominance of sight and sound in Western thought, even Saussure conceptualizes the signifier most often as the "sound-image" that captures our attention. I am suggesting here that what captivates can be initiated by any of the senses.
23. Anderson, *Creativity and the Philosophy*, 58–59.
24. As Anderson explains, Peirce did not make his aesthetic turn until the mid-1890s. See Anderson, *Creativity and the Philosophy*, 4.
25. His notion of aesthetics is developed more thoroughly by fellow pragmatist John Dewey. See, in particular, *John Dewey: The Later Works, 1925–1953*, ed. Jo Ann Boydston, vol. 10, *1934* (Carbondale: Southern Illinois University Press, 1987).
26. In testifying to the importance of aesthetics to Peirce's semiotic, Herman Parret indicates, "The aesthetic Siren profoundly motivates Peirce when he 'invents' abduction." Herman Parret, *The Aesthetics of Communication: Pragmatics and Beyond* (Netherlands: Kluwer Academic Publishers, 1993), 84.
27. Hans-Georg Gadamer, *Truth and Method*, trans. W. Glen-Doepel (London: Sheed & Ward, 1975), 62–63, 316–320.
28. Hans-Georg Gadamer, *The Relevance of the Beautiful and Other Essays* (New York: Cambridge University Press, 1986), 18.
29. Ibid., 15.
30. Ibid., 15.
31. Alexander Baumgarten, *Aesthetica* (Hildesham: George Olms, 1961), Sec. 1, quoted in Gadamer, *Relevance*, 17.
32. Anderson, *Creativity and the Philosophy*, 58.
33. Schiller, *On the Aesthetic Education*, 161.
34. Bennett, *The Enchantment of Modern Life*, 133.
35. Ibid., 131.
36. Ibid., 138.
37. Ibid., 132.

38. Ibid., 132.
39. Locke, *The De-Voicing of Society*, 17.
40. Roman Jakobson, "The Speech Event and the Functions of Language," in *On Language: Roman Jakobson*, ed. Linda Waugh and Monique Monville-Burston (Cambridge, MA: Harvard University Press, 1990).
41. Cavarero, *For More Than One Voice*, 216.
42. Ibid., 216.
43. Gregory Bateson, *Sacred Unity: Further Steps to an Ecology of Mind*, ed. Rodney E. Donaldson (New York: Cornelia and Michael Bessie Book, 1991).
44. Deborah Eicher-Catt, "The Logic of the Sacred in Bateson and Peirce," *The American Journal of Semiotics* 19, no. 1/4 (2003).
45. Emmanuel Levinas, *Emmanuel Levinas: Basic Philosophical Writings*, eds. Adriaan T. Peperzak, Simon Critchley, and Robert Bernasconi (Indianapolis: Indiana University Press, 1996), 45.
46. Cavarero, *For More Than One Voice*, 28–29.
47. Ibid., 26.
48. Ibid., 29.
49. In this regard, Levinas is in complete harmony with the symbolic interactionists, as developed in particular by George Herbert Mead.
50. Cavarero, *For More Than One Voice*, 30.
51. Ihde, *Listening and Voice*, 3.
52. Cavarero, *For More Than One Voice*, 20.
53. Ibid., 31.
54. Ibid., 27.
55. Ibid., 27.
56. Christoph Cox, "Beyond Representation and Signification: Toward a Sonic Materialism," *Journal of Visual Culture* 10, no. 2 (2011): 148.
57. Connor, *Dumbstruck*, 7.
58. David Oscar Harvey, "The Limits of Vococentrism: Chris Marker, Hans Richter and the Essay Film," *SubStance* 41, no. 2 (2012): 7.
59. Dolar, *A Voice and Nothing More*, 45.
60. Because of its relatedness to spontaneity and chance, this voice also demonstrates Peirce's notion of tychism or theory of chance. Peirce identifies chance with an indeterminate feeling. As he states in *The Collected Papers*, 6.265, "Wherever chance-spontaneity is found, there in the same proportion feeling exists. In fact, chance is but the outward aspect of that which within itself is feeling."
61. Anderson, *Creativity and the Philosophy*.
62. Bennet attributes these qualities to Henry David Thoreau. As she indicates, Thoreau appreciated both the wildness of nature and the experience of solitude because they disrupted "one's normal or default mode of being." See, Jane Bennett, *Thoreau's Nature: Ethics, Politics, and the Wild* (Lanham, MD: Rowman & Littlefield Publishers, Inc. 2002), xxii.
63. As explained by cultural theorist Frances Dyson, French philosopher Michel Serres believes that the sonic environment induced by electronic connectivity results in producing a constant "solipsism of endless iterations of transmissions that circle the globe with ever-increasing speed . . . [and these] can be heard as the tinnitus-like ring, the very high-frequency pitch, barely discernible, of electronic communication." See, Dyson, *The Tone of Our Times*, 108.
64. See, for example, Bilgrami, "Occidentalism;" Bilgrami, *Secularism, Identity, and Enchantment;* Johnson, "This Enchantment Is No Delusion."
65. Bennett, *The Enchantment of Modern Life*, 95.
66. Ibid., 92.
67. Ibid., 95.
68. Ibid., 94.
69. Bennett is quick to acknowledge that Bruno Latour, with his proposed network theory, is trying to dispel the dichotomy of nature and culture so prevalent in philosophical circles. I

believe Peirce's triadic structure successfully accounts for the way nature and culture intermingle within conscious experience.

70. Bennett, *The Enchantment of Modern Life*, 94.

71. Linda Simon, "Bewitched, Bothered, and Bewildered: William James's Feeling of 'If,'" in *The Re-Enchantment of the World: Secular Magic in a Rational Age*, eds. Joshua Landy and Michael Saler (Stanford: Stanford University Press, 2009), 39.

72. Ibid., 40.

73. Henry David Thoreau, *Journal*, 15 May 1853.

74. Johnson, "'This Enchantment Is No Delusion.'"

75. As detailed by Nicholas L. Guardiano, these ideas coalesced into the Transcendental Movement embraced by Thoreau and this movement greatly influenced the intellectual project of his New England neighbor, Charles Sanders Peirce. Guardiano, "Charles S. Peirce's New England Neighbors and Embrace of Transcendentalism," *Transactions of the Charles S. Peirce Society* 53, no. 2 (2017).

76. Zebuhr, "Sound Enchantment," 582.

77. Alexandra Morrison and Laura Zebuhr, "The Voice of Ambiguity: Simone de Beauvoir's Literary and Phenomenological Echoes," *Hypatia* 30, no. 2 (Spring 2015), 418.

78. Simon, "Bewitched, Bothered, and Bewildered," 40.

79. Zebuhr, "Sound Enchantment."

80. Johnson, "'This Enchantment Is No Delusion.'"

81. Zebuhr, "Sound Enchantment," 585.

82. Thoreau, *Journal*, 18 September 1858.

83. Zebuhr, "Sound Enchantment," 589.

84. Bennett, *The Enchantment of Modern Life*.

85. Some argue that the Internet represents the new *Wild West*, given the current lack of oversight. I argue that, while we may describe it as our new wild, it is unfortunately a hollow or reduced sense of the wild, as I am employing the term here. It is a wild that is thoroughly tethered to the semantic/symbolic system, an artifice indeed.

86. Helmuth Plessner, *Laughing and Crying: A Study of the Limits of Human Behavior*, trans. James Spencer Churchill and Majorie Grene (Evanston: Northwestern University Press, 1970), 45.

87. Ibid., xii.

88. Ibid., xii.

89. Semiotician John Deely claims we are semiotic animals. With this concept, he partially agrees with Plessner on the animal/human distinction. For Deely, as semiotic animals we participate in semiosis and at the same time are conscious of it, unlike animals. See John Deely, *Semiotic Animal: A Postmodern Definition of "Human Being" Transcending Patriarchy and Feminism* (South Bend: St. Augustine's Press, 2010).

90. Plessner, *Laughing and Crying*, 39.

91. Ibid., 44.

92. Ibid., 44.

93. Kim-Cohen, *In the Blink of an Ear*, 112.

94. Merleau-Ponty, "Indirect Language," 44.

*Chapter Seven*

# The Pivotal Nature of Voice

Interper-sónal *Relationality and Its Authenticity*

As we learned so far, the voice of enunciation as a phenomenological event is an action produced by the very "flesh of the soul,"[1] for we found that the voice shares an etymological link with spirit and breath. Dolar asserts that the voice as breath points to the soul given that it embodies our "quintessential corporeality and the soul."[2] This assertion implies, of course, the dialectical tensions in lived experience between materiality and immateriality and the intelligible and ineffable, the tensions that are at the very heart of existence as a lived ambiguity. From our discussions, we discovered that our natural vocality originates from an ineffable interior where literally and figuratively the heart of a person dwells.[3] I insist that such a hermeneutic of the voice renews our appreciation for the important phenomenological aspect of voice and, as a semiotic sign relation of firstness and secondness, the voice of the wild momentarily exceeds the symbolic, although it is necessarily bound to it just the same. Hence, we find that it is best to view the voice of enunciation as a fundamental medium of human experience that contributes to our natural unfolding as cultural human beings. My aim in the last chapter was to attest to this voice's originary aesthetic nature and function as a fully embodied materiality at the pre-logical level that inevitably calls us powerfully toward one another in the dyadic relation of secondness. Unlike the hyper-textual visual forms of information exchange that our digital age promotes, Dolar reminds us of the performative value of the voice in its sounding[4] in which we experience a very different degree of communicative intensity. The enunciating voice potentializes a mutuality of aesthetic co-presence as a semiotic process like no other sensory experience. Dolar confirms this natural materiality of the voice by stipulating that "the voice appears as the link which ties the signifier to the body. It indicates that the signifier . . . must have a point of origin and emission in the body."[5] Again, his statement explains how the voice negotiates a complex semiotic and phenomenological boundary. Detailing the voice within the complex semiotic relation of firstness and secondness, we discover why "firstness [is] the most elusive of Peirce's categories of experience."[6] As Peirce insists, firstness "is so tender that you cannot touch it without spoiling it."[7] It is only within its relation to secondness and mediation by thirdness that its aspects begin to come to the fore.

Herein, I extend my previous discussion on the qualities and functions of the voice of enunciation by detailing the key role it plays as an existential pivot point within human experience. By understanding its pivotal nature as a semiotic relation of firstness and secondness in thirdness, we begin to appreciate how the natural sounding of voices activates several dialectics and their subsequent semiotic and phenomenological recursive negotiations; nature and culture (as alluded to above), the body and language, the Greek's depiction of *zoe* and *bios*, Aristotle's *phone (semantike)* and *logos*, self and other, and listening and speaking. The pivotal point from which discourse as speaking and listening emerges within this auditory register is highly paradoxical, however, and accentuates our lived ambiguity as cultural beings, an ambiguity that Merleau-Ponty and Beauvoir so clearly delineated. As LaBelle asserts,

> The voice comes to us as an expressive signal announcing the presence of a body and an individual—it proceeds by echoing forward away from the body while also granting that body a sense of individuation, marking vocality with a measurable paradox. The voice is the very core of an ontology that balances presence and absence, life and death, upon an unsteady and transformative axis.[8]

Moreover, by keeping the voice of enunciation foremost in mind, our theory of human relationality necessarily shifts from an impersonal focus (enhanced by our appeals to merely the voice of articulation) to an actual *interper-sónal* one. This philosophical shift calls, in other words, for a re-signing of our traditional designation of interpersonal communication so as to emphasize the crucial *sonic* elements that we now understand inhere within immediate ear-to-ear events of speaking and listening. The additional accent on the sonic aspect of the word is intended to mark this very distinction. In this way, the sonic components that resonate in the voice of enunciation are heard and appreciated for the richness of being they carry within immediate ear-to-ear relations. In such cases of speaking with and listening to the voice of enunciation in its aesthetic wildness, we dispense with the dominant signifying systems, if only temporarily, and possibilize new contexts for meaning and understanding.

As we shall see, the voice of enunciation thus creates a necessary gap in human conscious experience, emphasizing the actual void of silence from which it springs. This gap affords us the very possibility of being powerfully enchanted by the sounding of the other, however, within inter-mediate experience. Because of its enchanting effects, this voice prompts a renewed indebtedness to relationality itself in our natural unfolding as cultural beings. The voice, after all we have learned, accentuates nearness as opposed to distance and autonomy.[9] I end this chapter by advocating that we attend to these interper-sónal qualities of discursive practices. This aesthetic sensibility will re-enchant our overall understanding of human communication. Within such enchanting experiences between self and other, we additionally find a promising semio-ethic—one that is produced within embodied interper-sónal relations. We discover that by attending to the important auditory aspects of speaking with and listening to this voice, we enhance our chances of constituting more authentic encounters with others. This enhanced attending proves to be the necessary and sufficient condition by which to counter the inauthentic enchantments we too often find in our current electronic culture that deprive us of a fuller sense of our humanity.

## THE PIVOTAL FUNCTION OF THE ENCHANTING SOUNDING OF VOICE

As I mentioned, generally enchantments are semiotically and phenomenologically constituted by way of an initial element of sensory, perceptual surprise, which leaves us temporarily transfixed on the existent. Our experiences of enchantment, no matter the sensory stimuli, are, therefore, quite paradoxical. That is, we simultaneously experience a disruption to everyday sense perception (the element of surprise) that produces a gap in the flow of experience at the same time that we are transfixed by the institution of that very gap. As Philip Fisher describes, a sense of wonder or enchantment creates a temporary "moment of pure presence." He says that "the moment of pure presence within wonder lies in the object's difference and uniqueness being so striking to the mind that it does not remind us of anything and we find ourselves delaying in its presence for a time in which the mind does not move on by association to something else."[10] In essence, Fisher is describing the semiotic aesthetic experience of firstness and secondness, where distinctions and differences begin to appear within our conscious awareness. This is, of course, the aesthetics of enchantment that lies at the heart of such experiences, recognized by so many scholars, the aesthetics which are powerfully affectual in their significant effects. Fisher also alludes to the fact that enchantments, as an element of surprise, serve as a disruption where we "bump up against [the] hard fact"[11] of relation itself, the mode of secondness as Peirce outlines.

In these ways, the voice of enunciation as an enchanting sign condition is no different than any visual cue. However, as we learned, the voice of enunciation in its enchanting effect breaks into conscious experience in a different way than other sensory stimuli, given its intense auditory qualities. When it comes to the auditory, the break is more prominent, given its penetrating nature and capacity to literally surround or inhabit us in its immateriality and sense of materiality simultaneously. Important to keep in mind, given our current digital age of distraction, is the fact that when we attend to this voice of the other, we may "delay in its presence for a time," as Fisher indicates. This means that we may allow ourselves to be enchanted by the other's voice by lengthening our attendant qualities to the other in a momentary mutuality of inter-mediacy. I submit that this orientation to the voice of the other helps to counteract our new distracting habits of discourse, where attention to the immediate other often takes a back seat to the lure of the textual and the electronic. As we shall see, this voice radically affects the flow and substance of our relationality in very distinct ways from what textual messages alone can offer.

Because it breaks into conscious experience as an auditory irruption, the enunciated voice emerges from the void of awareness as silence and constitutes that void semiotically and phenomenologically. Dolar compares the experience of silence to death, stipulating that, in contrast, with the voice we discover the first sign of life.[12] He continues, "We are social beings by the voice and through the voice; it seems that the voice stands at the axis of our social bonds, and that voices are the very texture of the social, as well as the intimate kernel of subjectivity."[13] It is important to recognize, therefore, that the voice of enunciation acts as an important pivotal point between the personal and the social, between the pre-cultural or natural world of experience (as a call of wildness) and the symbolic or cultural world of meaning and signification. As we shall hear, this voice activates a dialectical auditory movement between several nodes of experience by drawing attention to a temporary semiotic gap or breach in our stream of awareness and sense making as the relation of firstness and secondness transpires. At the same time, the voice of enunciation allows for the semiotic and phenomenological negotiation of that very gap. Dolar describes this pivotal feature of the voice as "paramount" and argues that it "opens a zone of undecidability, of a between-the-two, an intermediacy."[14] I will have more to say about this "zone of undecidability" as it relates to our lived sense of ambiguity further in my discussion.

For now, I pursue in more detail the pivotal nature and function of the voice of enunciation. While Dolar does not label this voice as wild in its naturalness, as I do, he refers to this voice as the lawless voice. In particular, Dolar attempts to extend the work of his mentor on the voice, especially as it relates to the sonorous voice. As mentioned, Lacan's object voice or the voice of excess is the presence/absence non-auditory voice. Dolar is bent on pursuing the audible register of this voice, its counterpart as the aesthetic voice that contributes to meaning quite indirectly and yet resonates just the same. His descriptions of this pre-cultural voice at the intersections of presence and absence, the natural and the cultural, the body and language, the ancient Greek's sense of *zoe* and *bios*, and self and other are instructive. By doing so, he encourages us to appreciate the pivotal role the sonorous voice has within human relations.

Taking up the dialectic between nature and culture, Dolar refers to Plato's *Symposium*, specifically the scene in which Aristophanes suffers from the hiccups. According to Dolar, this scene illustrates that even the involuntary intrusion of physiological processes can disrupt speech.[15] He states,

> This pre-cultural, non-cultural voice can be seen as the zero-point of signification, the incidence of meaning, itself not meaning anything, the point around which other—meaningful—voices can be ordered, as if the hiccups stood at the very focus of the structure. The voice presents a short circuit between nature and culture, between physiology and structure; its vulgar [or wild] nature is mysteriously transubstantiated into meaning *tout court*.[16]

I want to make several initial points about this passage as it pertains to the pivotal nature of the voice of enunciation.

First, Dolar recognizes that the pure voice of enunciation is similar to the involuntary irruption that hiccups entail. Both vocal emissions serve to disrupt and destabilize sedimented discursive practices (their aspect of secondness) by the fact that their resounding constitutes a zero-point of signification. In the case of the voice, it may be pre-cultural or pre-logical (not yet fully evolved in semiotic relations of secondness by thirdness), but it generates a semiotic process or action of semiosis nevertheless. Hence, we should remember that there is a natural aspect to the voice's sounding that is in many cases quite involuntary, even as it contributes to discourse.

Second, as a destabilizing force, this voice acts as a pivot or "short circuit" between our natural processes, of which speaking as sonority is a part, and our cultural acts of signification as linguistic creatures. This voice serves as a sign relation of secondness. Here, Dolar positions the pre-cultural sounding voice at the intersection of nature and culture and claims that this voice serves as a pivot point between the two. This idea supports my arguments that our understanding of human communication would benefit by acknowledging that speaking as a human action should be identified by both its natural and cultural components. The natural and the cultural elements share a similar relation within communicative experience as expression and perception; they constitute a reflexive, recursive dialectical pair. In other words, speaking with and listening to the voice of enunciation amplifies the dialectical relation between the natural and the cultural.[17]

Third, Dolar acknowledges that the sounding voice is ultimately an act or gesture of speaking. Its "apparent exteriority [to the symbolic] hits the core of the structure; it epitomizes the signifying gesture precisely by not signifying anything in particular, it presents the speech in its minimal traits, which may later get obscured by articulation."[18] Here, Dolar is highlighting this essential function of the voice at the same time that he is conceding that even this voice's destiny resounds within the voice of articulation as I have described it, the voice of signification. That is, the voice of enunciation eventually also serves our linguisticality even as it clearly announces particular aspects of our animality as a wildness. The key phrase that Dolar uses is "presents the speech," a phrase that endorses the notion of speaking speech, embodied in Merleau-Ponty's French phrase *parole parlante*. This is the aspect of the voice prior to its articulate sedimentation as speech spoken, or *parole parlée*. Speaking speech potentializes originary discourse.

It is clear to Dolar that the pre-cultural voice or the voice of enunciation should be appreciated for its uniqueness as a qualitatively distinct element in discourse at the same time that we should also appreciate it in relation to the signifying order of things. As I interpret Dolar, he is acknowledging that the sonorous voice may temporarily exist outside of the symbolic, but it is a *semiotic function* of discursive practices nonetheless. Here, he specifically extends the work of Lacan on this point by pinpointing the fact that the inaudible voice of excess of signification, to which Lacan refers, has its counterpart in the audible, and both function semiotically and phenomenologically in the constitution of discourse. In other words, the voice of excess is semiotic in both its audible and inaudible forms (Lacan's voice as *object a*). Dolar is thus claiming that the audible "voice and nothing more," the voice of enunciation, can exist prior to sedimentation within thirdness as an aspect of relationality. This voice should not be conceptualized, however, as a transcendent essence, as Dolar is quick to detail.[19] Dispelling the notion that the voice, and in particular the singing voice, should be conceptualized as transcendence, Dolar clearly states, "The voice as the bearer of a deeper sense, of some profound message, is a structural illusion, the core of a fantasy that the singing voice might cure the wound inflicted by culture, restore the loss that we suffered by the assumption of the symbolic order."[20] As I interpret this passage, he is advocating for an appreciation of the voice as a semiotic and phenomenological relational enactment. There exists, in other words, an audible aspect of the voice at the pivot point between silence and speaking, between self and other, and this voice must be recognized as an integral aspect of the semiotic process of relationality.[21] So the voice we are pursuing is not transcendent but should be understood as a reflexive one, thoroughly steeped within relationality. Furthermore, the subject is constituted within this recursion.[22]

For Dolar, the importance of this apparent "wound" cannot be overstated when it comes to appreciating the voice as a semiotic entailment. He points us to this wound and describes it as the phenomenological gap induced by the actual intersections of the natural and the cultural. As the void or silence that the audible voice announces, the voice thus plays an integral part in instituting and negotiating this gap.[23] Thus, the natural or phenomenological aspects of the voice along with its semiotic enunciation explicitly announce this very gap as a pivotal point within lived experience.

It is to an understanding of this semiotic and phenomenological gap as a function of the voice of enunciation that I now turn. I intend to show that as enunciation, the sounding voice acts as the important pivot between several semiotic and phenomenological dialectics: the body and language, the Greek's depiction of *zoe* and *bios*, Aristotle's *phone* (*semantike*) and *logos*, self and other, and listening and speaking. I lean heavily upon Dolar and Italian philosopher Georgio Agamben in this section to clarify my points. I ask my reader to keep in mind that all of these dialectics are activated as a semiotic and phenomenological consequence of sign relations.

## The Pivot Between Body and Language

To begin, we encounter the voice of enunciation at the intersection of the dialectical relation of body and language as a relation of firstness and secondness. While this relation was interrogated to some extent in the last chapter with my discussion of the voice of enunciation as a semiotic phenomenology, Dolar is explicit about why the voice we are pursuing is a rupture that expresses the delicate balance between its position as a bodily manifestation and its role in service to language. He states,

> Of course . . . [the voice] has an inherent link to presence, to what there is, to the point of endorsing the very notion of presence, yet at the same time, as we have seen, it presents a break, it is not to be simply counted among existing things, its topology dislocates it in relation to presence. And—most important in this context—*it is precisely the voice that holds bodies and languages together*. It is like their missing link, what they have in common. The language is attached to the body through the voice.[24]

As he clarifies, we need to understand that while the voice ties language to the body, it paradoxically does not belong to either—body or language.[25] This is the very voice and nothing more that he pursues. In its emission, the voice detaches from the body even as it remains a corporeal manifestation in its very passing. This same voice is in service to language, but, as we have discovered, it exceeds signification in its semiotic firstness as an aesthetic. It is here that we need to remind ourselves that even though the voice emits an interior (as Ong suggests) that perhaps rings true to someone's natural inclinations, it is not an interior that exists outside the structures of language. For if we accept the notion that our sense of self is socially, that is, culturally, derived, then we must conclude that our interior is the culmination of previous exterior discursive practices.[26] Philosopher Vincent Colapietro reminds us, following Whitehead, that "the human self in its present actuality is, at once, an inheritor of a determinate past and a benefactor of an indeterminate future."[27] So the very structure of language—through the slippage of signifying practices—also potentializes the wildness or the naturalness of our being as I conceive it. Dolar articulates it best when he says, "What is exposed [in the voice] . . . is not some interior nature . . . or a primordial inner life; rather, it is an interior which is itself the result of the signifying cut, its product."[28] This leads Dolar to conclude that this voice inheres within the "zone of overlapping, the crossing, the extimate."[29] The word *extimate* or *extimacy* is Lacan's word for describing the uncanny which manifests as an internal externality.[30] As we shall see, Agamben refers to this notion of extimacy when discussing the political dimensions of lived experience and finds in it a way to grasp the complexities of being political. It is best for us to conclude that the voice of enunciation is both an interior expression and an exterior perception and vice versa. Said differently, this voice always expresses its previous perceptions, a fact that harkens to a communicological approach to discourse. It is the uncanniness of this voice that now needs to be recaptured, given that the echoes of the acousmatic voices within cyberspace and on the Internet have seemed to replace its natural allure.

## The Pivot Between *Zoe* and *Bios*

Dolar argues that the voice serves at the explicit pivotal point between the ancient Greek's sense of *zoe* and *bios*, which also implies the pivot between Aristotle's sense of *phone* (*phone semantike*) and the *logos*. It is at these junctures within semiotic secondness that the political emerges. First, I'll address the pivot between *zoe* and *bios,* according to Agamben's interpretation of the Greeks.

According to the ancient Greeks, describing what we mean by the word "life" is a complicated affair.[31] Drawing from a passage in Aristotle's *Politics*, Agamben emphasizes Aristotle's use of the term *zoe* to refer to natural life and contends that "in the classical world . . . [the] simple natural life is excluded from the *polis* in the strict sense, and remains confined . . . to the sphere of the *oikos*, 'home.'"[32] Desiring to investigate this very exclusion of *zoe* in the life of the communal, Agamben appeals to Foucault's theory of biopolitics in which Foucault claims that in the modern era "natural life begins to be included in the mechanisms and calculations of State power."[33] Agamben thus emphasizes the distinctive yet overlapping mechanisms between *zoe* and *bios* as a way to discuss his theory of exclusion/inclusion (*extimacy*) when it comes to communal life and our experience of it.

Following Agamben's interpretation of the Greeks, we can understand *zoe* as naked or bare life, that is, life understood in its animality. The concept of *zoe* thus accentuates a function of living, like breathing and eating. It is life that is *supposedly* external to the political world. *Bios*, on the other hand, indicates "the form or way of living proper to an individual or group."[34] *Bios* is life lived in community, in the *polis*, according to Agamben. It is sociopolitical life that we constitute and share as humans. In terms of the distinction I have made about the voice, generally the voice of *zoe* shares affinities with the voice of enunciation, while the voice of *bios* resounds within articulation. Given that the Greeks acknowledge that both animals and men have in common the wild voice of enunciation, Dolar also equates this voice with bare life. This conceptualization validates my contention that the voice of enunciation has its inherent natural wildness that should be acknowledged as a necessary component of its structure. As described by Aristotle, this mere voice in its wildness indicates, that is, it serves as an index in semiotic terms. By this, Aristotle means that this voice indicates or points to an animal's sense of pleasure and pain. On this particular note, as you recall, Plessner would agree and applies this distinction also to humans. Laughing and crying, as involuntary vocal emissions, also indicate emotional responses, although for Plessner this is not their entire significance. While Plessner argues that laughing and crying are unique to humans, he does acknowledge they are forms of expressivity that share a rudimentary association with the centric positionality of animals. My contention is that this natural aspect of the voice most prominently indicates the co-presence of self and other and, because of its auditory nature, does so most profoundly.

Now for Dolar, what is most interesting about the mere voice of *zoe* is that it persists even when the voice of *bios* (the voice of articulation) seems to supersede it. This is important, given our pursuit of this voice within human relations and the capacity it might provide for more intense levels of calling to the other, aside from what is articulated in discourse. By persisting in its sounding, Dolar claims that this voice of *zoe* imposes the paradoxical position of *extimacy*. *Extimacy* is the simultaneous inclusion/exclusion to which Agamben specifies in his work in *Homo Sacer*. Dolar's description of this delicate pivot point of the voice is worth quoting. He states,

> For what presents a problem is not that *zoe* is simply presocial, the animality, the outside of the social, but that it persists, in its very exclusion/inclusion, at the heart of the social—just as the voice is not simply an element external to speech, but persists at its core, making it possible and constantly haunting it by the impossibility of symbolizing it. And even more: the voice is not some remnant of a previous precultural state, or of some happy primordial fusion when we were not yet plagued by language and its calamities; rather, it is the product of *logos* itself, sustaining and troubling it at the same time.[35]

When Dolar says that this voice is a product of *logos*, he is specifying two ideas that I have been explicating—first, that the voice of enunciation is heard as a result of its oppositional nature to the voice of articulation (and the inaudible voice as *object a*) and, second, that this voice does not exist *a priori* but is integral to the developing semiotic process of discourse. In the ancient Greek's framework, the voice of *zoe* is excluded from the political, but, as Dolar contends via Agamben, it is at the same time included by its very exclusion. This position supports Agamben's claims in *Homo Sacer*, according to Dolar, that there is no simple externality that exists as the Greek's *bios*. Instead, with Agamben and Dolar (and Foucault), we begin to see that the political is the result of an inclusive exclusion of naked life as it plays out within the social realm. And, more importantly, that *extimacy* is activated through the voice of enunciation (as a sign condition of secondness), the voice that persists even when we may consciously ignore it.

## The Pivot Between *Phone* and *Logos*

The discussion of *zoe* and *bios* leads seamlessly into Dolar's explication of the dialectic between *phone* (*semantike*) and *logos*. This is because, for Dolar, the political is constituted as a result of the division between the *phone* and the *logos*, Aristotle's *phone semantike,* the *phone* that serves the *bios*. He claims that "there is a huge divide between *phone* and *logos*, and everything appears to follow from there, despite the fact that *logos* itself is still wrapped in voice, that it is *phone semantike*, the meaningful voice which relegates the mere voice to prehistory."[36]

In defense of the mere voice of enunciation against the onslaught of the *logos* (interpreted as *phone semantic* and textual in nature), Dolar cites several "practical and empirically observable"[37] examples from Althusser's ideological state apparatuses—the church, the courts or legal system, and the university. We are reminded that each apparatus operates according to a highly codified and ritualized set of discursive practices. However, each also displays the performative value of the *viva voce* or the *phone* of *zoe*. In the case of the church, Dolar asserts that religious rituals cannot be performed without using the voice, chief among these are prayers and sacred formulas. Even though these rituals are detailed in sacred texts, their performative strength only comes from being voiced.[38] In such cases, it is the living voice, characterized as the voice of enunciation, that imbues such practices with their efficacy.

Dolar argues that secular examples in the court system and the legislature follow the same vocal pattern. In terms of court proceedings, part of the process and the depositions that have to be made are required to be vocal. Witnesses and defendants may have sworn statements that are, of course, textual, but they must take the stand in order to vocally express their positions. He reminds us in Aristotle's depiction of deliberative rhetoric that the voice serves as the medium of justice and democracy.[39] While in both the courts and the legislature there are written protocols, in the end such documents represent the faithful copy of the voice.[40]

The last example he uses is the university setting. He prompts us to remember that in Anglo-American educational settings the dissertation or doctoral thesis must be defended in the living voice.[41] While the research is completed and recorded in textual form, it is not until the dissertation defense that the candidate orally performs the knowledge gained and is subsequently awarded the degree. Even in everyday classroom settings, while students are required to read the textual material on the subject matter, it is expected that the teacher will give a living voice to it in the form of lectures and through oral discussion. While knowledge is stored in textual form, Dolar makes the case that it does not become effective until it is relegated to the voice.

In each of these cases, we find the oppositional nature of *phone (semantike)* and *logos*, or the voice and the letter. The delicate negotiation of the two in different contexts is highly codified and ritualized. We might conclude that the division of labor between *phone* and *logos* is a complementary one, by which Dolar means unproblematic. However, Dolar is quick to indicate that the pivot point between the two is necessarily a political one, evidencing that complementary relations are inherently hierarchical. Power struggles thus ensue to a certain extent between the living voice of enunciation and the *logos* in most all circumstances. What is more, according to Dolar, is that it is during intense moments of conflict that we find the living voice being put to a very different use and function. Instead of merely enacting or lending efficacy to the textual as *phone semantike*, according to Dolar, the living voice can also question the authority of the letter thereby supplanting it.[42] Again, this is the sign condition by which we find speaking speech or *parole parlante* instead of *parole parlée*, speech spoken. It is the very instantiation of discourse in any originary form that may signify the development of new habits of being and relating.

At the root of Dolar's discussion of the pivotal nature of the voice at the political nexus of *phone* and *logos*, or the voice and the letter, Dolar appeals once again to Agamben, particularly his book *Homo Sacer*. In it, Agamben describes the qualities and functions of sovereignty. As he sees it, sovereignty is based on exception, the ability to suspend the rules—to create or announce what he calls a "state of emergency" where "the usual laws are no longer valid, and the exception becomes the rule."[43] A state of emergency shares affinities, according to Dolar, with *zoe*—bare life where the non-political reigns (as cast by Aristotle). A state of emergency is declared at times when, in fact, bare life is most in danger, either by natural catastrophes or when "one is obliged, in the name of bare life, to cancel the validity of the normal rule of law."[44]

What I find most compelling about Dolar's discussion about sovereignty and the declaration of a state of emergency is his assertion about the voice.

For him, the voice (understood as the voice of enunciation) is analogous to sovereignty itself. He claims that

> *the voice is structurally in the same position as sovereignty*, which means that it can suspend the validity of the law and inaugurate the state of emergency. The voice stands at the point of exception which threatens to become the rule, where it suddenly displays its profound complicity with the bare life, *zoe* as opposed to *bios*, that Aristotle was talking about. The emergency is the emergence of the voice in the commanding position, where its concealed existence suddenly becomes overwhelming and devastating. The voice is precisely at the unlocatable spot in the interior and the exterior of the law at the same time, and hence a permanent threat of a state of emergency.[45]

Conceptualizing the voice of enunciation as an act of sovereignty resonates with the ideas I have been advancing. By its disruptive tone, this voice possibilizes a sovereignty from the sedimented habits of communal discourse and action that too often, we find, leave us psychologically bereft. As I argue, our digital age of distraction has produced and condoned a more superficial or impersonal way of being and relating. Given the increasing rates of depression and anxiety in America, perhaps it is time to listen to the declaration of this voice. As I hear it, this voice calls, if only momentarily, for a state of emergency when it comes to relationality itself, when it comes to our expressions and perceptions of one another. It can serve, therefore, to suspend the taken-for-granted ways of electronically relating and inaugurate, instead, a renewed appreciation for the wildness that inheres within lived relations. Because the voice of enunciation can disrupt the taken-for-granted in such a dramatic way (indicating its relation to secondness), speaking with and listening to this voice can inaugurate new habits of discourse that could prove to be more satisfying for self and other. In this way, we understand that the voice of enunciation is a thoroughly political voice. It enunciates the political in its very emission.

In a similar fashion as the pivot between body and language, the voice of enunciation holds together both the *zoe* and *bios* and the *phone semantike* and *logos*. And yet again, paradoxically, this voice creates the very boundary conditions between them. On discussing these dialectical relations, Dolar emphasizes how these dialectics overlap in a location—the intersection or void—in which the voice is precarious and elusive and yet serves a vital function as it holds the dialectics together.[46] As such, the voice of enunciation can instigate the political in its very sounding. This voice, in other words, provides "an opening, a pure enunciation compelling a response, an act, a dislocation of the imposing voices of domination."[47] It presents as speaking speech.

Cavarero is also keen on explicating this important political aspect of the voice when she attempts to redefine what political speech is by way of

Hannah Arendt's work, in particular *The Human Condition*. Taking her lead from Arendt, Cavarero shows that political speech is not merely "the signifying capacity of the speaker, the communicative capacity of discourse, or the semantic content of a given statement."[48] Instead, we discover that, à la Arendt, "speech is not a mere faculty that distinguishes man from animal, or a general capacity for signification that allows human beings to communicate with one another; rather, speech is first and foremost a privileged way in which the speaker actively, and therefore politically, distinguishes him- or herself to others,"[49] and this process is best understood as an accomplishment of the unique sounding voices of self and other.[50]

## *The Voices of Enunciation*—Romeo and Juliet

An illustration of the crucial pivot of the voice of enunciation between *zoe* and *bios* and *phone semantike* and *logos* within the interpersonal context is provided in Shakespeare's famous balcony scene in the play *Romeo and Juliet*. The star-crossed lovers are so because they quite literally exist at the very intersections of *phone* and *logos* (letter) and *zoe* and *bios*, the sign condition whose negotiation is ambiguous and difficult to master. Their personal agency is thwarted by the letters or names (*logos*)—Capulet and Montague—which ascribe to each of them a very distinct and different sociopolitical positionality or *bios*. Hence, their tragedy is played out as a struggle against the *logos* and *bios* that threaten to dominate their unadulterated love (*zoe*) for each other in its intense passion and wildness. Kottman points out that it is the balcony scene in particular in which the tragedy of their plight is momentarily suspended and we witness—or better, hear—the negotiation of their paradoxical situation and their attempts to set a new context of discourse for themselves that will resonate their *zoe*. It is the very battle waged against the *logos* and *bios* by the *phone*, the voice of enunciation.

Cavarero, in her hermeneutic of this famous play, declares that when Derrida offers his interpretation of the play in a brief essay from 1986 titled "Aphorism Countertime" the fact that the balcony scene itself is "centered on vocalic uniqueness"[51] totally escapes Derrida's awareness. Instead, Derrida's focus is on the problem of the proper name and the aphorism or countertime—"the mechanism of equivocations and delays—messages that arrive too late at their destination, and at the wrong time—which not only lead to the death of the two lovers, but also allow each one to see and to survive, albeit briefly, the other's death."[52] This is unfortunate on Derrida's part. For Cavarero, the scene most aptly reveals the power of the voice itself and the potential it has to disrupt the *logos* and *bios*. It reveals

> the ontological status of a unique being whose existence is not reducible to the name, or to language. . . . Recognizing Romeo's voice, the young girl recog-

nizes the uniqueness of the loved one, separable from the proper name ("thou art thyself, though not a Montague" [2.2.39]), which is communicated to her vocally. Thus the essential bond between voice and uniqueness [*zoe*]—theatrically underscored by a nocturnal darkness that empowers the exclusive role of the acoustic sphere—comes to the fore.[53]

Cavarero helps us understand that the entire scene is centered around the voice that we have been pursuing, "aside from the significance of the words that are pronounced."[54] This is most dramatically emphasized by the fact that the dialogue between them unfolds in darkness—they do not see each other, which enhances the importance of the auditory register. When Juliet's presumed soliloquy about her thoughts of love is answered by Romeo's voice, she recognizes him by it: "My ears have not yet drunk a hundred words of thy tongue's uttering, yet I know the sound."[55] Moreover, while the uniqueness of Romeo is attached to the actual name, it is the "physical, corporeal element of the voice—in contrast to a proper name, which belongs instead to the verbal register [that matters in the end]. The name is not flesh; still less is it singular flesh. The voice, however, is."[56]

It appears that Shakespeare well understood that the voice itself provides the pivot from which to negotiate the complex boundary between *phone semantike* and *logos*, and *zoe* and *bios*, elucidated so beautifully in this scene. By declaring that love itself is not a proper name, Shakespeare's characters also emphasize the important function of the aesthetic, illustrating how love itself is an aesthetic par excellence that powerfully shapes human experience. In the play, we witness love as a performative, as an aesthetic passion that calls the lovers in its enchanting effects to immediate action. It no longer becomes important that one is a Capulet and the other a Montague. Rather it is the *relation* itself that now matters, that now will define them. Furthermore, Shakespeare also demonstrates how the hate and animosity between the Capulets and the Montagues plays a significant aesthetic role in the lead characters' ultimate demise. In this sense, Shakespeare illustrates the very "poetry of human relations"[57] that exists at the heart of discourse and action that Merleau-Ponty would later identify in his work.

Harkening back to Agamben's notion, in this balcony scene, we hear the performative voice of enunciation most clearly, summoned as it is to declare a state of emergency when it comes to the dominating effects of the *logos* and *bios*. The voice activates the characters' struggle to instantiate a sense of interpersonal sovereignty between them that includes as it excludes. This voice declares their love as an exception, and we witness the consequence of such a declaration. While the voices of articulation are certainly present in the lovers' dialogue, we also hear the intense voices of enunciation in their political and aesthetic potency, in their capacity to declare a new context for their love and desire. Cavarero explains the functioning of these two voices:

> The dialogue between the two lovers develops on two intersecting registers. In one sense it is a dialogue of words, fully semantic, which connects the phrases of Romeo and Juliet, often in the form of question and answer. . . . However, it is [also] a dialogue of voices, an exchange of sonorous emissions that reciprocally communicate two embodied uniquenesses whose reality, in their "dear perfection," can do without the name, and even without speech. . . . Beyond the words, two voices invoke and convoke one another; they resound according to the musical rhythm of the relation.[58]

I submit this resounding is the very rhythm of *zoe*—naked as it is in its wild passion in the context of discourse, but pivotal all the same. As this scene plays out, we hear the voice of enunciation in its most enchanting hour.

Having elaborated on the pivotal function of the voice of enunciation as a political and poetic performative, I now turn to look more specifically at the voice in regard to self and other relations. The story of Romeo and Juliet serves as a wonderful prelude to this subsequent discussion. It is within this context of relationality that the question of ethics resounds most prominently as a sign relation of secondness.

## The Pivot Between Self and Other

In taking up the dialectical relation of self and other as they pertain to the voice of enunciation, we necessarily problematize ethics. This circumstance is not surprising, given that the voice has traditionally been associated philosophically with conscience and moral questions, described briefly below. It is also not surprising given Peirce's association of ethics as a normative science with secondness where, according to Peirce, distinctions and differences (such as self and other) are made within conscious experience. In its enunciation, this voice creates a disruption, and in its unfolding, it constitutes the semiotic relation of secondness in its "brute force,"[59] as Peirce would say.

The issue of ethics arises in secondness because it is within this semiotic relation that self-control becomes problematic. When we hear the other, after all, we are confronted immediately with questions about how to listen and respond, acts by which we temper subsequent discourse and action. Peirce theorizes self-control as secondness because for him it tempers both the formal impulse of reasoning (thirdness) and the sensuous aesthetics of firstness.[60] This idea Peirce credits to Schiller in his development of the play impulse.

As Dolar explains, the association of the voice in particular with ethics has a long philosophical history beginning with Socrates, who he calls a "creature of the voice."[61] Socrates attended to what he described as the daemon voice, the inner voice that did not encourage him to do certain things but instead dissuaded him from doing particular acts. For Socrates, this voice was derivative of the divine and thus was endowed with supernatural qualities. Of course, Socrates is often named as our last real oral philosopher.

Philosopher Jean-Jacques Rousseau, writing in the eighteenth century, believed that human consciousness should be viewed as altogether a vocal affair. Our existence, according to Rousseau, was a struggle between conscience (conceptualized as a voice of the soul) and passions, which were viewed as the voice of the body. Kant focused on separating any moral feelings or ties to the divine from reason, arguing that ethics should be grounded in reason alone. As explained by Dolar, Freud, a full century and a half after Kant, still displays the same faith in reason.[62] And as for Lacan, we learn from Dolar that ethics, to his way of thinking, are based upon an "insistence on desire, of desire as an uncompromising insistence."[63] For Lacan, therefore, to act ethically means that reason itself must always be desired.

It is at this juncture that Dolar addresses the work of Heidegger, suggesting that in it we find the voice in its "last and perhaps purest form."[64] This is because Heidegger's call of conscience developed in *Being and Time* is a call to ethical and moral responsibility with the very notion of voice at its core.[65] Yet Dolar is quick to remind us that for Heidegger, this pure call of conscience is not sonorous. This produces its uncanny nature. Thus, Being is only known through the mute or aphonic voice, the *die lautlose Stimme* and, more importantly, this voice is without any explicit content[66] but is profound nonetheless.

Based upon this very brief history of the relation between voice and ethics, we find that within the relation of self and other the voice is the nonsignifying, meaningless foundation of ethics.[67] By meaningless I do not believe that Dolar regards the voice as non-significant. In our pursuit of ethics, however, we must conceptualize the voice not as a divine, infallible emission when it comes to ethical conduct. Instead, the voice of pure enunciation, the voice beyond any statement of content per se in its audible form, begins to provide the "touchstone of morality"[68] that we have been pursuing at the pivotal juncture between self and other. For as Dolar suggests, with the voice of enunciation,

> we have to supply the statement ourselves. The moral law is like a suspended sentence, a sentence left in suspense, confined to pure enunciation, but a sentence demanding a continuation, a sentence to be completed by the subject, by his or her moral decision, by the act. . . . [This] voice does not command or prohibit, but it nevertheless necessitates a continuation, it compels a sequel.[69]

This voice of enunciation thus plays a crucial role as a pivot between self and other, which, like all the other dialectics we have explored, places it in an "ambiguous position"[70] within the sign relation of secondness. In the end, the voice of ethics is not the subject's own because it is a voice that comes from the Other.[71] So, it is not the voice of self entirely or the voice of the Other entirely, but the voice that emerges within relationality itself. The voice that enunciates the possibility of an ethical relation is precisely at the "curious intersection" between self and other. Dolar is quite explicit: "The voice is the element which ties the ... [self] and the Other together, without belonging to either.... We can say that the ... [self] and the Other coincide in their common lack embodied by the voice and that 'pure enunciation' can be taken as the red thread which connects the linguistic and ethical aspects of the voice."[72] The lack to which Dolar refers signifies merely the incompleteness of self and other in their own right, anticipating a completeness that only relationality will provide. Thus, the lack points to relationality itself as the necessary and sufficient condition from which self, other, and subsequent ethical conduct emerge.

It is at this moment that I return to the idea, expressed by Dolar following Lacan, that at these pivotal points between these various lived dialectics we discover that the voice "opens a zone of undecidability."[73] As we have seen from our discussions of these dialectics, the voice acts to produce both the semiotic and phenomenological boundary conditions from which these dialectics play out as a relation of secondness and thirdness. The negotiation of these boundary conditions creates an existential tension in lived experience, given that at these pivotal points contingency reigns, discontinuity persists, and ambiguity thrives, if only momentarily. The sounding voice in its irruption of the taken-for-granted in secondness necessarily prompts this felt tension and ambiguity to a degree unlike that which we experience by the visual. It also instigates our ensuing activity of choice making as its resolution. Even though our choice of actions as responses are sometimes made with little conscious deliberation (such as in the case of habits), the initial tension or ambiguity envelops this process just the same. Thus, these dialectics necessarily enunciate axiological judgments along with the ethical.

Dolar's reference to this zone of undecidability shares close affinities with Merleau-Ponty's sense of the "open, inexhaustible" horizons of experience that make our existential relations to the world inherently ambiguous.[74] As may be recalled from chapter 3, Merleau-Ponty theorizes that the tension of lived ambiguity comes in two forms he names "positive and negative ambiguity."[75] When we interpret this tension in a negative way, we often search for certainty or knowledge in its most rigid forms as a means of coping with the tension, often resulting in what I have described as speaking with or listening to merely the voices of articulation. For example, if we suffer from social anxiety, that is, an uncomfortableness with the immediate effect of this sounding voice of wildness, then we interpret this lived tension the voice produces as a negative ambiguity. We seek to mute it in our own discursive practices and also fail to listen to it in the discourse of others.

Turning to the hyper-textual and visually based medium of cyberspace and the Internet becomes a therapeutic move, therefore restoring temporarily a sense of existential certainty and stability. As reviewed earlier, the younger generations are already admitting an uncomfortableness they feel in immediate ear-to-ear relations and find ideal refuge in the textual world. Under such circumstances, we hear most clearly the voice of enunciation and interpret it as an index of negative ambiguity.

However, I claim that the voice of enunciation in its wildness, in contrast, can enable a positive ambiguity, given that its enchanting call signals an opportunity to conjure deeper and perhaps more satisfying levels of dialogic existence through its inherent heterogeneity. In its natural and wild unfolding, we may hear the sonority of this voice for the invigorating sense it offers, interpreting this voice as a positive ambiguity. As we shall see, its enchanting effects can enhance our appreciation of human communication as a condition of our very humanness. Merleau-Ponty refers to such an orientation or positive ambiguity in dialogic relations as instigating a "poetry of human relations."[76] This is a semiotic and phenomenological condition that he believes lies at the very heart of a healthy or pragmatic way of being in the world with others. Describing positive ambiguity as fostering a poetry of human relations also affirms our earlier description of the voice of enunciation as a heightened aesthetic resounding of semiotic and phenomenological firstness. As a distinctive auditory irruption into the taken-for-granted world, this enchanting voice promotes, and at the very least possibilizes, distinctive communicative choices. That is, this voice endorses particular stylized enactments that, according to Merleau-Ponty, counter mere redundant patterns of discourse and action. As a result, this voice fosters the kind of relations we inherently desire but too often dismiss in the frenzied world in which we live.

It seems as though Plato was onto something when in the *Republic*, referring to the significant effects of music (of which he was suspicious), he contends that music acts as a *pharmakon*, that is, a sign, an index—more specifically, of a both/and logic. In other words, the *pharmakon* displays a structural ambiguity. The word *pharmakon* is Greek, meaning both remedy and poison.[77] Plato theorized that inherent to music (and the auditory more generally) resides an ability to serve as both the remedy and the ultimate danger, the cure and the poison when it comes to facing life's challenges.[78] For Plato, then, the auditory function of music can conjure the spiritual or sublime that beyond a certain limit can also cause decay or the decline of spiritual faculties.[79] When it comes to speaking with and listening to the enchanting voice of enunciation, it appears that many of us view such relations as a threat, as instilling a negative ambiguity. We believe that its powerful call or summons makes us too vulnerable to the other, given that the openness that it calls for implies personal and psychological risk. We view the enchanting call of the wild as a dangerous one, perhaps because of its inherent heterogeneous contours. Our cultural tendency to diminish the value of this enchanting voice in our digital age of distraction testifies to the uncomfortableness or even fear that we now ascribe to it.

However, I insist that we will be much better off psychologically and socially if we begin to listen again to this voice and see it not as ruin but potential remedy in its manifestation as a positive ambiguity. As St. Augustine professed in a counter-fashion to Plato, music (and the auditory more generally) is, according to Dolar, a vehicle for manifesting the ineffable.[80] Above all, we are reminded once again that with the voice we discover a ritual efficacy through an originary performativity.[81] The voice of enunciation in its wildness serves, in other words, as this performative that counteracts the mere competent performance sounded by way of voices of articulation. It affords discursive shifts and slippage within the signifying order of things that can enhance our habitual relations with others. The voice of enunciation is the voice of our radical alterity. In other words, it announces quite clearly our means by which to attain an authentic sense of being and relating. It is to this topic that I now turn.

## THE ENCHANTING VOICE THAT CALLS US TO OUR AUTHENTICITY

As suggested earlier,[82] when we approach any communicative situation as the accomplishment of an aesthetic *logos*, as Merleau-Ponty notes, we actualize "authentic speech," that is, speech that is "primordial, creative, and expressive of existential meaning."[83] Authentic speech appreciates the particularity of a given discursive event. This authentic approach to our life-world is a "movement of disclosure . . . that strives to inhabit the everyday in a way that enables the intensification of the questionable-ness, uncanniness, openness . . . alterity, and, it is hoped, possibilities for things to become otherwise."[84] Such is the sign condition of authenticity. Authenticity inheres, in other words, within sign conditions of positive ambiguity.[85]

The voice of enunciation announces such opportunities to approach lived experience as a positive ambiguity. The positive ambiguity that the voice of enunciation emits through its enchanting auditory effects makes possible authentic enactments in speaking and listening. As the pivotal point within discursive relations, the voice of enunciation resoundingly calls us to our authenticity. One of the ways it accomplishes this is by declaring a state of emergency, as Agamben suggests. In this case, it is an emergency announcing a profound concern about our human relationality. It offers a way for us to reckon with our inauthentic tendencies of being and relating. This is a beneficial countermove that can dissuade appeals to the superficial, inauthentic modes of discourse that electronic forms of information exchange typically promote in their articulation. These inauthentic modes or habits of discourse and ways of thinking, as exemplified most directly in the world of cyberspace and on the Internet, I reviewed in chapter 3.[86] Now, I proceed to contrast these inauthentic modes or habits of discourse with their authentic counterparts. Like the inauthentic modes I discussed before, I address four areas of distinction in authentic encounters: the general phenomenological sign condition entailed, the mythical elements displayed, relations with Heideggerian thought, and the communicological relation induced. Each of these habits of discourse, prompted by the enchanting voice of enunciation, substantially conditions our orientation toward others in authentic ways.

In terms of its basic phenomenological sign condition, the voice of enunciation accents Peirce's category of firstness (the affectual and aesthetic) and its relation to secondness while it de-emphasizes or eclipses the symbolic level of thirdness. The voice of enunciation in its wildness produces an authentic enchantment by continually calling us to move recursively from thirdness (the symbolic and highly codified level of experience) to firstness (which is analogic and iconic) and then to secondness (the digital). This is because the voice enunciates the pre-logical aspects of being at the same time that it announces the self and other dialectic. This voice thus summons us from our momentary thirdness (our search for meaning) to firstness, to a moment of originary enunciation in tone and sensation. However, we must remember that this recursion to firstness is never semiotically a return to the thing itself or the sign itself in its originary state of appearance. This is because, as I have mentioned before, the state of firstness is always contextualized by our previous experiences of thirdness, that is, the cultural always informs the natural. This is Peirce's sense of infinite semiosis. So, the enchanting voice of enunciation as an authentic precursor in experience is not a return to some originary state. Instead, it is a phenomenological calling to the ineffable—the wild, the untamed aspects of existence that always lack full symbolic codification, closure, and sedimentation, if only briefly. This recursive call to firstness and its movement into secondness produces the phenomenological gap in experience that we have heard before. In such instances, the call or summons momentarily takes our breath away (a typical characterization of enchantment) as we listen to the voice of the other or, conversely, as we pay attention to our own breathing as vocal emission. As it is a call of the wild, the yet-to-be-tamed aspects of experience, this authentic call portends new ways of being in the world. This call can be highly productive and beneficial for both self and other, given that this moment exists outside the bounds of the symbolic flow of codification that meaning requires and thus promotes formation of new patterns of relating.

The recursion to the mode of firstness by the voice of enunciation explains why we typically associate enchantment in its authentic entailments in particular with the ancient concept of *mythos*. According to philosopher of culture Ernst Cassirer,[87] it is *mythos* that gives birth to subjective consciousness and culture. Cassirer tells us that mythical consciousness provides our first apprehension of the world and forms the basis for other levels of consciousness that follow—secondness, that is, ethics, and thirdness, that is, logic.[88] For Cassirer, myth "functions as the most basic and undeveloped symbolic form . . . and lies at the root of all human experience."[89] Here we discover the authentic essence of the magical, mythical worldview so often associated with enchantments in general and which paradoxically reflects a ubiquitous interconnectedness of all things—a concreteness to human experience that is quite beyond our typical machinations. This is indicative of Peirce's mode of firstness, that is, it is an undifferentiated or wholistic experience that is pre-logical.[90] An instance of the mythical, Lofts explains, produces an image that "stands before us as the concrete incarnation of the meaning it represents. It is so woven into our intuition of reality as to be indistinguishable from it."[91] While Lofts is referencing the iconic as visual here with his reference to "image," the same holds true when considering the auditory to the mythical in its iconic relation. Sound in general, as Ong suggests, conjures the mythical, and with Peirce and Cassirer we now understand why. Thus, it is the very penetrating nature of sound as speaking in immediate ear-to-ear contexts that lends human relations mythical elements. This is the closest we get to concrete experience with another given the inherent inter-mediacy of relation.

By experiencing authentic enchantment produced by the voice of enunciation, we thus enter briefly into a mesmerized state that can foster imaginative thinking and sensuous being and becoming. We often respond in such circumstances with musement, a condition of thought's productive play, as Peirce describes it.[92] This is radically different than the play of amusement that inauthentic enchantments conjure, as earlier described.[93] Musement is activated because of the intimate connection that our experience of the call of the voice of enunciation creates. The voice assumes a mimetic form—in the original Greek sense of the concept—that is visceral and poetic and produces an erotic identification.[94] As an object to consciousness, the enunciated voice activates an epistemological orientation to the world since it stimulates the evolution of the sign of relation. As we know, prior to Plato's separation of subjective experience from the objective, the ancient Greeks recognized that the intellect is thoroughly grounded in subjective affect.[95] Both Peirce and Merleau-Ponty acknowledge the salient aesthetic aspects within the developing *logos*.[96] Hence, we should not find it surprising that being authentically enchanted by the voice of enunciation awakens and heightens our sensory (phenomenological) experiences, producing an intense sense of affectual identification with the world. Moreover, this sign action conditions the very possibility for mutual respect in our dialogic encounters with others as we move into secondness. At the very least, the activation of *mythos* within the wild enchanting call of enunciation creates originary narratives about the mutuality of self and other. The form of this sign condition takes precedence over any substance of what is said or done. It is unfortunate that the power of this originary mythic consciousness is commodified by the consumerist orientation of cyberspace and the Internet and turned so frequently into mere myth or mythologies, as Barthes describes. Mythic consciousness is quite distinct, Barthes reminds us, from sedimented cultural mythologies.[97]

When it comes to understanding the authentic call of the voice of enunciation, Heideggerian thought also lends some insight. Unlike the "call of technology" that beckons us into the world of know-how, the call of conscience "summons the lived body"[98] to a mutuality of relation. As Michael Hyde explains, the call of conscience arouses a different kind of hearing since it brings us back to our very being and allows us to behold the beingness of others in their originary state of affect.[99] This condition emphasizes the ideal realm of mythical consciousness as just discussed. For Heidegger, it is through our emotions that we locate ourselves in the world. We thereby exhibit an existential care for self, other, and the world that undergirds our lived experience when we attend to this call.

Resembling Peirce's ideas about the mode of being known as firstness, Heidegger says that our involvement in the world is primordially enveloped in emotion or affect. Following this, we can now comprehend how the affectual aesthetic voice of enunciation produces a disposition toward the world—a state of mind/mood, as Heidegger would say—where we begin to care and become mutually beholden to others. Unlike his concept of they-ness, which represents our over-determined, everyday sense of being-in-the-world, the call of conscience is quite different. The call of conscience and our response to it are the very sign actions that summon us from our immersion in thirdness. It calls or enchants us to a mode of firstness from which authentic encounters may ensue.

Recall, however, that for Heidegger the call of conscience is a non-sonorous call. While the call of authentic conscience is mute and represents a clearing (in a visual/spatial sense), according to Heidegger, I believe it resonates within the auditory emissions of the pre-logical voice of enunciation. The voice in its originary enunciation serves as the semiotic opposition to the non-sonorous call of being—though, instead of providing a clearing within human experience (and to remain true to our auditory focus), the authentic call of enunciation serves as a *prelude* to the full accomplishment of meaning that evolves through secondness and thirdness. It thus creates an *interlude* in the everyday communicative routines of existence, complementing Heidegger's visual representation of a clearing.

The last area of distinction between the authentic call of the voice of enunciation and its inauthentic counterpart deals with the type of communicological relations that it promotes. The type of relation is significant, especially when we consider its impact on our relationality. As reviewed earlier, Gregory Bateson and his Palo Alto colleagues determined that relations between entities (be they people or countries) should be categorized as complementary or symmetrical, depending upon whether they are constituted on the basis of perceived differences between self and other (complementary) or similarities (symmetrical).[100] A complementary relationship is one based upon power differences and typically establishes a hierarchical relation between self and other—for example, the parent and child relation. Recall that symmetrical relations are based upon perceived similarities. Although they are based upon perceived differences, more often than not, complementary relationships build cooperation and mutual respect between the parties involved. This only transpires because self and other clearly understand their differences and respect the positionality those differences entail as an accomplishment of semiotic secondness.

Where the voice is concerned, complementary relationships emphasize a differential between us and the other—that necessarily calls us to the negotiating table in secondness and thirdness. Like the patterns of authentic enchantment more generally, our experience of speaking with and listening to the voice of enunciation summons us to negotiate the existential differential that inheres within most of our self and other relations. As I have previously suggested, this voice announces a radical alterity that awakens us to the notion of relationality itself. Nussbaum stipulates that when we experience awe or enchantment the experience resembles an existential bending or kneeling.[101] We discover that we are in the presence of something different or greater than ourselves, depending upon the context. This is why these kinds of enchanting experiences are often humbling.

In the case of the enchanting voice of enunciation, we experience a momentary existential condition of bending or kneeling to the voice of the other or to the radical alterity heard within our own. The enchanting voice of enunciation thus summons us to an obligatory moment of negotiation with the other that possibilizes authentic encounters. These type of relations, we are told, produce optimizing consequences between self and other. As Berman interprets Bateson, an optimizing system/environment interchange (an interchange between self and other) is one that reflects an appreciation for the complexity of recursive processes and, more importantly, seeks to preserve a balance of cooperative interaction between the two, given the differential involved.[102] This optimization process is quite different than maximization, which never takes account of the greater good or whole of the relation. Complementarity thus promotes optimization of the relation itself, which takes a willingness to negotiate with the different other. This type of sign action serves as a pre-condition for an ensuing ethical generosity prompted within secondness. This is because we approach our relationality acknowledging and appreciating from the outset the complexity of differences that always exist between oneself and another. This recognition of difference or alterity helps to build existential respect for and a deference to the other. The enchanting voice of enunciation activates this opportunity for optimizing relations. This is quite different from symmetrical relations that typically maximize power differences.

In sum, we find that instances of authentic enchantment by way of the voice of enunciation tend to optimize the semiotic phenomenological experience of firstness and secondness. The voice also activates the originary *mythos*, as opposed to the mythologized understanding of the world so often sedimented in inauthentic modes of enchantment. Although Heidegger's call of conscience is a non-sonorous one, we discover its audible counterpart in the voice of enunciation. We also discover that the voice of enunciation as authentic enchantment tends to produce complementary relations that humbly ground our orientation toward others and the world. Thus, the enchanting voice of enunciation displays what Schiller describes as an authentic, aesthetic sense of play,[103] i.e., an auditory flight of discourse and action that taps into the beautiful—what Gregory Bateson and Mary Catherine Bateson describe as the sacred.[104] I'll have more to say about this later on.

The enchanting voice of enunciation generates a unity of purpose and evokes a moral orientation toward the world, especially as the sign condition evolves into secondness and thirdness. As a semiotic and phenomenological interpretant, the voice of enunciation signifies an answering comprehension, or unique expression that resonates with the greater whole, the greater good. Susan Petrilli describes this as a productive pragmatic semio-ethic.[105] Petrilli understands that all sign actions carry a *response-ibility* with them, an obligation to honor the productive (hence pragmatic) future evolution of both poles of phenomenological experience (self and other). This wholistic way of thinking provides the very foundation of her semio-ethic. Drawing from her work, we can easily understand that the ethical inducement of action is altogether a semiotic and phenomenological affair.

The important role the enchanting voice plays in an affective model of semio-ethics must no longer be dismissed. Such an orientation is timely, given that socio-politically we are trying to thrive within an increasing culture of distraction that many have argued results in moral decay. Furthermore, I agree with Schiller, who contends that we cannot rationalize or completely think our way into becoming an ethical being. Schiller cautions that we will remain barbarians if we call upon intellect to carry more moral weight than it can bear. According to Jane Bennett "Schiller concludes that reason is ethically insufficient."[106] Appreciating the enchanting, aesthetic voice of enunciation provides a counter-theoretical move. It begins to open up a discussion about how best to advance dialogic relations in a mutually pragmatic, embodied semiotic. Petrilli's work in particular reminds us that semiotics, axiology, and ethics necessarily intersect and that this intersection must be interrogated for the kinds of responses and habits that may result. Our ethical intentionality in the world is significantly enhanced when we understand how the aesthetic resonates within the voice of enunciation. In addition, we benefit by understanding that the aesthetic conditions the very possibility of such an ethic as a semiotic phenomenological event of dialogue. Such an aesthetic ethic nourishes our understanding of relationality far beyond that which is offered by typical theories of dialogue.

It is now time to explicate one of the preliminary consequences of speaking with and listening to the enchanting voice of enunciation—that is, the co-constitution of truly *interper-sónal* levels of relationality in which authenticity and an ethics may flourish.

## *INTERPER-SÓNAL* RELATIONALITY AS A RE-ENCHANTMENT OF HUMAN COMMUNICATION

Most textbooks in interpersonal communication produced by the scholars of our discipline begin by defining interpersonal quantitatively. We learn that the interpersonal context, unlike group or organizational, involves just two people talking and listening to each other. Our texts, therefore, focus attention on honing skills that are thought to be productive for each party involved to create satisfying or harmonious relations within the self and other dynamic. This quantitative focus is certainly a way of defining interpersonal communication, but it is not the only way. Aside from its quantitative aspect, interpersonal interactions also entail primordial qualitative dimensions. These distinctions, I insist, deepen our understanding of the nature and scope of our experience of interpersonal communication.

On the qualitative front, we are informed that interpersonal forms of discourse, unlike impersonal forms I reviewed earlier, are distinct because of the greater degree to which the interaction itself stresses the personal or unique qualities of each interlocutor within the unfolding process of discourse.[107] This deeper level of perspective taking on the self and other relation, among other things, involves several aspects that oblige us to the relation itself in more profound ways. Such a perspective on the relational process (a) requires more psychological effort by both self and other as more intense levels of sharing and understanding are invoked; (b) necessitates a higher degree of tolerance for the uncertainty and unpredictability that natural discourse entails; and (c) requires a willingness of both parties to be vulnerable to the expressions/perceptions of self and other within the ongoing, unpredictable flow of the semiotic and phenomenological event of discourse. Dialogic philosopher Martin Buber, of course, identifies this distinction as the "I-Thou" relation. He contrasts this relation with the more impersonal modes of discourse that manifest what he calls "I-It" relations, relations that I previewed early on, given their prominence within electronic forms of information exchange.[108] By distinguishing between the two types of interaction, we see different semiotic and phenomenological effects in both kind and degree. That is, we are apt to learn different things about ourselves and others from each form of interaction and, because of their depth versus shallowness, more about ourselves and others from interpersonal than impersonal encounters.

If anything, impersonal modes are about personal expression with less regard for subsequent perceptions. While we can certainly express personal sentiments in a text, such as, "I love and miss you," the asynchronous interaction of a text or email lacks the voiced para-linguistic elements that lend the status of a genuine encounter, as Buber describes. Because we are not listening to the other in the true auditory sense of the word, we miss the qualities of feeling that the sonorous voice enunciates when speaking and listening. With impersonal interactions, given their inherent disembodied natures, our sense of the other as a qualitative feeling is diminished. As an object to consciousness, the semiotic qualities of impersonal interactions (derived always from a sense of the communal or culture) are also lessened. As a result, such impersonal interactions diminish the dynamism possible in interpersonal relations.

In my assessment, the quantitative definition of interpersonal is altogether inadequate. It does little to explain the complexities involved when we speak with and listen to each other. The description supplied by Buber comes much closer to acknowledging and understanding the contours and complexities involved in interpersonal interactions. Buber's work and the scholars who follow him have made a tremendous impact on our interpretation of the event of dialogue in a more nuanced way. However, even his rendition still misses the mark by failing to account fully for the importance of the voice within dialogic relations, particularly the wild, aesthetic voice of enunciation. Although we often teach our students to understand the voice within the non-verbal/oral dimensions of speaking—its para-linguistic function, in other words—unfortunately, the nuance of the embodied voice that we have been pursuing remains muted in such a version. This is because in such characterizations the voice is still defined by its function in service to the semantic, the voice of articulation. We typically highlight the linguistic elements of the voice (accent, inflection, or vocal variety) and neglect the important embodied aesthetic of the actual voice of speaking. I have never seen a text on interpersonal communication that specifically addresses the aesthetic elements of the voice.[109] By emphasizing the tonal qualities of the non-verbal/oral voice, we begin to address the aesthetic aspects. But, again, when these characteristics are mentioned in our texts, they are so only in their capacities as clues to help us unravel the meaning of a given message spoken by someone. The embodied aesthetic of the voice as a becoming *within dialogue* is not stressed, and so we fail to hear it in its integral function of developing a sense of relationality.

In his opening chapter of *Listening and Voice: A Phenomenology of Sound*, called "In Praise of Sound," Ihde asks us to reconsider the fundamental existential significance of sound. His insights help us in our goal of extending a theory of voice, especially as it relates to dialogic relations. Echoing Ong's position, Ihde recounts how the very beginning of human life is in the midst of word as spoken. "The center of word," he explains, "is in breath and sound, in listening and speaking."[110] Jean-Luc Nancy also advocates for a renewed esteem for the speaking voice and listening. When comparing the written word as visual form and the sonorous qualities of speaking, Nancy argues that the "sonorous . . . outweighs form." He goes on to say that the sonorous "does not dissolve . . . [visual form] but rather enlarges it; it gives it an amplitude, a density and a vibration. . . . The visual persists until its disappearance; the sonorous appears and fades away into its permanence."[111]

It is beneficial for us, therefore, to re-consider how speaking is our very breath transformed into sound, as Ihde suggests. As ancient myths describe, breath is equated with our very soul or spirit as it moves through the body. According to Nancy, our body should be understood as a "resonance chamber or column of beyond-meaning," which for him implies our "soul."[112] Soul, in other words, is thought to be incorporated in the sounding voice. Metaphorically expressed, to listen and to speak, therefore, is to inhale and exhale the world and to engage in the very "haleness or health of the air that for the ancients was spirit."[113] Thus, air has its life in sound and voice, and the silence of the invisible (soul) comes to life in sound. The actions of speaking and listening make the word incarnate—emphasizing the full embodiment of such modes of aesthetic communicative action. We thus invert the hierarchy and dominance of our visual orientation when we remember the sequence of the scriptures, "And God *said*, Let there be light."[114]

Addressing the saliency of oral discourse, Ihde explains: In the process of hearing the interiors of others, as opposed to the surface orientation of vision, "the auditory capacity of making present the invisible begins to stand out dramatically."[115] So it is beneficial for us to remember that the action of speaking and listening opens a level of depth and intimacy that mere writing can only hope to accomplish. In this way, we might venture that the sounding voice of the other reverberates in me as I listen, possibilizing a sonorous depth of shared connection that no written word (read asynchronistically) can immediately do. For "to be listening," Nancy asserts, "is to be at the same time outside and inside, to be open from without and from within, hence from one to the other and from one in the other."[116] Supporting this idea and extending it to wider levels of sociality, Ong argues that "because of the very nature of sound . . . voice has a kind of primacy in the formation of true communities."[117] The auditory voice is thus a vital source of our relationality.

By keeping the voice of enunciation foremost in mind, our theoretical understanding of human relationality changes from both an impersonal focus (which barely takes notice of the voice—and if so only in written form) and a commonsense understanding of interpersonal interactions that too often renders the aesthetic voice mute within the process of mere articulation. With the voice of enunciation in its aesthetic wildness, our philosophical attention shifts to the semiotic and phenomenological evolution of what I call an actual *interper-sónal* encounter. By re-signing our traditional designation of interpersonal by including the accent mark, I aim to accentuate, quite literally, the crucial *sonic* elements that we now understand inhere within all immediate ear-to-ear events of speaking and listening. Our renewed respect for the aesthetic voice of enunciation begins to recapture the saliency of the truly auditory nature of our being inclusive of its most enchanting effects.

This renewed respect corresponds to the originary meaning of the word *personal*. While the word personal is often associated with the visual metaphor of the mask—as in our word *persona*—it also implies *a being brought forth by sound*. From its Latin etymology, it is derived from *personare*, which means "to sound through." Thus, it is the mask of being that is *sounded through* that is the person's most important feature.[118] Locke helps clarify this important detail. In discussing the root of the word *personality*, he says,

> It comes from the Latin word *persona*, which in ancient Roman theater referred to an actor's mask and specifically to the mouthpiece through which the *sona*, or sound, passed. Since the mask identified the character and his fixed facial emotion, the actor's voice had total responsibility for mood variations and personality. Over time, the word *persona* come to mean the actor himself and eventually any person or "personality."[119]

In this sense, the auditory nature of sound gives the visual mask its incarnate depth and soul, thereby inverting the typical hierarchical relation of sound and sight. Given the traditional notion of the personal as only the mask, and the mask of an individual at that, my theoretical inversion is certainly warranted. To our dismay, yet again we discover the auditory being lost or replaced by its visual counterpart in these commonsense understandings of *persona*.

The wild voice of enunciation (as opposed to the written voice in its verbal/non-oral mode) begins to more deeply enable the *per-sónal* to come forth within dialogic relations. This voice is the primary aesthetic medium of the body that evokes our human relationality in its most immediate contexts. By attending to the voice of enunciation, the auditory call of the other resounds most intimately within our very being, if only momentarily. Hence, the voice of enunciation announces our spiritual and soulful capacities to enter into dialogic encounters that can prove to be more productive and satisfying. By emphasizing the auditory nature of our relationality, we understand that the actual per-sónal aspects of self and other come to the fore in the inter-mediacy of our sounding voices as enunciation.

By listening to this voice, we come to a renewed respect for the relation itself. We come to a felt embodied sense that, in such established interpersónal relations, the meaning given to the event of discourse *is* the salient emergent phenomenon. As a result, our typical appeals to the mere transmission of each party's individual meanings or codes begin to dissipate. The wild sonic components that resonate in the aesthetic voice of enunciation are heard and valued for the richness of being they carry within immediate ear-to-ear relations. Drawing once again from Peirce, in such genuine interpersónal encounters, the self and other as semiotic objects to phenomenological consciousness within secondness are thus perceived and valued as unique particularities (and not generalities). To be clear, as in all forms of discourse, the interchange of codes and messages within interper-sónal encounters plays an integral role in establishing interaction, but when our attention is drawn initially by the voice of enunciation, neither one dominates the communicative experience. Accordingly, we do not readily reduce the other to a type or consider them a mere token, a representative of a given group of people that we happen to be interacting with. Instead, we respect the genuine *tonality of the relation* so constituted as the key interpretant that nourishes the interaction. I am reminded of Ihde's warning: "Without voice the *per-sóna* recedes, and there is the possibility of 'depersonalization.'"[120]

Even an unconscious discrediting of the sounding voice dramatically reshapes our communicative experiences. This is partially due to the fact that sound initiates a different logic or semiotic than typical modes of visual interchanges. As Nancy says, sound as a phenomenon "does not stem from a logic of manifestation. It stems from a different logic, which would have to be called evocation. . . . While manifestation brings presence to light, evocation summons (convokes, invokes) presence to itself . . . [and, as evocation, it is] a call and, in the call, breath, exhalation, inspiration and expiration."[121] The voice of enunciation as evocation thus calls us existentially—to be genuinely enchanted by the other—by the immediate ear-to-ear presence of the other within the potentialities offered by discourse. The voice of enchantment that resonates so aesthetically in enunciation reminds us that speaking is, indeed, a "song of the flesh"[122] that, above all, activates authentic existence. Like few other visual stimuli—or auditory stimuli, for that matter—the enunciating qualities of this auditory voice thus activate relational enchantment in its fullest of capacities.

As such, we discover in the sounding voice of enunciation the aspects of speaking to which Merleau-Ponty calls our attention. As explained by James M. Edie, Merleau-Ponty well understood that words . . . never completely lose that primitive, strictly phonemic, level of "affective" meaning which is not translatable into their conceptual definitions. There is, he argues, an affective tonality, a mode of conveying meaning beneath the level of thought, beneath the level of the words themselves (which the phonological patterns permit to come into existence), which is contained the words *just insofar as they are patterned sounds*, as just the sounds which this particular historical language uniquely uses, and which are much more like a melody—a "singing of the world"—than fully translatable, conceptual thought.[123]

Furthermore, this singing of the world as speaking transpires at the pivotal point between the body and language. As we have heard, the voice of enunciation in its wildness produces an existential tension between body and language, *zoe* and *bios*, *phone semantike* and *logos*, and self and other that is qualitatively distinct from that of the written voice, primarily due to its penetrating, inhabiting nature. The voice as enunciation thus unfolds as a semiotic and phenomenological performative in its unique particularity. Indeed, the voice of enunciation creates an impulsion within lived experience that the ancient Greeks, who followed Dionysian ways of thinking, well understood. The sounding voice in its wildness invites us into authentic dialogue in a most immediate and profound way and gets at the very heart of the matter of discourse.

We possibilize a re-enchantment of human communication by attending to the distinct authentic call of alterity within oneself and another as enunciated by this embodied natural voice of discourse. It is there that we produce the resonance that nourishes our humanity, an interper-sónal resonance that affords us the opportunity to be communicatively resilient in our demanding digital age of distraction. The concluding chapter takes up these topics.

## NOTES

1. Dolar, *A Voice and Nothing More*, 71.
2. Ibid., 71.
3. I specify, however, that the meaning of this *interior* is not outside the bounds of signification. It is not, ironically, a transcendent interior, in other words, but an interior (a sense of self) that derives its ultimate meaning from the socio-cultural. The interior is imbued with a spiritual essence, given its association with soul and the breath, but my interpretations of these concepts are secular in tone.
4. Dolar, *A Voice and Nothing More*, 109.
5. Ibid., 59.
6. Colapietro, "Striving to Speak," 385.
7. Peirce, *The Collected Papers*, 1.358.
8. LaBelle, "Raw Orality," 149.
9. Dolar, *A Voice and Nothing More*, 79.
10. Philip Fisher, *Wonder, the Rainbow, and the Aesthetics of Rare Experiences* (Cambridge: Harvard University Press, 1998), 131.
11. Peirce, *The Collected Papers*, 2.324.
12. Dolar, *A Voice and Nothing More*, 14.

13. Ibid., 14.
14. Ibid., 13.
15. Ibid., 24.
16. Ibid., 26.
17. As we learned in chapter 5, the voice of articulation amplifies the cultural elements while it silences or muffles the natural.
18. Ibid., 28–29.
19. Many might assert that Ong's characterizations of the spoken word reflect such a transcendent view of the voice, a voice that exists beyond or in no relation to the material world. However, my reading of Ong affirms that he quite explicitly theorized the spoken word as a cultural byproduct. The spoken word may be an emission from one interior to another, as he claims, but that interior is culturally shaped through discourse and action. If our sensory perception is cultural, as he claims, then our expressions are as well.
20. Dolar, *A Voice and Nothing More*, 31.
21. The issue of the wound of culture to which Dolar refers, however, raises an interesting point in relation to the voice: If we accept such a premise—that we have indeed been wounded by the dominance of the voices of the symbolic order—then our acceptance, perhaps unwittingly, implies its opposite, that is, that we conceptualize ourselves as more natural beings to begin with. Social theorist Bernard Stiegler identifies this wound as a symbolic misery, a condition brought on by our growing appeals to the artificiality of the aesthetic through the symbolic mechanisms of a consumerist mindset. See Stiegler, *Symbolic Misery*, trans. Barnaby Norman (Cambridge: Polity, 2014).
22. Dolar, *A Voice and Nothing More*, 16.
23. Ibid., 31.
24. Ibid., 60.
25. Ibid., 73.
26. As Peirce would say, thirdness recursively becomes firstness and so on, displaying what he defines as infinite semiosis.
27. Colapietro, "Striving to Speak," 393.
28. Dolar, *A Voice and Nothing More*, 80.
29. Ibid., 81.
30. Ibid., 96.
31. As Agamben stipulates, "Plato mentions three kinds of life in the *Philebus*, and when Aristotle distinguishes the contemplative life of the philosopher (*bios theórétikos*) from the life of pleasure (*bios apolaustikos*) and the political life (*bios politikos*) in the *Nichomachean Ethics* . . . This follows from the simple fact that what was at issue for both thinkers was not at all simple natural life but rather a qualified life, a particular way of life." See Agamben, *Homo Sacer: Sovereign Power and Bare Life,* trans. Daniel Heller-Roazen (Stanford: Stanford University Press, 1998), 1.
32. Agamben, *Homo Sacer*, 2.
33. Ibid., 3.
34. Ibid., 1.
35. Dolar, *A Voice and Nothing More*, 106.
36. Ibid., 105.
37. Ibid., 107.
38. Ibid., 107.
39. Ibid., 109.
40. Ibid., 109. It is interesting to note that he mentions that even the president of the United States of America could not get away with only a written deposition but instead has to take the witness stand. Given the time of his writing, I think he is referring to the Clinton impeachment process. Unfortunately, in regard to the latest political controversy concerning Russian meddling in our elections and the possibility of collusion by our president, he was able to respond in writing to the questions posed by the special counsel. A good deal was made, however, about the fact that speaking in the immediacy of the moment for our current president was too great a risk to take, exemplifying the very point that Dolar is making.
41. Dolar, *A Voice and Nothing More,* 110.

42. Ibid., 113–4.
43. Agamben, *Homo Sacer,* 15.
44. Dolar, *A Voice and Nothing More,* 120.
45. Ibid., 120; emphasis added.
46. Ibid., 121.
47. Ibid., 122.
48. Cavarero, *For More Than One Voice,* vii.
49. Ibid., vii.
50. At the same time, the voice of enunciation can be drowned out audibly by the voice of articulation. This is Altusser's notion of interpellation. See Dolar, *A Voice and Nothing More,* 122.
51. Cavarero, *For More Than One Voice,* 234.
52. Ibid., 234–5.
53. Ibid., 235.
54. Ibid., 237.
55. William Shakespeare, *Romeo and Juliet,* ed. Brian Gibbons (London: Metheusen, 1980), 2.2.58–59. References are to act, scene, and line.
56. Cavarero, *For More Than One Voice,* 238.
57. Merleau-Ponty, "An Unpublished Text," 5.
58. Cavarero, *For More Than One Voice,* 241.
59. Here Peirce is equating our sense of actuality with something that is experienced as a brute fact. In other words, in secondness we come upon effort, resistance, and struggle. See Peirce, *The Collected Papers,* 1.322.
60. Petry argues that Peirce conceives of self-control as a struggle involving resistance, dualisms, and a polarized consciousness, all aspects indicative of secondness. On his concept of self-control, Peirce was influenced quite directly by Friedrich Schiller, who outlined the "play impulse" as the harmonizer between the sensuous and the formal. Petry also instructs that Peirce's view of ethics and his notion of self-control changed over time. Eventually, Peirce reconciled the idea of self-control with his prior moralistic view of ethics. Peirce decides that his prior view, with an external focus on right and wrong, was inadequate. He comes to see that this type of morality/ethics "chokes its own stream" because it destroys its own vitality by resisting change. See Edward S. Petry, "The Origin and Development of Peirce's Concept of Self Control," *Transactions of the Charles S. Peirce Society* 28, no. 4 (1992), 677. Peirce went on, therefore, to link his notion of ethics and self-control with the aesthetic that was highly contextual in tone. So, Peirce believes in the end that "if one is self-controlled, there is a continuity between the present and the future, and consequently, one need not await the future in order to have a reasonable concept of it," Edward S. Petry, "The Origin and Development," 684.
61. Dolar, *A Voice and Nothing More,* 85.
62. Ibid., 93.
63. Ibid., 93–94.
64. Ibid., 95.
65. Ibid., 95.
66. Ibid., 97.
67. Ibid., 98.
68. Ibid., 98.
69. Ibid., 98–99.
70. Ibid., 102.
71. Ibid., 102.
72. Ibid., 103.
73. Ibid., 13.
74. Maurice Merleau-Ponty, "An Unpublished Text," 5.
75. Ibid., 11.
76. Ibid., 9.
77. Cavarero, *For More Than One Voice,* 227.

78. Derrida, in his essay "Plato's Pharmacy," applies this distinction of the *pharmakon* as both a remedy and a ruin to the process of writing. In this essay, Derrida is also addressing Plato's references to the *pharmakon* in the *Phaedrus*. In the *Phaedrus*, Plato is interrogating the Egyptian legend whereby writing is presented as a good and as an evil; for the Egyptian god Theuth, writing is a remedy; for King Thamus, it is a poison. Cavarero offers insight in *For More Than One Voice*, 227.
79. Dolar, *A Voice and Nothing More*, 47.
80. Ibid., 50.
81. Ibid., 55.
82. Chapter 3
83. Richard L. Lanigan, *Semiotic Phenomenology of Rhetoric: Eidetic Practice in Henry Grattan's Discourse on Tolerance* (Washington: University Press of America, 1984), 14.
84. Smith, "Intensifying Phronesis," 101.
85. Eicher-Catt, "The Authenticity in Ambiguity."
86. However, as I argued, we are unfortunately seeing these electronic patterns of abbreviated discourse being used more and more in ear-to-ear relations.
87. Ernst Cassirer, *The Myth of the State* (New Haven: Yale University Press, 1946).
88. For a more thorough description of these distinctions, see Eicher-Catt and Catt, "Peirce and Cassirer."
89. Peter Savodnik, "Ernst Cassirer's Theory of Myth," *Critical Review* 15, no. 3–4 (2003).
90. Charles Sanders Peirce, "Logic as Semiotic: The Theory of Signs," in *Philosophical Writings of Peirce,* ed. Justus Buchler, (New York: Dover Publications, 1940).
91. S. G. Lofts, *Ernst Cassirer: A "Repetition" of Modernity* (Albany: State University of New York Press, 2000), 92.
92. Peirce, "A Neglected Argument."
93. Eicher-Catt, "Enchantment and the Serious Play."
94. This concept of mimesis was rebuked by Plato, of course, given his desire to replace it with the value of objective observation and experience.
95. For an insightful discussion on this point, see Berman, *The Re-Enchantment*, 70–73.
96. According to Richard Prawat, Dewey follows Peirce and comes to appreciate "that the estehic and ethical dimensions of inquiry are just as important as the logical." See Prawat, "Dewey and Peirce, the Philosopher's Philosopher," *Teachers College Record* 103, no. 4 (August 2001), 681. As a result, Prawat claims that Dewey's development of an aesthetic appreciation of inquiry, a hallmark of his philosophy, is derived in part from Peirce's understanding of the aesthetics within thought's development.
97. Roland Barthes, *Mythologies*.
98. Michael Hyde, "Human Being and the Call of Technology," in *Toward the 21st Century: The Future of Speech Communication,* eds. Julia Wood and Richard Gregg (Cresskill, NJ: Hampton, 1995), 58.
99. Michael Hyde, "The Call of Conscience: Heidegger and the Question of Rhetoric," *Philosophy and Rhetoric* 27, no. 4, 1994.
100. Watzlawick, Bavelas, and Jackson, *Pragmatics of Human Communication*.
101. See Martha Nussbaum, *Upheavals of Thought: The Intelligence of Emotions* (Cambridge: Cambridge University Press, 2001).
102. Berman, The *Re-Enchantment*, 255.
103. Schiller, *On the Aesthetic Education*.
104. Bateson and Bateson, *Angels Fear*.
105. Susan Petrilli, *Sign Crossroads*, 53.
106. Jane Bennett, "How is it, Then, That We Still Remain Barbarians?" *Political Theory* 24, no. 4, 1996, 653.
107. A good example of this perspective is the following text: John Stewart, Karen E. Zediker, and Saskia Witteborn, *Together: Communicating Interpersonally: A Social Construction Approach,* 6th edition (Los Angeles: Roxbury Publishing Company, 2005).
108. Martin Buber, *Between Man and Man* (New York: Macmillan, 1965).
109. While not textbooks, the aesthetic elements of the voice are addressed in other disciplinary publications such as: Norie Neumark, Ross Gibson, and Theo Van Leeuwen, eds. *Voice:*

*Vocal Aesthetics in Digital Arts and Media* (Cambridge, MA: MIT, 2010); Herman Parret, *The Aesthetics of Communication: Pragmatics and Beyond* (Netherlands: Kluwer Academic Publishers, 1993).

110. Ihde, *Listening and Voice*, 3.
111. Nancy, *Listening*, 2.
112. Ibid., 31.
113. Ihde, *Listening and Voice*, 3.
114. Genesis 1:3.
115. Ihde, *Listening and Voice*, 70.
116. Nancy, *Listening*, 14.
117. Ong, *The Presence of the Word*, 124.
118. See: "Personare," *To:Sound:Through*. Accessed August 30, 2019. https://tosoundthru.wordpress.com/2011/11/11/personare-to-sound-through/
119. Locke, *The De-Voicing of Society*, 33.
120. Ihde, *Listening and Voice*, 153; emphasis added, although it is his division of the word.
121. Nancy, *Listening*, 20.
122. Cavarero, *For More Than One Voice*, 15.
123. James M. Edie, forward to *Consciousness and the Acquisition of Language*, by Maurice Merleau-Ponty, trans. Hugh J. Silverman (Evanston: Northwestern University Press,1973), xviii.

*Chapter Eight*

# Resonance, Resilience, and Re-Enchantment

*Voicing the Heart of the Matter*

In chapter 7, I appealed to Shakespeare's play *Romeo and Juliet* as an example of why the sounding voice of enunciation presents us with the opportunity to hear the uniqueness of the other as an originary source of being in our pursuit of a genuine interper-sónal relationality. This example provided me with a foundation from which to construct my concept of interper-sónal resonance, an exemplar of authentic enchantment in relationality. Herein, I develop these ideas further using Foucault's notion of the nameless voice as an auditory anchor. I argue that such enactments of discourse, with their focus on achieving interper-sónal resonance, counter the tendency to speak only the voiceless name within instances of articulation. I also extend my ideas about interper-sónal resonance by distinguishing between the experience of resonance and echo, re-interpreting Jean-Luc Nancy's 2007 conceptualization in his tightly woven text *Listening*.[1] To accomplish this, I reference the myth of *Echo and Narcissus* as a symbol of both resonance and love lost. I contend that relationality, especially as practiced through interper-sónal encounters, is a salient event of discourse. This is because interper-sónal encounters bring us to the very heart of the matter when it comes to understanding healthy and productive discursive habits. I submit that interper-sónal encounters point to the heart or existential stasis point from which authentic relatedness may unfold in its natural temporal flow. I equate this flow with a sense of existential musicality, which inheres within auditory events of speaking and listening heart-to-heart. Tracing the word *salient* etymologically, we find its correlation to the Latin word *resilient*. Consequently, I remind my readers that the sounding voices of self and other within our most immediate interper-sónal encounters call us to a precious moment in time in which our subjectivities may actually alter or shift—enabling us to reposition ourselves within our semiotic webs of meaning, to improvise new ways of being and relating. These encounters offer a remedy for the relational hardships we may be facing in our digital age.

I end the chapter with a brief summary of this book. I argue that it is through the resonance created between the sounding voices of self and other that we may actualize authentic enchantments of relationality. These moments of aesthetic enchantment cultivate the resiliency we seek in today's fast-paced, media-saturated environment by recovering a sense of our musicality as vibrant communicative creatures as we "sing the world"[2] together.

## THE VOICE OF ENUNCIATION AS THE NAMELESS VOICE

Recall from chapter 5 that the voice of articulation closely resembles Foucault's conceptualization of the voiceless name. That is, voices of articulation serve the Law of Representation.[3] When we speak with the voice of articulation, the naming of experience often takes precedence over the actual auditory event of speaking. Such practices of discourse align with Merleau-Ponty's sense of sedimented speech or *parole parlée* (speech spoken). They also exemplify Foucault's aphorism "I lie" when "I speak." We are condemned to speak a language that precedes us, and so our words are already a deception to a certain extent.

Conversely, by attending to the voice of enunciation in interper-sónal dialogue, we temporarily subvert the rationality of discourse in the Law of Representation. Our individual per-sónalities escape being eclipsed by the representational status of the word or *logos*. Speaking with and attending to the voice of enunciation thus possibilizes the Law of Communication, as both Foucault[4] and Merleau-Ponty[5] describe it. We avoid being reified as a "disguised object"[6] of discourse, or what Heidegger identifies as a *they-self*.[7] Instead, we become subjects exercising a full sense of existential agency and volition within a praxis of discourse. In Foucault's aphorism that declares "I speak," we understand that the speaking and listening subject resounds within discursive practices and averts becoming merely a "deictic ghost"[8] of speech.

Together, the voices of enunciation create the nameless voices of discourse in all their sonic vitality. It is within the chorus[9] created by these nameless voices that we momentarily move beyond a seemingly unquestioned objectified reality. We move beyond seeing self and other as mere objects of discourse. We move beyond mere representational practices to the actual praxis of communication. We are able to co-constitute originary and meaningful discourse in its natural unfolding as a semiotic process and phenomenological event. We exemplify, in other words, speaking speech (*parole parlante*) in the process of speaking with and listening to the voices of enunciation. As the Law of Communication announces, intersubjectivity is embodied in subjectivity, and acts of communication precede acts of representation in language.[10]

As we now understand, we speak and listen within the social matrix or intersection of culture and *per-són*, within the reflexive discursive structure Foucault identified as "I lie/I speak." And the voice of enunciation acts as the pivotal point within this social matrix in which improvisations of speaking and listening may occur. Our voice of enunciation serves as a vital element within this social matrix and should be accounted for in our interrogations of it. For the voice of enunciation accentuates the variability and vitality that inhere within every interper-sónal encounter over the apparent semiotic constraints imposed by cultural markers. With a renewed understanding of interper-sónal relations, we come to a greater appreciation for the nameless voice that Foucault thought so important. It is time to attend to its calling, to its evocation.

At this point, I turn to another story of relationality, one that illustrates the consequences of ignoring or devaluing the voices of enunciation and their role in establishing vital interper-sónal resonance.

## LOVE AND RESONANCE LOST—
## THE MYTH OF *ECHO AND NARCISSUS*

If Shakespeare's balcony scene in the play *Romeo and Juliet* reminds us of the value of attending to the voices of enunciation as a pre-condition from which the *zoe* of love naturally unfolds between self and other, then the myth of *Echo and Narcissus* provides us with its representative opposite. The former illustrates the tragedy of love when the *bios* and the *logos* successfully over-determine human action, despite the clear pronouncement of love's enunciation within the all-important acoustic sphere of relationality. We witness the difficulty that the lovers endure when they try to declare a state of emergency and make a new rule, the relational exception of love in an ambivalent socio-political climate.

The story *Echo and Narcissus* represents the tragedy of unrequited love, the manifest result of a failure to negotiate the delicate balance between the visual and the auditory in human discourse.[11] Such an account thus dramatizes the human hardship of failing to maintain a healthy tension between the dominance of the visual and an appreciation for the auditory aspects of speaking and listening. This myth of *Echo and Narcissus* is told by Ovid, the Roman poet, in *The Metamorphoses*[12] and serves as a cautionary tale when it comes to love's enactment. Ovid illustrates how the visual and auditory elements within relationality, when gone awry or unchecked, impact human relations in dramatic, negative ways. *Romeo and Juliet* and Ovid's story present us with love's tragedy, although from very different angles. As we learned from the earlier explication of *Romeo and Juliet*, "the voice is the way in which the exquisitely human uniqueness emits its essence."[13] We appreciate this notion in Ovid's myth as well, although its truth is learned by exploring its opposite manifestation.

The famous myth of *Echo and Narcissus* illustrates two dangers in relations of self and other. Narcissus represents the danger of focusing too much on the self to the detriment of relationality, represented by his insatiable absorption of his own reflection in a pool of water. He spurns real relations.[14] This visual desire prevents him from any focus on or attention to the other, especially the other's auditory emissions. As Strate remarks, media theorist Marshall McLuhan

> saw in Narcissus a parallel to modern individuals who fall in love with their gadgets, their tools, machines, and media. . . . McLuhan argued that by and large we bypass the fact that our technologies are extensions of ourselves; we have become so alienated from our extensions that we do not recognize them as being made in our own image. . . . [Thus Narcissus represents] the numbness that we feel in regard to technology. . . . The numbness that we feel misleads us into perceiving of technology as a nothingness, rather than the something that influences almost every aspect of our lives.[15]

On the other hand, Echo's character signifies the danger to the self that transpires when we are no longer able to initiate relationality as an auditory phenomenon—as a genuine voiced relation. Consequently, her very *per-sóna* or self, her vitality as a human being, has been silenced by the goddess Juno as a punishment for previously being too talkative. Hence, Echo can no longer initiate dialogue with others. She also cannot "sing" the originary musicality of discourse.[16] She can only repeat the emissions she has heard, becoming literally only an echo: "She becomes a vocal nymph who only echoes sounds."[17] Interestingly, in both Freud's and McLuhan's analyses of the myth, Echo is a neglected character.[18] Given that Echo represents the loss of the voice in either its articulated or enunciated form, this neglect should no longer be surprising; it merely echoes (pun intended) the long history of neglect when it comes to the voice in philosophical literature.

Echo is representative of a de-voiced creature of human relationality. Her capacity for originary speech to declare her love for Narcissus is taken away—and with it, an ability to instantiate a fullness of relationality. The love that might have been between Echo and Narcissus is unrequited. Echo cannot vocally share anything of herself; the auditory dialogue from which a self emerges is silenced and reduced to a mere echo. Narcissus is restricted to only love of self within the visual sphere. He initially sees Echo when she is embodied in feminine form, but his attention is focused only on himself. Her echoing or voice does nothing to tear him away from his own image. Important to our understanding of the voice, Narcissus explains to Echo that "I'd die before I'd give myself to you!"[19] Although Narcissus hears the voice of the other in her echo, he interprets that echo as a danger to his self-presence. He realizes that the echo is not an originary voice of another to which he is obligated or called to respond. Rather, for him, it is only a hollow representation of voice that merely haunts in its articulation and reverberation. When Narcissus refuses Echo, she withers away and becomes only a disembodied voice. But even her voice is "not *her* voice; it does not possess an unmistakable timbre, and it does not signal a unique person. It simply obeys the physical phenomenon of the echo, repeating even the timbre of the other's voice."[20]

Narcissus is de-voiced in a certain sense as well, since Echo's repetition of his words does not allow for a fully fledged auditory interlocutor with whom he might engage. If the "voice is always *for* the ear," as Cavarero attests, then "it is always relational."[21] This is not the case for Narcissus. He carries on monologues with himself while he focuses on the visual. The love that could have occurred between them does not come to pass. Ovid's story tells of their "impossible reconciliation,"[22] love and resonance lost. Because of their failure to create love through the auditory attention to their voices of enunciation, the tensive pivotal point between self and other is never actualized.

As I indicated earlier, the pivotal voice of enunciation establishes an existential tension between self and other that is qualitatively distinct from that of the visual or written word. This tension is vital for human relations. Nancy clarifies the importance of this auditory tension when it comes to speaking and listening. Referring to the action of listening, Nancy's theory reminds us that the verb *ecouter*, "to listen," implies a "tension, an intention, and an attention . . . literally, to stretch the ear. . . . It is an intensification . . . [which arouses] a concern, a curiosity or an anxiety."[23] As he stipulates, "in all saying (and I mean in all discourse, in the whole chain of meaning) there is hearing, and in hearing itself, at the very bottom of it, a listening."[24] This same tension holds true, of course, on the side of speaking. While all sensory perceptions imply this tensive aspect to a certain degree, Nancy claims that the auditive pair of speaking and listening "has a special relationship with sense in the intellectual or intelligible acceptance of the word."[25] In describing hearing and listening as sense, he contends "perhaps it is necessary that sense not be content to make sense (or to be *logos*), but that it want also to resound."[26] Following Nancy we hear that sound as the speaking voice "intends" its audience as it necessarily places the relational pair in tension to each other.[27] Cavarero implies a similar notion when she reminds us that the etymology of the Latin *vox* (voice), comes from *vocare*, which means "to call" or "invoke."[28] She goes on to say that "in the play of voices that invoke each other, the sequence of emissions configure a reciprocal dependence . . . [a] dependence that is inscribed in the very relationality of invocation."[29] This dependence is none other than the tensive point of contact.

As a result, Nancy proposes that we need to understand that aside from sense making as *logos*, the auditory pair of speaking and listening demonstrates "a fundamental resonance . . . as a first or last profundity of 'sense' itself."[30] This is because of sound's inhabiting nature as bodily expression/perception that gives rise to the process of sense making itself, as we see demonstrated in the voice of enunciation in its enchanting wildness. I will take up this sense of resonance of which he speaks shortly as it applies to my concept of establishing interper-sónal relations.

For now, I want to stress that Nancy implicitly acknowledges the voice of enunciation as I described and its important tensive properties in establishing relationality. Concerning this inherent tensive manner within speaking and listening he claims that

> *to say* is not always, or only, to speak, or else to speak is not only to signify, but it is also, always, to dictate, *dectare*, that is, at once to give saying its *tone*, or its *style* (its tonality, its color, its allure) and for that or in that, in that operation or in that *tenseness* of saying, *reciting* it, reciting it to *oneself* or letting itself recite *itself* (make itself sonorous). . .[31]

Nancy's reference to "diction" is quite similar to my sense of the voice in its wild, enchanting enunciation. It is the "I say" of speaking in its originality as auditory gesture that, when attended to, can thoroughly enchant.[32]

In Ovid's myth, we clearly see that Echo cannot establish, through any originary expressions of her own, the salient tension of discourse that is required in order to identify herself as a semiotic dynamical object to Narcissus.[33] Her speaking voice as mere echo represents only a hollow and empty gesture—reducing the tensive power of the auditory to its spatial-only capacities.[34] Furthermore, as in any experience of the natural phenomenon of echo, with her soundings we get a sense of space, distance, and surface, not temporality, nearness, and depth.

Similarly, Narcissus cannot establish relationality as a full auditory phenomenon because he is only attending to the visual representation of himself and not the other represented by Echo. Likewise, he is not able to realize Echo as a semiotic dynamical object through the tensive qualities of voiced self and other relations. The result is that their relation, although represented by quite disparate categories of sight and sound, lacks the existential tension required to bring a full sense of relationality to fruition as an auditory phenomenon. Each of them suffers from a skewed and diminished sense of self based on the lack of any interper-sónal resonance.[35] If we accept Peirce's idea that "the movement of love is circular, at one and the same impulse projecting creations into independency and drawing them into harmony,"[36] then love's movement is certainly not manifested between Echo and Narcissus. This is not the case in the balcony scene in *Romeo and Juliet*. Here, a satisfying resonance is established between self and other as the tensive aspects of their social positioning actually heighten their experience and bring them together in dialogue. "In the balcony scene," suggests Cavarero, "there is . . . the acoustic work of a resonance,"[37] in which "beyond the words, two voices invoke and convoke one another; they resound according to the musical rhythm of the relation."[38] It is to the possibility of invoking this important musicality of resonance in relationality that I now turn.

## INVOKING RESONANCE WITHIN RELATIONALITY

The existential tension between self and other produced in-tensely as an auditory enchanting phenomenon occurs within the sign condition I identify as *resonance*. This is in direct opposition to the existential *dissonance* that our culture of distraction seems to promote. Resonance, as an embodied interper-sónal phenomenon, that is, an in-tense phenomenological experience between two interlocutors, is a powerful contributor to healthy self and other relations. Resonance indicates the acquisition of a mutuality of co-presence beyond what any other sense perception can offer.[39] Nancy recognizes this existential tension of the auditory. He states that "sound is what places its subject, which has not preceded it with an aim, in tension, or under tension."[40] The enchanting voice of enunciation as evocation thus surrounds us with a felt sense of "pressure, an impulsion"[41] to listen and respond.

According to its use and understanding within the musical sphere, the term *resonance* comes from Latin and means to "resound" or a "sounding out together" of two vibrational objects.[42] In order to achieve resonance, however, these objects (or sound instruments) must vibrate at the same frequency. In the case of interper-sónal encounters, resonance thus occurs when self and other achieve, in a figurative sense, a mutuality of vibrations in their speaking and listening. Nancy describes resonance as a "womb[*matrice*]-like constitution"[43] or auditory matrix. When applied to the interper-sónal context, this definition stresses the in-tense interconnected auditory qualities of self and other that together produce it. Resonance thus emphasizes the fact that sonic relationality itself creates this very auditory matrix of vibrational in-tensity.

Nancy describes resonance as a "complex of returns [*renvois*] whose binding is the resonance."[44] However, he does not clearly differentiate the return of sound as echo from the idea of resonance. He claims that the resonant subject exemplifies "an intensive spacing of a rebound that does not end in any return to self without immediately relaunching, as an echo, a call to that same self."[45] For Nancy, resonance thus implies the operation of an echo. Although Nancy claims that the echo is an important factor in speaking and listening as a signal of the presence of self and other (including the other within one's own voice), I insist that our notion of echo must be developed beyond his conceptualization. This is especially true if we want to appreciate the constitution of relationality as a genuine interper-sónal sign condition.[46] I believe the myth of *Echo and Narcissus* supports making such a theoretical distinction between resonance and echo.

As I hear it, an echo serves to only minimally confirm a previously articulated presence of self or other as a resounding phenomenon. In this sense, I concur with Nancy that an echo is a semiotic deferral, like Derrida's sense of trace.[47] However, I suggest that while resonance *is* a re-sounding and, in that way, resembles an echo, resonance is also substantially different from an echo in terms of form and function. An echo represents the very lack of voice in its origin as a sign condition of Peirce's firstness or immediacy. An echo is merely the auditory equivalent of the visual idea of reflection, that is, the bouncing back from an external surface, which, of course, gives the echo its spatial sense and diminishes its auditory power and felt sense of immediacy. When these ideas are applied to the voice, as Dolar indicates, this echo acquires an autonomy as it also impacts the other,[48] but not, I submit, in an originary existential or dynamical semiotic way. In other words, the echo is the actualization of a disembodied voice, similar to the acousmatic voice, where the originary source gets lost in its very articulation and mediation. Echo represents a sign condition of Peircean secondness. The brute force of the voice is encountered as a semiotic difference, the mere other, as Nancy suggests. Peirce would say that the echo represents only an immediate object to consciousness and not a dynamical one. An immediate object presents itself as a generality and asks very little of us in terms of response and interpretation. It is what it is. The immediate object is quite unlike its dynamical opposite. The dynamical object is an experience imbued with particularity, and possibly changed as a result of our interpretive semiosis.[49] The echo of the other that we may hear, even in our own experience of speaking, "fades away into its permanence"[50] while asking nothing of us interper-sónally in reply.

Echo is a repetitious sound that does not summon us to originary speech—*parole parlante*. It is speech spoken—*parole parlée* par excellence. However, given its repetitious quality, echo does share affinities with chanting, although their affinity stops abruptly there. Chanting is speech speaking (which can, of course, transform in its enunciation to articulated *parole parlée*). However, its repetitious nature in its originary sounding serves as an existential prompt or call to the other and, as we have heard, in very intense and profound ways. This is what gives the experience of auditory enchantment its powerful allure. There is an invocation and an evocation to chanting, unlike our experience of a mere echo. Most important, chanting inaugurates the timbre and rhythm of *zoe*, as Eastern religions and practices know quite well. I develop this idea of the musicality of discourse in more detail below. Chanting thus calls us back to naked life (*zoe*), if you will. It calls us to the phenomenological, to the natural embodied flow of existence and offers a moment in which to existentially connect to that flow. We are called out in the process of chanting to intersubjective experience. We are called out to experience the sacred unity of life and to actively participate in sustaining such a sacredness by our responses.[51] The repetitious character of an echo does not operate in the same way. Echoes can be temporarily enchanting but not to the degree that resonance is, especially when experienced between self and another.

Resonance is produced in self and other relations by more than a mere echo. The echo is only a repetitious act of discourse with no originary dynamical movement of expression and perception. When resonance occurs within the matrix of self and other through originary auditory enunciations, the existential boundary between self and other is momentarily breached. The voice that now speaks and addresses me seems to come from the whole unity of experience of which I am a part. While echo signifies a bouncing back and return of a now-disembodied voice, a resonance established between self and other signifies the mutual accomplishment of auditory enunciations that figuratively vibrate at the same wave length.

A note of clarification is needed here. While we may say in a commonsense way that we achieved a sense of resonance with another through the non-sonorous practice of writing, this is not a genuine resonance as I describe it. Following Nancy on this point, "resonance . . . [is] a sonorous materiality, vibration that animates the auditory apparatus as much as the phonatory apparatus."[52] It is best to think of resonance as a re-sounding evoked by the interper-sónal sign condition established as a matrix, auditorily, in-tensively, and reflexively between self and other. We each can be characterized as a "reverberation chamber"[53] for ourselves as we hear the other within our own speaking, as Nancy suggests. More importantly, a reverberation chamber is produced within the always present void or gap that exists between self and other that relationality itself exposes. It is best for us to imagine that void as an especially rich acoustic space and not merely a visual one. The enchanting voice of enunciation in its wildness calls us to our relationality, invoking the void that exists between self and other, a void that acts as the potential resonance chamber by which we find oneself as another, as auditory beings. While sound itself (whether produced by me or by an instrument) can most certainly produce an echo, this echo is a simple iconic sign (as when my speaking already is the object of my own listening). On the other hand, resonance occurs when a shared, vibrational quality of feeling or auditory sense perception is produced between speaker and listener. Resonance is the semiotic and phenomenological byproduct of the sonorous vocal emissions of self and other, when vocality as enunciated is co-valued in its mutual vibrational sounding.

Employing Peirce, we can understand resonance as the accomplishment of the firstness of thirdness, the immediacy of mediation[54] that produces a *tone*, not merely the echo of repetition in secondness. With resonance understood as *tone* and implying its musical origins, we are reminded that "musical tone for Langer has an unmistakably *sensuous* value, its effect has a *vital* value, and it has deep *personal* import."[55] Resonance is thus a shared dynamical sensuous object relation between speaker and listener as intersubjective auditory experience takes on a vital role within human relations. Resonance is prompted when the wild voice of enunciation is clearly heard and attended to. It stands to reason that when resonance occurs, so too does communication, at a level and a depth much more intense than ordinary exchanges of messages or information in their textual form. As Nancy submits, "Communication is not transmission, but . . . *a sharing* . . . an unfolding, a dance, a resonance. Sound [as resonance] . . . is first of all communication in this sense."[56] Cavarero agrees when she asserts that in such instances of resonant vocality, "there is nothing yet to be communicated, if not communication itself in its pure vocality."[57] When it comes to dyadic encounters, the accomplishment of resonance is an auditory experience by way of speaking with and listening to the enchanting voice of enunciation. This accomplishment signifies the constitution of genuine interper-sónal relations. Moreover, and in a reflexive fashion, it is by way of interper-sónal relations that we have the in-tense, sensory experience of resonance that sustains our very human relationality.

## THE MUSICAL CONTOURS OF SPEAKING AND LISTENING AS AN AESTHETIC

An important thread in Nancy's explication of resonance that I want to draw out concerns the auditory aspects of speaking and listening that help to constitute resonance as the very sign condition that it is. I hinted at these aspects above, but I now want to make them more explicit and argue for their saliency in producing interper-sónal relations. Susanne Langer's philosophical project on the aesthetic dimensions of music will prove helpful. As she notes in *Philosophy in a New Key,* music rests "on the foundation of tensions and resolutions"[58] (like sound, resonance, and relation itself), and as a special enunciation of feeling, music shares formal properties with "the inner life."[59] The inner life to which she refers is none other than the affectual sense of being in its very aesthetic expressiveness, an aesthetic of discourse that we have been pursuing within its auditory mode. Acknowledging the relation between musicality and our inner lives, Langer claims that "quite generally the inner processes, whether emotional or intellectual, show types of development which may be given names, usually applied to musical events, such as: *crescendo* and *diminuendo, accelerando* and *ritardando*."[60] Parret concurs when, citing Schopenhauer, he contends that "music offers the most intimate translation of inner being, precisely because it remains estranged from the world of space.... [Music represents] the pure time of Becoming."[61]

Hence, within an aesthetic frame provided by music, we begin to appreciate that a sense of existential musicality inheres within auditory events of speaking and listening as enunciation. Philosopher Michel Serres agrees when he states that "Meaning presupposes music, and could not emerge without it.... It inhabits the sensible, it carries all possible senses. It vibrates in the secret recesses of our conversations, continually underpins our dialogues, our exchanges presuppose it, it knows in advance harmonies and discords . . . and [it has] paved the way for our collective existence."[62] Recollecting the correlation between sound and time more generally, we now understand why "music, in the hierarchy of fine arts, is the art of time par excellence."[63] To unpack these ideas, I begin with Nancy's sense of resonance, one that implies and further extends this notion of an inherent musicality to speaking and listening.

According to Nancy, resonance brings together in unity and distinction two things: rhythm and timbre, both of which indicate a musicality. He stipulates,

> Rhythm and timbre—between them holding melodic and harmonic possibility—outline, in a way, the matrixlike constitution of resonance when it is placed in the condition of the phrasing or of the musical sense, that is to say, when it is offered to listening. This condition is that of diction or "dictation" in general: de-clamation, ex-clamation, ac-clamation, previous to music as well as to language, but common to them both while still dividing them, and at the same time the presence of each one of the two in the other: presence of sense as resonance, sonorous impulse, call, out-cry, address.[64]

Similar to Cavarero's reference to the rhythmic dynamic of resonance within the dialogic encounter of Romeo and Juliet in the balcony scene, in the passage above Nancy identifies an inherent rhythm/timbre that plays out within instances of resonance. This rhythm/timbre gives resonance its penetrating quality as a true auditory experience. Nancy argues that within affectual experience such as resonance we find a "fundamental rhythmic"[65] movement as an integral aspect of our subjectivity. Langer agrees when she stipulates (citing Gestalt psychologist d'Udine) that the gestures of feeling associated with music "reveal to us, bit by bit, the essential characteristic of Life: movement. All living creatures are constantly consummating their own internal rhythm."[66] Bachelard also supports this notion when he claims, according to Parret, that "it is rhythm that provides the primordial element"[67] to existence.

Nancy goes on to claim that experience itself entails a rhythmic flow that corresponds to the temporality that we are (on this point, he echoes Heidegger). Nancy says that this sense of rhythm is "not only as scansion (imposing form on the continuous) but also as an impulse (revival of the pursuit)."[68] Nancy acknowledges that rhythm as well as timbre act as pivotal points in the constitution of our experience of resonance—or, said differently, rhythm and timbre punctuate experience and, as such, enliven possibilities within lived experience, especially in the context of interper-sónal relations. Nancy thus concludes that our subjectivities are altogether the product of sonic encounters. In sound, we experience the pulsating spirit of Dionysus and, more importantly, we submit to this spirit in a way that transforms us "from possessed to creator."[69] Hence, we are beings "moving and fluid, syncopated, beaten out,"[70] like the rhythmic drum and the timbre that accompanies it, all the while contributing to this very rhythm. Cavarero claims that the Western metaphysical tradition, starting with Plato, has tried repeatedly to "neutralize" this inherent musicality of our existence by specifically attacking the voice.[71] As Cavarero interprets Italian philosopher Calvino, there is a musicality to speech that resides in "the pleasure of giving one's own form to the sound waves."[72] This pulsating nature of speaking and listening as resonance thus testifies to its inherent musicality.[73]

I believe these aspects of resonance (rhythm and timbre) indicate the very *zoe* of music that inheres in our very being as lived. Like musical experience generally, within immediate ear-to-ear relations, we quite effortlessly move in such instances from passive listeners to active dancers or embodied participants in the percussive movements of life known as speaking and listening. In a similar fashion to choral and dance groups, we discover that the musicality of speaking and listening is "a physiological and sociological phenomenon. Obvious physical changes manifest emotional events of any depth, and choral singing is no exception: changes in pulse rate, respiration, adrenalin flow, and similar symptoms are present."[74] Phenomenologist Alfred Schutz also recognizes the importance of musicality in our understanding of human relationality when he asserts that in dialogue we possibilize a "mutual tuning-in relationship upon which all communication is founded . . . by which the 'I' and 'Thou' are experienced by both participants as a 'We' in vivid presence."[75] This is none other than the accomplishment of resonance I discuss. Like music, then, we appreciate that speaking and listening are not merely cognitive enactments of code conditions but that they also "extend beyond the 'mind' to the 'body',"[76] in their pulsating nature as truly embodied felt events. In this way, we hear that immediate ear-to-ear dialogue understood as musicality "is associated . . . primarily with . . . rhythm, movement, and overt physical enactment, a context in which it is perhaps scarcely surprising that participants experience a particular sense of active control and of personal creativity . . . a different and unique modality of human action *sui generis.*"⁷⁷

Merleau-Ponty also acknowledges the inter-twining of music and dialogue. He reminds us that as voiced beings in our originary enunciations, we "sing the world"⁷⁸ in response to the voices of silence and sedimented speech. Like Schopenhauer, Merleau-Ponty appreciates the way in which the musicality of speaking is becoming. He, perhaps more than any other phenomenologist, "has pointed to the intimacy of language [speaking] and music."⁷⁹ Recognizing the important links between speaking in its rudimentary form and singing, Merleau-Ponty is quite explicit, saying that

> our language is less emotional than its rudimentary forms. There would not have been an initial difference between the act of speaking and the act of singing. . . . The initial form of language, therefore, would have been a kind of song. Men would have sung their feelings before communicating their thought. Just as writing was at first painting, language at first would have been song, which, if it analyzed itself, would have become a linguistic sign. It is through the exercise of this song that men would have tried out their power of expression.⁸⁰

In addition to valuing our rhythmic, musical qualities as speakers and listeners as Merleau-Ponty suggests, Nancy also claims that timbre is the resonance of the sonorous. However, Nancy is quick to indicate that timbre is not something that can be viewed as a "single datum."⁸¹ Rather than try to distinguish timbre from pitch, duration, or intensity (recall Barthes's work), Nancy insists that none of these aspects of sound and voice exist without timbre; timbre is an integral aspect of sound, along with rhythm, in its generality. Recalling its German etymology in the word *klangfarbe*, Nancy reminds us that timbre is often referred to as the "color of sound."⁸² Dolar, as may be recalled, informs us that timbre, accent, and intonation are aspects of voice that are recalcitrant to the signifier.⁸³ By this, he means that timbre is like a "fingerprint" of the voice, giving voice its individuality as an emission from a particular speaker. Nancy wants us to understand that timbre is best described as the "sonorous matter" of speaking and listening, given that it "spreads out in itself and resounds in (or from) its own spacing."⁸⁴ He goes on to say that "timbre is thus the first correlative of listening,"⁸⁵ and I think Barthes would agree. We probably pay more attention to the timbre of someone's voice than the rhythm, unless the rhythm draws attention to itself.

As the ancient patrons of sound, voice, and music, it is not surprising that the Muses were celebrated in primarily oral-aural cultures, given the integral role they played in human affairs. As Robert Innis claims, "Langer holds that the idea that music mediates knowledge, gives us knowledge is the most persistent, plausible, and interesting doctrine of meaning in music."⁸⁶ In ancient times, the Muses were held in esteem because of this. Yet, over the centuries, our appeals to their iconic representation of the pursuit of knowledge through music, celebration, and play have drastically diminished. Citing the poem by Blake about the demise of the Muses, Ong writes,

> How have you left the ancient love
> That bards of old enjoy'd in you!
> The languid strings do scarcely move,
> The sound is forced, the notes are few.[87]

Continuing, Ong recounts the unfortunate historical trend in which the Muses come to be taken as only a "satiric, mock-epic device." He declares that "the eighteenth century was the critical period in the silencing of this once convincingly vocal group"[88] by writers and poets. Ironically, the very sense of what a poet is and does becomes conceptualized as "non-vocal and withdrawn, a 'loner'—quite the opposite of the gregarious oral bard."[89] This shift in perspective was due in large part to the rise of written language, of course, making music and its corollaries abject others. According to Langer, however, music needs to be distinguished from language. Langer makes clear that music is not a language. She states that "the analogy between music and language breaks down if we carry it beyond the mere semantic function in general, which they are supposed to share."[90] This is because, as Innis explains Langer,

> music has no fixed connotations as language does. It has no literal meaning. But we must not fall into the trap, Langer warns, of thinking that nothing can be known that cannot be named. The strength of musical expressiveness is found in music's power to articulate forms that language cannot. . . . Langer, therefore, will think of music as essentially, and in principle, more congruent with the forms of human feeling than language is.[91]

In any case, while music is distinct from language per se, that does not mean that auditory speaking and listening as musicality should be subservient to language. When we submit to the dominance of language, we only speak with and listen to the voices of articulation, as I suggest.

For the resonance that interper-sónal encounters creates is like music itself and should be celebrated for the power of its expressiveness as a performative of becoming. Speaking with and listening to the voices of enunciation is not about expressing "passion, love, or longing of such-and-such an individual on such-and-such an occasion, but passion, love or longing in itself."[92] We must not forget to attend to these important sounds and tones of intersubjective experience within immediate ear-to-ear relations nor should we try to "contrive" their soundings as a "direct endeavor," as Peirce suggests. For as Peirce reminds us, we must be patient as the musicality of interper-sónal resonance naturally unfolds between self and other. On this point, he contends, "We haunt in vain the sacred well and throne of Mnemosyne; the deeper workings of the spirit take place in their own slow way, without our connivance. Let but their bugle sound, and we may then make our effort, sure of an oblation for the altar of whatsoever divinity its savor gratifies."[93]

In support of the musicality of being that I am advancing, semiotician Naomi Cumming in her book *The Sonic Self*[94] recognizes the important semiotic and phenomenological functions that the materiality of sound in vocality serves in its reminiscence of musicality more generally. She draws parallels between musical performers' acts of sensuous vocality as singing and the everyday sensuousness that dialogic encounters with another may also exhibit. All of these notions support the idea that framing our immediate auditory speaking and listening as musical enactments is an important theoretical move. By doing so, we emphasize the sensuousness of lived experience as a powerful aesthetic phenomenon and honor the qualities of experience within Peirce's firstness as immediacy.

In coming back to our topic of resonance more directly, composed as we now know within the rhythm and timbre of musicality, Nancy asserts,

> In truth, resonance is at once listening to timbre and the timbre of listening, if one may put it that way. Resonance is at once that of a body that is sonorous for itself and resonance of sonority in a listening body that, itself, resounds as it listens. (At the same time, this resonance is not an immobile given, since timbre itself is an evolving process, and, consequently, listening evolves along with it.) . . . [Timbre] forms the first consistency of sonorous *sense* as such, under the rhythmic condition that makes it resound. . . . *Sense*, here, is the ricochet, the repercussion, the reverberation.[95]

As I interpret Nancy, this sense of the auditory is a primordial one.

Joining timbre and rhythm as the sign condition of resonance exemplified in the above quotation is not difficult for Nancy to do. This is because in Greek the literal meaning of timbre is *tympanon*, meaning "tambourine."[96] The tambourine is a percussion instrument, an instrument that beats out a rhythm as it signals a timbre. Most importantly, in the above passage, Nancy speaks to the overall percussive quality of resonance. Nancy is reminding us that speaking and listening always entail the joint qualities of timbre and rhythm, which, when attended to, can invoke an embodied sense of resonance. He wants us to hear that we are vibrant aesthetic creatures at the level of *zoe*. That is, we must acknowledge that our phenomenological existence is thoroughly enveloped by the vibratory elements that we speak and attend to within our aesthetic sounding. The process of speaking and listening as auditory relationality consists in optimizing these musical reverberations, if you will, which, under the right conditions, produce a resonance that confirms our ongoing participation in the temporal flux of life with others.

Experiencing the flux of life with others is manifest most fundamentally within immediate ear-to-ear relations. For as Schutz suggests, "only within this experience does the Other's conduct become meaningful to the partner tuned in on him—that is, the Other's body and its movements can be and are interpreted as a field of expression of events within his inner life."[97] And as Peter Martin attests, hearing dialogue in its immediate embodied musicality, "is a special, important and illuminating case of what must occur for any kind of human communication to take place and any intersubjective, social life-world to be sustained. In effect, the very form of existence of music is a microcosm of the very conditions of existence of the social macrocosm."[98] In pursing the importance of resonance as a genuine auditory phenomenon produced within interper-sónal relations, these theorists prove beneficial in our efforts to re-enchant our sense of human communication. They help clarify that the fundamental qualities of resonance are rooted within the very musicality of life—its rhythm and timbre.

As such, we begin to grasp why the resonance within interper-sónal relations affects us so deeply and intensely. Like our engagement with a favorite piece of music, we can become caught up in the flow of speaking, listening, or performing. We also begin to appreciate the aesthetic qualities of human communication that electronic forms of information exchange so often dismiss. Human communication becomes re-enchanted by speaking with and listening to the wild, aesthetic voices of enunciation in their embodied musical enactments. We begin to realize the possibility human communication holds as a profound auditory moment of lived musicality produced between self and other. Such realizations about the depth and in-tensity produced within sonorous moments of communication radically distinguish these types of encounters from the everyday, mundane exchanges of messages in which we participate, especially in their textual/visual form. Although the sonority of interper-sónal resonance currently may be fading in our everyday lives, I am convinced that we still can cultivate an attention to its musical reverberations. Peirce is also sure, following the aesthetic work of Schiller, that "the aesthetic process" of deliberating improving our "habits of feeling" is the way we also improve our mental activity.[99] This is especially true when we sense or attune to the existential rhythm and timbre of resonance announced within genuine interper-sónal relations. We are closer now to the heart of the matter.

## HEART-FELT COMMUNICATION

It is not surprising that when deeper embodied moments of interper-sónal relations are experienced we characterize them as speaking and listening heart-to-heart. I am reminded of psychologist and physician James Lynch's words on the importance of such kinds of intimate interactions. He stipulates that while "we think that talking is mental . . . when we speak to others, we're touching their hearts."[100] Although I am approaching heart-felt communicative experiences metaphorically, Lynch is quite literal about the relationship between our communication practices and the physical responses of our heart. His extensive research on the correlation between human relationships and our mental and physical well-being is quite illuminating. As he stipulates, "Human beings have varied, and at times profound, effects on the cardiac systems of other human beings."[101] Referring to studies done to document how human interactions might alter levels of serum cholesterol in patients suffering from heart disease, he says,

> Findings indicated that reassuring and supportive types of relationships could significantly lower the levels of serum cholesterol of patients in an intensive-care environment, while stressful human interactions could significantly elevate cholesterol levels. Within the hospital setting, the patients' serum cholesterol levels changed according to the nature of the human interactions they experienced.[102]

Lynch is drawing direct connections, therefore, between the kinds of interactions we have and our physical health.

I submit that we describe our heart-felt experiences as speaking heart-to-heart because the heart itself, in its natural rhythmic beating and timbre, represents to us the most concrete and embodied aspect of life to which we may refer. According to William McNeill, within such experiences of sharing the "rhythmic input from muscles and voice, after gradually suffusing through the entire nervous system, may provoke echoes of the fetal condition when a major and perhaps principal external stimulus to the developing brain was the mother's heartbeat . . . prolonged and insistent rhythmic stimuli may restore a simulacrum of fetal emotions to consciousness."[103] Speaking heart-to-heart means leaving behind temporarily the abstract world filled with symbols and significations that too often pull us away from one another—the symbolic world of Peirce's thirdness. Instead, we value that "the body is a dialogic instrument; it's not a machine."[104] As a dialogic instrument, we must always ask ourselves: How might we find resonance with another?

On such occasions of sharing heart-to-heart, we re-awaken our aesthetic nature as truly sentimental and sensuous creatures in an in-tense phenomenological way. Here I am not referring to a sense of the sentimental as nostalgia, although if we rarely experience such a heart-to-heart resonance with another, it might reflect such a conjuring of mutuality lost. Instead, I am using the term *sentimental* to recapture its meaning as a refined feeling or a delicate sensibility that we experience toward the other and/or relation itself as an in-tense aesthetic. Sentimentality toward the other or the relation itself implies acknowledging and enacting the very embodied aesthetic of life that we have been pursuing in our discussion of enchantment. I submit that sentimentality requires attending to the musicality of speaking and listening that when shared with another creates a "connection, or continuity . . . [which]

stems from the idea of a music received as a summons to the most profound and ineffable interiority, to 'sentiment' itself."[105] Here, Peirce adds insight. Describing sentiment as both a "strong feeling" and a "warmth of feeling," he cautions us to not dismiss these feelings in our logical pursuits. Without reducing sentimentality to a doctrine (as sentimentalism), Peirce admonishes us to remember that "great respect should be paid to the natural judgments of the sensible heart."[106] He goes on to suggest that

> the strong feeling is in itself, I think, an argument of some weight in favor of the agapistic theory of evolution——so far as it may be presumed to bespeak the normal judgment of the Sensible Heart. Certainly, if it were possible to believe in agapism without believing it warmly, that fact would be an argument against the truth of the doctrine. At any rate, since the warmth of feeling exists, it should on every account be candidly confessed.[107]

According to Vincent Colapietro, Peirce believes wholeheartedly that "our sentiments define us."[108] Quoting Peirce, "It is the instincts, the sentiments that make the substance of the soul. Cognition is only the surface, its locus of contact with what is external to it."[109]

These heart-felt moments of human communication are the most concrete and embodied experiences we can have. In these heart-felt moments, we realize that such occasions make life worth living. The deeply felt connection with another surpasses all the other experiences we might have, especially those heavily shaped by the symbolic. We cherish these moments of sentiment because they are the times when we are most touched by the other and feel their existence within the beat or pulse of the relation so constituted. Typically, this felt sense of touch is not merely a haptic encounter in its exteriority, although haptics can certainly play an integral role in its development. Instead, we say that our inner-most being is touched, signifying the embodied nature of resonance most profoundly. We are momentarily *enchanted*. In such circumstances, we declare that someone has *touched our hearts*, and we might gesture to the organ's actual location within our chests.

These verbal and non-verbal gestures to the actual heart of our being are also not surprising. For the physiological heart, which pulsates as a regular chanting of being, announces our very arrival and its secession our departure as living creatures. During the interim, we engage in the rhythm and musicality of dialogue from which we actualize occasions of in-tense sharing. Important to remember is that the heart is the only organ of the body in its natural state that is explicitly auditory in nature. The lungs contribute to the auditory nature of our being only when we purposely push air over the vocal folds. The auditory emission of the body in its natural flow comes only from the heart. As the primary emitter of sound in its embodied naturalness, the heart's salient beat is the natural rhythm of life in its bare nakedness, in its *zoe*. Like the percussive instrument it is, the beat of the heart resembles the primal pulsating and vibrations of life itself. It is as though the tribal cultures recognized this important aspect of the auditory nature of our being, given that the drum is used fundamentally as the *zoe* of music in dance and celebrations. In its most rudimentary enunciations, the drum signifies the very rhythm of life, before life becomes clothed by the articulations of melody and its various harmonics. I insist that the physical heart represents the prominence and necessity of the auditory in human experience and expressiveness, although we seldom think of it that way. Instead, we identify the heart with the action of sensing as sentimental in only its reductive form. Regrettably, this association is to the exclusion of the heart's prominent auditory nature and testament to our very embodied sonority.

When we experience resonance in interper-sónal relations as an aesthetic auditory attunement between self and other, we truly appreciate the embodied phenomenological nature of discourse and action. As the pivotal nature of the wild voice of enunciation attests, we exist as affectual creatures, as creatures *of the heart* at the same time that we are constrained to represent those ideas within the signifying system in which we are immersed, whether those expressions are verbal or non-verbal. The heart, both literally and figuratively, serves to signify the auditory sense of our being and possible attunement with others in the world. We have discovered that within resonance, as facilitated by a renewed value placed on interper-sónal relations and their aesthetic enchanting effects, we come to the very *heart of the matter*. We possibilize deeply satisfying engagements with others. With this renewed sense of human communication, we may create a truly enchanting life, one that is not delusionary but delights in its very musical constitution and performativity.

This discussion has focused attention on the aesthetic attunement of self and other within interper-sónal relations as resonance. As such, we have gone to the heart of the matter, that is, to the auditory uniqueness that we each are as discursive beings. However, I now want to extend the discussion and offer an important reminder. As vibratory creatures, we each have a heart that we figuratively protect or share with others as unique instantiations of *zoe*. Yet, when we create a resonance with another as an enchanting moment of interper-sónal relations, the relation so constituted also takes on the qualities of a beating heart, complete with its own musicality. In our individualistic culture, we often fail to recognize that relationships, while certainly the result of self and other engagement, are the thirdness of dyadic encounters. Relations have a life of their own, signified by their own rhythms and timbre. From a Peircean perspective, we see that relation itself is constructed as a dynamic interpretant, the signifying effect of the mediation of firstness (the aesthetic) and secondness (the ethical). This interpretant then serves to shape subsequent expressions and perceptions of both self and other. So, relationality itself beats with a rhythm and displays a timbre; in many ways, it becomes the musical score for our dialogic engagements.

What kind of dialogic score are we creating and then performing with others? Cavarero alludes to this musical aspect when she declares that the voices of Romeo and Juliet in the balcony scene serve to "invoke and convoke one another; they resound according to the musical rhythm of the relation."[110] John L. Locke, in his discussion on the de-voicing of society, makes a similar claim that "social talking thus has a heart of its own."[111] Bateson is always quick to remind us as well that we focus too much on the things of the world (for example, self and other) to the detriment of valuing the actual relation so constituted. It is always the particular "pattern which connects," the particularity of the relation that Bateson finds most sacred in human existence.[112] I have tried to stress that it is the auditory voicing of this relationality within an immediate encounter that becomes critical to its healthy evolution and endurance. We should now hear clearly why the enchanting voice of enunciation in its aesthetic wildness is a *salient* factor in human affairs. This voice enunciates the very heart of the matter when it comes to co-constituting a satisfying and meaningful relationality as musical resonance. Like music, immediate ear-to-ear relations are a functional necessity and a sufficient condition to social life. They should not be viewed as an inconvenience or nuisance. They are as vital to human existence "as bread: perhaps more so, since whereas an individual would die without food, without music [as ear-to-ear relations] a whole society, perhaps even the cosmos itself, might disintegrate."[113] I now offer a brief summary of this project: returning to the voice.

## RETURNING TO THE VOICE

Given that we are now culturally immersed in the digital age of distraction with its dominance of hyper-textual/visual modes of interaction, it is a good time to remind ourselves of the value of the speaking voice in its immediacy. As Locke attests, in such an electronic climate, "intimate talking, the social call of humans, is on the endangered behaviors list."[114] In his book, Locke recounts a patient who awoke from cancer surgery on his larynx to discover that his voice was removed along with the cancer cells. As a result, this patient lost his sense of who he was, his very *per-sónality* because he could no longer participate in voiced relations. Now we fully understand why. Our salient auditory capabilities are fundamental to our being. We articulate and enunciate the musical substance of who we are as vital aesthetic creatures within an unfolding relationality.

As we increasingly try to connect with one another in the predominant electronic form of the textual/visual, this fundamental aspect of our being is being gradually sacrificed for the sake of efficiency. As I documented, our new online habits of discourse, of always being *on the phone*, are insidiously and quite ironically undermining our essential vocality. Apparently 2008 was the watershed year in which the use of the digital phone for calling another and talking ear-to-ear was surpassed by texting, emailing, and sending image-based messages. It appears that we have increased our abilities to electronically connect with others and perhaps increased the volume of those connections. Unfortunately, these connections are predominantly superficial, impersonal in tone, and indicative of what dialogic philosopher Buber contends are "I-It" relations. These are relations where the other is merely considered an object among many that we may encounter. We quite literally take others at face value and don't look much farther. We can most certainly express a deep, personal sentiment to another by way of text. When we do, it is with the voice of articulation. Such an expression, therefore, makes a diminished impact, given that it is not auditory in nature. It does not penetrate the being of the other that a vocal emission would do within immediate ear-to-ear contexts of speaking and listening. About the importance of the sounding word (unlike a visual representation), Ong stipulates that sound uniquely

> binds interiors to one another as interiors. . . . [Thus] the spoken word moves from interior to interior, encounter between man and man is achieved largely through voice. The modes of encounter are innumerable—a glance, a gesture, a touch, even an order—but among these the spoken word is paramount. Encounters with others in which no words are ever exchanged are hardly encounters at all. The written word alone will not do, for it is not sufficiently living and refreshing.[115]

Additionally, the voices that echo in our electronic environments are acousmatic in the extreme cases and merely voices of articulation in our everyday practices. While social media are touted by technology enthusiasts as the new way to establish relations, we now see the other side, a dwindling of satisfying productive relations. Social media merely echo the larger consumerist trend fed by a capitalistic system that appears to be in runaway. The sheer quantity of electronic interactions is now staggering to think about—in the billions each day. Tech companies now feel the need to address digital wellness issues as a growing social concern. We are increasingly distracted consumers of information, and this often prevents us from establishing intimate satisfying relations. We are caught in an information theoretic perspective on discourse, which, regrettably, is silencing genuine communication.[116]

Sherry Turkle's research on the growing digital trends indicates that we increasingly desire to "text rather than talk." It is worth remembering what former Google executive James Williams says about the designs within cyberspace and on the Internet: that these designs exploit our cognitive vulnerabilities and speak to the lowest part of ourselves.[117] These revelations should give us pause. Less recent but no less off the mark, Ong claims that the new media we now have are beneficial but are also a "distracting boon. They overwhelm us and give our concept of the word special contours which can interfere with our understanding of what the word in truth is, and thus can distort the relevance of the word to ourselves."[118] Here he is referencing, of course, the spoken word—in particular within immediate ear-to-ear relations.

I explicated the inherent paradox of our use of the phone/*phone*. We are always *on the phone,* and yet the actual sounding of *phone* is receding as a valued aspect of our existential sensorium and as a means by which we establish our human relatedness. The current low status that the voice assumes in our everyday encounters is not, however, created soely as a result of new electronic forms of connectivity. I argue that the actual murder of the *phone* is the consequence of historically brandishing several murder weapons, one being a philosophical perspective that honors the visual and can be traced back to the influence of ancient Greece.

In any case, our most intimate attention that we can give to one another is being thwarted by the provocative yet inauthentic enchantments offered up so readily by new media. The result is the construction of an impersonal self, one that is left feeling untethered, anxious, and depressed, unable to cope productively with the onslaught of information and amusements it has helped to create. It is not surprising that we are witnessing an amazing rise in anxiety and depression in America, which indicates an overall existential dissonance or disenchantment with contemporary life. The statistics I reviewed on this social matter attest to this fact. Causal relations need not be established between these mental health issues and our increased usage of electronic forms of connecting. Their correlation is sufficient to warrant our concern. This is especially true if we bracket the bio-medical model that attributes mental health conditions to mere chemical imbalances in the brain. For example, philosopher and psychiatrist Thomas Fuchs and others are promoting an alternative perspective, claiming that psychological maladies are communicatively based.[119] In other words, mind is clearly a social product and not a progenitor of mental problems. This perspective brings us back to exploring the qualitative aspects of our social relations, given the importance they play in our lived experiences and our sense of well-being. Moreover, a focus on these disturbing societal issues should return us to the saliency of the auditory voice of enunciation within human affairs. Equating the de-voicing of society with "vocal cooling," Locke rightly claims that "we cannot reverse vocal cooling any more easily than readers of *Future Shock* could go out and slow down societal change. But we can begin to respond reflectively, a process abetted to some degree by having the concept 'de-voicing' in our lexicon."[120]

Paradoxically, we can begin to respond reflectively by returning to the ideas of Plato, especially as they relate to our discussion of the musicality within lived experience. In the *Republic,* Plato advocated that music could be viewed as both a remedy and a danger, a cure and a poison.[121] This idea is represented in his designation of the *pharmakon*, the indexical sign that points to this ambiguous semiotic and phenomenological boundary condition. When it comes to applying these ideas specifically to the voice, it appears that the echoes of the acousmatic voices and the voices of articulation within cyberspace, the Internet, and our everyday experiences should be heard with some degree of suspicion. This is because we can now hear how they represent a possible danger and poison to intimacy and genuine interpersónal relations. The sole use of these voices does not help in producing satisfying relations and fostering an ethical generosity toward the other. In addition to depression and anxiety, incivility is on the rise in America.[122] Even though the voices of articulation promote the efficiency of information exchange, ironically, it appears that our uncertainty as existential beings in the world continues to rise. As evidenced by the increase in America of mental anxiety and depression (not to mention attention-deficit disorders), it appears we are interpreting our social and personal contexts as a negative lived ambiguity. We are uncertain more than ever about who we are and who we should become. Because of this, we appeal to the ease of electronic exchanges, given that we find a measure of control in our writing and reading. If we don't like how we sound, we can certainly edit and rewrite. If we agree with McLuhan's depiction as interpreted by Strate "that any given medium or technology, in extending some aspect of the body . . . also amputates that organ,"[123] then we must seriously question the use of technology when it comes to *matters of the heart*. The dispersal of the figurative heart is accomplished by the aesthetics of new media (like Alexa's Valentine proposals). The meaning of the heart has been co-opted and re-programmed by Alexa and other such electronic devices, as well as re-vamped by consumerist logos and greeting card companies and the like. Regrettably, I'm not sure we even notice most of the time.

## RESILIENCE AND A RE-ENCHANTMENT OF HUMAN COMMUNICATION

On the other hand, it behooves us to now hear the voice of enunciation in all its wild, aesthetic musicality and appreciate its sounding. It provides us with a potential enchanting remedy to our media-frenzied environment that is pulling us further apart rather than bringing us together. As the pulsating musicality of existence, the sharing of these enchanting voices within immediate ear-to-ear contexts can make our encounters much more satisfying and productive, given that they offer us a level of communicative engagement beyond the mere superficial. They offer us the moments in which we might foster an actual sharing heart-to-heart, including the felt embodied reverberations of such experiences.

The act of sharing these voices of enunciation is thereby a salient event of discourse, especially in regard to our sense of well-being. Recall that the word *salient* shares the same etymology as the word *resilient*, that is, the Latin word *salire*, which means to jump or leap outward. In its typical usage, the word *salient* functions as an index—pointing to the *heart* or existential starting point. By association, the voices of enunciation invoke salient moments where intimacy and deep connections can truly resonate with heart-felt sentiments. The voice of enunciation offers us a remedy to the social and psychological afflictions we may be suffering, given that it potentializes our very well-being. As a possible cure, this enchanting voice resounding as it does in our most immediate ear-to-ear encounters actually calls us to a precious moment in time. It is a tensive moment, however, in which our subjectivities (and the inter-subjective nature of our relations) may actually shift—enabling us to reposition ourselves more productively within our symbolic webs of meaning.

Given its enchanting effects, the voice of enunciation is not delusionary (like the voice of articulation). Rather, it offers us the talking cure in the truest sense of the word. In its enunciation, we are reminded of Freud's insights about vocal therapy as the very foundation of analysis and mental healing. As Dolar reminds us, à la Freud, the voice is "the pivot of analysis."[124] Parallel to the relationship between analysand (the patient) and analyst, self and other in dialogue co-construct a potential therapeutic situation in which an equality of sharing can take place and healing can begin. Like the musicality of dialogue I am promoting, psychoanalysis, claims Dolar, can only be accomplished by the *viva voce*, in the living voice. As Dolar contends, analysis cannot be done via writing or even the telephone.[125] While we typically think of the analysand as the speaker and the analyst as the silent listener, Dolar indicates that

> a curious reversal takes place; it is the analyst, with his or her silence, who becomes the embodiment of the voice as the object. She or he is the personification, the embodiment, of the voice, the voice incarnate, the aphonic silent voice. . . . It is the silent voice of an appeal, a call, an appeal to respond, to assume one's stance as the subject. . . . Perhaps the whole process of analysis is a way to learn how to assume this voice. . . . . [In this sense] our fate as linguistic, ethical, political subjects has to be pulled to pieces and reassembled, traversed, and assumed.[126]

While definitely risky and producing a level of lived ambiguity, the personal and social rewards of this communicative action of "pulling to pieces and reassembly" of ideas are mentally worth it in the long run. By our willingness to engage the other in immediate auditory dialogue, we reflect an interpretation of life's challenges as a positive ambiguity. When we see such moments as opportunities for personal and social change, we sustain both self and other and the relations we co-construct.

Given the inherent therapeutic potential that inheres with such relations of the voice as resonance, it is clear why an opportunity to create resonance produces a resiliency that we cannot achieve alone. Recall the etymological association between the Latin word *resilire*, meaning to rebound—from which our word *resilience* is derived and the word *resonance*. To be resilient thus implies an ability to personally cope with life's challenges, to rebound from life's existential blows, and to move forward in pragmatic and productive ways. Interper-sónal relations as resonance are thus directly associated with a sense of phenomenological and semiotic resilience. Through speaking with and listening to the wild, enchanting voice of enunciation, we can create genuine interper-sónal relations as resonance and cultivate a resilience, a capacity to spring back or recover from personal or social problems we face. In such instances of auditory acuteness, we understand we are not completely alone—we *are* truly connected to another, and we now value that connection for the musically rich experience it provides. The sounding voice of enunciation presents us with momentary existential wagers that the authentic relationality of resonance will be worth the time and psychological effort we invest. In the end, we find that it is through the resonance created between particular sounding voices of self and other that we enable authentic enchantments of relationality that allow us to persist. I am convinced that these kinds of enchantments will foster the resiliency we seek in today's fast-paced, media-saturated environment.

If we feel an overall sense of disappointment in our lives, a sense of existential disenchantment, then critically reflecting upon the role of human communication in our lives is certainly warranted. For it is within the acoustic space of genuine interper-sónal relations that we discover a means to re-enchant our sense of relationality from which all life depends. By speaking with and listening to the enchanting voice of enunciation, we hear the wild call of humanity—summoning us to participate more actively in the rhythmic dance of cultural life. Not attending to the evocation enunciated by this voice actually severs the essential dialectic between the voiceless name (articulation) and the nameless voice (enunciation), as Foucault suggests. Such severing sacrifices "humanity itself."[127] Above all, by speaking with and listening to the voice of enunciation, we realize, once again, that in the "spoken word there is a dramaturgy of voice which is essentially musical."[128] And we all have our parts to sing.

## NOTES

1. Nancy, *Listening*.

2. Merleau-Ponty, *Consciousness and the Acquisition of Language*.
3. This problematic is discussed in Lanigan, "The Voiceless Name," 155–77.
4. See, for example, Foucault, *The Order of Things*.
5. See Merleau-Ponty, *Phenomenology of Perception*; Merleau-Ponty, *The Primacy of Perception: And Other Essays on Phenomenological Psychology, the Philosophy of Art, History and Politics*, trans. James M. Edie (Evanston: Northwestern University Press, 1964).
6. See Lanigan, "Somebody Is Nowhere," 83.
7. Heidegger, *Being and Time*, 163.
8. Lanigan, "Somebody is Nowhere," 84.
9. Although I do not further develop this idea of chorus in my discussion, it does resemble Julia Kristeva's sense of the semiotic *chora*. For her, the *chora* is the "preverbal and unconscious sphere, not yet inhabited by the law of the sign, where rhythmic and vocalic drives reign. . . . It precedes the symbolic system of language." See Cavarero, *For More Than One Voice*, 133.
10. Lanigan, "Foucault's Chinese Encyclopedia."
11. Dolar, *A Voice and Nothing More*, 40.
12. Ovid, *The Metamorphoses of Ovid*, trans. Michael Simpson (Amherst: University of Massachusetts Press, 2001).
13. Cavarero, *For More Than One Voice*, 240.
14. Isaac E. Catt, "Communicology and Narcissism: Disciplines of the Heart," *Journal of Applied Psychoanalytic Studies* 4, no. 4 (2002).
15. Strate, *Echoes and Reflections*, 106.
16. Cavarero, *For More Than One Voice*, 165.
17. Ibid., 165.
18. See Strate, *Echoes and Reflections*, 106.
19. Ovid, *The Metaphorphoses*, 3.391–2.
20. Cavarero, *For More Than One Voice*, 167.
21. Ibid., 169.
22. Ibid., 165.
23. Nancy, *Listening*, 5.
24. Ibid., 6.
25. Ibid., 5.
26. Ibid., 6.
27. By articulating that listening is at the bottom of discourse, Nancy is inverting the typical hierarchy in which we assume that speaking precedes listening. Of course, both speaking and listening create a unity of discourse within communication.
28. Cavarero, *For More Than One Voice*, 169.
29. Ibid., 170.
30. Nancy, *Listening*, 6.
31. Ibid., 35.
32. Ibid., 35.
33. The notion of "dynamical object/interpretant" comes from Peirce. As he indicates the dynamical object/interpretant is the "effect actually produced on the mind by the Sign" and not merely "the Object as the Sign represents it," which is the immediate object/interpretant. On this distinction see, Peirce, *The Collected Papers*, Vol. 8, ed. Arthur W. Burks (Cambridge, MA: Harvard University Press, 1958), 8.343.
34. Ihde, *Listening and Voice*, 69.
35. Strate's analysis of the myth illustrates what happens when we have an unbalanced sense of self. He declares that it represents a crisis of identity, to which I concur. For an additional interpretation of Ovid's myth from a communicological perspective, I refer you to Isaac E. Catt, "Rhetoric and Narcissism: A Critique of Ideological Selfism," *Western Journal of Speech Communication* 50, no. 3 (1986).
36. Charles Sanders Peirce, "Evolutionary Love," in *Chance, Love, and Logic: Philosophical Essays*, ed. Morris R. Cohen (New York: Harcourt, Brace & Company, 1923), 269.
37. Cavarero, *For More Than One Voice*, 240.
38. Ibid., 241.

39. It is interesting to note that in common nomenclature we use the word *resonance* to signify these types of deep relational experiences, and yet the word's association with its true auditory roots often escapes our notice. This is especially true when resonance is unfortunately characterized as a "common emotional worldspace" rather than an auditory phenomenon. See Ken Wilber, *A Brief History of Everything* (Boston: Shambhala, 1996), 99.

40. Nancy, *Listening*, 20.

41. Ibid., 20.

42. On resonance, see *Merriam-Webster*, s.v. "resonance (n.)," accessed August 10, 2019, https://www.merriam-webster.com/dictionary/resonance.

43. Nancy, *Listening*, 37.

44. Ibid., 16; brackets in original.

45. Ibid., 21.

46. Nancy appeals to the notion of echo, I believe, because he sees parallels to the concept of trace within writing, developed by Derrida. Echo is thus a deferral of speaking. Echo can be heard as a deferral; however, where I disagree with Nancy is with his making echo the inaugural prompt for speaking and listening as a communicative event.

47. Nancy, *Listening*, 13.

48. Dolar, *A Voice and Nothing More*, 40.

49. Peirce, *The Collected Papers*, 8.343.

50. Nancy, *Listening*, 2.

51. I disagree that echo serves as the origin of language or communication. For a counterperspective, see Garnet C. Butchart, "Echo: Or, on the Origin of Words," *Journal of Cultural Studies* 5, no. 1 (2018).

52. Nancy, *Listening*, 29.

53. Ibid., 27. Gaston Bachelard concurs when he describes man as a "sound chamber." See Bachelard, *Air and Dreams: An Essay on the Imagination of Movement* (Dallas: Dallas Institute Publications, 1988), 240.

54. Colapietro, "Qualitative Immediacy."

55. Robert E. Innis, *Susanne Langer in Focus: The Symbolic Mind* (Bloomington: Indiana University Press, 2009), 85.

56. Nancy, *Listening*, 41.

57. Cavarero, *For More Than One Voice*, 169.

58. Susanne K. Langer, *Philosophy in a New Key: A Study in the Symbolism of Reason, Rite, and Art* (Cambridge: Harvard University Press, 1942), 227.

59. Ibid., 228.

60. Ibid., 226.

61. Parret, *The Aesthetics of Communication*, 51.

62. Michel Serres, *The Five Senses: A Philosophy of Mingled Bodies,* translated by Margaret Sankey and Peter Cowley (London: Continuum, 2008), 123.

63. Parret, *The Aesthetics of Communication*, 51.

64. Nancy, *Listening*, 36–37.

65. Ibid., 38.

66. Jean d'Udine, *L'Art et le geste* (Paris: Alcan, 1910), 6, quoted in Langer, *Philosophy in a New Key*, 83. In light of these ideas, we may speculate that by also characterizing love as a circular *movement*, Peirce is drawing our attention to the evolutionary love that he believes undergirds our logical existence. On this, see Peirce, "Evolutionary Love," 267.

67. Parret, *The Aesthetics of Communication*, 59.

68. Nancy, *Listening*, 39.

69. Graham, *The Re-Enchantment of the World*, 173.

70. Nancy, *Listening*, 38.

71. Cavarero, *For More Than One Voice*, 11.

72. Ibid., 11.

73. Of course, the psychoanalytic tradition and especially Julia Kristeva acknowledge and heavily privilege rhythm as a vital aspect of language and discourse, claiming rhythm is the unconscious. See, Kristeva, *Revolution*.

74. Ray Robinson and Allen Winold, *The Choral Experience: Literature, Materials, and Methods* (New York: Harper & Row, 1976).
75. Alfred Schutz, *Making Music Together*, 161–2.
76. Ruth Finnegan, *The Hidden Musicians: Music-Making in an English Town* (Cambridge: Cambridge University Press, 1989), 340.
77. Ibid., 340.
78. Merleau-Ponty, *Consciousness and the Acquisition*.
79. Ihde, *Listening and Voice*, 154.
80. Merleau-Ponty, *Consciousness and the Acquisition*, 81.
81. Nancy, *Listening*, 41.
82. While Peirce does not explicitly explore the auditory dimensions of sign actions in his writings, he does refer at one point to the "scarlet trumpet sound," indicating a similar representation of sound as color. See Peirce, *The Collected Papers*, 1.358. Vincent Colapietro argues that it was "quite natural" for Peirce "to use the metaphor of light to characterize . . . the articulation of a doctrine of categories." See Colapietro, "A Lantern," 201.
83. Dolar, *A Voice and Nothing More*, 20.
84. Nancy, *Listening*, 40.
85. Ibid., 40.
86. Innis, *Susanne Langer in Focus*, 81.
87. William Blake, *Complete Poetry and Prose of William Blake,* ed. David V. Erdman (Berkeley: University of California Press [1965] 2008, quoted in Walter Ong, *The Presence of the Word*, 71.
88. Ibid., 71.
89. Ibid., 71.
90. Langer, *Philosophy in a New Key*, 232.
91. Innis, *Susanne Langer in Focus*, 84. Innis is using the word *articulate* in a different way than I have specified herein. Substituting the word *enunciate* aligns with the arguments I have advanced.
92. Richard Wagner, "Ein Glücklicher Abend," reprinted 1841 by Gatz, in *Musik-Aesthetik*, from the *Gazette Musicale*, nos. 56–58, quoted in Langer, *Philosophy in a New Key*, 221–22.
93. Peirce, "Evolutionary Love," 282.
94. Naomi Cumming, *The Sonic Self: Musical Subjectivity and Signification* (Bloomington: Indiana University Press, 2000). Cumming takes an explicit Peircean approach to musical performance.
95. Nancy, *Listening*, 40.
96. Ibid., 42.
97. Schutz, *Making Music Together*, 178.
98. Peter J. Martin, *Sounds and Society: Themes in the Sociology of Music* (Manchester and New York: Manchester University Press, 1995), 200.
99. Barnouw, "'Aesthetic' for Schiller and Peirce," 615.
100. "The Consequences of Loneliness: Interview with James Lynch," Earl E. Bakken Center for Spirituality & Healing, accessed April 4, 2019, https://www.takingcharge.csh.umn.edu/consequences-loneliness-interview-james-lynch.
101. James Lynch, *The Broken Heart: Medical Consequences of Loneliness* (New York: Basic Books, 1977), 11.
102. Lynch, *Broken Heart*, 132.
103. William H. McNeill, *Keeping Together in Time: Dance and Drill in Human History* (Cambridge MA: Harvard University Press, 1995), 7.
104. "The Consequences of Loneliness."
105. Nancy, *Listening*, 55.
106. Peirce, "Evolutionary Love," 274.
107. Ibid., 276.
108. Colapietro, "Emersonian Moods," 181.
109. Pierce, *The Collected Papers,* 1.628.
110. Cavarero, *For More Than One Voice*, 241.
111. Locke, *The De-Voicing of Society*, 26.

112. Bateson and Bateson, *Angels Fear*.
113. Wilfred Mellers, Introduction, in Christopher Ballantine, *Music and its Social Meanings* (London: Gordon & Breach, 1984), ix.
114. Locke, *De-Voicing of Society*, 19.
115. Ong, *Presence of the Word*, 125.
116. Lanigan, *Phenomenology of Communication*.
117. Williams, *Stand Out of Our Light*, 29.
118. Ong, *Presence of the Word*, xxvii–xxviii.
119. Fuchs, *Ecology of the Brain*.
120. Locke, *De-Voicing of Society*, 196.
121. Dolar, *A Voice and Nothing More*, 46.
122. See Stephen L. Carter, *Civility: Manners, Morals, and the Etiquette of Democracy* (New York: Harper, 1998).
123. Strate, *Echos and Reflections*, 131.
124. Dolar, *A Voice and Nothing More*, 123.
125. Ibid., 123.
126. Ibid., 124.
127. Cavarero, *For More Than One Voice*, 210. Cavarero describes this as the essential dialectic between speaking and speech.
128. Ihde, *Listening and Voice*, 156.

# Bibliography

Agamben, Giorgio. *Homo Sacer: Sovereign Power and Bare Life*. Trans. Daniel Heller-Roazen. Stanford: Stanford University Press, 1998.
Anderson, Douglas R. *Creativity and the Philosophy of C. S. Peirce*. Boston: Martinus Nijhoff Publishers, 1987.
Androne, Dakin, and Artemis Moshtaghian, "A Doctor in California Appeared via Video Link to Tell a Patient He Was Going to Die. The Man's Family Is Upset." *CNN*, March 11, 2019. https://www.cnn.com/2019/03/10/health/patient-dies-robot-doctor.
Aristotle. *Metaphysics*. Translated by John Warrington. London: J. M. Dent and Sons, 1956.
Bachelard, Gaston. *Air and Dreams: An Essay on the Imagination of Movement*. Dallas: Dallas Institute Publications, 1988.
Barnouw, Jeffrey. "'Aesthetic' for Schiller and Peirce: A Neglected Origin of Pragmatism." *Journal of the History of Ideas* 49, no. 4 (1988): 607–632.
Barthes, Roland. *The Grain of the Voice: Interviews 1962–1980*. Translated by Linda Coverdale. Los Angeles: University of California Press, 1991.
Barthes, Roland. *Mythologies*. Translated by Annette Lavers. New York: Hill and Wang, 1972.
Barthes, Roland. *The Pleasure of the Text*. Translated by Richard Miller. New York: Noonday Press, 1975.
Barthes, Roland. *S/Z*. Translated by Richard Miller. New York: Noonday, [1970] 1974.
Bartky, Sandra Lee. *Femininity and Domination: Studies in the Phenomenology of Oppression*. New York: Routledge, 1990.
Bateson, Gregory. "The Cybernetics of 'Self': A Theory of Alcoholism." In *Steps to an Ecology of Mind*, 309–37. New York: Ballantine Books, 1972.
Bateson, Gregory. *Mind and Nature: A Necessary Unity*. New York: E. P. Dutton, 1979.
Bateson, Gregory. *Sacred Unity: Further Steps to an Ecology of Mind*, edited by Rodney E. Donaldson. New York: Cornelia and Michael Bessie Book, 1991.
Bateson, Gregory. *Steps to an Ecology of Mind*. New York: Ballantine Books, 1972.
Bateson, Gregory, and Mary Catherine Bateson. *Angels Fear: Towards an Epistemology of the Sacred*. New York: Bantam Books, 1987.
Baudrillard, Jean. *Simulations*. Translated by Paul Beitchman, Paul Foss, and Paul Patton. New York: Semiotext[e], 1983.
Baumgarten, Alexander. *Aesthetica*. Hildesham: George Olms, 1961.
Bennett, Jane. *The Enchantment of Modern Life: Attachments, Crossings, and Ethics*. Princeton: Princeton University Press, 2001.
Bennett, Jane. "How Is It, Then, That We Still Remain Barbarians?" *Political Theory* 24, no. 4 (1996): 653–672.

Bennett, Jane. *Thoreau's Nature: Ethics, Politics, and the Wild.* Lanham, MD: Rowman & Littlefield Publishers, Inc. 2002.

Bennett, Jane. *Vibrant Matter: A Political Ecology of Things.* Durham: Duke University Press, 2009.

Berman, Morris. *The Re-Enchantment of the World.* Ithaca: Cornell University Press, 1981.

Bernardino, Jacopo. "The Role of Marketing in the Infantilization of the Postmodern Adult." *Fast Capitalism*, October 1, 2013. https://www.uta.edu/huma/agger/fastcapitalism/10_1/bernardini10_1.html.

Bettelheim, Bruno. *The Uses of Enchantment: The Meaning and Importance of Fairy Tales.* New York: Vintage Books, 1976.

Bilgrami, Akeel. "Occidentalism, the Very Idea: An Essay on Enlightenment and Enchantment." *Critical Theory* 32, no. 3 (2006): 381–411.

Bilgrami, Akeel. *Secularism, Identity, and Enchantment.* Cambridge: Harvard University Press, 2014.

Blake, William. *Complete Poetry and Prose of William Blake,* edited by David V. Erdman. Berkeley: University of California Press, (1965), 2008.

Bodie, Graham D., and Nathan Crick. "Listening, Hearing, Sensing: Three Modes of Being and the Phenomenology of Charles Sanders Peirce." *Communication Theory* 24, no. 2 (May 2014): 105–23.

Bonev, Anton. "The Impact of the Digital Age on Human Engagement." *Medium,* July 13, 2017. https://medium.com/the-looking-glass/the-impact-of-the-digital-age-on-human-engagement-aaa42d526453.

Bourdieu, Pierre, and Loïc J. D. Wacquant. *An Invitation to Reflexive Sociology.* Chicago: University of Chicago Press, 1992.

Bowles, Nellie. "Human Contact Is Now a Luxury Good." *The New York Times,* March 23, 2019. https://www.nytimes.com/2019/03/23/sunday-review/human-contact-luxury-screens.html.

Bradford, Alina. "5 Awesome Ways to Use Alexa on Valentine's Day." *CNET,* February 13, 2019. https://www.cnet.com/how-to/alexa-on-valentines-day/.

Brophy, Philip. "Vocalizing the Posthuman." In *Voice: Vocal Aesthetics in Digital Arts and Media,* edited by Norie Neumark, Ross Gibson, and Theo Van Leeuwen, 361–382. Cambridge, MA: Massachusetts Institute of Technology, 2010.

Buber, Martin. *Between Man and Man.* New York: Macmillan, 1965.

Buber, Martin. *I and Thou.* Translated by Walter Kaufmann. New York: Touchstone, 1970.

Bull, Michael and Les Back, eds. *The Auditory Culture Reader.* Oxford and New York: Berg, 2003.

Butchart, Garnet C. "Echo: Or, on the Origin of Words." *Journal of Cultural Studies* 5, no. 1 (2018): 1–14.

Butler, Judith. *Excitable Speech: A Politics of the Performative.* New York: Routledge, 1997.

Butler, Judith. *Gender Trouble: Feminism and the Subversion of Identity.* New York: Routledge, 1990.

Calvino, Italo. *Under the Jaguar Sun.* Translated by William Weaver. New York: Harcourt Brace, 1988.

Capeller, Ivan. "Sounds, Signs and Hearing: Towards a Semiotics of the Audible Field." *Athens Journal of Philology* 5, no. 1 (2018): 45–60.

Carey, James. *Communication as Culture: Essays on Media and Society.* Boston: Unwin Hyman, 1997.

Carlsen, Arne, and Lloyd Sandelands. "First Passion: Wonder in Organizational Inquiry." *Management Learning* 46, no. 4 (2015): 373–90.

Carr, Nicholas. *The Shallows*: *What the Internet Is Doing to Our Brains.* New York: W. W. Norton & Company, 2011.

Carter, Stephen L. *Civility: Manners, Morals, and the Etiquette of Democracy.* New York: Harper, 1998.

Cassirer, Ernst. *The Myth of the State.* New Haven: Yale University Press, 1946.

Catt, Isaac E. "Charles Sanders Peirce." In *Encyclopedia of Communication Ethics: Goods in Contention,* edited by Ronald C. Arnett, Annette M. Holba, and Susan Mancino, 369–73. New York: Peter Lang, 2018.

Catt, Isaac E. "Communication Is Not a Skill: Critique of Communication Pedagogy as Narcissistic Expression." In *Communicology: The New Science of Embodied Discourse*, edited by Deborah Eicher-Catt and Isaac E. Catt, 131–50. Madison: Fairleigh Dickinson University Press, 2010.

Catt, Isaac E. "Communicology and Narcissism: Disciplines of the Heart." *Journal of Applied Psychoanalytic Studies* 4, no. 4 (2002): 389–411.

Catt, Isaac E. "Communicology and the Ethics of Selfhood Under the Regime of Antidepressant Medicine." In *Philosophy of Communication Ethics: Alterity and the Other*, edited by Ronald C. Arnett and Pat Arneson, 285–304. Madison: Fairleigh Dickinson University Press; Lanham: Rowman & Littlefield, 2014.

Catt, Isaac E. *Embodiment in the Semiotic Matrix: Communicology in Peirce, Dewey, Bateson, and Bourdieu*. Madison: Fairleigh Dickinson University Press, 2017.

Catt, Isaac E. "Rhetoric and Narcissism: A Critique of Ideological Selfism." *Western Journal of Speech Communication* 50, no. 3 (1986): 242–53.

Catt, Isaac E., and Deborah Eicher-Catt. "Communicology: A Reflexive Human Science." In *Communicology: The New Science of Embodied Discourse*, edited by Deborah Eicher-Catt and Isaac E. Catt, 15–29. Madison: Fairleigh Dickinson University Press, 2010.

Cavarero, Adriana. *For More Than One Voice: Toward a Philosophy of Vocal Expression*. Translated by Paul A. Kottman. Stanford: Stanford University Press, 2005.

"Cell Phone Addiction." Psychguides. Accessed August 30, 2019. https://www.psychguides.com/behavioral-disorders/cell-phone-addiction/signs-and-symptoms/.

Chion, Michel. *Audio-Vision: Sound on Screen*. New York: Columbia University Press, 1994.

Chion, Michel. *The Voice in Cinema*. Translated by Claudia Gorbman. New York: Columbia University Press, 1999.

Chonchúir, Mórna Ní, and John McCarthy. "The Enchanting Potential of Technology: A Dialogical Case Study of Enchantment and the Internet." *Personal and Ubiquitous Computing* 12, no. 5 (June 2008): 401–9.

Classen, Constance. *Worlds of Sense: Exploring the Senses in History and Across Cultures*. New York: Routledge, 1993.

Clerkin, Bridget. "Death by Text Message? Stats Show How Technology Is Killing Us." *DMV.org*, April 28, 2017. https://www.dmv.org/articles/death-by-text-message-stats-show-how-technology-is-killing-us/.

Colapietro, Vincent. "Emersonian Moods, Peircean Sentiments, and Ellingtonian Tones." *The Journal of Speculative Philosophy* 33, no. 2 (2019): 178–199.

Colapietro, Vincent. "A Lantern for the Feet of Inquirers: The Heuristic Function of the Peircean Categories." *Semiotica* 136, no. 1 (2001): 201–216.

Colapietro, Vincent. *Peirce's Approach to the Self: A Semiotic Perspective on Human Subjectivity*. Albany: State University of New York Press, 1989.

Colapietro, Vincent. "Qualitative Immediacy and Mediating Qualities: Reflections on Firstness as More Than a Category," *Semiotics 2018*, DOI: 10.5840/cpsem201813.

Colapietro, Vincent. "Striving to Speak in a Human Voice: A Peircean Contribution to Metaphysical Discourse." *The Review of Metaphysics* 58, no. 2 (2004): 367–98.

Connor, Steven. *Dumbstruck: A Cultural History of Ventriloquism*. New York: Oxford University Press, 2000.

"The Consequences of Loneliness: Interview with James Lynch." Earl E. Bakken Center for Spirituality & Healing, accessed April 4, 2019. https://www.takingcharge.csh.umn.edu/consequences-loneliness-interview-james-lynch.

"Continuous Partial Attention." The Attention Project, accessed April 15, 2019. https://lindastone.net/qa/continuous-partial-attention/.

Cox, Christoph. "Beyond Representation and Signification: Toward a Sonic Materialism." *Journal of Visual Culture* 10, no. 2 (2011): 145–61.

Crary, Jonathan. *24/7: Late Capitalism and the Ends of Sleep*. New York: Verso, 2014.

Crawford, Matthew B. *The World Beyond Your Head: On Becoming an Individual in an Age of Distraction*. New York: Farrar, Straus and Giroux, 2015.

Cumming, Naomi. *The Sonic Self: Musical Subjectivity and Signification*. Bloomington: Indiana University Press, 2000.

Curry, Patrick. "Enchantment and Modernity." *PAN: Philosophy Activism Nature* 9 (2012): 76–89.
Deely, John. *Semiotic Animal: A Postmodern Definition of "Human Being" Transcending Patriarchy and Feminism*. South Bend: St. Augustine's Press, 2010.
Deledalle, Gérard. *Charles S. Peirce's Philosophy of Signs: Essays in Comparative Semiotics*. Bloomington: Indiana University Press, 2000.
Denizet-Lewis, Benoit. "Why Are More American Teenagers Than Ever Suffering from Severe Anxiety?" *The New York Times*, October 11, 2017. https://www.nytimes.com/2017/10/11/magazine/why-are-more-american-teenagers-than-ever-suffering-from-severe-anxiety.html.
"Depression." World Health Organization. Accessed August 30, 2019. https://www.who.int/news-room/fact-sheets/detail/depression/.
Derrida, Jacques. *Of Grammatology*. Translated by Gayatri Spivak. Baltimore: Johns Hopkins University Press, [1967] 1976.
Derrida, Jacques. *Speech and Phenomena*. Translated by David B. Allison. Evanston: Northwestern University Press, 1973.
Derrida, Jacques. *Writing and Difference*. Translated by Alan Bass. Chicago: University of Chicago Press, 1967.
Dewey, Caitlin. "What the Heck Is Pokémon Go? An Explainer for the Out-of-Touch And/Or Old." *The Washington Post*, July 11, 2016. https://www.washingtonpost.com/news/the-intersect/wp/2016/07/11/what-the-heck-is-pokemon-go-an-explainer-for-the-out-of-touch-andor-old/?utm_term=.18997aedc819.
Dewey, John. *Human Nature and Conduct*. New York: The Modern Library, Random House, 1922.
Dewey, John. *John Dewey: The Later Works, 1925–1953, Vol. 10, 1934*, edited by Jo Ann Boydston. Carbondale: Southern Illinois University Press, 1987.
"Distracted Walking a Major Pedestrian Safety Concern." *Safety.com*, April 15, 2019. https://www.safety.com/distracted-walking-a-major-pedestrian-safety-concern/.
Dockrill, Peter. "America Really Is in the Midst of a Rising Anxiety Epidemic." *Science Alert*, May 9, 2018. https://www.sciencealert.com/americans-are-in-the-midst-of-an-anxiety-epidemic-stress-increase.
Dolar, Mladen. *A Voice and Nothing More*. Cambridge: MIT Press, 2006.
Ducharme, Jamie. "'Phubbing' is Hurting Your Relationships. Here's What It Is." *Time*, March 29, 2018. http://time.com/5216853/what-is-phubbing/.
Dyson, Frances. *The Tone of Our Times: Sound, Sense, Economy, and Ecology*. Cambridge, MA: Massachusetts Institute of Technology, 2014.
Eco, Umberto. *A Theory of Semiotics*. Bloomington: Indiana University Press, 1976.
Edie, James M. Forward to *Consciousness and the Acquisition of Language*, by Maurice Merleau-Ponty, xi–xxxii. Translated by Hugh J. Silverman. Evanston: Northwestern University Press, 1973.
Eicher-Catt, Deborah. "The Authenticity in Ambiguity: Appreciating Maurice Merleau-Ponty's Abductive Logic as Communicative Praxis." *Atlantic Journal of Communication* 13, no. 2 (2005): 113–34.
Eicher-Catt, Deborah. "Enchantment and the Serious Play of A(musement)." *Language and Semiotic Studies* 4, no. 2 (2018): 128–43.
Eicher-Catt, Deborah. "The Logic of the Sacred in Bateson and Peirce." *The American Journal of Semiotics* 19, no. 1/4 (2003): 95–126.
Eicher-Catt, Deborah. "A Prelude to a Semioethics of Dialogue: The Aesthetics of Enchantment in a New Key." *Language and Dialogue* 7, no. 1 (2017): 100–19.
Eicher-Catt, Deborah. "Recovering the Voice of Embodied Dialogue: Edward Sapir's Contribution to Communicology." *International Journal of Communication* 20, no 1–2 (2010): 9–33.
Eicher-Catt, Deborah, and Isaac E. Catt, eds. *Communicology: The New Science of Embodied Discourse*. Madison: Fairleigh Dickinson University Press, 2010.
Eicher-Catt, Deborah, and Isaac E. Catt. "Peirce and Cassirer, 'Life' and 'Spirit': A Communicology of Religion." *Journal of Communication and Religion* 36, no. 2 (2013): 77–106.

Ellul, Jacques. *The Humiliation of the Word*. Translated by Joyce Main Hanks. Grand Rapids: Eerdmans, 1985.
Ewen, Stuart. *All Consuming Images: The Politics of Style in Contemporary Culture*. New York: Basic Books, 1988.
Fader, Sarah. "Social Media Obsession and Anxiety." Anxiety and Depression Association of America, November 2018. https://adaa.org/social-media-obsession-and-anxiety.
Fanelli, Matthew. "Getting Consumers' Attention Across Every Screen They Have at Home." *eMarketer*, December 1, 2017. www.emarketer.com/Article/Getting-Consumers-Attention-Across-Every-Screen-They-Have-Home/2016798.
Farrell, Thomas J. Preface to the 2000 paperback edition of *The Presence of the Word: Some Prolegomena for Cultural and Religious History*, by Walter Ong, xiii–xxix. Binghamton: Global Publications, State University of New York, [1967] 2000.
Filmer, Paul. "Songtime: Sound Culture, Rhythm and Sociality." In *The Auditory Culture Reader*, edited by Michael Bull and Les Back, 91–112. New York: Berg, 2003.
Finnegan, Ruth. *The Hidden Musicians: Music-Making in an English Town*. Cambridge: Cambridge University Press, 1989.
Fisher, Philip. *Wonder, the Rainbow, and the Aesthetics of Rare Experiences*. Cambridge: Harvard University Press, 1998.
Foucault, Michel. *The Order of Things: An Archaeology of the Human Sciences*. New York: Vintage Books, 1973.
Frank, Mark G., Darrin J. Griffin, Elena Svetieva, and Andreas Maroulis, "Nonverbal Elements of the Voice." In *The Social Psychology of Nonverbal Communication*, edited by Aleksandra Kostic and David Chadee, 92–113. London: Palgrave Macmillan, 2015.
"Frequently Asked Questions," Pristiq, accessed August 30, 2019. https://www.pristiq.com/faqs.
Frischmann, Brett, and Evan Selinger. *Re-Engineering Humanity*. Cambridge: Cambridge University Press, 2018.
Fuchs, Christian. *Social Media: A Critical Introduction*. 2nd ed. Thousand Oaks: Sage, 2017.
Fuchs, Thomas. *Ecology of the Brain*. Oxford: Oxford University Press, 2018.
Furedi, Frank. "The Ages of Distraction." *Aeon*, April 1, 2016. https://aeon.co/essays/busy-and-distracted-everybody-has-been-since-at-least-1710.
Furness, Graham. *Orality: The Power of the Spoken Word*. New York: Palgrave Macmillian, 2004.
Gadamer, Hans-Georg. *The Relevance of the Beautiful and Other Essays*. Translated by Nicholas Walker. New York: Cambridge University Press, 1986.
Gadamer, Hans-Georg. *Truth and Method*. Translated by W. Glen-Doepel. London: Sheed & Ward, 1975.
Gelernter, David. "The Danger Is Not Machines Becoming Humans, but Humans Becoming Machines." Big Think, December 13, 2013. https://bigthink.com/in-their-own-words/the-danger-is-not-machines-becoming-humans-but-humans-becoming-machines.
Gergen, Kenneth J. *The Saturated Self: Dilemmas of Identity in Contemporary Life*. New York: Basic Books, 1991.
Giroux, Henry A. and Grace Pollock, *The Mouse that Roared: Disney and the End of Innocence*. Lanham, MD: Rowman & Littlefield, 2010.
Graham, Gordon. *The Re-Enchantment of the World: Art Versus Religion*. Oxford: Oxford University Press, 2007.
Graham, Philip W. "Space and Cyberspace: On the Enclosure of Consciousness." In *Living with Cyberspace: Technology and Society in the 21st Century*, edited by John Armitage and Joanne Roberts, 156–164. London: Continuum, 2002.
Greenberg, Gary. *Manufacturing Depression: The Secret History of a Modern Disease*. New York: Simon & Schuster, 2010.
Guardiano, Nicholas L. "Charles S. Peirce's New England Neighbors and Embrace of Transcendentalism." *Transactions of the Charles S. Peirce Society* 53, no. 2 (2017), 216–245.
Gusdorf, Georges. *Speaking (La Parole)*. Translated by Paul T. Brockelman. Chicago: Northwestern University Press, 1965.

Hagerty, Alexa. "Speak Softly to the Dead: The Uses of Enchantment in American Home Funerals." *Social Anthropology* 22, no. 4 (2014): 428–42.

Haraway, Donna. "A Cyborg Manifesto: Science, Technology, and Socialist-Feminism in the Late Twentieth Century." In *Philosophy of Technology: The Technological Condition: An Anthology*, edited by Robert C. Scharff and Val Dusek, 429–50. Malden: Blackwell Publishing, 2003.

Hartmans, Avery. "This Beautiful Credit-Card-Sized Phone Just Might Cure Your Smartphone Addiction." *Business Insider,* January 10, 2017. https://www.businessinsider.com/light-phone-features-photos-2017-1.

Harvey, David Oscar. "The Limits of Vococentrism: Chris Marker, Hans Richter and the Essay Film." *SubStance* 41, no. 2 (2012): 6–23.

Hawkes, Terence. *Structuralism and Semiotics*. Berkeley: University of California Press, 1977.

Heidegger, Martin. *Being and Time*. Translated by John Macquarrie and Edward S. Robinson. Oxford: Blackwell, 1962.

Henriques, Julian F. "Sonic Dominance and the Reggae Sound System Session." In *The Auditory Culture Reader*, edited by Michael Bull and Les Back, 451–80. New York: Berg, 2003.

Hoffmann, Bill. "Report: Depression Is Skyrocketing in America." *Newsmax,* May 10, 2018. https://www.newsmax.com/newsfront/survey-depression-surge-america/2018/05/10/id/859531/.

Horkheimer, Max and Theodor Adorno. *Dialectic of Enlightenment*. Translated by John Cumming. Frieberg: Herder and Herder, 1972.

Howe, Louis E. "Enchantment, Weak Ontologies, and Administrative Ethics." *Administration & Society* 38, no. 4 (2006): 422–46.

Howe, Neil. "Why Millennials are Texting More and Talking Less." *Forbes*, July 15, 2015. https://www.forbes.com/sites/neilhowe/2015/07/15/why-millennials-are-texting-more-and-talking-less/#c5a207259752.

Howes, David. "Introduction to Sensory Museology." *The Senses and Society* 9, no. 3 (2014): 259–67.

Husserl, Edmund. *Experience and Judgement: Investigations in a Genealogy of Logic*. Translated by James S. Churchill and Karl Ameriks. Evanston: Northwestern University Press, 1973.

Hyde, Michael. "The Call of Conscience: Heidegger and the Question of Rhetoric." *Philosophy and Rhetoric* 27, no. 4 (1994): 374–396.

Hyde, Michael. "Human Being and the Call of Technology." In *Toward the 21st Century: The Future of Speech Communication,* edited by Julia Wood and Richard Gregg, 47–79. Cresskill, NJ: Hampton Press, 1995.

Hyde, Michael. *The Interruption That We Are: The Health of the Lived Body, Narrative, and Public Moral Argument*. Columbia: University of South Carolina Press, 2018.

Ihde, Don. *Listening and Voice: Phenomenologies of Sound*. Albany: State University of New York Press, 2007.

Ingemark, Camilla Asplund. "The Chronotope of Enchantment." *Journal of Folklore Research* 43, no. 1 (2006): 1–30.

Innis, Robert E. *Susanne Langer in Focus: The Symbolic Mind*. Bloomington: Indiana University Press, 2009.

Jackson, Maggie. *Distracted: The Erosion of Attention and the Coming Dark Age*. Amherst: Prometheus Books, 2008.

Jakobson, Roman. *Six Lectures on Sound and Meaning*. Boston: Institute of Technology Press, 1942.

Jakobson, Roman. "The Speech Event and the Functions of Language." In *On Language: Roman Jakobson,* edited by Linda Waugh and Monique Monville-Burston, 69–79. Cambridge, MA: Harvard University Press, 1990.

James, William. *The Principles of Psychology*, edited by Frederick Burkhardt, vol. 1. Cambridge: Harvard University Press, (1890) 1981.

Jenkins, Richard. "Disenchantment, Enchantment and Re-Enchantment: Max Weber at the Millennium." *Max Weber Studies* 1, no. 1 (November 2000): 11–32.

Johnson, Rochelle L. "'This Enchantment Is No Delusion': Henry David Thoreau, the New Materialisms, and Ineffable Materiality." *Interdisciplinary Studies in Literature and Environment* 21, no. 3 (Summer 2014): 606–35.
Jhally, Sut. *The Spectacle of Accumulation: Essays in Culture, Media, and Politics.* New York: Peter Lang, 2006.
Karp, David A. *Speaking of Sadness: Depression, Disconnection, and the Meanings of Illness.* New York: Oxford University Press, 1996.
Kelley, Trista. "Study: You are More Likely to Die Walking with Headphones." *Times Union*, January 17, 2012. https://www.timesunion.com/news/article/Study-You-are-more-likely-to-die-walking-with-2578662.php.
Kestenbaum, Victor. *The Phenomenological Sense of John Dewey: Habit and Meaning.* Atlantic Highlands: Humanities Press, 1977.
Kim, Kyung Hee. "The Creativity Crisis: The Decrease in Creative Thinking Scores on the Torrance Tests of Creative Thinking." *Creativity Research Journal* 23, no 4 (2011): 285–95.
Kim-Cohen, Seth. *In the Blink of an Ear: Toward a Non-Cochlear Sonic Art.* New York: Continuum, 2009.
Kimbrough, Andrew McComb. "The Sound of Meaning: Theories of Voice in Twentieth-century Thought and Performance." Dissertation, Louisiana State University, 2002.
Kirsch, Irving. *The Emperor's New Drugs: Exploding the Antidepressant Myth.* New York: Basic Books, 2010.
Kopf, Abbie. "A New Report Shows That Diagnosis Rates for ADHD Have Risen 30% in 8 Years." *USA Today*, March 29, 2019. https://www.usatoday.com/story/sponsor-story/bluecross-blue-shield-association/2019/03/29/new-report-shows-diagnosis-rates-adhd-have-risen-30-8-years/3309871002/.
Korzybski, Alfred. *Science and Sanity: An Introduction to Non-Aristotelian Systems and General Semantics.* Fort Worth: Institute of General Semantics, [1933] 1994.
Kottman, Paul A. Translator's introduction to *For More Than One Voice: Toward a Philosophy of Vocal Expression*, by Adriana Cavarero, vii-xxv. Translated by Paul A. Kottman. Stanford: Stanford University Press, 2005.
Kristeva, Julia. *Revolution in Poetic Language.* Translated by Margaret Waller. New York: Columbia University Press, 1984.
LaBelle, Brandon. "Raw Orality: Sound Poetry and Live Bodies." In *Voices: Vocal Aesthetics in Digital Arts and Media,* edited by Norie Neumark, Ross Gibson, and Theo Van Leeuwen, 147–171. Cambridge, MA: Massachusetts Institute of Technology, 2010.
Langer, Susanne K. *Philosophy in a New Key: A Study in the Symbolism of Reason, Rite, and Art.* Cambridge: Harvard University Press, 1942.
Langsdorf, Lenore. "The Primacy of Listening: Toward a Metaphysics of Communicative Interaction." In *Postphenomenology: A Critical Companion to Ihde,* edited by Evan Selinger, 37–47. Albany: State University of New York Press, 2006.
Lanigan, Richard L. "Foucault's Chinese Encyclopedia: *Le Même et L'Autre.*" In *The Human Science of Communicology: A Phenomenology of Discourse in Foucault and Merleau-Ponty*, 142–54. Pittsburgh: Duquesne University Press, 1992.
Lanigan, Richard L. *The Human Science of Communicology: A Phenomenology of Discourse in Foucault and Merleau-Ponty.* Pittsburgh: Duquesne University Press, 1992.
Lanigan, Richard L. *Phenomenology of Communication: Merleau-Ponty's Thematics in Communicology and* Semiology. Pittsburgh: Duquesne University Press, 1988.
Lanigan, Richard L. "The Self in Semiotic Phenomenology: Consciousness as the Conjunction of Perception and Expression in the Science of Communication." *The American Journal of Semiotics* 15–16, no. 1–4 (2000): 91–111.
Lanigan, Richard L. *Semiotic Phenomenology of Rhetoric: Eidetic Practice in Henry Grattan's Discourse on Tolerance.* Washington: University Press of America, 1984.
Lanigan, Richard L. "Somebody Is Nowhere: Michel Foucault on Rhetoric and the Discourse of Subjectivity in the Human Sciences." In *The Human Science of Communicology: A Phenomenology of Discourse in Foucault and Merleau-Ponty*, 81–113. Pittsburgh: Duquesne University Press, 1992.

Lanigan, Richard L. "The Voiceless Name and the Nameless Voice." In *The Human Science of Communicology: A Phenomenology of Discourse in Foucault and Merleau-Ponty*, 155–77. Pittsburgh: Duquesne University Press, 1992.

Lannamann, John W. "The Politics of Voice in Interpersonal Communication Research." In *Social Approaches to Communication*, edited by Wendy Leeds-Hurwitz, 114–31. New York: Guilford Press, 1995.

Levin, Thomas Y. "Before the Beep." In *Voices: Vocal Aesthetics in Digital Arts and Media* edited by Norie Neumark, Ross Gibson, and Theo Van Leeuwen, 17–32. Cambridge, MA: Massachusetts Institute of Technology, 2010.

Levinas, Emmanuel. *Emmanuel Levinas: Basic Philosophical Writings*, edited by Adriaan T. Peperzak, Simon Critchley, and Robert Bernasconi. Indianapolis: Indiana University Press, 1996.

Levine, Donald N. *The Flight from Ambiguity: Essays in Social and Cultural Theory*. Chicago: University of Chicago Press, 1985.

Levy, Pierre. *Becoming Virtual: Reality in the Digital Age*. Translated by Robert Bononno. New York: Plenum Press, 1998.

Locke, John L. *The De-Voicing of Society: Why We Don't Talk to Each Other Anymore*. New York: Simon & Schuster, 1998.

Locklin, Reid B. "Sacred Orality, Sacred Dialogue: Walter J. Ong and the Practice of Hindu-Christian Studies." *Journal of Hindu-Christian Studies* 26 (2013), 80–90.

Lofts, S. G. *Ernst Cassirer: A "Repetition" of Modernity*. Albany: State University of New York Press, 2000.

Longo, Giuseppe O. "Body and Technology: Continuity or Discontinuity?" In *Mediating the Human Body: Technology, Communication, and Fashion*, edited by Leopoldina Fortunati, James E. Katz, and Raimonda Riccini, 23–29. Mahwah: Lawrence Erlbaum Associates, 2003.

Lynch, James. *The Broken Heart: Medical Consequences of Loneliness*. New York: Basic Books, 1977.

Lyons, Sara. "The Disenchantment/Re-Enchantment of the World: Aesthetics, Secularization, and the Gods of Greece from Friedrich Schiller to Walter Pater." *Modern Language Review* 109, no. 4 (2014): 873–95.

Macallan, Helen and Andrew Plain, "Filmic Voices." In *Voice: Vocal Aesthetics in Digital Arts and Media*, edited by Norie Neumark, Ross Gibson, and Theo Van Leeuwen, 243–266. Cambridge, MA: Massachusetts Institute of Technology, 2010.

MacIntyre, Alasdair. *After Virtue: A Study in Moral Theory*. Notre Dame: University of Notre Dame Press, 1981.

Madsen, Virginia and John Potts, "Voice-Cast: The Distribution of the Voice via Podcasting." In *Voices: Vocal Aesthetics in Digital Arts and Media*, edited by Norie Neumark, Ross Gibson, and Theo Van Leeuwen, 33–59. Cambridge, MA: Massachusetts Institute of Technology, 2010.

Marina, Elantseva. "The Infantilization of Western Culture," Accessed August 30, 2019. http://theconversation.com/the-infantilization-of-western-culture-99556.

Martin, Peter J. *Sounds and Society: Themes in the Sociology of Music*. Manchester and New York: Manchester University Press, 1995.

Marwick, Alice E. *Status Update: Celebrity, Publicity, and Branding in the Social Media Age*. New Haven: Yale University Press, 2013.

McCarthy, John, Peter Wright, Jayne Wallace, and Andy Dearden. "The Experience of Enchantment in Human–Computer Interaction." *Pers Ubiquit Comput* 10, no. 6 (2006): 369–78.

McLuhan, Marshall. *The Gutenberg Galaxy: The Making of Typographic Man*. Toronto: University of Toronto Press, 1962.

McLuhan, Marshall. *Understanding Media: The Extensions of Man*. New York: McGraw Hill, 1964.

McNeill, William H. *Keeping Together in Time: Dance and Drill in Human History*. Cambridge, MA: Harvard University Press, 1995.

McPherson, David, and Charles Taylor. "Re-Enchanting the World: An Interview with Charles Taylor." *Philosophy & Theology* 24, no. 2 (2012): 275–94.
Mellers, Wilfred. Introduction to *Music and its Social Meanings*, ix-xiii. By Christopher Ballantine. London: Gordon & Breach, 1984.
Merleau-Ponty, Maurice. *Consciousness and the Acquisition of Language*. Translated by Hugh J. Silverman. Evanston: Northwestern University Press, 1973.
Merleau-Ponty, Maurice. "Indirect Language and the Voices of Silence." In *Signs*. Translated by Richard C. McCleary, 39–83. Chicago: Northwestern University Press, 1964.
Merleau-Ponty, Maurice. *In Praise of Philosophy and Other Essays*. Translated by John Wild, James Edie, and John O'Neill. Evanston: Northwestern University Press, [1953] 1963.
Merleau-Ponty, Maurice. *Phenomenology of Perception*. Translated by Colin Smith. New York: Humanities Press, [1945] 1962.
Merleau-Ponty, Maurice. "The Primacy of Perception and Its Philosophical Consequences." In *The Primacy of Perception: And Other Essays on Phenomenological Psychology, the Philosophy of Art, History and Politics*. Translated by James M. Edie, 12–42. Evanston: Northwestern University Press, 1964.
Merleau-Ponty, Maurice. *The Primacy of Perception: And Other Essays on Phenomenological Psychology, the Philosophy of Art, History and Politics*. Translated by James M. Edie. Evanston, Northwestern University Press, 1964.
Merleau-Ponty, Maurice. *The Structure of Behavior*. Translated by Alden L. Fisher. Boston: Beacon Press, 1963.
Merleau-Ponty, Maurice. "An Unpublished Text by Maurice Merleau-Ponty: A Prospectus of His Work." In *The Primacy of Perception: And Other Essays on Phenomenological Psychology, the Philosophy of Art, History and Politics*. Translated by James M. Edie, 3–11. Evanston: Northwestern University Press, 1964.
Meyrowitz, Joshua. *No Sense of Place: The Impact of Electronic Media on Social Behavior*. New York: Oxford University Press, 1985.
Miller, Stephen. *Conversation: A History of a Declining Art*. New Haven: Yale University Press, 2006.
Mohan, Pavithra. "Google and Facebook Now Own 85% of Internet Ad Growth." *Fast Company*, May 31, 2017. https://www.fastcompany.com/4039263/google-and-facebook-now-own-85-of-internet-ad-growth.
Moncrieff, Joanna. *The Myth of the Chemical Cure: A Critique of Psychiatric Drug Treatment*. Houndmills: Palgrave MacMillan, 2008.
"Monthly Number of Game Console Users in the United States from 2nd Quarter 2012 to 2nd Quarter 2017 (In Millions)." *Statista*, accessed April 10, 2019. https://www.statista.com/statistics/320315/number-users-game-consoles-usa/.
Morin, Amy. "Depression Statistics Everyone Should Know." Verywell, July 26, 2019. https://www.verywellmind.com/depression-statistics-everyone-should-know.
Morrison, Alexandra and Laura Zebuhr. "The Voice of Ambiguity: Simone de Beauvoir's Literary and Phenomenological Echoes." *Hypatia* 30, no. 2, (Spring 2015): 418–433.
Mosher, Loren. "Are Psychiatrists Betraying Their Patients?" *Psychology Today*, September 1, 1999. https://www.psychologytoday.com/us/articles/199909/are-psychiatrists-betraying-their-patients.
Mull, Amanda. "Talk to People on the Telephone: It's Time to Start Calling Your Friends Again." *The Atlantic*, September 16, 2019. https://www.theatlantic.com/health/archive/2019/09/ring-ring-ring/598129/.
Mumford, Lewis. *The Myth of the Machine: Technics and Human Development*. New York: Mariner Books, 1971.
Mushengyezi, Aaron. Review of *Orality: The Power of the Spoken Word*, by Graham Furness. *Language in Society* 36, no. 4 (2007): 605–08.
Nancy, Jean-Luc. *Listening*. Translated by Charlotte Mandell. New York: Fordham University Press, 2007.
Neumark, Norie. "Doing Things with Voices: Performativity and Voice." In *Voice: Vocal Aesthetics in Digital Arts and Media*, edited by Norie Neumark, Ross Gibson, and Theo Van Leeuwen, 95–118. Cambridge, MA: Massachusetts Institute of Technology, 2010.

Neumark, Norie, Ross Gibson, and Theo Van Leeuwen, eds., *Voice: Vocal Aesthetics in Digital Arts and Media*. Cambridge, MA: Massachusetts Institute of Technology, 2010.

Nietzsche, Friedrich. *The Birth of Tragedy*, edited by Michael Tanner. Translated by Shaun Whiteside. London: Penguin Books, [1886] 1993.

Niose, David. "Political Discourse is Getting Dangerously Anti-Intellectual." *Psychology Today,* December 30, 2015. https://www.psychologytoday.com/us/blog/our-humanity-naturally/201512/political-discourse-is-getting-dangerously-anti-intellectual.

North, Paul. *The Problem of Distraction*. Stanford: Stanford University Press, 2012.

Nussbaum, Martha. *Upheavals of Thought: The Intelligence of Emotions*. Cambridge: Cambridge University Press, 2001.

Nutt, Amy Ellis. "Why Kids and Teens May Face Far More Anxiety These Days." *Washington Post,* May 10, 2018. https://www.washingtonpost.com/news/to-your-health/wp/2018/05/10/why-kids-and-teens-may-face-far-more-anxiety-these-days/?noredirect=on.

Ong, Walter J. *The Barbarian Within: And Other Fugitive Essays and Studies*. New York: Macmillan, 1962.

Ong, Walter. "Grammar Today: 'Structure' in a Vocal World." *Quarterly Journal of Speech* 43, no. 4 (1957): 399–407.

Ong, Walter. *Orality and Literacy: The Technologizing of the Word*. New York: Routledge, (1982) 2002.

Ong, Walter. "Orality, Literacy, and Modern Media." In *Communication in History: Technology Culture, Society*. 3rd ed., edited by David Crowley and Paul Heyer, 49–55. New York: Longman, 1999.

Ong, Walter. *The Presence of the Word: Some Prolegomena for Cultural and Religious History*. Binghamton: Global Publications, State University of New York, [1967] 2000.

Ong, Walter. Review of *Saving the Text: Literature/Derrida/Philosophy*, by Geoffrey H. Hartman. *Philosophy and Rhetoric* 15, no. 4 (October 1982): 274–77.

Ong, Walter J. "Wired for Sound: Teaching, Communications, and Technological Culture." In *The Barbarian Within: And Other Fugitive Essays and Studies*, 220–229. New York: Macmillan Company, 1962.

O'Reilly, Tim. "Web 2.0: Compact Definition?" *Radar,* October 1, 2005. http://radar.oreilly.com/2005/10/web-20-compact-definition.html.

Ovid. *The Metamorphoses of Ovid*. Translated by Michael Simpson. Amherst: University of Massachusetts Press, 2001.

Parret, Herman. *The Aesthetics of Communication: Pragmatics and Beyond*. Netherlands: Kluwer Academic Publishers, 1993.

Peirce, Charles Sanders. "The Categories Defended," *Essential Peirce: Selected Philosophical Writings,* Vol. 2, 1893–1913, edited by The Peirce Edition Project, 160–178, Bloomington: Indiana University Press, 1998.

Peirce, Charles Sanders. *The Collected Papers of Charles Sanders Peirce*. Vols. 1–6, edited by Charles Hartshorne and Paul Weiss. Cambridge: Belknap Press of Harvard University Press, 1931–1935.

Peirce, Charles Sanders. *The Collected Papers*, Vol. 8, edited by Arthur W. Burks. Cambridge, MA: Harvard University Press, 1958.

Peirce, Charles Sanders. *The Essential Peirce: Selected Philosophical Writings*. Vol. 1, *1867–1893,* edited by Nathan Houser and Christian Kloesel. Bloomington: Indiana University Press, 1992.

Peirce, Charles Sanders. "Evolutionary Love." In *Chance, Love, and Logic: Philosophical Essays*, edited by Morris R. Cohen, 267–300. New York: Harcourt, Brace & Company, 1923.

Peirce, Charles Sanders. "Logic as Semiotic: The Theory of Signs." In *Philosophical Writings of Peirce,* edited by Justus Buchler, 98–119. New York: Dover Publications, 1940.

Peirce, Charles Sanders. "A Neglected Argument for the Reality of God." In *The Essential Peirce: Selected Philosophical Writings*. Vol. 2, *1893–1913,* edited by Peirce Edition Project, 434–450. Bloomington: Indiana University Press, 1998.

Peirce, Charles Sanders. "The Principles of Phenomenology." In *Philosophical Writings of Peirce,* edited by Justus Buchler, 74–97. New York: Dover Publications, 1940.

"Personare." *To:Sound:Through*. Accessed August 30, 2019. https://tosoundthru.wordpress.com/2011/11/11/personare-to-sound-through/.
Peters, John Durham. "The Voice and Modern Media." In *Kunst-Stimmen*, edited by Doris Kolesch and Jenny Schrödl, 85–100. Berlin: Theater der Zeit, 2004.
Petrilli, Susan. *Sign Crossroads in Global Perspective: Semioethics and Responsibility*, edited by John Deely. New Brunswick: Transaction Publishers, 2010.
Petry, Edward S. "The Origin and Development of Peirce's Concept of Self Control." *Transactions of the Charles S. Peirce Society* 28, no. 4 (1992): 667–690.
Picard, Rosalind W. *Affective Computing*. Cambridge: MIT Press, 1997.
Plato. *Complete Works*, edited by John M. Cooper. Indianapolis/Cambridge: Hackett, 1997.
Plessner, Helmuth. *Laughing and Crying: A Study of the Limits of Human Behavior*. Translated by James Spencer Churchill and Marjorie Grene. Evanston: Northwestern University Press, 1970.
Postman, Neil. *Amusing Ourselves to Death: Public Discourse in the Age of Show Business*. New York: Viking, 1985.
Prawat, Richard S. "Dewey and Peirce, the Philosopher's Philosopher." *Teachers College Record* 103, no. 4 (August 2001): 667–721.
Przybylski, Andrew K., and Netta Weinstein. "Can You Connect with Me Now? How the Presence of Mobile Communication Technology Influences Face-to-Face Conversation Quality." *Journal of Social and Personal Relationships* 30, no. 3 (May 2013): 237–46.
Restak, Richard. *The New Brain: How the Modern Age Is Rewiring Your Mind*. Emmaus: Rodale Publishers, 2003.
Ritzer, George. *Enchanting a Disenchanted World: Revolutionizing the Means of Consumption*. Thousand Oaks: Pine Forge Press, 1999.
Ritzer, George, and Todd Stillman. "The Postmodern Ballpark as a Leisure Setting: Enchantment and Simulated De-McDonaldization." *Leisure Sciences* 23, no. 2 (2001): 99–113.
Robinson, Ray, and Allen Winold. *The Choral Experience: Literature, Materials, and Methods*. New York: Harper & Row, 1976.
Rothman, Joshua. "A New Theory of Distraction." *The New Yorker*, June 16, 2015. https://www.newyorker.com/culture/cultural-comment/a-new-theory-of-distraction.
Saler, Michael T. "Modernity, Disenchantment, and the Ironic Imagination." *Philosophy and Literature* 28, no. 1 (2004): 137–49.
Sapir, Edward. *Culture, Language and Personality: Selected Essays*. Berkeley: University of California Press, 1966.
Satariano, Adam, Elian Peltier, and Dmitry Kostyukov. "Meet Zora, the Robot Caregiver." *The New York Times*, November 23, 2018. https://www.nytimes.com/interactive/2018/11/23/technology/robot-nurse-zora.html.
Saussure, Ferdinand de. *Course in General Linguistics*. Translated by Wade Baskin. New York: McGraw Hill, [1906–1911] 1959.
Savodnik, Peter. "Ernst Cassirer's Theory of Myth." *Critical Review* 15, no. 3–4 (2003): 447–58.
Schafer, Murray. "Open Ears." In *The Auditory Culture Reader*, edited by Michael Bull and Les Back, 25–39. New York: Berg, 2003.
Schafer, Murray. *The Tuning of the World*. New York: Knopf, 1977.
Schiller, Friedrich. *On the Aesthetic Education of Man*. Mineola: Dover Publications, [1795] 2004.
Schlichter, Annette. "Do Voices Matter? Vocality, Materiality, Gender Performativity." *Body and Society* 17, no. 1 (2011): 31–52.
Schrage, Michael. "Time to Hang Up on Voice Mail." *Harvard Business Review*, September 30, 2013. https://hbr.org/2013/09/time-to-hang-up-on-voice-mail.
Schutz, Alfred. *Making Music Together, Collected Papers II: Studies in Social Theory*, edited by Arvid Brodersen. The Hague: Martinus Nijhoff, 1964.
Schwartz, Casey. "Finding It Hard to Focus? Maybe It's Not Your Fault. The Rise of the New 'Attention Economy.'" *The New York Times*, August 14, 2018. https://www.nytimes.com/2018/08/14/style/how-can-i-focus-better.html.

Schwartz, Oscar. "Why Beating Your Phone Addiction May Come at a Cost." *The Guardian*, March 13, 2019. https://www.theguardian.com/technology/2019/mar/13/digital-wellness-phone-addiction-tech?CMP=twt_gu.

Scott, D. Travers. *Pathology and Technology: Killer Apps and Sick Users*. New York: Peter Lang, 2018.

Sebeok, Thomas A. *Global Semiotics*. Bloomington: Indiana University Press, 2001.

Sebeok, Thomas A. *The Play of Musement*. Bloomington: Indiana University Press, 1981.

Serres, Michel. *The Five Senses: A Philosophy of Mingled Bodies*. Translated by Margaret Sankey and Peter Cowley. London: Continuum, 2008.

Shakespeare, William. *Romeo and Juliet*. Arden edition, edited by Brian Gibbons. London: Metheuen, 1980.

Shannon, Claude, and Warren Weaver. *The Mathematical Theory of Communication*. Urbana: University of Illinois Press, 1949.

Shepherd, John. *Music as Social Text*. Cambridge: Polity, 1991.

Sherry, Patrick. "Disenchantment, Re-Enchantment, and Enchantment." *Modern Theology* 25, no. 3 (2009): 369–86.

Simon, Linda. "Bewitched, Bothered, and Bewildered: William James's Feeling of 'If.'" In *The Re-Enchantment of the World: Secular Magic in a Rational Age*, edited by Joshua Landy and Michael Saler, 38–55. Stanford: Stanford University Press, 2009.

Slaughter, Aubrey. "Cyberspace." The Chicago School of Media Theory, accessed March 23, 2019. https://lucian.uchicago.edu/blogs/mediatheory/keywords/cyberspace/.

Smith, Andrew R., Isaac E. Catt, and Igor E. Klyukanov, eds. *Communicology for the Human Sciences: Lanigan and the Philosophy of Communication*. New York: Peter Lang, 2018.

Smith, Daniel L. "Intensifying Phronesis: Heidegger, Aristotle, and Rhetorical Culture." *Philosophy and Rhetoric* 36, no. 1 (2003): 77–102.

Smith, John E. "Being, Immediacy, and Articulation." *The Review of Metaphysics* 24, no. 4 (June 1971): 593–613.

Soukup, Paul A. "Looking is Not Enough: Reflections on Walter J. Ong and Media Ecology." *Proceedings of the Media Ecology Association* 6 (2005): 1–9.

Spiegelberg, Herbert. *The Phenomenological Movement: A Historical Introduction*. The Hague: Martinus Nijhoff, 1971.

Standish, Paul. "The Disenchantment of Education and the Re-Enchantment of the World." *Journal of Philosophy of Education* 50, no. 1 (2016): 98–116.

Sterne, Jonathan. *The Sound Studies Reader*. New York: Routledge, 2012.

Sterne, Jonathan. "The Theology of Sound: A Critique of Orality." *Canadian Journal of Communication* 36 (2011): 207–25.

Stewart, John, Karen E. Zediker, and Saskia Witteborn. *Together: Communicating Interpersonally: A Social Construction Approach*. 6th edition. Los Angeles: Roxbury Publishing Company, 2005.

Strate, Lance. *Amazing Ourselves to Death: Neil Postman's Brave New World Revisited*. New York: Peter Lang, 2014.

Strate, Lance. *Echoes and Reflections: On Media Ecology as a Field of Study*. Cresskill, NJ: Hampton Press, 2006.

Stiegler, Bernard. *The Re-Enchantment of the World: The Value of Spirit Against Industrial Populism*. Translated by Trevor Arthur. New York: Bloomsbury, 2014.

Stiegler, Bernard. *Symbolic Misery*. Vol. 1, *The Hyper-Industrial Epoch*. Translated by Barnaby Norman. Cambridge: Polity, 2014.

"Striking a Balance in the Age of Digital Distraction." MCW19, accessed March 4, 2019. https://www.mwcbarcelona.com/session/striking-a-balance-in-the-age-of-distraction.

Sugiyama, Satomi, and Jane Vincent. "Social Robots and Emotion: Transcending the Boundary Between Humans and ICTs." *intervalla* 1, no. 1 (2013): 1–6.

Taylor, Charles. *The Ethics of Authenticity*. Cambridge: Harvard University Press, 1991.

Thass-Thienemann, Theodor. *Symbolic Behavior*. New York: Washington Square Press, 1968.

Thiebaud, Jane R. "Effects of Technology on People: Living F2F Conversation and Social Interaction." *Proceedings of the Media Ecology Association* 11 (2010): 117–127.

Thibeault, Matthew D. "Sound Studies and Music Education." *Journal of Aesthetic Education* 51, no. 1 (Spring 2017): 69–83.
Thoreau, Henry David. *Journal.* September 18, 1858.
Thorpe, JR. "7 Bizarre Historical Beliefs About Women's Voices." *Bustle,* October 27, 2016. https://bustle.com/articles/191686-7-bizarre-historical-beliefs-about-women's-voices.
Tiwari, Maniui and Maneesha Tiwari, "Voice—How Humans Communicate?" *Journal of Natural Science, Biology, and Medicine* 3, no. 1 (2012): 3–11.
Tracey, Sarah J. "Let's Talk: Conversation as a Defining Moment for the Communication Discipline." *Health Communication,* DOI: 10.1080/10410236.2019.1593081.
Turkle, Sherry. *Alone Together: Why We Expect More from Technology and Less From Each Other*. New York: Basic Books, 2011.
Turkle, Sherry. *Reclaiming Conversation: The Power of Talk in a Digital Age*. New York: Penguin Books, 2015.
Turner, Victor. *Dramas, Fields, and Metaphors: Symbolic Action in Human Society*. Ithaca: Cornell University Press, 1974.
Tyler, Jo A. "Reclaiming Rare Listening as a Means of Organizational Re-Enchantment." *Journal of Organizational Change Management* 24, no. 1 (2011): 143–57.
Tyler, Stephen A. "The Vision Quest in the West, or What the Mind's Eye Sees." *Journal of Anthropological Research* 40, no. 1 (Spring 1984): 23–40.
Tyson, Frances. *The Tone of Our Times: Sound, Sense, Economy, and Ecology.* Cambridge, MA: Massachusetts Institute of Technology, 2014.
Udine, Jean d'. *L'Art et le geste*. Paris: Alcan, 1910.
Valenstein, Elliot. *Blaming the Brain: The Truth About Drugs and Mental Health*. New York: Free Press, 1998.
Van Leeuwen, Theo. "Vox Humana." In *Voice: Vocal Aesthetics in Digital Arts and Media,* edited by Norie Neumark, Ross Gibson, and Theo Van Leeuwen, 5–15. Cambridge, MA: Massachusetts Institute of Technology, 2010.
Vincent, Jane and Leopoldina Fortunati, eds. *Electronic Emotion: The Mediation of Emotion via Information and Communication Technologies*. Oxford: Peter Lang, 2009.
Waelhens, Alphonse de. "A Philosophy of the Ambiguous." In *The Structure of Behavior*, by Maurice Merleau-Ponty, xvii–xxvii. Translated by Alden. L. Fisher. Boston: Beacon Press, 1963.
Wagner, Richard. "Ein Glücklicher Abend," in *Musik-Aesthetik, Gazette Musicale,* nos. 56–58, reprinted by Gatz, 1841.
Watzlawick, Paul, Janet Beavin Bavelas, and Don D. Jackson. *Pragmatics of Human Communication: A Study of Interactional Patterns, Pathologies, and Paradoxes*. New York: W. W. Norton & Company, 1967.
Weber, Max. *The Protestant Ethic and the Spirit of Capitalism*. Translated by Talcott Parsons. London: Unwin Hyman, 1989.
Weheliye, Alexander G. *Phonographies: Grooves in Sonic Afro-Modernity*. Durham: Duke University Press, 2005.
"What Is an Influencer?" Influencer Marketing Hub, accessed March 19, 2019. https://influencermarketinghub.com/what-is-an-influencer/.
Whitaker, Robert. *Anatomy of an Epidemic: Magic Bullets, Psychiatric Drugs, and the Astonishing Rise of Mental Illness in America*. New York: Crown Publishers, 2010.
Wilber, Ken. *A Brief History of Everything*. Boston: Shambhala, 1996.
Williams, James. *Stand Out of Our Light: Freedom and Resistance in the Attention Economy*. Cambridge: Cambridge University Press, 2018.
Wolf, Maryanne. "Skim Reading Is the New Normal: The Effect on Society Is Profound." *The Guardian,* August 25, 2018. https://www.theguardian.com/commentisfree/2018/aug/25/skim-reading-new-normal-maryanne-wolf.
Zebuhr, Laura. "Sound Enchantment: The Case of Henry David Thoreau." *New Literary History* 48, no. 3 (Summer 2017), 581–603.
Zengotita, Thomas de. *Mediated: How the Media Shapes Your World and the Way You Live in It*. New York: Bloomsbury, 2005.

Zimmerman, Michael E. *Eclipse of Self: The Development of Heidegger's Concept of Authenticity*. Athens: Ohio University Press, 1981.

Zraick, Karen. "Teenagers Say Depression and Anxiety Are Major Issues Among Their Peers." *The New York Times*, February 20, 2019. https://www.nytimes.com/2019/02/20/health/teenage-depression-statistics.html.

Zumthor, Paul. *Oral Poetry: An Introduction*. Translated by Kathryn Murphy-Judy. Minneapolis: University of Minnesota Press, 1990.

# Index

abduction: amusement and, 90; inauthentic enchantment and, 86; Peirce on, 86–87, 90; Trump and, 90
accessibility, 29, 50
Acousmatics, 101
acousmatic voice, 97, 242; authenticity and, 101; babble and, 143; Chion and, 100–101; cinema and, 101; disacousmatization and, 103; Dolar on, 101; ear-to-ear relations and, 103–104; enchantment and, 102; floating signifiers and, 102; impersonal self and, 110; Macallan and Plain on, 103; Neumark on, 102; relationality and, 101; self and, 112; source of, 100–101, 103
addiction, 34; Weizenbaum on, 35
ADHD (attention-deficit/hyperactivity disorder), 242; distraction and, 46–47
Adorno, Theodor, 89, 102; *Dialectic of Enlightenment* by, 87
advertising, 43n64; social media, 37; Williams on, 37–38
aesthetics: art of conversation and, 169; authentic enchantment and, 79; Bennett and, 166; enchantment, 8, 189; *erfahrung* and, 164, 165, 167–168; *erlebnis* and, 164, 167; ethics and, 164, 166; firstness and, 164, 169, 193; Gadamer and, 164, 165–166, 168; heart-felt communication and, 237;

Internet, cyberspace and, 82–83; *logos* and, 164; music, song and, 167; Peirce and, 164, 165–167, 170–171, 184n24, 184n26, 236; Schiller and, 166; sound and, 32; of sounding voice, 164–168; Thoreau and, 178; voice, 166–167, 212–213; voice of enunciation and, 167, 168, 187
Agamben, Georgio, 193, 195, 196, 197, 200, 217n31; extimacy and, 194; on *zoe* and *bios*, 194–195
age of attention, 107
AI. *See* artificial intelligence
Alexa, 31; Amazon Echo and, 18n3; anthropomorphism and, 2; *Love Notes* and, 1; love podcast and, 1–2; manipulation and, 61–62; Valentine's Day uses of, 1–3, 242
*Amazing Ourselves to Death* (Postman), 58
Amazon Echo. *See* Alexa
ambiguity, 244–245; Beauvoir and, 178, 182; enchantment and, 179; Merleau-Ponty and, 178, 182, 203, 204; negative, 75, 76, 91, 102, 104, 107, 110, 128, 203–204; voice of enunciation and, 204, 205. *See also* existential ambiguity; positive ambiguity
American Psychological Association, 111
amusement, 68; abduction and, 90; distracted consciousness and, 88; inauthentic enchantments and, 87,

265

88–92; Peirce and, 88–89; signs and, 88
Anderson, Douglas, 162, 184n24
animals, 181, 186n89
*The Animal That Therefore I Am* (Derrida), 173
anthropology of senses, 72
anxiety, 11, 111, 198, 203, 242; enchantment and, 112; Karp on, 112; relationships and, 111
Apollo (god), 124
Apple, 25, 84
Aquinas, Thomas, 122
Arendt, Hannah, 129, 199
Aristotle, 180; Classen and, 121, 149n11, 150n62; *phone semantike* and, 136, 142, 168–169, 193, 196; senses and, 122; visual and, 138; wild and, 195; *zoe* and, 194
artificial intelligence (AI), 53; Minsky and, 60
art of conversation, 10, 157, 170–171; aesthetics and, 169; Miller on, 10; phenomenology and, 170
attention: distraction and, 50; etymology of, 49; fluency of thought and, 51; inattention, 49, 50; neuroscience and, 49; sound and, 52; visual, 52; Williams on, 52
attention-deficit/hyperactivity disorder. *See* ADHD
attention economy, 45; Williams on, 47
Augustine (saint), 49, 205
authentic enchantment, 74, 77, 78; aesthetic awareness and, 79; firstness and, 78; relational tonality and, 8; resonance and, 222; thirdness and, 78; voice of enunciation and, 207–208
authenticity: acousmatic voice and, 101; Heidegger and, 77; Merleau-Ponty on, 77, 205; Taylor and, 77; voice of enunciation and, 205–206

babble: Heidegger on, 144; Internet and, 143; voice of articulation and, 143
baby boomers, 111
Bachelard, Gaston, 232
Baidu, 35
*The Barbarian Within* (Ong), 10

Barthes, Roland, 75–76, 84, 184n11; grain of voice and, 12, 131, 148; myth and, 83
Bartky, Sandra Lee, 82
Bateson, Gregory, 19n24, 240; on inauthentic enchantment, 86; messages and, 145; on news of difference, 142–143; on redundancy, 82; relationality and, 168; on sacred, 79–80, 171; symmetrical relations and, 91, 209, 210
Bateson, Mary Catherine, 79–80
Baudrillard, Jean, 62
Baum, L. Frank, 101
Baumgarten, Alexander, 165
Beattie, James, 49
Beauvoir, Simone de, 178; ambiguity and, 178, 182
Bennett, Jane, 89, 102–103, 178, 180, 185n62, 185n69; aesthetics and, 166, 167; wild and, 176–177
Bentham, Jeremy, 52–53
Bergson, Henri, 174
Berman, Morris, 209; *The Re-Enchantment of the World* by, 79
Bettelheim, Bruno, 85; fairytales and, 83, 94n54
bewilderment, 179
Bible, 84, 173
*bios*, 188, 191, 193, 194, 196, 216; Agamben and, 194–195; Dolar and, 195; *Romeo and Juliet* and, 199, 199–200; voice of enunciation and, 198
*The Birth of Tragedy* (Nietzsche), 124
*In the Blink of an Ear* (Kim-Cohen), 182
body and language, 198; Dolar on, 193
Bourdieu, Pierre, 38
brain, 56; Carr on, 61; neuropathways of, 9; neuroplasticity and, 56, 61
*Brave New World* (Huxley), 26, 58–59
breath, 213; Dolar and, 187; Levinas and, 173
Brophy, Philip, 42n36
Buber, Martin, 59; on "I-It" relations, 106, 169, 241; interper-sónal and, 212; "I-Thou" relation and, 36, 37, 57, 110, 211–212
Butler, Judith, 137–138, 152n123

Cambridge Analytica, 35
Carey, James, 18n14
Carr, Nicholas, 48; brain functioning and, 61; on intellectual ethic, 56; intellectual technologies and, 56; *The Shallows* by, 56; on shallow thinking, 106; on skim reading, 56
Cassirer, Ernst: on myth, 83; *mythos* and, 207
catfishing, 38–39
Cavarero, Adriana, 138, 151n70, 157, 184n11, 198–199, 230; Derrida and, 134, 136, 137; firstness and, 160–161; *For More Than One Voice* by, 129; on invocation of voice, 225–226; Levinas and, 172, 172–174; *logos* and, 129, 150n62; on murder of *phone*, 120; music and, 232; psychoanalysis and, 130; *Romeo and Juliet* and, 199–200, 201, 240; voice and, 129–130, 133–134, 140, 156, 225
chanting, 228–229
Chion, Michael, 5, 97; acousmatic voice and, 100–101
choice and autonomy, 47, 61, 74, 203
Classen, Constance, 26–27; Aristotle and, 121; on modes of consciousness, 128; on senses, 120, 121, 122, 149n10; on visual, 123
Colapietro, Vincent, 72, 92n4, 141, 157, 194; on firstness, 92n6–93n7; sentimentality and, 238
Colbert, Stephen, 109
communication, 18n12, 144; connectivity and, 5, 109; informational retrieval compared to, 1; Jakobson and, 169; Ong on, 59, as shared meaning, 4; technologies, 4; techno-social dilemma and, 59. *See also* heart-felt communication; interper-sónal communication
connectivity: communication and, 5, 109; efficiency and, 3–4; FOMO and, 108; impersonal self and, 110; relationality and, 35. *See also* video and logo-centric connectivity
Connor, Steven, 115n10, 155, 174
consumerism, 47

content: FOMO and, 108; of messages, 142–144; social media and abbreviated, 105
conversation. *See* art of conversation
couch potato syndrome, 26
Crawford, Matthew, 47
cultural loss: human interaction as, 53; thinking deeply as, 53; trust as, 52–53
culture: industry, 87; social media and cultural capital, 38; visual, 30. *See also* oral-aural culture
culture of distraction, 11; cultural loss and, 52–53; relationality and, 52
Cumming, Naomi: music and, 235; *The Sonic Self* by, 235
cyberspace. *See* Internet and cyberspace

Deely, John, 186n89
democratization, 34
depression, 11, 198, 242; enchantment and, 112; suicide and, 111
Derrida, Jacques, 119–120, 175; *The Animal That Therefore I Am* by, 173; Cavarero and, 134, 136, 137; *différance* and, 135, 136; linguistics and, 135, 138, 139–140; metaphysics of presence as phonocentrism and, 120, 124, 134–138; Ong and, 135; *pharmakon* and, 219n78; on phonocentrism, 152n97; Plato and, 136, 139; *Romeo and Juliet* and, 199–200; Saussure and, 135, 170; visual and, 136–137; voice and, 135, 137
Descartes, René, 122
Dewey, John, 219n96; on habits, 3, 6, 13, 24; *Human Nature* by, 6
*Dialectic of Enlightenment* (Adorno and Horkheimer), 87
*différance*, 135, 136
digital wellness, 4, 241; tracking applications and, 34
Dionysus (god), 124, 125, 135, 138, 232
disacousmatization of voice, 103
disenchanting enchantments, 8; inauthentic enchantment and, 114; Ritzer on, 79
disenchantment, 245; existential dissonance and, 11; Jenkins on, 7; Weber on, 7, 11
Disney, 84–85

distraction, 40, 45, 55; accessibility and, 50; ADHD and, 46–47; attention and, 50; choice and, 47; engagement and, 57; James on, 49; Peirce on, 50–51; Williams on, 57–58. *See also* culture of distraction

Dolar, Mladen, 47, 99, 138, 157, 193, 217n40; on acousmatic voice, 101; *bios* and, 195; on body and language, 193; breath and, 187; on court proceedings and dissertation, 196–197; echo and, 228; on ethics, 201–203; extimacy and, 195; on impersonal voice, 104; lawless voice and, 175, 190; linguistics and, 140; *logos* and, 130–131, 195–196, 197; on murder of *phone*, 120; phenomenology and, 157; *phone semantike* and, 197; phonology and, 140, 156; Plato and, 191; on political voice, 100; psychoanalysis and, 244; religious rituals and, 196; sounding voice and, 191–192; on sovereignty, 197–198; voice and, 100, 124–125, 139, 144, 149n2, 217n21; voice of articulation and, 147; voice of enunciation and, 159–160, 190, 191, 192; *zoe* and, 195–196; zone of undecidability and, 203

driving: cellphone bans, 46; distracted driving deaths, 46

Dyson, Frances, 100, 143, 185n63

ear-to-ear relations, 25, 57, 119, 127, 144, 170, 204, 241; acousmatic voice and, 103–104; catfishing and, 39; distracted consciousness and, 107; immediacy of, 86, 97; music and, 232–233, 240; mythical and, 207; re-enchantment of, 67, 99; relationality and, 8, 39; secondness and, 163; voice of enunciation and, 167–168, 169, 175, 188; vulnerability and, 10

echo, 221, 229; Dolar and, 228; enchantment and, 229; Nancy and, 228, 247n46; *parole parlée* and, 228; resonance and, 228, 229

*Echo and Narcissus*, 221; Ovid and, 223–224, 226; relationality and, 224, 225, 226; resonance and, 226–227; self and other in, 224

echolalia, 114

Edie, James M., 215–216

Elliot, Norbert, 53

Ellul, Jacques, 9, 30

email, 86, 98, 241

emojis, 30

empathy, 11

enchanté (enchanted to meet you), 17

enchantment, 6, 11, 67, 99; acousmatic voice and, 102; aesthetic, 8, 189; ambiguity and, 179; anxiety, depression and, 112; communicology and, 67; disempowerment and, 8; echo and, 229; with electronic media, 11, 12; Fisher and, 189; flow and, 72; French greetings and, 17; habits of perception and, 71–72; heart-felt communication and, 238; hyper-textual/visual connection and, 81, 179; ironic imagination and, 8; music and song and, 243; mystery and, 7; phenomenology and, 68–69, 72, 73; relationality and, 63; ritual and, 73; sacred and, 79; as sensory trope, 19n31; signs and, 68–74; techno-social dilemma and, 63; Thoreau and, 179–180; voice of enunciation and, 158, 162, 168, 183, 189, 205, 209, 211, 215, 229, 240, 244; wild and, 178; Williams and, 63. *See also* disenchanting enchantments

engagement, 57, 126, 239–240, 244; ethical, 176

Enlightenment, 49

énoncé (to state or express), 149n2; Foucault and, 148; voice of enunciation and, 159

enunciation: relationality and, 39. *See also* voice of enunciation

*erfahrung*, 164, 165, 167–168

ethics: aesthetics and, 164, 166; Dolar on, 201–203; relationality and, 203; Schiller and, 210; secondness and, 201; semio-ethics, 210; semiotics and, 211; voice of enunciation and, 202–203

existential: boundaries, 23; dissonance, 11, 113; Peirce and the, 64n26; positionality, 23–24

existential ambiguity, 81–82; Merleau-Ponty and, 63, 67, 74–75, 82, 93n24, 131; negative ambiguity, 75, 76; positive ambiguity, 75–76, 131; relationality and, 76
extimacy: Agamben and, 194; Dolar and, 195; voice of enunciation and, 196

Facebook: abbreviated content and, 106; advertising and, 37; Cambridge Analytica and, 35; Generation Z and, 35; photo sharing on, 30; user statistics, 35
Facebook Messenger, 35, 106
fairytales: Bettelheim and, 83, 94n54; inauthentic enchantment and, 83
Farrell, Thomas, 137, 142, 154n172; voice and, 135
fear of missing out (FOMO), 111–112; Generation Z and, 108; impersonal self and, 108; social media and, 39
female voice, 129–130, 150n34, 151n67
fight-or-flight responses, 50
Filmer, Paul, 131
firstness, 68–70, 71, 72, 92n5, 114, 177, 179, 188; aesthetics and, 164, 169, 193; Anderson on, 162; authentic enchantment and, 78; Cavarero and, 160–161; Colapietro on, 92n6, 93n7; discontinuity and, 175; inauthentic enchantment and, 80, 82; lawless voice and, 175; music and, 235; myth and, 83; relationality and, 239–240; symbolic and, 83; tone and, 92n6; voice of enunciation and, 157, 160, 161–162, 175, 193, 206, 210
Fisher, Philip, 189, 190
FOMO. *See* fear of missing out
Foucault, Michel, 53, 132, 157, 166, 245; *énoncé* and, 148; "I lie/I speak" and, 147, 148, 156; Law of Communication and, 146; Law of Representation and, 146; nameless voice and, 145, 156, 183, 221, 223; *parole parlée, parole parlante* and, 147; voiceless name and, 120, 146, 147, 183, 222
Frankfurt, Harry, 58
FreeConvo, 21n48
Friedman, Maurice, 57

Frischmann, Brett, 61
Fuchs, Christian, 35, 43n68
Fuchs, Thomas, 112, 242
Furedi, Frank, 49
Furness, Graham, 150n59; *Orality* by, 40

Gadamer, Hans-Georg, 87; aesthetics and, 164, 165–166, 168; *erfahrung* and, 164, 165; *erlebnis* and, 164, 167
General Semantics, 117n61
Generation Z, 9; control and, 108; Facebook and, 35; FOMO and, 108; "I-It" relations and, 106
Gibson, Ross, 21n57
Gibson, William: Internet and, 29; *Neuromancer* by, 29
Google, 35; advertising by, 37
Google+, 35, 42n53
GPS, 31
Graham, Gordon, 124
Graham, Phil, 29
grain of voice, 12, 131, 148
Guardiano, Nicholas L., 186n75
Gusdorf, Georges, 16–17

habits: Dewey on, 3, 6, 13, 24; new normal, 24–25; Peirce on, 6, 9, 13; of perception, 28–29, 71–72; radical reflection and, 24
Haraway, Donna, 60
*Harvard Business Review*, 9
heart-felt communication: aesthetics and, 237; enchantment and, 238; interpersónal, 236; Lynch on, 236–237; rhythm, timbre and, 237, 238–239; sentimentality and, 237–238; thirdness and, 237; *zoe* and, 239
Heidegger, Martin, 19n30, 202, 208; authenticity and, 77; on babble, 144; call of conscience and, 208, 210; everydayness and, 75; on technology, 85, 86; on *they-self*, 86, 91, 147, 222
Henriques, Julian, 126–127
Homer, 125, 129–130, 176
*homo technologicus*, 60
Horkheimer, Max, 89, 102; *Dialectic of Enlightenment* by, 87
*Human Nature* (Dewey), 6

Husserl, Edmund, 24; phenomenology and, 27
Huxley, Aldous, 26, 58–59
Hyde, Michael, 85, 94n45, 208
hyper-textual/visual connection, 9–10, 30, 159; enchantment and, 81, 179; inauthentic enchantment and, 88; Internet, cyberspace and, 43n69; relationality and, 92

Ihde, Don, 52, 120, 128, 138; *Listening and Voice* by, 213; on sound, 31; speaking and, 213; voice and, 132, 157
"I-It" relations, 106, 169, 241
impersonal self, 97; acousmatic voice and, 110; connectivity and, 110; FOMO and, 108; inauthentic enchantment and, 110, 242; mediated voice and, 104; social media and, 106
inauthentic enchantment, 6–7, 63, 74, 78, 188; abduction and, 86; amusement and, 87, 88–92; Bateson, G., on, 86; disenchanting enchantments and, 114; firstness and, 80, 82; hyper-textual/visual connection and, 88; impersonal self and, 110, 242; Internet and, 80–87; myth and, 83–84; narcissism and, 113; Peirce and, 113–114; profane experience and, 80; relationality and, 92; sounding voice and, 99; symmetrical relations and, 91; thirdness and, 78, 83; voice of articulation and, 142
information transfer, 4–5
Innis, Robert, 231, 234
Instagram: photo sharing on, 30; user statistics, 35–36
intellectual technologies, 56
Internet and cyberspace, 113; aesthetic and, 82–83; babble and, 143; codified information and, 81; cyberspace compared to, 29; Gibson, W., and, 29; hyper-textual/visual connection and, 43n69; Korzybski and, 117n61; Law of Representation and, 146; mediation of, 81; myth and, 84; perception and, 28–29; redundancy and, 82; time spent on, 34–35; voice and, 146; Web 2.0, 35; wild and, 186n85. *See also* acousmatic voice
interper-sónal communication, 20n47, 110, 188, 189, 211; Buber and, 212; etymology of, 214; greetings, 17; heartfelt, 236–237; Peirce and, 215; qualitative focus of, 211–212; quantitative focus for, 211, 212; re-enchantment and, 216; relationality and, 221–222, 228; resonance and, 221, 226–227, 230, 234, 236, 239; sonic elements of, 214; voice of enunciation and, 222, 223
"It Can Wait" campaign, 46
"I-Thou" relation, 36, 37, 57, 110, 211

Jackson, Maggie, 48, 49, 55–56; on cultural loss, 52–53
Jakobson, Roman, 140, 153n136, 169
James, William, 6, 88; on distraction, 49–50; wild and, 177, 178
Jenkins, Richard, 7
Johnson, Samuel, 51
JPMorgan Chase, 9

Kant, Immanuel, 41n18, 129, 202
Karp, David, 112
Kim-Cohen, Seth, 182; *In the Blink of an Ear* by, 182; voice of enunciation and, 182
Korzybski, Alfred, 117n61
Kristeva, Julia, 246n9, 247n73

LaBelle, Brandon, 100, 188
Lacan, Jacques, 12, 119–120, 202; non-sonorous voice and, 157; signs and, 151n72, 161, 192; voice and, 130, 140, 155; voice of articulation and, 159
Langer, Susanne: language and, 234; music and, 230–232, 233, 234
Lanigan, Richard L., 146; Law of Representation and, 146
Lannamann, John W., 18n2, 132
Latour, Bruno, 185n69
lawless voice, 183; Dolar and, 175, 190
Law of Communication, 222, 223
Law of Representation, 154n166, 222; Foucault and, 146; Internet, cyberspace and, 146; Lanigan and, 146; *logos* and, 147; voiceless name and, 146, 147;

voice of articulation and, 147
Levin, Thomas, 98
Levinas, Emmanuel: breath and, 173; Cavarero and, 172, 173–174; *logos* and, 171; *pneumatism* and, 173; relationality and, 174; on Saying and Said, 171–172, 173–174; signs and, 172
Levi-Strauss, Claude, 153n152
Levy, David, 53
Light Phone, 42n50
linguistics: Derrida and, 135, 138, 139–140; Dolar and, 140; murder of *phone* and, 141; phonology and, 140; relationality and, 140; voice of articulation and, 141
*Listening* (Nancy), 221
*Listening and Voice* (Ihde), 213
Locke, John L., 33, 114, 214, 240; on senses, 122; speaking voice and, 240; on vocal cooling, 242
Locklin, Reid, 127
Lofts, S. G., 207
logo-centric connectivity. *See* video and logo-centric connectivity
*logos*, 81, 124, 133, 136, 156, 193, 216; aesthetic, 164; Cavarero and, 129, 150n62; Dolar and, 130–131, 195–196, 197; Law of Representation and, 147; Levinas and, 171; Merleau-Ponty and, 76–77, 82, 95n77, 164, 207; Nancy and, 225, 226; Ong and, 147; Peirce and, 207; *phone semantike* and, 194, 196, 197, 198; *Romeo and Juliet* and, 199–200; signs and, 72; thirdness and, 81, 164; voice and, 133–134, 141
*Love and Sex with Robots* (Levy), 53
*Love Notes*, 1
Lynch, James, 3, 5; on heart-felt communication, 236–237

Macallan, Helen, 41n31, 102; on acousmatic voice, 103
marketing, 30
Martin, Peter, 236
Marx, Karl, 36
Massachusetts Institute of Technology, 5
McDonaldization, 8; Ritzer and, 88
McLuhan, Marshall, 20n35, 25–27, 121, 224, 242; senses and, 123

McNeill, William, 237
McPherson, David, 7
Mead, George Herbert, 6, 105
media, 105; changes in history, 25–26; functions of, 26; literacy, 149n8
media ecology, 20n41
Merleau-Ponty, Maurice, 24, 132, 215–216; on abduction, 86; ambiguity and, 178, 182, 203, 204; on authenticity, 77, 205; on babble, 143; existential ambiguity and, 63, 67, 74–75, 82, 93n24, 131; inauthenticity and, 77; *logos* and, 76–77, 82, 95n77, 164, 207; music and, 233; *parole parlée* and, 222; on perception, 28; on situation and reaction, 29; speaking and, 157–158; voice of enunciation and, 156, 159. *See also* existential ambiguity
messages: Bateson, G., and, 145; content of, 142–144; non-verbal, 151n85; relationality and, 142, 144–145; secondness and, 169; signs and, 145
metaphysics of presence as phonocentrism, 120, 124, 134–138
Meyrowitz, Joshua, 23
millennials, 9; "I-It" relations and, 106; texts and, 107; Turkle research on, 38, 104, 108
Miller, Stephen, 10; on art of conversation, 10–11
Minsky, Marvin, 60
Mitchell, William J., 103
Moment, 34
*More Than One Voice* by (Cavarero), 129
Morrison, Alexandra, 178
murder of *phone*, 119, 128–129, 138, 242; Cavarero and Dolar on, 120; linguistics and, 141
Muses, 233; Ong on, 234
Mushengyezi, Aaron, 40
music and song, 131, 151n67, 236; aesthetics and, 167; Cavarero and, 232; chanting and, 228–229; Cumming and, 235; ear-to-ear relations and, 232–233, 240; enchantment and, 243; firstness and, 235; Langer and, 230–231, 234; language and, 234; Merleau-Ponty and, 233; Muses and, 233–234; in oral-aural culture, 125; Peirce and, 234; Plato and,

156, 204, 242; relationality and, 232; resonance and, 232, 235–236; rhythm, timbre and, 231, 232, 233, 235; Schutz and, 232; voice of enunciation and, 243, 245; *zoe* and, 232, 238–239

myth: Apple and, 84; Barthes and, 83; Cassirer on, 83; Disney and, 84–85; firstness and, 83; inauthentic enchantment and, 83–84; Internet, cyberspace and, 84; Muses and, 233–234. *See also Echo and Narcissus*

*mythos*: Cassirer and, 207; voice of enunciation and, 207–208

nameless voice, 245; Foucault and, 145, 156, 183, 221, 223; voice of enunciation and, 222

Nancy, Jean-Luc, 213, 215; echo and, 228, 247n46; listening and, 225, 246n27; *Listening* by, 221; *logos* and, 225, 226; resonance and, 227–228, 229, 231, 232; on rhythm and timbre, 231, 232, 233, 235; senses and, 126; speaking and, 213, 225, 246n27; voice of enunciation and, 226; *zoe* and, 235

narcissism, 91; inauthentic enchantment and, 113

National Assessment of Adult Literacy, 53

National Highway Traffic Safety Association (NHTSA), 46

Neumark, Norie, 21n57, 92, 115n7; on acousmatic voice, 102

*Neuromancer* (Gibson, W.), 29

neuroplasticity, 56, 61

new normal habits, 24–25

NHTSA. *See* National Highway Traffic Safety Association

Nietzsche, Friedrich, 47; *The Birth of Tragedy* by, 124

North, Paul, 50

Nussbaum, Martha, 209

Ong, Walter, 3, 4, 21n52, 25, 41n15, 213; *The Barbarian Within* by, 10; on communication, 59; death of, 29; depersonalization and, 142; on depersonalization of sound, 31; Derrida and, 135; *logos* and, 147; on media changes in history, 26; on Muses, 234; on oral-aural culture, 30, 33, 38, 160; orality and, 5; phenomenology and, 163; primary orality and, 31, 33; on print, 43n69; radio and, 30–31; secondary orality and, 26, 32–33, 119; senses and, 26–27, 123; sensorium and, 28, 71–72; signs and, 69; on sound, 72–73, 93n20, 125–126, 152n119, 161–162, 163, 241; on sounding voice, 40, 132; spatializing of voice and, 99; spoken word and, 217n19, 241; time and, 161; on visual, 72–73, 93n20, 120–121, 125, 127, 163; on word, 32

*On the Aesthetic Education of Man* (Schiller), 87

*on the phone*, 6, 12, 25, 32, 67, 114, 134, 241, 242

oral-aural culture, 26; Muses in, 233–234; music in, 125; Ong on, 30, 33, 38, 160; tribal qualities of, 38

orality: vocality and, 133. *See also* primary orality; secondary orality

*Orality* (Furness), 40

O'Reilly, Tim, 35

Ovid, 223–224, 226

*parole parlante*, 76, 77, 78, 100, 133, 149n2, 192; Foucault and, 147; voice of enunciation and, 156, 223

*parole parlée*, 77, 80, 100, 133, 149n2, 183, 192; chanting and, 228–229; echo and, 228; Foucault and, 147; Merleau-Ponty and, 222; semiotic closure and, 81; voice of articulation and, 145

Parret, Herman, 231, 232

Pascal, Blaise, 47, 79

pedestrians: cellphone bans for, 46; traffic accidents and, 46

Pedraza, Milton, 55

Peirce, Charles Sanders, 27, 28, 83, 88, 92n4, 175, 185n60, 218n59; on abduction, 86–87, 90; aesthetics and, 164, 165–167, 170–171, 184n24, 184n26, 236; amusement and, 88–89; color and, 248n82; consciousness and, 163; on distraction, 50–51; doubt and, 178; dynamical object/interpretant and, 246n33; existential categories of, 64n26; on habits, 6, 9, 13; inauthentic

enchantment and, 113–114; intentionality and, 93n10; interper-sónal communication and, 215; interpretant and, 70; *logos* and, 207; love and, 247n66; music and, 234–235; play of musement and, 87; pragmatism and, 13; self-control and, 88, 89, 218n60; semiosis and, 166, 171, 206; sentimentality and, 238; voice and, 140, 150n34, 167. *See also* signs
perception: habits of, 28–29, 71–72; Internet, cyberspace and, 28–29; Merleau-Ponty on, 28; Ong on sensory, 26–27; phenomenology and, 27–28
Peters, John Durham, 132
Petrilli, Susan, 210–211; on signs, 71, 72
Petry, Edward S., 218n60
*phainein*, 27
*pharmakon*, 204, 242; Derrida and, 219n78
phenomenology, 150n59, 156, 203; art of conversation and, 170; Dolar and, 157; enchantment and, 68, 72, 73; Husserl and, 27; Ong and, 163; perception and, 27–28; *phainein* and, 27; signs and, 27, 70; sound and, 52
phone: cellphone bans, 46; distracted driving deaths and, 46; presence of, 6; usage, 6
*phone* (voice), 3, 5, 12, 40
phone calls: Light Phone and, 42n50; office voice mail, 9; text compared to, 9, 241
*phone semantike*, 216; Aristotle and, 136, 142, 168–169, 193, 196; *logos* and, 194, 196, 197, 198; *Romeo and Juliet* and, 199, 200
phonocentrism: Derrida on, 152n97; metaphysics of presence as, 120, 124, 134–138
phonology: Dolar and, 140, 156; linguistics and, 140
phubb, 6
Pinterest, 35
Plain, Andrew, 41n31, 102; on acousmatic voice, 103
Plato, 18n10, 130, 207, 217n31; Derrida and, 135–136, 139; Dolar and, 191; music and, 156, 204, 242; on secular, 7; sound and, 139

Plessner, Helmuth: dialectics of expressivity and, 181; expressions and, 180–181, 195; voice of enunciation and, 182; wild and, 181
*pneumatism*, 173
*Pokémon Go*, 46
positive ambiguity, 75–76, 131; voice of enunciation and, 204, 205
post-human age, 45, 54, 55
Postman, Neil, 25, 87; *Amazing Ourselves to Death* by, 58; on television, 26
Prawat, Richard, 219n96
primary orality: Ong on, 31, 33; secondary orality and, 33
print-typography culture, 26
psychoanalysis, 94n54, 247n73; Cavarero and, 130; Dolar and, 244
Pythagoras, 101

*Reclaiming Conversation* (Turkle), 11
*The Re-Enchantment of the World* (Berman), 79
*The Re-Enchantment of the World: The Value of Spirit Against Industrial Populism* (Stiegler), 113
relationality, 5, 23, 45, 104, 240, 245; acousmatic voice and, 101; Bateson, G., and, 168; culture of distraction and, 52; ear-to-ear relations and, 8, 39; *Echo and Narcissus* and, 224–225, 226; enchantment and, 63; enunciation and, 39; ethics and, 203; existential ambiguity and, 76; firstness and, 239; hyper-textual/visual connection and, 92; inauthentic enchantments and, 92; interper-sónal communication and, 221–222, 228; Levinas and, 174; linguistics and, 140; messages and, 142, 144–145; music and, 232; resonance and, 222; robots and, 53–54, 55; secondness and, 201, 239; social connectivity and, 35; social media and, 39; social robots and, 109; socio-economics and, 54–55; sounding voice and, 34, 39; thirdness and, 80, 192; vocality and, 9–10; voice and, 132, 189; voice of articulation and, 145; voice of enunciation and, 148, 183, 188

resonance, 247n39; authentic enchantment and, 222; echo and, 228, 229; *Echo and Narcissus* and, 226–227; interper-sónal communication and, 221, 226, 226–227, 230, 234, 236, 239; music and, 232, 235; Nancy and, 227–228, 229, 231, 232; relationality and, 222; resilience and, 245; rhythm, timbre and, 231, 232, 233, 235; *Romeo and Juliet* and, 231; tone and, 230; voice of enunciation and, 230, 245

Restak, Richard, 9

rhythm and timbre: heart-felt communication and, 237, 238–239; resonance and, 231, 232, 233, 235

Ritzer, George, 8; on disenchanting enchantments, 79; McDonaldization and, 88

robots: love, 53; relationality and, 53–54, 55; social, 54; Sox as, 55; Zora as, 54

*Romeo and Juliet* (Shakespeare), 221, 224; Cavarero and, 199–200, 201, 240; Derrida and, 199–200; *logos, bios* and, 199–200; *phone semantike* and, 199, 200; resonance and, 231; voice of enunciation and, 223; *zoe* and, 199–200, 201, 223

Rothman, Joshua, 47

Rousseau, Jean-Jacques, 202

sacred: Bateson, M., and Bateson, G., on, 79–80, 170; enchantment and, 79

Saler, Michael, 19n27; on ironic imagination, 8

Sapir, Edward, 132

Saussure, Ferdinand de, 70, 139, 184n22; Derrida and, 135, 170; on hierarchy, 170

Savodnik, Peter, 83

Schaeffer, Pierre, 101

Schafer, R. Murray, 99, 127

Schiller, Friedrich, 201, 210, 218n60; aesthetics and, 166; ethics and, 210; *On the Aesthetic Education of Man* by, 87; on play, 58

Schlichter, Annette, 137–138, 152n123

Schopenhauer, Arthur, 231, 233

Schutz, Alfred, 110, 235–236; music and, 232

Scott, D. Travers, 21n51

Sebeok, Thomas, 72

secondary literacy, 33

secondary orality: audience and, 33; Ong on, 26, 32–33, 119; primary orality and, 33

secondness, 68–70, 71, 72, 85–86, 179, 188, 201; ear-to-ear relations and, 163; ethics and, 201; messages and, 169; relationality and, 201, 239–240; self-control and, 201; voice of enunciation and, 157, 160, 161, 191, 193, 206, 210

self-control, 35, 107, 166; Peirce and, 88, 89, 218n60; secondness and, 201

Selinger, Evan, 61

semio-ethics, 210

semiotic closure: *parole parlée* and, 81; thirdness and, 81

semiotics. *See specific topics*

senses: anthropology of, 72; Aristotle and, 122; Classen on, 120, 121, 122, 149n10; Descartes on, 122; Greek philosophers and, 121; Locke on, 122; McLuhan and, 123; Nancy and, 126; Ong and, 26–27, 123

sensorium: Ong and, 28, 71–72; sounding voice and, 40

sentimentality: Colapietro and, 238; heart-felt communication and, 237–238; Peirce on, 238

Serres, Michel, 100, 108, 185n63

Shakespeare, William. *See Romeo and Juliet*

*The Shallows* (Carr), 56

shallow selves, 109–110

Shannon, Claude, 4

Shepard, John, 127

signs, 88, 104, 125, 150n44, 157, 162, 168, 180, 248n82; amusements and, 88; enchantment and, 68–74; Lacan and, 151n72, 161, 192; Levinas and, 172; *logos* and, 72; messages and, 144; Ong and, 69; Petrilli on, 71, 72; phenomenology and, 27, 70; semiosis and, 70–71, 105, 158, 166, 170, 175, 203, 206; time and, 163. *See also* firstness; impersonal self; secondness; thirdness

Simmel, Georg, 47

Simon, Herbert, 48
Simon, Linda, 177; on bewilderment, 179; wildness and, 179
Sirens, 125, 129–130, 176
Siri, 31
skim reading, 40, 53; Carr on, 56
Snapchat, 35
social media, 23, 35, 241; abbreviated content and, 105–106; advertising, 37; catfishing and, 38–39; cultural, social capital and, 38; defining, 36; FOMO and, 39; impersonal self and, 106; influencers, 37; intimacy, vulnerability and, 36; quality and, 106; relationality and, 39; self-esteem and, 38–39; self-validation and, 38–39; users, 35
social robots: relationality and, 109; Turkle on, 109
socio-cultural environments, 25–26
socio-economics, 54–55
Socrates, 201–202
*The Sonic Self* (Cumming), 235
Soukup, Paul, 28
soul, 47
sound: aesthetics and, 32; attention and, 52; color and, 248n82; digitized, 31–32; hierarchy and, 138, 149n20; Ihde on, 31; Ong on, 72–73, 93n20, 125–126, 152n119, 161–162, 163, 241; Plato and, 139; recording technology and, 98–99; sense of, 123–129; Shepard and, 127; time and, 98, 127, 160, 161
sounding voice, 23, 29, 33; aesthetics of, 164–168; digitized, 31–32, 98–99; Dolar and, 191–192; inauthentic enchantment and, 99, 100; mediation of, 31, 99–100, 104; Ong on, 40, 132; relationality and, 34, 39; sensorium and, 40; soul and, 47; Turkle on, 104; voice of enunciation and, 215; wild and, 216. *See also* enunciation
sovereignty: Dolar on, 197–198; voice of enunciation and, 198
Sox, 55
space and visual, 98, 107, 127, 136–137
Sterne, Jonathan, 133
Stiegler, Bernard, 88, 217n21; on desire, 89–90; *The Re-Enchantment of the World: The Value of Spirit Against Industrial Populism* by, 113
Stone, Linda, 50
Strate, Lance, 25–26, 58, 59, 242, 246n35
suicide, 111
surveillance, 52
symmetrical relations, 90–91; Bateson, G., and, 91, 209–210; inauthentic enchantment and, 91–92

Taylor, Charles, 7, 91; authenticity and, 77
techno-culture, 12; existential dissonance and, 11
techno-social dilemma, 45, 58, 67; communication and, 59; enchantment and, 63; *homo technologicus* and, 60; information and communication in, 59; play and, 58; re-engineering humanity and, 61; smart technology manipulation and, 61–62; Turkle and, 62
television: politics and, 26; Postman on, 26
texts, 36, 86, 98, 104, 204, 241; calls compared to, 9, 241; millennials and, 107; shared meaning and, 4; vocality and, 9
Thass-Thienemann, Theodor, 138
*they-self*, 86, 91, 147, 222
Thiebaud, Jane R., 132
thirdness, 68–70, 71, 72, 114, 133, 162, 168, 169, 188, 206; authentic enchantment and, 78; heart-felt communication and, 237; inauthentic enchantment and, 78, 83; *logos* and, 81, 164; relationality and, 80, 192; semiotic closure and, 81; technology and, 85
Thoreau, Henry David, 176, 185n62; aesthetics and, 178; enchantment and, 179–180; wild and, 176–177
Thorpe, JR, 151n67
timbre. *See* rhythm and timbre
tracking mechanisms, 18n9
Trump, Donald: abduction and, 90
Turkle, Sherry, 5, 8, 18n3, 60, 91, 241; Colbert and, 109; on intimacy reminders, 106; on love robots, 53; millennial research of, 38, 104, 108; on new normal habits, 25; *Reclaiming Conversation* by, 11; on social robots, 109; on sounding voice, 104; techno-social dilemma and, 62

Twitter, 35, 105

Van Leeuwen, Theo, 21n57, 36–37
verbal, 133
verbo-centric, 5–6
video- and logo-centric connectivity, 30, 34, 79; audio and, 31; email and, 86, 98, 241. *See also* texts
virtual, 62
visual: Aristotle and, 138; attention and, 51–52; Classen on, 123; Derrida and, 136–137; hierarchy and, 138, 149n20; Ong on, 72–73, 93n20, 120–121, 125, 127, 163; sense of sight, 123–129; space and, 98, 107, 127, 136–137
vocality, 3, 138, 170; orality and, 133; relationality and, 10; soul and, 13; text and, 9
voco-centric, 5–6
voice, 10; aesthetic, 166–167, 212–213; Cavarero and, 129–130, 133–134, 140, 156, 225; Derrida and, 135, 137; devaluation of, 12; digitized, 31–32; disacousmatization of, 103; Dolar and, 100, 124–125, 139, 144, 149n2, 217n21; Farrell and, 135; female, 129–130, 150n34, 151n67; grain of, 12, 131, 148; Ihde and, 132, 157; intelligibility and, 12–13; Internet, cyberspace and, 146; Lacan and, 130, 140, 155; *logos* and, 133–134, 141; non-verbal, 151n85; Peirce and, 140, 150n34, 167; political, 100; poststructuralist theory and, 12; relationality and, 132, 189; song and, 131, 151n67; source of, 103; spatializing of, 98. *See also specific topics*
voice (Greek: *phone*), 3, 5, 12, 40
voiceless name, 245; Foucault and, 120, 146, 147, 183, 222; Law of Representation and, 146, 147; voice of enunciation and, 222
voice mail, 9
voice of articulation, 119, 141, 149n2, 157, 159, 163, 212; abstraction and, 141; babble and, 143; depersonalization and, 142; Dolar and, 147; inauthentic enchantment and, 142; Lacan and, 159; Law of Representation and, 147; linguistics and, 141; *parole parlée* and, 145; relationality and, 145; voice of enunciation and, 155
voice of enunciation, 119, 149n2, 155–156, 175, 194, 242; aesthetics and, 166–167, 168, 187; authentic enchantment and, 207–208; authenticity and, 205–206; Dolar and, 159–160, 190–191, 192; ear-to-ear relations and, 167, 169, 175, 188; enchantment and, 158, 162, 168, 183, 189, 205, 209, 211, 215, 229, 240, 244; *énoncé* and, 159; ethics and, 202–203; extimacy and, 196; firstness and, 157, 160, 161, 162, 175, 193, 206, 210; gap in consciousness and, 188–189, 190; interper-sónal communication and, 222, 223; irruption and, 175; Kim-Cohen and, 182; Merleau-Ponty and, 156, 159; music and, 243, 245; *mythos* and, 207–208; nameless voice and, 222; Nancy and, 226; *parole parlante* and, 156, 223; *phone semantike*, *logos* and, 198; Plessner and, 182; positive ambiguity and, 204, 205; relationality and, 148, 183, 188; resonance and, 230, 245; *Romeo and Juliet* and, 223; salient, 244; secondness and, 157, 160, 161, 191, 193, 206, 210; self, other and, 201–205; sonic voice and, 160, 215; sounding voice and, 215; sovereignty and, 198; time and, 162–163; voiceless name and, 222; voice of articulation and, 155; wild and, 158, 176, 177, 182, 183, 216, 229, 239; *zoe, bios* and, 198
vulnerability: ear-to-ear relations and, 10; social media and, 36

wealth, 55
Weaver, Warren, 4
Web 2.0, 35
Weber, Max, 6; on disenchantment, 7, 11
Weheliye, Alexander, 138
Weizenbaum, Joseph, 35
WhatsApp, 35
wild: Aristotle and, 195; Bennett and, 176–177; enchantment and, 178; Internet, cyberspace and, 186n85; James and, 177, 178; Plessner and, 181;

Simon, L., and, 179; sounding voice and, 216; Thoreau and, 176–177; voice of enunciation and, 158, 176, 177, 182, 183, 216, 229, 239
Williams, James, 18n8, 24–25, 39, 241–242; on advertising, 37–38; age of attention and, 107; on attention and attention economy, 47, 51; on distraction, 57–58; enchantment and, 63
*The Wizard of Oz* (film), 101
*The World Beyond Your Head* (Crawford), 47

Yahoo, 35

YouTube, 35, 37

Zebuhr, Laura, 178, 179–180
Zengotita, Thomas de, 34
*zoe*, 188, 191, 193, 194, 196, 216; Agamben and, 194–195; Aristotle and, 194; Dolar and, 195–196; heart-felt communication and, 238–239; music and, 232, 239; Nancy and, 235; *Romeo and Juliet* and, 199–200, 201, 223; voice of enunciation and, 198
Zora, 54
Zumthor, Paul, 132–133

# About the Author

**Deborah Eicher-Catt** (Ph.D., Rhetoric and Philosophy of Communication, Southern Illinois University at Carbondale, 1996) is professor of communication arts and sciences at Penn State, York. She is founding member and fellow of the International Communicology Institute, past president of the Semiotic Society of America, and past chair of the Philosophy of Communication Division for the National Communication Association. She has won numerous awards for her scholarship and teaching, including the prestigious Pennsylvania State University Alumni Teaching Award. In addition to fifty published peer-reviewed articles, book chapters, review essays, and encyclopedic entries, she has guest-edited several academic journal issues and co-edited (with Isaac E. Catt) *Communicology: The New Science of Embodied Discourse* (2010).